Intimate Strangers

When Louis Antoine de Bougainville reached Tahiti in 1768, he was struck by the way in which 'All these people came crying out *tayo*, which means friend, and gave a thousand signs of friendship; they all asked nails and ear-rings of us.' Reading the archive of early contact in Oceania against European traditions of thinking about intimacy and exchange, Vanessa Smith illuminates the traditions and desires that consistently led Bougainville and other European voyagers to believe that the first word they heard in the Pacific was the word for friend. Her book encompasses forty years of encounters from the arrival of the *Dolphin* in Tahiti in June 1767, through Cook's and Bligh's voyages, to early missionary and beachcomber settlement in the Marquesas. It unpacks both the political and emotional significances of ideas of friendship for late eighteenth-century European, and particularly British, explorations of Oceania.

VANESSA SMITH teaches in the Department of English at the University of Sydney. She is the author of *Literary Culture and the Pacific: Nineteenth-Century Textual Encounters* (1998) and co-editor of *Exploration and Exchange: A South Seas Anthology 1680–1900* (2000) and *Islands in History and Representation* (2003).

Critical Perspectives on Empire

Editors

Professor Catherine Hall
University College London

Professor Mrinalini Sinha
Pennsylvania State University

Professor Kathleen Wilson
State University of New York, Stony Brook

Critical Perspectives on Empire is a major new series of ambitious, cross-disciplinary works in the emerging field of critical imperial studies. Books in the series will explore the connections, exchanges and mediations at the heart of national and global histories, the contributions of local as well as metropolitan knowledge, and the flows of people, ideas and identities facilitated by colonial contact. To that end, the series will not only offer a space for outstanding scholars working at the intersection of several disciplines to bring to wider attention the impact of their work; it will also take a leading role in reconfiguring contemporary historical and critical knowledge, of the past and of ourselves.

A full list of titles published in the series can be found at:
www.cambridge.org/cpempire

Intimate Strangers

Friendship, Exchange and Pacific Encounters

Vanessa Smith

CAMBRIDGE
UNIVERSITY PRESS

CAMBRIDGE UNIVERSITY PRESS
Cambridge, New York, Melbourne, Madrid, Cape Town, Singapore,
São Paulo, Delhi, Dubai, Tokyo, Mexico City

Cambridge University Press
The Edinburgh Building, Cambridge CB2 8RU, UK

Published in the United States of America by
Cambridge University Press, New York

www.cambridge.org
Information on this title: www.cambridge.org/9780521728782

First published 2010

Printed in the United Kingdom at the University Press, Cambridge

A catalogue record for this publication is available from the British Library

Library of Congress Cataloguing-in-Publication Data
Smith, Vanessa.
  Intimate strangers : friendship, exchange and Pacific encounters / Vanessa
  Smith
    p.   cm.
  ISBN 978-0-521-43751-6 (Hardback) – ISBN 978-0-521-72878-2 (pbk.)
  1. Friendship–Oceania   2. Friendship–Great Britain   3. East and West.
  I. Title.
  BF575.F66S625 2010
  303.48'24096–dc22
                                                              2010014313

ISBN 978-0-521-43751-6 Hardback
ISBN 978-0-521-72878-2 Paperback

For Gabrielle Smith

I found my account in having such a friend.

James Cook, *Voyage of the* Resolution *and* Adventure *1772–1775*

Contents

Illustrations

Acknowledgements

I've learnt much in the process of writing this book about how difficult it is to disentangle the languages of debt and friendship, and it's a book indebted to many friends. For the generosity of their insights, references, reading and hospitality, I thank Judith Barbour, Gillian Beer, Danielle Bobker, David Chappell, Hervé-Marie Le Cleac'h, Guy Davidson, Robert Dixon, James Drown, Mark Eddowes, Markman Ellis, Kim Evans, Vanessa Finney, Annegret Gottwald, the Grafton Terrors, Harriet Guest, Alexis Harley, David, Lorna and Shel Hershinow, Mark Johnston, Pamala Karol, Ulrich Kinzel, Catarina Krizancic, Harry Liebersohn, Kate Lilley, Paul Lyons, James Mackenzie, Andy Martin, Roslyn Mayled, Donna Merwick, Geoff Moggridge, Nancy and Al Morris, Keao NeSmith, Jennifer Newell, Sandhya Patel, Lee Quinby, Merrilee Robb, Bob Suggs, Ari'i Tai Tani, Teriitauairohutu Tetumu, Nicholas Thomas and Richard Yeo. I'm especially grateful to Elizabeth Wilson for her galvanizing critical engagement with this project, to Rod Edmond, for island and other conversations, and to Greg Dening and Noel Rowe, who offered me so much by way of conversation and example. My thanks and love always to Georg and Jan Gottwald, and Vivian, Sybille, Gabrielle and Nick Smith, who have given me all the best kinds of support and encouragement.

I wish to express my appreciation to the Australian Research Council for awarding me a QEII fellowship to conduct this research, and to the librarians and staff of Fisher Library and the Mitchell Library, State Library of NSW, Sydney; the National Library, Canberra; the Bishop Museum Archive, Hamilton Library, Hawaiian Historical Society Library and Mission Houses Museum Library, Honolulu; the Service des Archives Térritoriales, the Société des Etudes Océaniennes, the Académie Tahitienne and the Musée de Tahiti et Ses Isles, Tahiti; the Phillips Library, Peabody Essex Museum, Salem, Massachusetts; the Centre des Archives d'Outre-Mer, Aix-en-Provence; and the British Library, the British Museum and the National Archives, London. In particular I'd like to thank Paul Niva at the Musée de Tahiti et Ses Isles,

Coulin Yoan at the Académie Tahitienne, Desoto Brown and Patty Belcher at the Bishop Museum Archive, and Barbara Dunn at the Hawaiian Historical Society for giving thought to the questions this project posed. I am grateful to Michael Watson and Kathleen Wilson for their early and sustained enthusiasm for the project, and their editorial guidance.

Versions of sections of this work have appeared in *Pacific Studies* 27, nos 1–2 (March/June 2004), *Eighteenth-Century Studies* vol. 41, no. 2 (2008), *Leviathan: A Journal of Melville Studies* 11, no. 2 (June 2009), and *Parergon* 26, no. 2 (2009).

This book is dedicated to my perceptive and generous sister Gabrielle Smith, who has always understood everything about friendship.

Introduction
'Amicable signs'

It is to be observed that friendship, from whatever mercenary
cause it was entered into is inviolate and is a kind of real relation
in Tahiti.

– William Pascoe Crook

I believe no European in future will ever know what their ancient
Customs of receiving Strangers were.

– William Bligh

The naturalist George Forster got his first glimpse of the Tahitian coast-
line on the morning of 16 August 1773. Looking out from the deck of the
Resolution, he watched the dawn break over the island and the inhabitants
awake, perceive the ship and launch their canoes. His initial encounter
with Tahitian people was subsequently described in *A Voyage Round the
World*, written in English and published in 1777:

One of the[canoes] approached within hale. In it were two men almost
naked, with a kind o[f] turban on the head, and a sash round their waist.
They waved a large green leaf, and accosted us with the repeated exclamation
of *tayo*! which even without the help of vocabularies, we could easily translate
into the expression of proffered friendship. The canoe now came under
our stern, and we let down a present of beads, nails, and medals to the men.
In return, they handed up to us a green stem of a plantane [*sic*], which was
their symbol of peace, with a desire that it might be fixed in a conspicuous part
of the vessel. It was accordingly stuck up in the main shrouds, upon which
our new friends immediately returned towards the land. In a short time we
saw great crouds of people on the seashore gazing at us, while numbers in
consequence of this treaty of peace, which was now firmly established, launched
their canoes, and loaded them with various productions of their country. In less
than an hour we were surrounded by an hundred canoes, each of which carried
one, two, three, and sometimes four persons, who placed a perfect confidence
in us, and had no arms whatsoever. The welcome sound of *tayo* resounded
on all sides, and we returned it with a degree of heart-felt pleasure, on this
favourable change of our situation. (G. Forster 2000:143–4)

1

What is this word, '*tayo*', that is so integral to Forster's sense of having arrived?[1] He presents the term as at once unfamiliar and transparent. At this stage in Oceanic encounter it is neither. Forster was travelling on James Cook's second voyage to the Pacific. Cook learned to say '*tayo*' during his earlier visit to Tahiti in the *Endeavour*, between 12 April and 12 July 1769. The records of his English predecessors in Tahiti, the captain and crew of the *Dolphin*, who claimed the island for King George III (as 'King George's Island') and remained there from 19 June until 28 July 1767, do not register the word (Robertson 1948; Rensch 2000:330–1). But Louis Antoine de Bougainville, whose ships the *Boudeuse* and *Étoile* spent just twelve days at Tahiti in April 1768, recorded it in both his journal and the published version of his voyage. Bougainville's botanist Commerson included it in his rudimentary vocabulary of Tahiti (Taillemite 1977:499–500). George's father, Johann Reinhold Forster, who was with him on board the *Resolution* when it made landfall at Tahiti, had only the year before, with George's assistance, translated Bougainville's account into English. The scene that greeted father and son off the Tahitian coast had been anticipated in Bougainville's text, which reports (in Forster's translation): 'we had much to do to warp in amidst the croud of boats and the noise. All these people came crying out *tayo*, which means friend, and gave a thousand signs of friendship, they all asked nails and ear-rings of us' (Bougainville 1967:217). The word '*tayo*' then, far from being novel to the voyagers, 'resounds on all sides' in early European narratives. It was already, by the time George Forster wrote, *the* recognizable Tahitian word: the first word to translate across the beach, the first word to appear in European accounts, the signifier of contact itself. Forster's concern at this stage, however, is to attribute the spontaneous and heartfelt response provoked by hearing the word, not to its learned familiarity, but to its universal translatability.

This book begins with this idea of friendship as in some way self-evident. It explores the traditions and desires that lead European voyagers such as Forster to assert instant and instinctive recognition of *taio* and cognate Oceanic friendship terms; consistently to believe that the first word they heard in the Pacific was the word for friendship. My study encompasses forty years of early European–Oceanic encounter, beginning with the arrival of the *Dolphin* in Tahiti in June 1767, and ending with the beachcomber Edward Robarts's departure from the Marquesas

---

[1] There are a number of variations to the spelling in European accounts. Unless context demands otherwise, I have adopted *taio*, which is favoured in recent anthropological discussion and conforms to the Tahitian alphabet.

in 1806. I look at key moments and accounts of imperial exploration: the three Cook voyages of the *Endeavour* (1769–71), the *Resolution* and *Adventure* (1772–5) and the *Resolution* and *Discovery* (1776–80); the wreck of the East India trader the *Panther* in Palau in 1783; Bligh's *Bounty* and *Providence* voyages of 1788–9 and 1791–2; Vancouver's visits to Tahiti and Hawaii in 1791 and 1792; and the London Missionary Society's inaugural missionary voyage of 1796–9. And although the majority of the accounts under consideration are British, I also look at records of the visit of Bougainville to Tahiti in 1769, the reconnoitres of Spanish ships and the sojourn of Spanish missionaries in Tahiti-iti from 1772 to 1775, and the 1804 visits to the Marquesas and Hawaii of the Russian exploring expedition under Adam von Krusenstern, all of which occurred during what Harry Liebersohn has recognized as a cosmopolitan era of exploration, that took in 'a broad swath of Europe as well as the wider world' (Liebersohn 2006:2). Although I touch on contacts and friendships in Tonga, Hawaii, New Zealand, the Marquesas, Easter Island, Niue, Vanuatu, Palau and Pitcairn, the island of Tahiti, more than any other part of Oceania, is focal to this study, because of its centrality to the European encounter with Pacific cultures: Harriet Guest has written of the 'accretional logic' by which 'Cook and his fellow journalists conceived of the different island cultures they encountered through their similarity or difference to Tahiti' (Guest 2007:21). All of the texts I examine give detailed accounts of friendship-making between crew members and islanders, of a kind that is seen to be improvised on local terms. All but the *Dolphin* journalists name their Tahitian friendships *taio*. The account of the *Missionary Voyage* of 1799 echoes the terms of George Forster's and Bougainville's arrival scenes, focusing also on crowding, the absence of arms and the familiar yet unfamiliar word, with only a slight tincture of English to dilute the impression of classic first encounter:

Being so numerous, we endeavoured to keep them from crowding on board; but in spite of all our efforts to prevent it, there were soon not less than one hundred of them dancing and capering like frantic persons about our decks, crying, 'Tayo! tayo!' and a few broken sentences of English were often repeated. They had no weapons of any kind among them ... (J. Wilson 1799:56)

Such a sustained rhetoric over some thirty years of European–Oceanic contact solicits closer attention. Why was it necessary, in these early days of scientific imperialism and then missionary enterprise, to be received in a spirit of friendship?

This question is particularly relevant to the British voyages that bear the main weight of my investigation. The secret Instructions to the

French and Spanish captains Bougainville and Boenechea do not contain explicit injunctions regarding friendship-making. However, those for each of Cook's voyages to the Pacific set forward, alongside plottings of course and guidelines for the collection of specimens, explicit strategies for engaging with Pacific communities. The Instructions to the *Endeavour* voyage of 1768–71, which constitute the prototype, encapsulate many of the themes of this book in their attempt to tread rather than blur a line between friendliness and suspicion, exploitation and interaction, the individual and the crowd:

> You are to endeavour by all proper means to cultivate a friendship with the Natives, presenting them such Trifles as may be acceptable to them, exchanging with them for Provisions (of which there is great Plenty) such of the Merchandize you have been directed to Provide, as they may value, and shewing them every kind of Civility and regard. But as Captn Wallis has represented the Island to be very populous, and the Natives (as well there as at the other Islands which he visited) to be rather treacherous than otherwise you are to be Cautious not to let your self be surprized by them, but to be Constantly on your guard against any accident. (Cook 1955:cclxxx)

In islands whose natural abundance is persistently assumed, where 'Natives' exchange from a position of 'great Plenty', Cook is advised to 'cultivate a friendship' through prestation and trade.[2] How this kitchen garden of intimacy is to be established in the fertile wilderness is not, however, clear. The Instructions propose both the trivial and the useful as models of exchange. Gifts to local people should be 'Trifles': items of little value, implicitly deceptive,[3] whose value is nonetheless acknowledged to be significantly determined by the needs and desires of the recipients. Equally the anticipated natives are figured as potentially treacherous and generous, their islands both bounteous and 'very populous'. Once a vision of the crowd displaces the proposed singularity of 'a friendship', 'guard' replaces 'regard'. As a guide to the formation of friendship, the instructions are notable for the absence of any reference to verbal communication. There are no instructions for the acquisition of local languages, no models of phatic communion, and the presentation of objects serves as substitute for words.

---

[2] For the relationship between cultivation, culture and civility, see Williams 1983:87, Young 1995:30–1 and Hall 2000:10–12.

[3] The *Oxford English Dictionary* defines 'trifle' as both 'a small article of little intrinsic value' and 'a false or idle tale told to deceive, cheat or befool . . . a lying story, a fable, a fiction'.

Additional Instructions for the *Endeavour* apply the injunction concerning friendship to the projected discovery of a great Southern Continent. In the event of such a discovery, Cook is instructed:

> You are likewise to observe the Genius, Temper, Disposition and Number of the Natives, if there be any, and endeavour by all proper means to cultivate a Friendship and Alliance with them, making them presents of such Trifles as they may Value, inviting them to Traffick, and Shewing them every kind of Civility and Regard; taking Care however not to suffer yourself to be surprized by them, but to be always upon your guard against any Accident.
>
> You are also with the Consent of the Natives to take possession of Convenient Situations in the Country in the Name of the King of Great Britain; or, if you find the Country uninhabited take Possession for His Majesty by setting up Proper Marks and Inscriptions, as first discoverers and possessors. (Cook 1955:cclxxxiii)

In new territory, the appearances of friendship are to be established before friendship may proceed: information concerning the character and force of the native population, which in the case of Tahiti had already been supplied by Captain Wallis, must be obtained as a necessary preface to friendly overtures. A space of potential misinterpretation thus opens between the recognition and dissemination of the signs of friendship that is a recurrent site of interpretative tension throughout Cook's voyages. Friendship projected onto the unknown, rather than a context of previously encountered peoples, is doubly contingent. Its terms may be rendered instantly redundant by the absence of any local population, or practically redundant by the perception of local resistance. These alternatives, in turn, mark the boundaries of a European desire for amicable relations that it is both fantastic and territorial, only dreamed of and yet already subject to contract. The reiterated injunction to 'take possession' either with the consent of inhabitants or, in their absence, 'by setting up Proper Marks and Inscriptions', underscores, once again, the neglect of any direction for verbal exchange, begging the question of how 'consent' might be communicated.[4] This in turn leaves friendship an overladen term: made to carry the burden of European good intentions for the benefit, ultimately, of European conscience rather than putative native subjects.

It is in another supplementary text to the *Endeavour* voyage, Morton's *Hints*, that acts of communication are adumbrated. Proffered by James Douglas, 14th Earl of Morton, who was president of the Royal Society

---

[4] Greg Dening has unpacked the relationship between an English politics of 'possession' and the setting up of markers in his seminal essay 'Possessing Tahiti' (Dening 1996:128–67).

(1764–8), the *Hints* are a more tentative document than the Instructions. Written in the conditional tense, rather than the future infinitive of the Instructions, they constitute a set of suggestions rather than an official code of conduct, which exemplifies the 'gentle method' they advocate for communicative exchange. I want to draw particular attention to Morton's parenthetical anticipation of a potential scene of miscommunication between Native and European. Morton writes:

Conquest over such people can give no just title; because they could never be the Aggressors.

They may naturally and justly attempt to repel intruders, whom they may apprehend are come to disturb them in the quiet possession of their country, whether that apprehension be well or ill founded. (Cook 1955:514)

Here Morton recognizes that subject positions at the scene of encounter are unequivocally dictated by the relationship to territory. Entitlement not only positions Europeans and Natives as subjects and objects of any act of violence – as aggressors and defenders: it must equally, in the brief space of contact, allow local interpretation to govern communication, to the extent that even Native *mis*interpretation of European communicative overtures, and even where it produces acts of violence, will always constitute true interpretation.

It is in this context, of a relationship to interpretation already spelled out by a relationship to territory, that Morton introduces his suggested techniques of communication. He writes, 'There are many ways to convince them of the Superiority of Europeans, without slaying any of those poor people', and goes on to describe a series of complex performances that he hopes will play this dual role, creating a substitute for violent interaction, and miming the European into a position of superiority. He advocates:

By shooting some of the Birds or other Animals that are near them; – Shewing them that a Bird upon wing may be brought down by a Shot. – Such an appearance would strike them with amazement and awe. – Lastly to drive a bullet thro' one of their hutts, or knock down some conspicuous object with great Shot, if any such are near the Shore.

Amicable signs may be made which they could not possibly mistake. – Such as holding up a jug, turning it bottom upwards, to shew them it was empty, then applying it to the lips in the attitude of drinking. – The most stupid from such a token, must immediately comprehend that drink was wanted.

Opening the mouth wide, putting the fingers towards it, and then making the motion of chewing, would sufficiently demonstrate a want of food. (Cook 1955:514–15)

The order of examples here enacts its intended effect, substituting 'amicable signs' for violence. Unlike the 'shock and awe' tactics of recent warfare, Morton's strategies of 'amazement and awe' are conducted at one remove, on animals and dwellings understood to serve a primarily symbolic function, as effective substitutes for human harm. The 'amicable signs' that follow enact a more ludicrous performance: in the doubly belaboured context of described mime, verbs proliferate to convey the most basic of actions, designed to satisfy the most essential of needs. And in both the indirect ultimatum of marksmanship and the clumsy theatre of mimed communication, Morton's *Hints* betray the strain under which they operate, as they work to deflect conflict, and to keep the hands of those engaged in an expedition of scientific discovery clean of the violence of imperial contact. Yet the *Hints* stand out among the instructive texts of Cook's voyages in advocating performances at which 'the Natives' constitute the projected audience. Morton's emphasis is not simply on sketching the separate scenes of a cross-cultural pantomime: he is also concerned to anticipate local responses, to second-guess native interpretation. If the communicative model he offers is hardly fluent or interlocutory, retaining the disjunction of theatre and audience, this is also partly the product of attempting to imagine and describe relations that have not yet been set in place.

That friendship was a significant part of the imperial project of discovery was manifest not just in the ways voyaging was proposed, but in the ways in which territory was mapped as a consequence. Instructions in hand, Cook charted the Pacific according to codes of friendship, repeatedly getting it wrong. Niue was called Savage Island after an angry encounter on the beach; Tonga with its cultivated landscape and strong trade ethos became the 'Friendly Islands', although this was later exposed as a misnomer in the account of the beachcomber John Mariner, who ascertained, during his longer sojourn in Tonga (1806–10), that friendly appearances had disguised a conspiracy to attack and plunder Cook's ships (Martin 1817:58). Vancouver, whose Instructions, in the wake of Cook's death, propose conciliation rather than a more optimistic cultivation of friendship:

> You are therefore hereby strictly charged to use every possible care to avoid disputes with the natives of any of the parts where you may touch, and to be particularly attentive to endeavour, by a judicious distribution of the presents, (which have been out on board the sloop and tender under your command, by order of Lord Grenville) and by all other means, to conciliate their friendship and confidence (Vancouver 1984:286)

labours to convince the chief Maquinna at 'Friendly Cove' in Nootka Sound that he, too, is a friendly cove. The history of contact at Nukuhiva in the Marquesas can be mapped onto a geographical distinction between the 'friendly' bay of the Tei'i and the 'unfriendly' valley of the Taipi.[5] Euro-American cartography describes an affective geography that can certainly be read as reflecting the tendency of imperial nomenclature to reify arbitrary attributions. But the authority of such designations must then equally be registered as unstable: the imperatives of naming are not simply classificatory, reflecting a vulnerability to immediate emotional impression.

Morton's 'amicable signs', like Forster's 'exclamation of *tayo*', are presented as unequivocal and transparent: communications 'which they could not possibly mistake'. In both directions across the beach, the project of European voyaging wishes to maintain the easy communication of friendly intention. How do we begin to assess this desire? Within disciplines and interdisciplinarily, the topic of friendship has increasingly engaged academic attention.[6] However, intimacy and affect have tended to be considered in relation to individual societies rather than across cultures. Sociology has methodologically confined itself within cultural borders, examining the relationship between friendship, class and culture, and the variable operations of instrumentality and affect in Euro-American friendship formation.[7] And while the operations of friendship, as I tentatively suggest in conclusion, may be the elided question of anthropological fieldwork, few anthropological texts look at cross-cultural friendship outside of, or indeed within, the local informant relationship. *The Compact*, a collection of essays that constituted the first sustained treatment of friendship in modern anthropology, argued that 'western idealistic notions of friendship' were non-transferable, and that friendships were best considered as

[5] I have discussed this psychogeography of Nukuhiva in V. Smith 2005.
[6] In 1998 two of America's leading literary theoretical journals, *South Atlantic Quarterly* and *Critical Inquiry*, devoted special issues to questions of intimacy and friendship. Peter Murphy's introduction to the *SAQ* collection of essays on 'Friendship' described it as 'a remarkably nodal concept, lying at the intersection of ethics and politics, eroticism and companionship, the personal and the public' (Murphy 1998:1). He acknowledged a resurgence of popular cultural and theoretical interest in friendship (a topic more typically displaced in modernity by a focus on love or desire). However, he expressed disappointment in philosophical interventions such as Jacques Derrida's *Politics of Friendship* and Allan Bloom's *Love and Friendship*, where friendship has seemed to serve as a cypher for other types of relationship, for citizenship or love. Lauren Berlant's 'Intimacy' issue of *Critical Inquiry* focused on the modes of narrative desire that inform the pursuit of intimacy. Her introductory essay drew attention to the 'tacit fantasies, tacit rules, and tacit obligations' that govern intimate relations, while registering the contradictions that intimacy throws up between desires for domesticity and disruption (Berlant 1998: 287). These symposia were preceded by interdisciplinary collections on friendship from Porter and Tomaselli, Rouner, and Adams and Allan.
[7] In particular seminal pieces by Paine 1969a, 1969b; Wolf 1966; Cohen 1961; Silver 1989, 1990, 1997; Adams and Allan 1998; and Pahl 2000.

'social compacts' conforming with the practices of individual societies (Leyton 1974:ix). Twenty-five years later, Sandra Bell and Simon Coleman's *The Anthropology of Friendship* (1999) broached the question of cross-cultural friendship only tangentially, noting the risk of instating any absolute distinction between western and non-western modes of friendship, and advocating attention to degrees of 'social process and ambiguity' that temper what anthropologists tend to see as the rigidly structured formal patterns of friendship within non-western societies. Robert Brain's engaging study *Friends and Lovers* (1976) offered an early broadly comparative anthropological foray into the topic of friendship, which he argued had been sidelined by the dominant anthropological emphasis on kinship relations, a critique that still widely pertains.

It is where questions of friendship touch the territories of history and Empire that cross-cultural contexts become compelling. Yet studies of intimacy and Empire encounter notable resistance. A single representative case – the response in the *Journal of American History* to Anne Stoler's controversial 'Tense and Tender Ties' essay – is sufficient to gauge the level of contention encountered by scholars seeking to take the affective turn to Empire studies. Stoler sought to draw attention to what she termed, following Albert Hurtado, 'the intimate frontiers of Empire', arguing, in relation to nineteenth- and early-twentieth-century colonial contexts, that 'colonial state projects ... attended minutely to the distribution of appropriate affect (what sentiments could be shown toward, and shared with, whom)' (Stoler 2001a:830, 832). While the novelty of her approach lay in its extension of the colonial archive to the domain of intimate rather than its mode of analysis, which reiterated the Foucauldian power/knowledge model of much post-colonial criticism, her respondents seemed anxious to distance themselves from her focus on positive affect. 'What's Love Got to Do with It?' asked Ramón Gutiérrez, drawing attention to what he regarded as the elision of violence towards women in Stoler's analysis (Gutiérrez 2001). The desire to reinstate what was perceived as an inevitably sidelined focus on negative affect among her respondents indicated a suspicion that to attend to private feelings and the modes of relationship they fostered was necessarily to abandon the proper task of exposing the work of Empire.[8] Stoler strenuously resisted this binarization in her response, arguing convincingly that intimacies 'are the grounds of contestations', and that

---

[8] More convincingly, to my mind, Mary Renda drew attention to Stoler's privileging of sexual over other forms of intimacy, a critical tendency I will explore throughout this book (Renda 2001:882–7). The privileging of kinship over friendship in anthropological discussion, highlighted by Brain (1976), is a parallel phenomenon.

'to study the intimate is *not* to turn away from colonial dominations, but to relocate their conditions of possibility and relations and forces of production' (Stoler 2001b:894).

There is much, both in the history of European interaction in the Pacific, and in recent critical practice, to prompt a straightforward exposition of the relationship between the script of Empire and a theatre of false friendship. It has become a commonplace of critiques of imperialism that sentimentalism, a discourse that informs ideas of friendship brought by Europeans to the Pacific, was complicit in palliating the violence of Empire. Peter Hulme eloquently expresses this thesis, claiming that 'Sentimental sympathy began to flow out along the veins of European commerce in search of its victims' (Hulme 1986:229).[9] Texts such as Morton's *Hints* can be easily exposed in their very self-conscious delicacy as far from provisional manifestos of power, while expressions of 'proffered friendship', 'perfect confidence' and 'heart-felt pleasure' attributed or testified by Forster can be readily translated into their opposites. Scenes of contact become inevitable scenarios of anxious distrust and disingenuous sentiment. If texts such as the Instructions seem to beg a retrospective scepticism, so equally might the ways in which the word *taio* emerges in voyaging accounts as the literal embodiment of phatic communion: 'a type of speech in which ties of union are created by a mere exchange of words' (*OED*). But converting friendship instinctively to a signifier of insincerity does little more than invert Forster's idealized preconceptions. It is, furthermore, a gesture anticipated in the rhetoric of voyaging. 'We came to destroy under the specious mask of friendship', Forster wrote of the *Resolution*'s encounters at Tanna in the New Hebrides (Forster 2000:551); 'They are all too susceptible under the smile of dissembled friendship', acknowledged George Keate of the Palauans (Keate 2002:254). This book seeks instead to build a picture of the operation of languages of friendship within the politics of Empire whose sophistication lies not in debunking, but in recognizing the compelling pull of potential friendship ties in those very contexts that would most seem to preclude their possibility.

Scepticism regarding friendship claims is not simply an attitude imposed by recent critics upon scenarios of early contact. Anxious scepticism charges European accounts of Oceanic friendship. The *taio* relationship seems particularly open to reproaches of calculation. At the centre of Forster's description of mutually understood friendly greetings

---

[9] June Howard has drawn attention to this same statement of Hulme's in a judicious article that appraises late-twentieth-century critical perspectives on sentimentalism (Howard 1999:72).

is another mutually, if less explicitly, understood language of exchange. The 'expression of proffered friendship' entails the proffering of gifts, the securing of the emblem of peaceful relations and the commencement of trade in those 'various productions' so essential to the replenishment of the voyagers. It is not long before this formalized connection between friendship-making and exchange leads Forster to regard trade as the tenor and *taio* as simply the vehicle of friendship's metaphor. Five days after experiencing the idealized arrival scene, Forster starts to suspect that 'it was not without some interested motives, that they attended upon us'. Not only trade, but thieving and begging have displaced a universal emotional responsiveness as the perceived motivations behind Tahitian friendliness. Forster now reports that:

Their general behaviour towards us was good-natured, friendly, and I may say officious; but they watched every opportunity of conveying away some trifles with amazing dexterity, and many among them, whenever we returned the kind looks they gave us, or smiled upon them, thought that a proper time to take advantage of our good disposition, and immediately with a begging tone said, *tayo, pöë,* 'friend, a bead!' which, whether we complied with or refused, did not alter their good temper. When these petitions became too frequent, we used to mock them, by repeating their words in the same tone, which always produced a peal of good-humoured laughter amongst them. (G. Forster 2000:159)

The emerging understanding, on the European side of what *taio* signifies, and on the Tahitian of what contact enables it to encompass, allows here for reciprocal mockery. Levity is engaged on both sides, in its dual sense of both playfulness, and a lightness of investment in the outcomes of play. In David Samwell's account from Cook's third voyage, on the other hand, claims for superlative and calculated friendship succeed each other so immediately that the prevailing tone is sarcasm rather than mockery. Samwell's journal entry for 20 September 1777, which overplays its third voyager's hindsight, gives the following description of daily life for the British crew members at Matavai Bay:

Those who have leisure amuse themselves ashore among the Houses or in paying Visits to their particular friends or Tayo, who always on such Occasions entertain them with great Kindness & make them Presents of Cloth or some other Articles, for which they will take nothing in return till they come & see their Friend on board where many of them spend most part of their time. Tho' a Tayo will behave in general with great appearance of friendship and Fidelity, yet they are not to be trusted for if a fair Opportunity offers of stealing some considerable Prize they cannot resist the Temptation. (Cook 1967: II, 1061)

Samwell goes on to narrate the tale of a shipmate who came to grief 'for putting Confidence in an Otaheite Tayo' (Cook 1967: II, 1062). There is precisely nothing 'particular' about this purportedly symptomatic portrait of 'particular' friendship, in which shifts from 'great Kindness' to 'great appearance' are simply a question of change of location, from the hospitable context of shore to the temptations of shipboard. Yet concerns about the relationship between friendship and self-interest have, as I will argue in detail in Chapter 3, a long and vexed heritage within European thought. This book therefore seeks to avoid reducing encounter to economic subtext, a manoeuvre hermeneutically indistinguishable from Samwell's sceptical exposition of Tahitian infidelity, while aiming to show that a relationship between friendship claims and material interests was not simply enacted but brought under scrutiny in the transactions of European–Oceanic encounter.

More generally, this study seeks to recognize that friendship's fraught ethics elude easy hindsight. Friend is the word we think we can see behind. The urge to translate it, and like Forster, to naturalize that act of translation, is powerful. Friendship leaves itself open to interpretation. It is readily reconstrued as patronage or lust; a foil for sexuality or an excuse for exploitation; as simply utilitarian; as obviously sentimental. The extent to which we see through friendship to what is nested within it, be it desire or exploitation, serves to register our social sophistication, our political commitment, our capacity for retrospection. Yet in friendship, literary criticism also encounters its own limitations. Eve Kosofsky Sedgwick introduced her groundbreaking analysis of the heterosexual/homosexual divide, *Epistemology of the Closet*, with an expression of frustration at the crude structures that tend to shape interpretation of intersubjective relations. She noted that 'a tiny number of inconceivably coarse axes of categorization have been painstakingly inscribed in current critical and political thought: gender, race, class, nationality, sexual orientation are pretty much the available distinctions' (Sedgwick 1990:22), and that these offer us little purchase on what she called 'the piercing bouquet of a given friend's particularity' (Sedgwick 1990:23). In her study of Victorian women's friendships, Sharon Marcus highlights the insufficiency of Fredric Jameson's model of symptomatic reading for understanding friendship. Where Jameson famously advocated 'diagnostic revelation of terms or nodal points implicit in the ideological system which have, however, remained unrealized in the surface of the text', defining the critical task as locating 'a latent meaning behind a manifest one' (Jameson 1981:48, 60; quoted Marcus 2007:74), Marcus proposes that friendship demands a different mode of reading – one that she challengingly terms 'just reading'. She argues that tracing representations of (in her case female, in mine cross-cultural) friendship requires that the critic 'not claim to plumb hidden depths but to account more fully for what texts present on their surface but critics have failed to notice' (Marcus 2007:75). Within eighteenth-century studies too, a longstanding acknowledgement of the ideological function of sentiment in repressing consciousness of power relations has been increasingly mitigated by recognition of the self-awareness of literary sensibility. Subtle readings of the conflicted representation of sensibility in literary and political documents by critics such as Adela Pinch (1996), Julie Ellison (1999) and Caleb Crain (2001) among others, have demonstrated a growing recognition of the ideological self-reflection within texts of sentiment and sociability. As Ellison expresses it, 'Sensibility is the *admitted* connection between speculation, mood, and power' (Ellison 1999:7).[10]

Like these scholars, I have become acutely aware in focusing on friendship of what our critical imperatives fail to register. However, the questions this book raises for thinking about Euro-American models of friendship and modes of critical practice were prompted, first and foremost, not by engagement with Euro-American philosophical and critical traditions, but by an interest in eighteenth-century Tahitian ways of thinking about friendship, and the forms of fascination they provoked in accounts of cross-cultural encounter. The dialogues on friendship that occurred on Oceanic beaches during the early contact period were both as rebarbative and as embedded as those taking place in British coffee houses or French salons – indeed, I would argue that they were more provocative for being framed by extraneous contact rather than internal critique. I have tried to do justice to their continued capacity to disrupt hermeneutic expectations, through a sustained focus on the resistances to analysis that I have encountered in trying to assess what such friendships mean. If a friendship claim seems to beg us to know better, this book argues that the topic of friendship therefore also has the capacity to reflect back the complacencies of our scepticism: our interpretative drive to locate the object of analysis behind the apparent, or to claim authority in retrospect. I will suggest in Chapter 3 that the tension between an attempt to describe what friendship adds up to and a declaration of its ineffability, its status outside description, is integral to western ethical

---

[10] Although I engage with criticism of eighteenth-century sociability and literary sentiment in this study, I consider my topic here to be friendship rather than these much canvassed discourses. Indeed, I would argue that a preference for discussion of discourses of sociability over practices of friendship within eighteenth-century studies is another aspect of the symptomatic evasiveness that the topic of friendship engenders critically. An exception to this tendency is of course Janet Todd's seminal study *Women's Friendship in Literature* (1980), with its clear and valuable categories of sentimental, erotic, manipulative, political and social friendship – all of which become variously complicated in the masculine contexts of cross-cultural encounter that I discuss.

thought. In examining some of the friendships of early contact in Oceania, I want to temper my own scepticism regarding motivations on both sides with a recognition of friendship's ontological irreducibility. The friendships I look at here, between men of very different cultures, might be shuffled so quickly behind trump cards of racial othering or homosociality that they need never be held in mind. By exploring the dilemmas that friendship's particular imbrication with exchange in certain Pacific societies posed for European voyagers I seek, rather than exposing a series of false fronts, to explore the complexity of thought and emotion that any embarkation on friendship entails. This involves respecting the sophistication of eighteenth-century subjects, and weighing intentions as well as outcomes. I focus, not on what particular friendship claims represent, connote or imply, but rather what they enabled.[11]

A study of friendship is uniquely poised to address issues of two-sidedness that are inherent to any engagement with the archive of Oceanic contact. Such research is necessarily subject to accusations of unevenness associated with extrapolating a picture of preliterate communities from the accounts of literate visitors. Like the historical record, there are two sides to every friendship, and often only one subject who testifies. We rarely encounter the perfect symmetry of two little boys with two little toys, with their friendship's exemplary reciprocity. However carefully we 'brush history against the grain', how is it possible to flesh out the other side of friendships reified in one-sided descriptions? A book that provides much inspiration for my attempt to complicate eighteenth-century European encounters with Oceanic cultures, Jonathan Lamb's *Preserving the Self in the South Seas 1680–1840* nonetheless demonstrates the perils of imbalance for such a project. Lamb proposes that European, and particularly British, imperial exploration was not the coherent policy of a consistent, enlightened subject that it has often been assumed to represent, but rather a fraught endeavour of increasing bewilderment, apt to dissolve rather than, in any simple sense, reconstitute European cultural certainties. He argues that this model of

---

[11] This gesture, which strategically embraces a kind of naïveté with regard to motive, might parallel Leela Gandhi's defence of 'immaturity' as 'the ethical and philosophical hallmark – the crucial ingredient' of a politics of friendship (Gandhi 2006:12), if the immaturity here is understood to be not her utopian politics so much as a rejection of the assumption that friendship can only ever be an intermediary term in our understanding: the thing to be seen beyond, of which eventual understanding must dispose. It is a rejection of the critical 'maturity' that assumes 'friend' is a double entendre.

fragile and defended selfhood can be extended equally to both sides of the Pacific cross-cultural encounter; that

the uncertainties that troubled the stability of the European self were intensified in the South Pacific at the same moment that they were being reflected in the Polynesian self, which was in turn being forced out of its tribal identity into a state more labile and less defended. On both sides of the line of encounter, people became directly interested in the issue of self-preservation. (Lamb 2001:5)

This reference to 'sides of the line' literalizes Greg Dening's metaphor of the beach – a tentatively equilibrial space in which ascribed meaning and cultural certainty are rendered provisional (Lamb, Smith and Thomas 2000:xix) – as simply a line in the sand, across which Lamb sets up binary equivalences between European and Polynesian experience (matching, for instance, the infatuations of the stock exchange with shamanism, or the dissolutions of scurvy and leprosy). The discrepancy between our knowledges of each side of the beach is disposed of by assertion: 'I assume, then, no metaphysical division between the European self and its so-called other. There is not on one side an "I" capable of writing a history into which the subaltern "I" on the other side is speechlessly incorporated as its predicate' (Lamb 2001:5).

To 'assume ... no metaphysical division' between subjects becomes more feasible when the focus of analysis is a politics of relationship rather than reflection: when what is being established is affiliation rather than selfhood. The term friendship, rather like the phenomenon it embodies, is one whose discrete valences are created between subjects in particular contexts of contact. Whatever the solipsisms inherent to a one-sided archive, when the topic of friendship is addressed writers are forced to some degree to think about subjects interacting. The anxieties that riddle their egos become recognizably constituted, not just by a relationship to the discourses of their home culture, but to the regard or rebuff with which they are met in unfamiliar contexts. Indeed, this is the minimum that can be argued for friendship as a critical trope. In her brilliant study of the role of friendship in anti-colonial politics, Leela Gandhi has further proposed, after Jacques Derrida, privileging 'the trope of friendship as the most comprehensive philosophical signifier for all those invisible affective gestures that refuse alignment along the secure axes of filiation to seek expression outside, if not against, possessive communities of belonging' (Gandhi 2006:10). Following Jean-Luc Nancy, she espouses a notion of *compearance*, focusing on 'the *between* as such: you *and* I (between us) – a formula which in the *and* does not imply juxtaposition, but exposition' (Gandhi 2006:19).

As Gandhi elucidates, 'the ethics of compearance defiantly contravenes the embargo on relationality through which power, colonial or otherwise, orchestrates its divisions and exclusions' (Gandhi 2006:20). Where Lamb, precisely, brings two sides of the beach into fascinating 'juxtaposition', this study seeks, with Gandhi, to engage friendship as a name for the 'exposition' of the '*between* as such'.

Yet this book is ultimately focused not on a universalized but on a culturally particular notion of friendship (*taio*), and the possibilities formulated in the space between Oceanic and European versions of friendship. The word *taio*, also documented as *tayo, tio* and *tyo* by the British and Spanish, and as *taillot* in some French accounts, offers a particularly interesting case for the type of analysis I propose, since it has largely disappeared from the Tahitian lexicon. Contemporary Tahitians do not recognize the term, and it does not appear in the most recent Maohi dictionary. Anthropologists concur in restricting its frame of reference to highly specific bond friendships, which are regarded as having become essentially obsolete. Its use in European accounts, however, seems to encompass a less restricted range of meanings, from the general term of welcome it embodies in Forster's account to carefully ritualized friendship based upon name-exchange. If there is little agreement regarding what Polynesians meant by *taio*, there is equal uncertainty about what Europeans saw themselves to be doing in expressing or entering into friendships in Oceanic contexts. For these reasons, it might join Greg Dening's list of Pacific models and metaphors, as a concept whose meanings were shaped, agreed and contested performatively, across the beach, in a context of relative historical provisionality.[12] On the other hand, two defining, and to Europeans potentially contradictory, aspects of *taio* seem to emerge with increasing consistency in the accounts under consideration here: an insistence on particularity and an emphatic link between friendship bonds and capacities for trade. It is this nexus that allows *taio*, in my reading, to challenge European disavowals of a relationship between the specialness of friendship and the circuitry of exchange.

This study, then, attempts to keep several balls in the air. It tries to recover both a language and a practice of friendship-making from eighteenth-century Oceania, and its European equivalents. It imagines the kinds of questions that Europeans might have been forced to ask of their broader philosophies and more instrumental policies of friendship when these two cultures of intimacy encountered one another.

---

[12] Greg Dening, private communication.

It acknowledges that, by obsessing upon the emotional motives of Oceanians, European observers animated an affective agency that in turn obscures the imbalance of power latent in encounter. But it recognizes that, if friendship has the capacity to expose Empire's trade in false feeling, it also reveals the limitations of our abilities to read the motives behind Empire. Furthermore, it reflects on the potential of friendship to challenge wider complacencies of readerly sophistication, by being both more obvious and more elusive than we are trained to register. In exploring such questions, I have adhered to only a limited chronology, retracing scenes and emphasizing certain encounters over others. I have favoured long quotations from logbooks and journals in order to allow readers to assess for themselves the claims I am making for the texts of contact. And I have drawn freely on sources from Plato to Agamben to think through the implications of these scenes and their representations. Such interpretative flexibility seems warranted by the urgency of the questions early cross-cultural friendships still ask, and by their sustained capacity to baffle easy answers.

The book is divided between broad scenes of encounter and sets of particular friendships. Chapter 1 considers the crowding that is such a critically ignored feature of the Pacific island arrival scene. Despite the excitement and fear generated in accounts of early contact by the experience of being overwhelmed by strange bodies, Pacific beaches tend not to be regarded as crowded places, while studies of groups and their psychology have always represented the crowd as an inherently metropolitan phenomenon. The chapter considers the kind of context that these initial crowd scenes presented for deciphering what is the inevitable first word of Pacific contact – *taio* or its cognates. The second chapter explores what might be possible to understand was proffered in the invitation to become a *taio*. I look at the conundrum that Pacific friendship posed for the European imagination in its apparently paradoxical insistence both on the particularity of the friendship and on the entailments, material and prestigious, of the initial exchange of names that sealed the relationship. My concern here is the range of subtexts that must be brought to bear, in both voyage accounts and anthropological studies, to interpret a cultural system understood as exemplarily different. Questions of status, gender, wealth, cultural ritual and sexuality become foils for describing a mode of intimacy that is hard to hold in focus precisely because of its capacity to reflect back issues regarding the possibility of genuine feeling across such boundaries.

Chapter 3 offers a way of contextualizing European responses to Oceanic gestures of friendship, by analysing traditions of thinking about gift-giving and friendship. I am not concerned to provide a comprehensive analysis of Enlightenment philosophies of friendship and exchange, but rather to place these in a broader tradition that links current thinking with long-established paradigms. The chapter therefore ranges between Classical, Enlightenment and Post-modern theories of friendship, and explores a twentieth-century literature on gift exchange that was formulated substantially in relation to Oceanic encounters. My argument here is that European thought has been consistently troubled by the entanglement of friendship with self-interest, and that it is the absence of a commensurate disavowal in Oceanic understandings of friendship that disturbs European descriptions and performances of cross-cultural friendship-making. In Chapter 4, I place European scepticism about Oceanic friendship claims in the context of broader philosophical concerns about the capacity of individuals to evaluate the emotions of others as genuine or false. I turn here to the example of mourning in Tahiti, which incorporates an element of excess, including practices of self-mutilation, whose ethical value must be negotiated within European accounts. The dismissal of such practices as false theatrics reads also as a justification of comparative European reserve that chimes with contemporary philosophical writing on the emotions, in seeking to invest performativity with suspicion.

Part II is a series of experiments in reading through friendship. Taking the models established in the first section as starting points, and particularly the emphasis on particularity of relationship axiomatic to the *taio* bond, Part II wagers that friendship knows something that we can only discover by focusing, concomitantly, on the particular in our readings. To understand Empire's relationships purely as instantiations is to fail to do justice to historical and cultural subjects. While never ignoring how status anxiety, cultural blindness, discursive confidence or incipient authority could colour gestures of friendship, I question the assumption that such gestures are reducible to the sum of these parts. The hope of relationship as well as the knowledge of its frequent failure are present in the texts I examine. Acknowledging these can give our sense of encounter new texture.

If the first section of the book anatomizes friendship, the second embodies it in particular relationships. In Chapter 5 I look at Oceanians who joined European voyages – Ahutoru, who accompanied Bougainville to France; Tupaia, who sailed with the *Endeavour*; Mai and Lebuu, who visited London from the Society and Palau islands, respectively. Perceived by both their European contemporaries and recent scholarship through the lens of curiosity, I propose instead reconceptualizing voyaging Oceanians and Europeans as fellow travellers, whose knowledge and authority could only effectively emerge interrelationally.

In Chapter 6 I take seriously William Bligh's claim that friendship was the immediate cause of the *Bounty* mutiny. The various and conflicted accounts of the mutiny rehearse the same issues that I trace within cross-cultural friendship – of calculation and sentiment, disingenuousness and loyalty – within the fraught contexts of rebellion and trial. Friendship itself becomes a term of accusation and defence. In the final chapter I discuss a friendship that was imagined rather than realized, between an English missionary William Crook and an English beachcomber Edward Robarts who just missed meeting each other in the Marquesas. Their explicit or unacknowledged need of one another's friendship allows me to reconsider the relative force of the foreign and the familiar in forging intimacy, and reciprocally, to speculate on the significance of friendship to ethnographic observation.

The examples in this section of the book are primarily of friendships between men. This reflects the fact that most of the Europeans in Oceania in the later eighteenth century were men, and that the majority of *taio* bonds described are between males. It seems important, though, not to map this evidence too straightforwardly onto an analysis of gendered power relationships. Robert Williamson isolated the *taio* relationship as overriding a marital injunction towards fidelity in Polynesian females, noting that 'In Tahiti a man's wife was considered as common property with his *tayo*' (Williamson 1939:187). His observation, as we will see in Chapter 2, is contentious however: there are friendships recorded throughout Oceania between men and high-ranking women, including Purea's with Samuel Wallis and Joseph Banks, and 'Itia's with George Tobin in Tahiti, and a number of Robarts's in the Marquesas, where polyandry was also widely practised. However, although Claude Lévi-Strauss's claim that within gift economies 'the woman herself is nothing other than one of these gifts, the supreme gift among those that can only be obtained in the form of reciprocal gifts' (Lévi-Strauss 1969:65) has received compelling challenges from feminist scholarship (Rubin 1975), the understanding that women are among the objects of *taio* exchanges prevails in European accounts of early contact. In Chapter 2 I think about the ways in which *taio* both confirms and confronts Eve Sedgwick's thesis of relationship between men as predicated on Lévi-Strauss's paradigm of a 'male traffic in women' (Sedgwick 1985:16; Rubin 1975).

My three case studies in Part II are each an exemplary failure, rather than a model intimacy. As such, they differ from the kinds of friendship analysed by Leela Gandhi, which were articulated with political self-awareness and frequently with exquisite nuance. The individuals I discuss are for the most part not prone to self-reflection, and the friendship they seek is sometimes hypocritical or rudimentary. More often than not it is in the details of their failure that they illustrate both the lineaments and limitations of crude structures of power for describing friendship relations. Just as *taio* emerges as a complex compound of economics and affect, never fully reducible to one or the other, so these cross-cultural friendships are neither the pure products of the global relations that enable them nor of the emotional responses they engender. They announce absences rather than achieved presences in the historical record. They involve illiterate sailors with preliterate Polynesians, Oceanic travellers to and European travellers from metropolitan London, and a friendship dreamed up from the spare details of a missed encounter. Part of the exercise of the second section of the book is to make a case for close reading as the appropriate hermeneutic of particular friendship, and to show that, in the details of such stories, grand narratives are troubled as well as affirmed. Refusing to accept that this closeness of focus, in both subject matter and critical practice, involves a depoliticization of cultural relation, I argue that it is only through attention to specificity that we can do justice to historical subjects and to the complex irresolution of both the questions they asked differently and the questions we share. That friendships are never the sum of their records makes it more thinkable that cross-cultural friendships, too, require a scholarship understood not to be redressing an imbalance, but exploring both the constitutive and precarious aspects of imbalance and cultural difference.

Part I

Making contact

1 Crowd scenes

What beings surround me?
– Hume

If 'friend or foe' is the implicit first question of cross-cultural contact, in the Pacific it is articulated in a context that has disappeared from view: that of the crowd.[1] In the literature of early European encounter in Oceania, crowds are everywhere, and the experience of the mass is presented as overwhelming. Gauging crowd feeling – ascertaining whether the bodies that surround one are fascinated or afraid or aggressive – is imperative to the instigation of trade, and the possibility of obtaining essential supplies. Robertson's account of the *Dolphin* surrounded by hostile canoes at 'King George's Island' in 1767 contrasts with Bougainville's depiction of pirogues manned by clamorously friendly Tahitians crowding his vessel less than a year later, but both observers give a sense of the immediate effect of mass scrutiny and the need for interpretation it instigates. The focus of this book is the relationship for which crowd scenes set the stage: the highly particularized connection of *taio*, through which access to local resources is ultimately mediated. That term or its cognates – almost invariably the first word of early European–Oceanic encounter – emerges, again almost invariably, from the crowd scene. In European accounts, it seems, the named friendship requires the background of the unnamed mass to become distinguishable. On the other hand, as reports of the death of James Cook show, the hostile crowd remains intransigently collective: harbouring rather than surrendering up its guilty individual.

---

[1] Paul Lyons, discussing nineteenth-century American representations of Pacific islanders, suggests that 'fear and friendship … comprise poles of the discursive continuum along which Euro-Americans anticipate and/or retrospectively organize their relations with Oceanians … Recurrently in the archive, "friends" are those from whom there is nothing to fear' (Lyons 2006:98). As should already be clear, however, my own analysis seeks to acknowledge friendship as a concept charged with resonances that exceed the logic of binarism.

Pressing, exhilarating, unnerving as a presence within accounts of contact, the Oceanic crowd has nonetheless remained curiously elusive of critical attention. There are a couple of notable exceptions: Marshall Sahlins has focused on crowd dynamics in support of his thesis that the Hawaiian reception of Cook amounted to deification (I will look at his analysis later in this chapter), and Greg Dening's substantial body of work on the theatricality of Pacific encounter, with its recognition of a 'dialectic between audience and actors' (Dening 1996:118), opens up a space for the examination of group reaction.[2] Yet the Oceanic crowd becomes the primary focus of analysis exclusively in studies of population, where accounts of crowding are scrutinized in an attempt to gauge the impact of European disease and cultural decimation upon the lives of Pacific peoples. Within this field, however, there is no consensus. The Hawaii State statistician Robert Schmitt, responding to David Stannard's intervention in the Hawaiian population debate, quotes his own observation that 'Guesses of the size of crowds – a frequent element in ... pre-censal estimates – are notoriously unreliable, typically producing totals two or three sizes the actual number' (Stannard 1989:115). His comment, which articulates an assumption behind much work on Oceanic populations, taps into a broader conservative discourse on crowds that represents such manifestations as *inherently* unreliable, by virtue of their capacity to camouflage individual motive within collective action. Norma McArthur's study of pre-contact population figures (McArthur 1967) equated conservative estimates with scholarly rigour, and, as Stannard pointed out, there has been a concomitant tendency within more recent Pacific scholarship to reduce the dimensions of the crowd as an expression of resistance to the fatal impact thesis (Stannard 1989:xvi). Other population studies, such as Eleanor Nordyke's *The Peopling of Hawai'i*, have repeated conservative estimates of pre-contact figures to support a representation of islands under siege from post-contact population influx (Nordyke 1989:13–27). Among scholars concerned to reduce their dimensions, crowd scenes are implicitly presented as scenes of fantasy, to be dispelled by 'realistic' computation. Stannard, on the other hand, reassesses the same documents of contact from Hawai'i to present a compelling case for maximizing estimates of pre-contact Oceanic populations. The same crowds, then, have been read alternatively as metonym or symptom: as part of a larger whole or as sign of a special event. This chapter aligns itself with Stannard's work in focusing on the crowd as an absent presence within recent Pacific

---

[2] Dening's structuring of *Mr Bligh's Bad Language* (1992) as a series of 'Acts' has provided a model for this chapter's division into 'Scenes'.

scholarship, that produces a contradiction in our current account of early contact. In addressing both the importunate materiality and subsequent invisibility of the crowd within European accounts of the Pacific, I acknowledge the silent accommodation of representation to a reality of depopulation, while also asking what it might mean for a persistent European romanticization of Pacific islands to think of them as crowded places.

Retrieving a sense of the Oceanic crowd from the archive is an intricate process: and not merely because crowd scenes are composed of history's extras. Against the insistent representation of the press of bodies on the beach, of the throng and bustle of contact, must be weighed the force of a collective European imagining of islands as inherently uncrowded; the populous city's other; blank terrain for the metropolitan subject, castaway or self-exiled, to act out or self-fashion.[3] The image of the desert island morphs too easily into that of the deserted or decimated Pacific island, ravaged by imported disease or weapons or intoxicants, by slaving and blackbirding. Romantic fantasies and post-contact realities converge to depopulate islands. And yet, to focus simply on the tragic history of depopulation is, ironically, frequently to reiterate other romantic tropes, of loss and lapse, and to diminish the force of new crowds active in modern Oceanic contexts.[4] By retrieving the crowdedness of Pacific islands in this chapter, I am setting a physical scene for my discussion of cross-cultural friendships that acknowledges the robust presence of Oceanic multitudes at the time of contact. In friendship-formation, particular bodies emerge from the crowd's collective body, forging bonds that contribute to its dissolution, but also instantiate its resilience.

Scene I: The Bay

Only the mass makes it possible for the sexual object to become intoxicated with the hundred stimuli which it produces.

– Walter Benjamin

---

[3] For an extended discussion of the European imaginative investment in islands, see Edmond and Smith 2003:1–18.

[4] Epeli Hau'ofa has made a related point in a series of important essays (1993, 1995, 1998). He argues that the tendency to perceive Pacific islands as 'tiny, isolated dots in a vast ocean' promoted the notion that 'the countries of Polynesia and Micronesia are too small, too poor and too isolated to develop any meaningful degree of autonomy'. As Hau'ofa points out, this is 'an economistic and geographic determinsitic view of a very narrow kind, that overlooks culture history' (Hau'ofa 1993:7, 6). The conspicuous absence of the crowd from Pacific scholarship may be partially attributed to the same geographic determinism. A significant way in which Oceanic crowds have re-emerged as a presence in the Pacific in recent years is through protest movements of various kinds, in particular against weapons testing. This is reflected in both scholarly and fictional writing from Oceania, for example Hau'ofa 1998:400 and Morales 2002.

A year before he departed for the Pacific as botanist on James Cook's second voyage of exploration, Johann Reinhold Forster translated Bougainville's account of his arrival in Hitia'a, Tahiti in April 1768. Bougainville had described an enthusiastic welcome from the Tahitians that began in the harbour:

> As we came near the shore, the number of islanders surrounding our ships encreased. The periguas were so numerous all about the ships, that we had much to do to warp amidst the croud of boats and the noise ... The periguas were full of females; ... Most of these fair females were naked; for the men and the old women that accompanied them, had stripped them of the garments which they generally dress themselves in. (Bougainville 1967:217–18)

The ship's cook singled out a partner from the female throng, but Bougainville reported that, 'He had hardly set his feet on shore, with the fair whom he had chosen, when he was immediately surrounded by a croud of Indians, who undressed him from head to feet. He thought he was utterly lost, not knowing where the exclamations of those people would end, who were tumultuously examining every part of his body' (Bougainville 1967:219). The crowd on the beach encourages the cook to proceed with a public coupling, a task for which he has, however, been disabled by the shock of exposure. His illegitimate landing pre-empts and parodies the sanctioned arrival ceremony subsequently described by Bougainville:

> When we were moored, I went on shore with several officers, to survey the watering-place. An immense croud of men and women received us there, and could not be tired with looking at us; the boldest among them came to touch us; they even pushed aside our clothes with their hands, in order to see whether we were made exactly like them ... They sufficiently expressed their joy at our arrival. (Bougainville 1967:220)

The formal landing must now figure as a re-enactment of the cook's first encounter; an official public undressing that more successfully channels the narcissistic thrill produced by the fascination of the crowd, by explicitly retrieving this fascination as a form of tribute.

Bougainville and his crew experience arrival through a staged series of crowd scenes – in harbour and on shore, official and unofficial – that are not simply imperial triumphal. Against the backdrop of the crowd, in a spirit of 'intoxication' that appears oblivious to the distinctions of race, class and sex, individuals engage in a kind of competitive self-objectification that risks abashment in pursuit of exaltation. The crowd here – primarily feminine, and both insistently and generously seductive – is in distinct contrast to the version of the Tahitian crowd found in George Robertson's account of the *Dolphin*'s visit to Tahiti the previous year. The boats that crowd around the English vessel are manned primarily by males. Where women are proffered it is as a lure, that must initially be ignored in the interests of safety:

their [*sic*] was upwards of five hundred canoes round the ship, and at a Moderate Computation there was near four thousand men – most of the trading canoes which lay round the ship, and dealt with our people, had a fair young Girl in Each Canoe, who playd a great many droll wanton tricks, which drew all our people upon the Gunwells to see them, when they seemd to be most merry and friendly some of our people observd great numbers of stones in every canoe, this created a little suspition. (Robertson 1948:154)

In Bougainville's text, threat becomes, bathetically, an isolated case of performance anxiety. The current of excitement that runs through the crowd is picked up by the crew in a movement that traces the trajectory of voyeurism. Freud argues that the scopophilic instinct shifts its focus from an extraneous object to the subject's own body, and includes a significant auto-erotic element (Freud 1984:127).[5] In Bougainville's crowd scenes, the French crew members rediscover an excitement or experience a panic about their individual bodies in the light of crowd enthusiasm: often simultaneously.

The crowd acts as both stimulus and prophylactic. Bougainville's surgeon Vivez writes of Tahitian women, 'as soon as we landed, they gave us half their clothing displaying every sign of passion and leaving us only with regret, and all the discomfort we felt, we who were not on our guard against this lack of scruples and the preconceptions of our climes, that we were unable to express our vulcanism in public because the crowd did not leave us' (Dunmore 2002:232). Where Vivez suggests that desire and the crowd are incompatible, the florid account of his fellow crew member, volunteer Charles-Félix-Pierre Fesche betrays a more conflicted attitude to the offer of public sex. Describing in engorged prose a scenario in which a 'young girl aged 12 or 13' offers herself explicitly while her parents look on, Fesche concludes:

The summons was very appealing and the athlete caressing her was too skilled in the art of fencing not to take her right away had not the presence of the surrounding 50 Indians, through the effect of our prejudices, put the brake on his fierce desires, but however great the ardour that drives you, it is very difficult to overcome so quickly the ideas with which you have been brought up ... It is only someone who is doing or thinks he is doing evil who fears the light. We hide

---

[5] Barbara Benedict has argued that 'rather than sexual discovery motivating the pleasure of curiosity, as Freudian thought suggests, it is the historical phenomenon of curiosity that sexualizes discovery' (Benedict 2001:8). I would suggest, however, that Freud's discussion of voyeurism makes precisely that point. I have discussed the scopophilic dimension of the project of 'discovery' elsewhere (Smith 2003:117).

in order to carry out such a natural action, they do it in public and often. Several Frenchmen, less susceptible to delicacy, found it easier, that same day, to shrug off these prejudices. (Dunmore 2002:257)

Despite his attempt to round his fable off with a moral about natural humanity, Fesche is clearly aroused as much as inhibited by the presence of the crowd. Prince Nassau-Siegen, who was a passenger on Bougainville's ship and appears to have been the experienced 'athlete' described by Fesche, also takes the event as a lesson in overcoming social shame, attempting to contextualize the ritual through a specious comparativist framework: 'If wise people carry out these ceremonies in association with the planting of seeds, why should the reproduction of the finest species of things ever created not also be a public festival?' (Dunmore 2002:283). Serge Tcherkézoff has convincingly argued that Tahitian invitations to participate in public sex can best be understood in terms of local ritual practice and mythical belief. According to Tcherkézoff these encounters were focused rather than uninhibited, reflecting the desire to acquire the *mana* of the European through conception rather than libidinal play (Tcherkézoff 2004: 405–509). Tcherkézoff's hypothesization of the Tahitian perspective focuses on the youth of the female participant and on rituals of undressing and dance, without reflecting on the role of the crowd in the libidinal economy of the scene. Yet the crowd is essential to a further dimension in which the Tahitian girls are co-opted into European desire. The presence of the crowd enables the figuration of the Tahitian girl as unselfconscious. It offers the French crew members a theatre in which to divest themselves of those purportedly cultural scruples that are the barrier between their behaviour and the 'natural'. And this rhetoric of naturalization strains in turn against a competing voyeuristic drive in the narrative that is released and fuelled by the presence of the crowd.[6]

In the task of translating Bougainville, we might speculate, Forster learned what to anticipate from an Oceanic arrival scene. He learned to expect to be overwhelmed. It wasn't until 17 August 1773, over five years after Bougainville, that the botanist experienced his own Tahitian landfall at Vaitepiha Bay on Tahiti-iti. During a difficult anchoring, he

---

[6] Matt Matsuda offers a compelling and intricate analysis of the ways in which 'sensuality and erotic attraction' became 'consituents of a French presence in the Pacific': he argues that French colonialism, as a broad Pacific island and rim phenomenon, was 'amorously defined' (Matsuda 2005:3). An alternative, much discussed British scene of public sex in Tahiti, taken up by Tcherkézoff among others, is the 'Point Venus scene' described by Cook and redacted by Hawkesworth (Cook 1955:93–4; Hawkesworth 1773: II, 128). For a detailed discussion of the ambiguities of Cook's depiction of the scene, which, like Tcherkézoff's, focuses on the potentially ambivalent compliance of the female subject, see Rennie 1998.

had been called upon to participate in unaccustomed deckhand labour, and as a result was suffering from exhaustion and an injured foot. His account of the arrival is marginal: he writes that the pain from his exertions '& the intense heat ... caused me a Faintness & in the night I awoke from a pain in my breast [... The next morning] I saw such a crowd of people about our Ships, that it is hardly credible' (Forster 1982:326). Like Bougainville's and Robertson's, Forster's experience of the crowd channels a fluctuating sense of being physically besieged; here by fatigue and illness rather than desire or hostility. The crowd externalizes his sense of sudden self-distrust, becoming the locus of an incredulity at what his eyes witness that might otherwise reflect upon his own physical distress: 'it is hardly credible'. George Robertson observes that the varying physical and mental dispositions of crew members infected their perceptions of the crowd as hostile or benign. Noting that about thirty seamen were ill when the *Dolphin* arrived at Tahiti, he comments astutely on how resilience and temperament factored into the ways in which the promise of shore, and the generosity or aggression of its crowds, were weighed:

We past the most of this night in various reflections according to the Different dispositions of the people, the Greatest part of the Ships Company made sure of finding all sorts of refreshments, and lookd upon all the Deficultys of procuring them to be nothing. Oythers supposed nothing could be hade without blows, and made a great many Iddle suppositions, with respect to the savage Disposition of the natives and some thought it imposable to Land here. (Robertson 1948:142)

Reading the crowd becomes a reflection, in the first instance, of the individual's state of mind.[7]

Certainly Robertson's own account of the crowd that surrounded his ship is prey to temperamental fluctuations. He seems concomitantly conscience-struck by the possibilities of misreading that emerge in recounting the *Dolphin*'s encounter with the crowd at sea. Initially, massed canoes are construed as threat: 'at this time their [*sic*] was a great number of their canoes allong side, and they began to be a Little surly – this made us fire a nine pound shot over their heads'; 'we observed a great Number of Canoes surrounding her, which made us supose they meant to Attack her, the Capt. therefor Orderd her signal to be made and fird a nine pounder' (Robertson 1948:137, 138).

---

[7] Robertson's reflections here anticipate a later European and American literary interest in the crowd as psychological projection. Walter Benjamin's essay on the *flâneur* references, among others, the writings of Baudelaire and Edgar Allan Poe in exploring the relation between mental states and the shifting shapes of the crowd (Benjamin 1983:50).

Interwoven with references to such demonstrations of violence, presented as performative in status, but more than occasionally targeted, are mentions of attempts to signal friendship; 'making all the freindly signs that we could think of', which are matched by Tahitian 'signs of friendship to entice our people ashoar' (Robertson 1948:144, 148). By the time a clear premeditated attack takes place it is so enmeshed in contradictory signals of violence and friendship on both sides that crowd behaviour becomes, in Robertson's account, less a fulfilment of the predictable than a problem of misreading. Performances segue into violence, revealing their performative aspect, on both sides. The crowd 'behaved freindly', but at a signal threw stones: the sentries fired 'in hopes that would frighten them' but to no effect, and so the 'Great Guns' shoot among them. The superiority of European firepower is registered in Robertson's subsequent description of the guns' effect, 'which struck such terror amongs the poor unhapy croad that it would require the pen of Milton to describe, therefore too mutch for mine' (Robertson 1948:154). The adjectives 'poor unhapy', rarely associated with collectives, switch the focus from the strength of massed bodies to the broken condition of those attacked, and the crowd becomes suddenly reduced to a figure of pathos. It is not clear whether Robertson's reference to Milton here is merely an invocation of the canonical author, or a more specific reference to the sympathetic complexities engaged by Milton's depiction of the crowd of fallen angels: 'So thick the aerie crowd / Swarm'd and were straitn'd; till the Signal giv'n' (Milton 1674: Book I, ll.775–6). The *Dolphin*'s response to the Tahitian crowd was the most violent encounter ever recorded between Europeans and Tahitians, and even as Robertson attempts to justify the violence that was perpetrated, a different sense of proportion causes the crowd to shrink and shift in retrospect, its motives, then so clearly hostile, now thrown into question.

Scene II: The Beach

> The people were very civil & no way molested them except their Numbers which Novelty had made follow him.
>
> – Samuel Wallis

The crowd that surrounds and overruns the ship is only the more intrepid part of the greater multitude that lives on shore. As ships coast Pacific islands, crew members read between the crowds that venture out and those that stay on land. Captain Samuel Wallis was severely ill during a large part of the *Dolphin*'s stay at Tahiti, and thus witnessed the bloodier part of the crew's interactions with the islanders at a

Figure 1. The crowd in the bay watched by the crowd on shore:
'A representation of the attack of Captain Wallis in the Dolphin by the
natives of Otaheite', from John Hawkesworth, *An account of the voyages
undertaken by the order of His present Majesty*, 1773.

distance or vicariously. In his log, he describes his vantage point on the
crowd, suggesting that its vast numbers were sufficient provocation to a
violence on his crew's part that by implication becomes defensive:
'I being very ill came & looked out of the Gallery Windows':

a great Number of the Inhabitants appeared from amongst the trees on each side
of the River, and approached our people that were on the Beach who made them
signs to keep at a distance at the same time we saw from the Ship, vast Crouds of
People coming over the Hills, from every way seeming in great haste and severall
hundred canoes came round a Point about a Mile from the Ship, being full of
Men, and from a Creek to the Eastward, a great Number More and they all
pull'd close along shore & made directly for our Boats – On this I made the
signall for the Boats to come of[f] ... (Wallis 1766–8: I, 1, 3)

Robertson's account of the attack by and on the Tahitian canoes includes
an awareness of a further crowd on shore acting as audience and goad
(see Figure 1):

Whilst this skirmish lasted all the Bay and tops of the Hills round was full of
Men Women and children to behould the onset and I dare say in great hopes
of sheering all our nails and Toys, besides the pleasure of calling our great

Canoe their own, and having all of us at their mercy, to ill or well use us as they thought most proper – but in place of that, when they came all running doun to receive their Victorious friends, how terrible must they be shockd, to see their nearest and dearest of friends Dead, and toar to peces in such a manner as I am certain they neaver beheald before – to Attempt to say what this poor Ignorant creatures thought of us, would be taking more upon me than I am able to perform. (Robertson 1948:156)

The crowd on shore converts the bay into an amphitheatre, allowing Robertson to imagine the sentiments of an audience disappointed of expected outcomes. Again, a level of poignant identification is achieved once the massed body of the crowd is re-envisaged in terms of particular relations of friendship. Friendship is the connection through which sympathy can be channelled. The projection of personalized relations into a scenario that overtly demonstrates the disequilibrium of European and indigenous power exemplifies a rhetorical manoeuvre described by Markman Ellis as 'paradigmatically sentimental': 'troping the potentially dangerous (... insurrection) – a sublime figure of power – into the personal' (M. Ellis 1996:98). Yet we might also note that where he imaginatively transforms broadscale violence into a violation of friendship, Robertson finds himself not more facile in managing the politics of encounter, but demonstratively bereft of words.

The crowd disguises status. This creates problems for Europeans in trying to establish individuals of significance with whom to parley. Bougainville eventually fixes on tattooing as a mark of distinction, one so remote from his own culture that he must stress its veracity:

As for indications of social differences, I believe (and this is not a joke) that the first one, the one that distinguishes free men from slaves, is that free men have their buttocks painted. Then the amount of paint on the buttocks and other parts of the body, the beard and moustaches, the length of the nails, hair hanging down or gathered up over the head, these nuances distinguish, I believe, the various degrees. (Dunmore 2002:64)

It is nuance that distinguishes, and the crowd is not a nuanced space. The collective body of the crowd does not disclose individual bodily difference, let alone details such as degree of buttock tattooing or nail length. Pierre Bourdieu has exhaustively and circuitously analysed the notion of distinction as a structure of relations: arguing that the system of class conditions is 'a system of differences, differential positions' each defined 'by everything which distinguishes it from what it is not and from everything it is opposed to; social identity is defined and asserted through difference' (Bourdieu 1984:170–1). The crowd does not allow for the space between subjects that renders relations and their distinctions visible. Therefore, attempts to control the crowd in Oceanic contact scenes are partly about making hierarchies of relation apparent. In J. R. Forster's account of his arrival, the capitalized Captain and Chief work together to establish the significance of their interaction by separating themselves from the crowd: 'had the Capt not exerted himself a whole crowd of [the Chief's] followers would have entered the boat; but we took none in but the Chief & his wife ... The crowd was great, but when they came too near, there were men with long poles who beat the crowd unmercifully & broke several poles upon them' (Forster 1982:338). The journal of Don Raimundo Bonacorsi, lieutenant on the 1772–3 voyage of the *Aguila* to ascertain the possibility of establishing a Catholic mission in Tahiti, records, by contrast, a relatively seamless movement from crowd scene to particularized friendship between high-ranking crew members and Tahitians:

When they came on board the first time, swarming up the side from their canoes and clambering in from the portholes, they kept repeating the word '*Tayo*' (which means 'friend' in our language) and were not content until we answered them with the same word and embraced them. And the 'Heris,' [*ari'i*] as they call them, or caciques, for the most part each took one of us for his particular *tayo* to such good effect that we could never separate ourselves from such an one for an instant. (Corney 1913–18: II, 51)

Extracting significant faces from the crowd is imperative to identify individuals of distinction, who control resources, and thus to convert scenarios of theft into relations of trade. The crowd is always potentially a crowd of thieves: the theft that is ubiquitous in European accounts is carried on most effectively in a press of bodies. Yet rank cannot wholly resolve the ambiguity the crowd provokes in the European mind. Bougainville, who also observed that the 'cacique ... drives them away with a stick when they bother us', noted that the Hitia'a *ari'i* (chief) Reti 'saw the return of items stolen from us even though he himself is a great thief, but he wants to be the only one to steal in his kingdom', while the account of Caro, second-in-command of the *Étoile*, elaborates: 'The king is the first and greatest of the thieves' (Dunmore 2002:64, 206).[8] Bonacorsi quickly identifies a general 'proneness to steal whenever an opportunity presents itself to them', adding that 'even the Chiefs were not exempt from this propensity' (Corney 1913–18: II, 57). Contact muddles relations of distinction: the individual of significance achieves, not social separation from the thief, but rather a monopoly on theft.

---

[8] Bonacorsi's and Bougainville's term 'cacique' is derived from the colonial Spanish term for Latin American chiefs.

In these earliest Tahitian encounters, the segue from crowding and theft to individuated relations of trade, so effectively promoted, as we shall see, through *taio* and cognate Pacific friendships, is clumsily managed in ways that equally serve to breach hierarchies of distinction. After further reciprocal violence on land, Robertson records, the crew of the *Dolphin* seeks to commence trade with the Tahitians. Wary now of the crowd, 'the Gunner only allowed one old man to bring a fowl and some fruit over and weaved the oythers back' (Robertson 1948:169). Wallis gives a different account of the motivation, which he acknowledges was the result of bad behaviour on the part of a crew member: 'Punished Wm Welch for Cheating one of the Inhabitants of a Cock, & ordered that no man should trade with them but with an Officers Leave' (Wallis 1766–8: I, 2). Robertson, however, is intent on the ways in which the policy impedes trade: 'as Mr Harrison allowd non but the old man to bring any trade over the River, he was not able to bring a tenth part of what they hade in the time'. The numerous potential relationships between members of the crowd and the ship are funnelled into a monopoly of exchanges between two designated individuals, with the crowd held at bay on each side:

the Captn gave strick Orders to the Gunner not to let any of our men go across the River, nor to allow above two or three of the Natives to come on our side, neather was he to allow any of the men to trade with the Natives, but to carry on all the trade himselfe, this made our trade go on but slowly and prevented discoverys of all kinds for some time. (Robertson 1948:169)

Robertson's concern is that, in the arbitrary exchange relationship of gunner with old man, hierarchy is overridden:

Some of the Young Gentlemen who was on the spot thought oytherways, they say this gave Umbrage to oyther people of the Island, particularly to some who hade the Appearance of the first rank, and this old man was only of the middle rank, and seemd to pay a great deal of respect to some of the others, who seemd to have servants with them, and great plenty of stock, but would send non of it over by the old man. (Robertson 1948:170)

Behind two arbitrarily selected individuals, the crowd and the comestibles and curiosities, it brings bottleneck. The false hierarchy that the 'Young Gentlemen' identify here is a reflection of the situation of the crew. Robertson later spells out the breach of shipboard rank that may have led to the officers' identification of infringements of status within the crowd:

[The first Lieutenant, William Clarke, would not] permitt any of the young Gentlemen to trade for any thing, this in my Oppinion was behaving very Ungentile to all the Young Gentlemen, several of them having past for Officers, and the rest all young Gentlemen ready and willing to learn the Duety of a seaman and Officer – ... I cannot help thinking a Gunner a very improper person to command any Gentleman that has served his time in the Navy upon the King's Quarter Deck. (Robertson 1948:175)[9]

In the mediated monopoly of these early exchanges, the crowds of both ship and shore remain crowds, unstratified and, therefore, still unknown. It is only towards the end of his account of Tahiti, when a 'queen' is identified in the high-ranking Purea, that crowd behaviour becomes properly resolved. Robertson writes, 'she laid hold of my hand and introduced me to all the principale people, and made them all shake hands with me ... We then set out Arm in Arm for the Palace, and all the Principale part of the Inhabitance came after us. When we got in Sight of the Palace a great number of people came out to receive us' (Robertson 1948:212). As has been pointed out numerous times, the identification of Purea as 'queen' was a misconception.[10] It is one that allows, however, for the definitive salvaging of crowd behaviour as homage rather than threat. In the slippage of the word 'principale' between signifying quantity and distinction, the crowd at last becomes ordered to Robertson's satisfaction (see Figure 2).

The first British and French visits to Tahiti constitute, discursively and historically, two poles of exploitative encounter: one regrettably violent, the other emphatically libidinal. Their contact does not get much beyond the crowd scene: the *Dolphin*'s crew are the only Europeans in the archive of Tahitian encounter not to register the word *taio*; the French seem more excited by public coupling than individualized sexual connection. In later accounts, however, the crowd scene emerges as one of traffic, rather than a prelude to traffic. Yet the trade relations instantiated in the crowd remain poised between potentials for theft and violence and for a novel erotics. The crowd's animated collective enacts a fraught problematic of cross-cultural encounter, in which selves become identified with cultural artifacts, and evaluation is at once arbitrary and absolute. The crowd is also a market, and, as Walter Benjamin

---

[9] Robertson quibbles constantly with this figure throughout his account, whom he refers to as 'Growl' and 'Lieut. Knowall', over issues of rank and authority. As Stuart Murray recognises, 'No other journal of the late eighteenth century comes close to Robertson's for the interpenetration of these issues of text, authority and representation' (Murray 2004:72).

[10] For example, Kerry Howe notes, 'Wallis took the reputation of her sovereignty back to Europe, but he was quite mistaken. She certainly had respect in the Matavai Bay region because of high family ties there, and she was married to Amo, tribal chief of Papara in the Teva-i-uta tribal coalition, who also had kin ties in the Matavai area. Purea therefore had influence ... but was by no means a queen of the island' (Howe 1984:129). On the shared investment of Purea herself and European voyagers in the notion of Purea as queen see Arii Taimai 1976:51; Henry 1928:15; Dening 1996:148; Salmond 2003:50–5.

Figure 2. The crowd reconfigured in homage: 'A representation of the surrender of the island of Otaheite to Captain Wallis by the supposed Queen Oberea', from John Hawkesworth, *An account of the voyages undertaken by the order of His present Majesty*, 1773.

observed, it inflates the commodity: 'The concentration of customers which makes the market, which in turn makes the commodity into a commodity, enhances its attractiveness to the average buyer' (Benjamin 1983:56). This was equally the case outside the metropole. When Johann Reinhold Forster arrived in Tonga, the presence of the crowd announced the commencement of trade, heralding a feverish exchange of commodities: 'The shore & rocks were crowded with people. They harraed when we came near, & immediately began trading with us, & offered us Cloth & other trifles to sell viz. Mother of Pearl Shells, which they hung on their breast; brasselets of mother of Pearl; Fishhooks; little Paddles & Stools of Clubwood; Bows & Arrows, Clubs' (Forster 1982:337). Although he tries to dismiss the items displayed as trifles, there is much evidence of the 'unregulated desire' for acquisition that Harriet Guest has elucidated in this passage and other accounts of Tonga from Cook's voyages (Guest 2007:111–12). To the degree that either party determines what Guest calls the 'terms of trade' in first contact, this is surely the prerogative of the Oceanic crowd, both by virtue of numbers and by the fact that it supplies items of subsistence, as well as fluctuating commodities. Yet desire on both sides is, indeed, unregulated in a practical sense, since the value of the items is at the moment of contact literally up for grabs. Benjamin portrayed the petty bourgeoisie of Baudelaire's Paris as not yet 'aware of the commodity nature of their labour power'; thus enjoying an identification with the commodity 'with all the pleasure and uneasiness which derived from a presentiment of its own destiny as a class' (Benjamin 1983:59). So too, the exchanges of early contact may be charged with the presentiment of a subsequent relationship of power, but they are characterized also by a pleasurable identification of self with object that turns eminent women into queens, sailors into both sought after objects and speculative connoisseurs. Once again, this seems predicated on a dialectic of scopophilia, in which the desire to be looked at is inextricable from the desire to observe.

Scene III: The City

A mixed mob of ferocious men, and of women lost to shame . . .
                                                        – Edmund Burke

Although the crowd has been the object of a substantial body of historical analysis and theoretical speculation, it has almost exclusively been discussed as a metropolitan phenomenon. Historians and sociologists who seek to determine the individual composition and motivations of the collective, and psychologists who posit a crowd mentality or will distinct from individual consciousness, though theoretically opposed, agree in representing the crowd as a product of urbanization. Elias Canetti's *Crowds and Power* proposed that 'Men might have gone on disregarding [the crowd] if the enormous increase of population in modern times, and the rapid growth of cities, had not more and more often given rise to its formation' (Canetti 2000:20–1). John Plotz's *The Crowd: British Literature and Public Politics*, while taking Canetti to task for his evocation of a monolithic crowd mentality, concurs that, in the English context, crowds materialized in important new ways with urban expansion: 'When London became the first postclassical city of one million inhabitants around 1800, quantity changed the quality of the city's life . . . Mundane outdoor life came to include random encounters with strangers, inexplicable aggregations, sudden eruptions of violence, and permanent sites for encountering others *en masse*' (Plotz 2000:1). For both Canetti and Plotz, the crowd is a phenomenon naturalized in relation to a concept of crowdedness. Once metropolitan spaces become crowded, crowds will perforce 'erupt' (Plotz 2000:1; Canetti 2000:20): they are the by-product of population density.

The challenge of this chapter, on the other hand, is to disassociate metropole and crowd: to imagine crowds aggregating in spaces not conceived of as crowded. There is little precedent for such an approach. Studies that have hitherto gestured towards an interpretation of the crowd as paradigmatic of self–other relations tend nonetheless to retain an urban focus. Mark Harrison prefaces his *Crowds and History* with the observation that

Our association of differentness and foreignness – of the alien and the threatening – with the existence of faceless far-away hordes is an aspect of human psychology with crucial implications for the formulation of social policy and foreign relations the world over. The supposed intimidation represented by mythical packs of strangers is what makes possible international and intercultural mass violence. (Harrison 1988:xiii)

Yet Harrison pulls back from the broader implications of this statement to focus his study on four British urban communities. His remarks counterpoint a conservative tradition that associates the crowd with the eruption of the foreign or 'primitive' within urban society (Le Bon 2004:19, 28, 32). Stanley Tambiah's *Leveling Crowds* (1996) examines the role of collective violence in peripheral (South Asian) settings of ethnonationalist conflict, but his case studies remain urban. George Rudé's seminal work on the crowd in the eighteenth century looks at rural village and market-town crowds in pre-industrial Britain and France. However, he emphatically characterizes the period he discusses as transitional: his telos is still 'the new "industrial" society' (Rudé 1964:5). Durkheim's discussion of the manifestations of a collective 'effervescence' linking the modern crowd with totemic religious cultures avoids the metropolitan bias, but this is with the objective of comprehensively analysing totemic religion: he is not primarily a theorist of the crowd (Durkheim 2001:154–62).

Although crowding is typically figured as a metropolitan phenomenon, it is associated in some of its more politicized European forms with rural production and the spectre of famine. In the English context, as Walter Shelton, Thomas Ashton and Richard Sheldon, as well as Rudé, have all shown, the eighteenth century was one of chronic food rioting (Shelton 1973:21; Ashton 1959:159; Sheldon 2004:204–47; Rudé 1964:33–46).[11] Shelton's particular focus is on the waves of hunger rioting in southern England in 1766, the year before Wallis laid claim to Tahiti for George III. The popular disturbances were, he argues, caused by high food prices,

[11] For the French side of this history, see Steven Laurence Kaplan's discussion of cereal dependence in old regime Europe (Kaplan 1976).

coinciding with the movement of wheat to ports. Elsewhere I have argued that this economic climate provides a context for the representation of Tahiti and other Oceanic islands as spaces of bounty (Smith 2006). Yet island crowds also harboured a potential for scarcity, resisted in most voyaging accounts but occasionally surfacing in images which link famine to horrific manifestations of crowd theatre. William Pascoe Crook reports that during a famine following the failure of the breadfruit crop on Tahuata in the Marquesas in 1797:

Many perished with hunger among whom was a woman named Houo ... Her relation to the chiefs family, so far from affording her support, yeilded [*sic*] her no relief from the savage mockery of her half-starved neighbours. Her flesh being entirely wasted from her bones, her strength therefore perfectly exhausted, the natives amused themselves with giving her a slight push, which was sufficient to bring her to the Ground, against which her bones rattled like those of a Skeleton. (Crook 2007:107)

European readings of the crowd in bays and on beaches were always in part about ascertaining an issue of provision: they indexed the island's potential for bounty or scarcity. But here again the crowd could offer mixed messages. Did a mass of bodies indicate a sustaining natural fertility or competition for limited resources? Crook's description of the emaciated woman mocked by the group that surrounds her offers a horrific counterpoint to the spectacles of public sex that titillated the first European visitors to Tahiti.

The scene might also recall some of the more notorious theatre of the French Revolution, in which aristocratic ties equally, 'so far from affording ... support, yeilded ... no relief from the savage mockery of ... half-starved neighbours'. The French Revolution is generally regarded as the historical impetus for later theorizations of crowd psychology (Rogers 1998:2; McClelland 1989:6; Ginnekin 1992:3; Tambiah 1996:267; Nye 1975:63).[12] In the nineteenth century, seminal works by Thomas Carlyle, Hippolyte Taine, Jules Michelet, Gabriel Tarde and, most famously, Gustave Le Bon attempted to account for the mass mobilization of the underclass by figuring the multiple bodies of the crowd as motivated by collective will. From assumptions about the metropolitan constitution of the crowd grew attendant claims about the effects of urban anonymity (Engels 1952:24), which found poetic embodiment in Walter Benjamin's theorization of Baudelaire's figure of

---

[12] Susan Barrows associates later-nineteenth-century crowd theory not only with the revolution of 1789, but more specifically with its aftermath in the European revolutions of 1848, the suppressed Paris uprising of 1871 and 'the chaos of the Third Republic' in France (Barrows 1981:43, 7–42; compare Nye 1975).

the *flâneur*. Benjamin writes of the crowds of Berlin, Paris and London as confluences in which the individual may seek to hide; to achieve a paradoxical solitude. He comments on the uniformity of bodies in the urban crowd, 'in which no one is either quite transparent or quite opaque to all others' (Benjamin 1983:49). This is, of course, a very different experience of crowding from that registered by European voyagers, who *stand out* in the crowd that surrounds them. So successfully has the crowd been elided with the modern city, that experiences of crowding within situations of imperial contact, where the shock and pleasure for the European visitor is of being encompassed by bodies that are different rather than the same, and thus of being simultaneously singled out and engulfed, have consistently been interpreted as experiences of othering rather than of crowding (Pratt 1986:35). Yet to adopt Plotz's terminology, the Pacific beach became in the late eighteenth century a 'permanent site' where encounters, both staged and frighteningly random, took place, and voyagers experienced 'inexplicable aggregations' and 'sudden eruptions of violence'. Account after account records the experience of being inundated by the crowd: being noticed and enveloped by a mass of bodies emerges as a trope of encounter, through which the visitor constitutes and authorizes their experience.

The presence of peripheral crowd scenes within accounts of first contact raises a number of questions about the politics of encounter. What are the dynamics of identification that take place within the crowd, and how do they figure or alter in crowds that assemble at scenes of contact? Is the dialectical relationship between the body of the individual and the body of the crowd in any way comparable to that between recognition and repudiation that takes place in confrontation with cultural difference? We might also rethink through the crowd the dynamics of authority and voyeurism played out in cross-cultural observation. Most often the Oceanic crowd is represented as a spontaneous demonstration of curiosity about European bodies and culture. The European desire to perceive crowding as a testimony to cultural fascination might be seen as another aspect of a broad European project of self-elevation (Obeyesekere 1992:177). Yet surely something more complex is at stake here. If, as I intimated in my reading of Bougainville, Europeans relish as often as they are disconcerted by the experience of being sampled, fondled, of having their artifacts or their skin marvelled at, they are enjoying in a more immediate sense a process of objectification than of veneration. While curiosity has become an important field of inquiry for recent scholarship, the focus has been upon European curiosity about other societies: on cultures of collecting and connoisseurship, that testify to a European desire to look, to hoard, to possess (Benedict 2001;

Leask 2002; Elsner and Cardinal 1994).[13] What of the desire to be valued, exposed, fingered by the curious, that is the corollary of scopophilia and that is so sublimely gratified by the crowd?

As Gillian Beer has observed, any concomitant withdrawal of attention was registered harshly in European discourse:

> The absence of wonder or surprise was one of the phenomena that most disconcerted Western travellers in their encounters with indigenous people and which they described as most animal-like. Curiosity was so strong a driving force in Western expeditions, and so valued as a disinterested or 'scientific' incentive as opposed to the search for material gain, that the absence of an answering curiosity was felt as rebuff or even insult. (Beer 1996:62)

Scientific imperatives aside, recognizing the dialectical relationship between inattention and scopophilia can nuance our picture of the dynamics of encounter. Well into the nineteenth century, in situations where it is clear that they were not making first contact, travellers insisted on the novelty of their status as representative Europeans. The fantasy of entering territory where 'no white woman had previously set foot' recurs throughout the Fijian letters of Constance Gordon-Cumming, written between 1875 and 1877, which highlight the author's nonchalant intrepidity by depicting her capacity to conjure domesticity (*My Fijian Home*) within a recently cannibal context. Visiting a village of whose residents she claimed 'most of whom were, till within the last two years, uncompromising cannibals, and who, moreover, have never before beheld the face of a white woman' (though it had for some years been under missionary influence), Gordon-Cumming constructed a theatre space – 'I have hung up my plaid-curtain and mosquito-net, thereby greatly interesting a crowd of spectators, who had previously watched the wonderful process of consuming chocolate and biscuits' – favouring performance over hospitality as her mode of interaction (reprinted in Lamb, Smith and Thomas 2000:295, 297–8).

The same titillation at being the object of attention informs a related set piece that recurs in descriptions of Oceanic crowd scenes, where islanders purportedly marvel at the colour and texture of European skin. Melville plays with this scenario in *Typee*, his novel based on a brief sojourn on the Marquesan island of Nuku'hiva in 1842. In the valley of

---

[13] The focus on curiosity as a European prerogative responds to, and to some degree rearticulates, what Harriet Guest has identified as an assumption that 'curiosity and civilization are ... intimately intertwined'. She notes that in the late eighteenth century, 'curiosity was one of the characteristics that those allocated to the lowest rungs of the ladder of cultivation were thought to lack, whereas, in contrast, its impartial or indiscriminate avidity was seen as a hallmark of high civilization' (Guest 1996:xli).

Taipi, the protagonists Tommo and his friend Toby have 'the whiteness of our limbs' scanned: two sailors who have already presented themselves as a cut above the average find their pretensions confirmed when their skin is fingered with connoisseurship: 'They felt our skin, much in the same way a silk mercer would handle a remarkably fine piece of satin.' Melville recognizes that the desire to deduce primacy of contact from such a reception is a compelling fantasy: 'their singular behavior almost led me to imagine that they never before had beheld a white man; but a few minutes reflection convinced me that this could not have been the case'. He has Tommo settle instead for the runner-up title of 'first white men who ever penetrated this far back into their territories' (Melville 1996:94–5). The nineteenth-century fantasies of first encounter Melville parodies, which seek to re-engage tropes of the crowd scene – of the surrounded and marvelled at western body – are perhaps compensatory. They reinvigorate all the Oceanic bodies that have disappeared in the interim, and wish away the bodily contacts that were responsible for their decimation. If later visitors can still imagine that their skin is being seen for the first time, they can also fantasize that their belated first contact remains pristine, unsullied by the destructive interactions that have preceded it. Such marvelling responses on the part of Oceanians may in fact equally have been gestures of mimicry or hospitality: the two faces of a canny recognition of those western fantasies of primacy that are being acted out in such scenarios. Yet given the voyeuristic excitement we have identified as an aspect of cross-cultural crowd dynamics, perhaps what is being registered here is a kind of narcissistic alienation effect, in which the European's own body is seen *as if* for the first time, through the projected and internalized gaze of the excited mass.

Scene IV: The Rocks

> Contagion is particularly dangerous in crowds.
>
> – Montaigne

Axiomatic to crowd psychology is the notion that the crowd can turn. If massed individuals are regarded as having one mind, that mind is fickle. 'They may be animated in succession by the most contrary sentiments' wrote Gustave le Bon (Le Bon 2004:19). Herbert Blumer argues that, 'not having a body of definitions or rules to guide its behavior and, instead, acting on the basis of impulse, the crowd is fickle, suggestible and irresponsible' (Blumer 1969:73). Alan Kerckhoff, following Blumer, regards the 'erratic behavior, and increased suggestibility' of individuals in crowds as exemplifying an 'hysterical contagion' (Kerckhoff 1970:83). Charles Tilly highlights the capacity of crowds to 'shift rapidly into collective violence and then (sometimes just as rapidly) back into relatively peaceful relations' (Tilly 2003: 229). Elias Canetti discusses at length the tendencies towards 'reversal' and 'transformation' within crowds (Canetti 2000). More recently, John Plotz has summed up the arguments against crowd psychologizing, pointing in particular to an ahistoricist tendency in such crowd theories to figure 'an inarticulable essence' to the crowd. While his argument that 'claims about the innate and timeless qualities of "the" crowd were made tactically in order to describe and contain the unruly energies of suffrage-minded working-class assemblies' (Plotz 2000:4) is convincing in relation to the commonly understood metropolitan territory of the crowd, notions of mass psychology remain helpful as we begin to consider crowds outside the precincts of the city: not least because crowd psychology maps onto and incorporates a discourse of savage unknowability.[14] In this section I will argue that ignoring crowd psychology in the Oceanic context reiterates a refusal to recognize Oceanic crowds, which in turn exemplifies scholarship's broader analytic compartmentalization of metropolitan and peripheral societies.

The turning of the crowd at Kaleakekua Bay on 14 February 1779, which resulted in the death of James Cook upon the rocks of the foreshore, has in turn become a fiercely contested scene within Pacific scholarship. The thesis that Cook was identified in the Hawaiian mind with the god Lono, originally proposed by Gavan Daws (Daws 1968a; 1968b:1–29), was masterfully developed by Marshall Sahlins into an encompassing interpretation that brought together historical and structural anthropological analysis. Sahlins's detailed investigation of the correspondences between events leading up to Cook's death and those of the Hawaiian ritual calendar provoked an impassioned attack from Gananath Obeyesekere, who focused on agendas of local politics rather than mythical ritual and drew attention to the compromised nature of Sahlins's sources, which were primarily the work of mission-trained nineteenth-century Hawaiian historians (Kamakau 1992; Malo 1951). It has now become impossible for scholars engaging with Cook's legacies to avoid returning to this scene and this debate. Anne Salmond, Nicholas Thomas and John Gascoigne all assess the relevance of the Lono analogy in their studies of Cook's voyages, Rod Edmond has offered a judicious analysis of the post-colonial implications of the Sahlins/Obeyesekere debate, and recently Glyn Williams has devoted

---

[14] Kathleen Wilson notes the widespread tendency to compare French Revolutionaries to 'savages' (K. Wilson 2003:91).

Figure 3. The crowd on the rocks: Francesco Bartolozzi, 'The Death of Captain Cook', 1784.

an entire volume to a comprehensive re-evaluation of the events and implications of the death (Salmond 2003:386–416; Thomas 2003: 386–404; Gascoigne 2007:214–19; Edmond 1997:51–61; Williams 2008). I want here, nonetheless, once again to review that scene and that debate, since it is my argument that readings of Cook's death have been stymied by the same blindness to Oceanic crowds that I have identified in broader scholarship. In trying to establish whether structured ritual or universal rationalism influenced the events of Cook's reception, both Sahlins and Obeyesekere effectively systematized crowd behaviour, neglecting the ways in which ritual can devolve into unstructured activity and an encompassing irrationalism.

Sahlins's compelling analysis of Cook's reception and death in Hawaii makes sense of the crowd and the friendships and exchanges it instantiates in mythical-religious terms. He argues that Cook was received in Hawaii as the representation of the god Lono, a figure of peace and productivity, during the Makahiki festival, the time of Lono's ascendancy. In a series of remarkable coincidences, aspects of Cook's voyaging around the Hawaiian islands corresponded to the rituals of Makahiki; particularly his prolonged circumnavigation of the island group, prior to his second Hawaiian landfall on Hawai'i island and his initial, scheduled departure. However, when the *Resolution* sprung its foremast and Cook's ships were forced back to Hawai'i to make repairs, it was the season of the warlike god Ku, Lono's rival, who was represented by the Hawaiian *ali'i*[15] Kalei'opu'u. Cook/Lono became in this context a threatening figure, to be attacked rather than revered. Sahlins thus relates the crowd of welcome to the festival spirit of the Makahiki and its subsequent absence to the inappropriateness of Cook's return within the Hawaiian ritual calendar:

During the first hectic days at Kealakekua … 10,000 Hawaiians crowded on the waters and shores of the Bay – and all over the ships – in exuberant welcome of Lono. The welcome of 17 January 1779 had been the greatest reception any European voyager ever had in this Ocean … Now, on 11 February, the Bay was quiet, relatively empty of people and these, according to some accounts, showed nothing like the same amicability. (Sahlins 1972:23)

In a later version of his thesis, Sahlins describes Cook's initial welcome as the Pacific exploration crowd scene *par excellence*:

Nor in all his experience had Captain Cook ever seen so many Polynesians assembled as were here in Kealakekua Bay. Besides the innumerable canoes, Hawaiians were clambering over the *Resolution* and *Discovery*, lining the beaches, and swimming in the water 'like shoals of fish'. Perhaps there were 10,000, or five times as many people as normally lived there. (Sahlins 1985:105)

This is the apotheosis of the crowd: the most crowded crowd of Cook's experience, and one whose density is also abnormal in Polynesian terms. When it later turns hostile it will be transformed in Sahlins's prose, in a classic rhetorical move, into a 'mob exulting over him' (Sahlins 1985:106).[16]

What does Sahlins make of the crowd? Something pretty close to what John Plotz would recommend. He eschews psychology, and instead both historicizes and systematizes. He doesn't require a collective mentality; 'we need not suppose that all Hawaiians were convinced that Captain Cook was Lono; or, more precisely, that his being Lono meant the same to everyone' (Sahlins 1985:121). He makes a distinction between the unfolding of the event 'as individual action and as collective representation' and reads between these two planes of interpretation, asserting nonetheless the ordered logic of the group dynamic: 'those recurrent dimensions of the event in which we recognize some cultural order' (Sahlins 1985:108). Finally, he parses the crowd, eliciting from what

---

[15] Chief: equivalent to Tahitian *ari'i*.
[16] For a detailed exploration of the rhetorics of crowd and mob, see McClelland 1989.

has appeared a collective action the salient individual. For, as he notes, this has remained a resiliently collective execution: 'In historical texts dating from this day [of Cook's death] to fifty-odd years later, some eight or ten different men are identified as "the man who killed Captain Cook", referring to the one who first stabbed him with the iron dagger' (Sahlins 1985:108). Tracing social status and motive, Sahlins proceeds to identify the individual culprit from among the crowd on the Kealakekua rocks. Yet this detective work, even as it historicizes faces in the crowd in what might be regarded as an inherently politicized manoeuvre, is also a form of crowd control. The exulting 'mob' that Sahlins described earlier is reduced to one coherently motivated and manageable individual.

Gananath Obeyesekere's critique of Sahlins, which aims to 'restore . . . the dimension of reflectiveness and rationality to Hawaiian thought' (Obeyesekere 1992:95), inevitably performs a similar operation on the crowd, thus moving it further still from notions of contagious collective behaviour. Indeed the kinds of cultural presumption Sahlins highlights in his rebuttal of Obeyesekere become nowhere more apparent than in his treatment of the crowd as possessing one highly rational mind. Thus, rejecting Sahlins's interpretation of the Makahiki crowd as the definitive Oceanic crowd, Obeyesekere writes of the crowd phenomenon that greeted Cook on Hawai'i simply that 'large crowds would surely have been inevitable, because the ships had been cruising around the islands for over seven weeks, rousing the curiosity and sense of expectation of the native population'. He is concerned to represent the crowd as primarily motivated by a desire to give rather than take: as generous rather than importunate: 'The remarkable feature about the Hawaiian experience is the Hawaiians' extreme generosity with food and provisions' (Obeyesekere 1992:46). He chastises Sahlins with manipulating figures to create, from the example of a single woman, 'the impression that the decks of the ships were crowded with women gleefully shouting' as the houses of their countrymen were torched (Obeyesekere 1992:68). Conversely, he reprimands Sahlins for reducing the potential crowd of Cook's assailants to one, rightly observing that 'nice sociological distinctions' are not apparent in crowd scenes, and that individual culprits are hard to uncover: 'It should also be remembered that the melee in which Cook was killed took only a few minutes and by all accounts was a scene of confusion' (Obeyesekere 1992:185).

Sahlins's subsequent demolition of Obeyesekere's thesis, *How 'Natives' Think: About Captain Cook, for Example*, places a new emphasis on the phenomenon of the crowding that greeted Cook's ships. In an earlier article, 'Captain Cook at Hawaii', Sahlins had directed attention towards a novel source of evidence: 'the whole history of popular desire and delight that parallels the chroniclers' descriptions of incidents and events' (Sahlins 1989:412). In particular he emphasized two facets commonly associated with metropolitan crowding: spontaneous agglomeration and democratic constitution. He represented the Makahiki crowd as a mass movement: 'it was spontaneous and popular, not just something whipped up by the powers-that-were'; 'the ordinary people, were really excited' (Sahlins 1989:412, 413). Emphatically, he recuperated this crowd for a 'history from below'.[17] Dismissing 'a priori and tired ideas about how the ruling classes dupe the masses', Sahlins argued that

On the contrary, the Hawaiian celebration of Cook as Lono was from the beginning a collective movement, even as Lono was traditionally a popular god ... Likewise, the Makahiki, which celebrated the advent of Lono as a *fête* of pleasure and *communitas*, was a popular festival, marked for a time by the eclipse of the established order, or its royal rituals and human sacrifices, by the reign of a carnival king. And in the same way again, the veneration of Captain Cook in the Makahiki season of 1778–9 was a popular demonstration, spreading spontaneously around the island of Hawai'i even faster than his ships could carry him, so that, by the time he reached Kealakekua, he was greeted by a rejoicing people. (Sahlins 1989:413–14)

The crowd Sahlins describes here is a ritual crowd, but one with a mind of its own. Its responses are structured yet voluntary. I will return to this notion shortly, but first I want to look at where this crowd takes Sahlins in his rebuttal of Obeyesekere.

In *How 'Natives' Think*, the paradox of collective spontaneity is repeatedly invoked by Sahlins to portray the particular flavour of the Makahiki festival and Cook's incorporation within it. Of Lono he writes: 'His annual return, coinciding with the return of the sun and the revival of nature, is the occasion of collective joy' (Sahlins 1995:27). He juxtaposes a call for renewed attention to Hawaiian 'attitudes, gestures and emotions' with a sense of their ritualized – that is, recurrent and collective, dimensions (Sahlins 1995:36). His culminating description of the arrival of Cook as Lono stresses its 'epiphanal dimensions', the 'tumultuous scene', the 'pandemonium', the 'shoals of people swimming about' and the jubilation of 'the people who, in great numbers, clambered aboard the ships. And on board as well as in the water, on the shore and in their canoes, people were singing, dancing, shrieking, clapping and jumping up and down' (Sahlins 1995:47). Although Sahlins is himself careful to balance a sense of the ritual and spontaneous

---

[17] Examples of this approach to the crowd include Rudé, Thompson, and Stallybrass and White.

elements of crowd behaviour – just as his broader project is concerned to balance the mythical and historical dimensions of encounter – he quotes approvingly naval historian Richard Hough, who depicted the scene at Kealakekua as one of mass hysteria:

Neither the thieving, nor the unprecedented numbers, accounted for the hysterical element, which grew rather than diminished as this day of noise and pandemonium wore on. It was rather as if the ships had by chance arrived at some culmination in the lives of this community, a climax that would affect their destiny. Polynesian excitement was one thing, and they were familiar with that. In this bay the whole population gave the impression of being on the brink of mass madness. (Hough 1979:185; Sahlins 1995:47)

What Hough is prepared to countenance, and Sahlins will only footnote, is a notion of crowd behaviour as motivated by a collective psychology that eludes control. Hough's terminology is redolent of Canetti's typologies of crowd rhythm and discharge. It is 'on the brink' and capable of transformation. Sahlins's ritual crowd on the other hand recalls Canetti's domesticated religious crowd: 'the faithful are gathered at appointed places and times and, through performances which are always the same, they are transported into a mild state of crowd feeling sufficient to impress itself on them without becoming dangerous, and to which they grow accustomed' (Canetti 2000:25). Hough's hysterical crowd with its capacity for fickle transformation becomes, through Sahlins's analysis, an explicable, indeed logical crowd. The question it throws up: 'What did it mean?' (Sahlins 1995:47), can be answered. This ritual crowd is precisely not fickle, changeable, hysterical. It is necessarily not the same crowd that killed Cook. It is a joyous crowd that will be displaced by the inherently psychically different ritual crowd of a different ritual season.

Yet the crowd also unravels efforts at consistent interpretation. Having asserted the demographic and ideological unity of the Kealakekua crowd, Sahlins goes on to contradict this, and to refigure the crowd as a stratified, multi-vocal and socially manipulable space. He now writes:

It need not be supposed that all Hawaiians were equally convinced that Cook was Lono, or, more precisely, that his being 'Lono' meant the same to everyone ... The special enthusiasm of the old folks ... may not have been shared by the entire population, especially the people working priestly estates ... The priestly herald preceding Cook and making everyone prostrate at the cry of 'Lono' was not the only indication that the Hawaiian powers-that-be had unique possibilities of objectifying their own interpretations. (Sahlins 1995:65)

Such concessions make way for the reiteration of Sahlins's thesis that the crowd surrounding Cook at his death can be reduced to an identifiably motivated individual. In the service of his unfolding interpretation, the crowd morphs from a psychically unified to a socially constituted body.

In tracing the shifting representation of the crowd in debates about Cook's death, I hope to have given some indication of the way in which crowds remain both instrumental to and elided within Pacific scholarship. They are either extraordinary phenomenon or irrelevance. And this is because the crowd is not *seen*. Is the crowd that assembles at Kealakekua so numerically different from the thousands that Robertson estimated thronged Matavai Bay to greet the *Dolphin*, or is it simply that crowds so infrequently figure in subsequent European representation of the Pacific that *we* cannot encompass them? Sahlins's call for greater attention to the emotions of the multitude needs to be sustained across different Oceanic scenarios and beyond singular events. Where Sahlins focuses constructively on the crowd in relation to Cook's reception in Hawai'i, he loses sight of it at the scene of his death, opting to reduce the crowd to the single culprit. It is integral to Sahlins's interpretation that the crowds of Cook's reception and of his death are ritually constituted and therefore inherently different crowds, rather than one fickle body: crowds of Carnival and Lent, performing alternately rather than reacting unpredictably. What happens if we instead read Cook's death as a crowd phenomenon that exceeds the cultural particularities of ritual and exemplifies elements of a more universalized mass dynamic? In pursuing this possibility I want to sidestep rather than ignore the ethnographic particularities whose contributions to Cook's death seem to have become the sole arena for contests of interpretation, and to propose that the Hawaiian crowd might have behaved, and might be understood, like a metropolitan crowd, in terms of a crude crowd psychology. In other words as a perversely motivated collective, rather than as always a conglomerate of ethnographic subjects.

On the night of 13 February 1779, the *Discovery*'s cutter was removed from the ship while anchored in Kealekekua Bay. Cook resolved to take Kalei'opu'u hostage to secure its return. Initially the *ali'i* came willingly with Cook: however, his wife and two lesser chiefs argued against his departure, and he became resistant. Meanwhile, at the other end of the bay, Marines had killed a high-ranking *ali'i* and news of his death travelled towards Cook via the crowd. I want to suggest that Cook's death was the result of crowd feeling.

The most detailed descriptions of the death come from Charles Clerke, commander of the *Discovery* and Cook's second in command, from David Samwell, surgeon's mate, and from the Marine lieutenant Molesworth Phillips, who was on shore with Cook in the period immediately leading up to his death. These accounts, written from different perspectives on ship and shore, and with different degrees of evident narrative shaping, concur in figuring the death as a crowd event. Clerke, who watched through a spyglass from the ship – a position similar to Wallis's when the *Dolphin* attacked the Tahitian crowd – emphasizes the crowd's constituent indeterminacy and confusion: 'I could not distinguish Persons in that confused Croud', 'Capt Cook and four Marines had fallen in this confounded fray' (Cook 1967:534). His sense of the crowd appears to have been shaped by his own impotence as he watches from afar. Depicting the crowd as confounding and its actions as unpremeditated initially allows him to avoid questions of culpability. Yet ultimately he acknowledges that the crowd renders the British command culpable. Clerke concludes: 'Upon the whole I firmly believe matters would not have been carried to the extremities they were had not Capt Cook attempted to chastize a man in the midst of this multitude' (Cook 1967:538).

Samwell, on the other hand, who subsequently published *Narrative of the Death of Captain Cook* (1786), and was the most ambitious in literary terms of the three narrators, represents the crowd as a tactical body. 'It became necessary to resist the Impetuosity of the Indians who in a body of several Thousands of people were pressing upon them, and ready to seize on the first advantagious [sic] opportunity of falling upon our Men should they turn their Backs to them & retreat with Precipitation and Disorder,' he writes. After two Hawaiians were shot, 'The Ardour and Impetuosity of the Indians were by this a little repressed, they were staggered & the body of them fell back' (Cook 1967:1197). The 'staggered' Hawaiian crowd comprising a less dense body, Samwell argues, this was the moment for the Marines to have acted as one: to recognize their own crowd force. Instead they behaved as the classic panicked crowd described by Canetti: 'The individual breaks away and wants to escape from it because the crowd, as a whole, is endangered . . . the more blows he inflicts and the more he receives, the more himself he feels. The boundaries of his own person become clear to him again' (Canetti 2000:27). Cook's small crowd of Marines disintegrated before the crowd of Hawaiians: 'no sooner had the Marines made the general Discharge but the body of them flung down their pieces and threw themselves into the water, on this all was over, the Indians immediately rushed down upon them' (Cook 1967:1197–8). This scenario, in which firearms and thus Europeans lose their authority, and friends become foes as the Oceanic crowd recognizes its collective power, had been exactly anticipated by Cook in his published account of his second voyage:

Three things made them our fast friends, Their own good Natured and benevolent disposition, gentle treatment on our part, and the dread of our fire Arms; by our ceaseing to observe the Second the first would have wore of[f] of Course, and the too frequent use of the latter would have excited a spirit of revenge and perhaps have taught them that fire Arms were not such terrible things as they had imagined, they are very sencible of the superiority they have over us in numbers and no one knows what an enraged multitude might do. (Cook 1969:398)

In Samwell's account, the Hawaiian crowd is impetuous, but not confused as in Clerke's view: rather, it takes strategic advantage of confusion. The Marines, on the other hand, enact and suffer the negative effects of crowd confusion: 'the boats Crew were busy in taking the Marines in who had escaped from the Indians, which creating unavoidable confusion & disorder in such a small boat prevented them entirely from using their fire arms & giving assistance' (Cook 1967:1199). Samwell's Hawaiian crowd is represented, by contrast, as achieving coordination even within confusion. This is something different from Sahlins's effort to make sense of the crowd by breaking it down to motivated individuals. Samwell emphasizes, rather, the self-reflexive force of the crowd precisely as a multitude: one that understands and utilizes its own collective capacities.

Molesworth Phillips's eyewitness report confirms that it is the unexpected ability of the Hawaiians to act together – to behave as a crowd – that contravenes his party's expectations:

The business was now a most miserable scene of confusion – the Shouts and Yells of the Indians far exceeded all the noise I ever came in the way of, these fellows instead of retiring upon being fir'd at, as Capt Cook and I believe most People concluded they would, acted so very contrary a part, that they never gave the Soldiers time to reload their Pieces but immediately broke in upon and would have kill'd every man of them ... (Cook 1967:536)

Phillips's claim is that the ineffectualness of guns was in this context unanticipated, but what in fact emerges as truly unaccountable is the collective action of the crowd. We might compare his report with Robertson's evocation of the Tahitian first encounter with European weapons, cited earlier, where he described how the *Dolphin*'s guns 'struck such terror amongs the poor unhapy croad'. If the *Dolphin*'s inaugural encounter with Oceanic crowds has provided a template of crowd panic on which Cook's crew in part bases its assumptions, the Hawaiians adopt another mode of crowd behaviour. Acting as a body they revolt, thrusting confusion back against Cook and his marines, where it is registered in synaesthesia: 'all the noise I ever came in the way of'. It is as a crowd, rather than as either Sahlins's or

Obeyesekere's contingent collection of coherently motivated individuals, that Hawaiians inspire Europeans with a sense of the limits of their power.[18] The descriptions of the death of Cook are descriptions of European loss of command, of European loss of control. In Canetti's words, 'no-one has been appointed executioner; the community as a whole does the killing' (Canetti 2000:50).

Scene V: The Island

> Though my house is quite full in the morning, though I go down to the forum hemmed in by droves of 'friends', I can find no one out of that great crowd with whom I can freely make a joke or sigh familiarly.
> – Cicero

If it seems important to recognize that a model of universalized crowd behaviour might pertain as well to islands as to cities, however, it remains necessary to acknowledge that Oceanic crowds are in many ways specific in their manifestations. The remainder of this chapter will attempt to hold both these aspects of crowd dynamics in mind through a reading of William Bligh's 1792 account of the *Bounty* voyage, a text whose constitutive events coincided with the early riots of that 'original' crowd scene, the French Revolution (Dunphy 1982:281–2). The account, though written in the first person and derived from Bligh's log, was published while he was back in the Pacific completing his breadfruit mission. It therefore received some editorial shaping from James Burney, who had been twice in the Pacific with Cook, and whose own experience of Tahiti also resurfaces in Bligh's narrative (Du Rietz 1962:115–25).[19]

The *Bounty* voyage had been undertaken at the instigation of Joseph Banks, to convey breadfruit cuttings to the West Indies for cultivation as a staple food for plantation slaves. At Tahiti Bligh negotiated for breadfruit plants in exchange for 'valuable presents' purportedly sent directly by George III (Bligh 1979:73). The officers and crew spent five and a half months on Tahiti-nui, first at Matavai and then at Pare, while the breadfruit cuttings were established. The mutiny that took place only

---

[18] My interpretation here, in privileging the unstructured and uncontained, rather than ritualized, aspects of crowd behaviour and their political import, glosses the suggestion of Stallybrass and White, following Terry Eagleton, that 'the "licensed release" of carnival is ... simply a form of social control of the low by the high and therefore serves the interests of that very official culture which it apparently opposes' (Stallybrass and White 1986:13).

[19] Rolf du Rietz went so far as to argue that 'Bligh's *Voyage* should henceforth be stated as having been written partly by James Burney and partly by William Bligh (on whose journal and directions Burney of course still based his compilation.)' (Du Rietz 1962:120) This suggestion does not appear to have been taken up.

three and a half weeks after the ship's departure was attributed by Bligh to the friendships forged during this prolonged sojourn: intimacies filtered from an initial encounter with a crowd impelled by curiosity that was indexed to specific relationships – of trade, of ceremonial and social protocol.

Bligh's arrival at Matavai Bay on 26 October 1788 is narrated as a now familiar succession of crowd scenes: 'As we drew near, a great number of canoes came off to us . . . They crowded on board in vast numbers, notwithstanding our endeavours to prevent it, as we were working the ship in; and in less than ten minutes, the deck was so full that I could scarce find my own people' (Bligh 1979:59). The crowd that obstructs the process of landing is an authenticating presence, as the use of the word 'endeavours' perhaps unconsciously confirms. It links Bligh's voyage to a tradition that includes Wallis's, Bougainville's and Cook's arrivals in Tahiti, while affirming the continued novelty and significance of European visits to the Tahitians. This doubled recognition offered by the agglomeration of the crowd is further complicated once the ship anchors. Now the 'own people' the commander has difficulty identifying among the pressing throng become pre-eminent members of the Matavai community. He writes, 'The ship being anchored, our number of visitors continued to increase; but as yet we saw no person that we could recollect to have been of much consequence. Some inferior chiefs made me presents' (Bligh 1979:61). These individuals of consequence have, of course, been singled out from the crowd on former voyages: they are the named Tahitians of previous explorers' accounts, including Cook's final voyage, on which Bligh had served as master of the *Resolution*. In his log, Bligh makes a point of giving 'an account of some principal People and their descendants here who have been Spoke of in our earliest Voyages' (Bligh 1937: II, 62–3). Recognizing these familiar faces within the crowd, as well as accounting for the animals and plants left by Cook, and retracing Cook's footsteps and friendships, becomes an important aspect of Bligh's project to represent himself as Cook's inheritor. He had been the only officer on Cook's last voyage not to receive promotion when the *Resolution* and *Discovery* returned to London, after falling out with Lieutenant James King over Bligh's handling of events leading up to Cook's death. Greg Dening has insightfully analysed the ways in which Bligh overvalued the mission as a chance to redeem his career (Dening 1992:65). To claim relation to Cook by reforging his connections in Tahiti was surely among the over-determined imperatives of Bligh's voyage.

The concern to identify individuals of distinction among the multitude is at the same time ironized in a number of ways in Bligh's account. After noting that 'my table at dinner was generally crouded', he questions his capacity to establish the extent of the crowd or the degree of consequence of its individual members, commenting,

> Almost every individual of any consequence has several names, which makes it frequently perplexing, when the same person is spoken of, to know who is meant. Every chief has perhaps a dozen or more names in the course of thirty years; so that the person who has been spoken of by one visitor, will not perhaps be known to another, unless other circumstances lead to a discovery. (Bligh 1979:82)

As I will explain in Chapter 2, practices of name exchange ensure that the individual of consequence proliferates in Tahiti, thwarting the European's attempt to forge connections based on hierarchy established over the course of a series of significant contacts, and reducing the grand task of 'discovery' to the lesser project of establishing identity. In Bligh's log, a more expansive discussion of this phenomenon is prefaced by the comment, 'I should speak of a variety of Cheifs from other districts who have visited us, but as it would be nothing but a catalogue of Names, it can be of no use' (Bligh 1937: I, 384). Here Bligh seems to make a different kind of distinction between the recorded crowd and the physical crowd, implying that the inability to distinguish individuals is one that may persist in reading, but which is overcome through the praxis of contact.

A more telling irony, however, is Bligh's identification of the disabled as immediate figures of distinction among the multitude. In a crowd scene at the house of the Matavai chief Poeno, Bligh relates, 'The people ... thronged about the house, in such numbers, that I was much incommoded by the heat, which being observed, they immediately drew back. Among the croud I saw a man who had lost his arm just above the elbow; the stump was well covered, and the cure seemed as perfect as could be expected from the greatest professional skill' (Bligh 1979:63). Here the disabled body alone stands out from the collective body of the crowd, registering as the sole figure of consequence. In his log, Bligh distinguishes individuals for obesity, a cancerous nose and jaw, a lost eye, deformed limbs and ulcerations (Bligh 1937: I, 391, 389, 403; II, 30). Yet despite the focus on these figures as exceptions, there is an implication that they might be representatives of a different crowd, of the ill and infected, for whom Bligh is keen to disclaim responsibility.[20] Observing that 'Scropulous Patients were I to encourage them would be innumerable,' he concludes,

---

[20] Such grotesque bodies are indeed, according to Stallybrass and White, inherently of the crowd: the grotesque aesthetic features a 'somatic conception ... which was usually multiple, teeming, always already part of a throng' (Stallybrass and White 1986:21).

I do not beleive that they have superior blessings with respect to health; we already see them with dreadful Cancers, Consumptions, Fevers, Fits and the Scropula in a Shocking degree, and we may infer many incidental diseases besides. The fertile Country and delightfull Climate of the Society Islands does not therefore exempt its Inhabitants from the attendant miseries of ill health. (Bligh 1937: II, 31)[21]

During his subsequent visit in the *Providence*, Bligh would find that what was in the process of emerging as the highest-ranking Tahitian name commemorated the legacies of disease:

It surprised me to find, that both Iddeah & Tynah were called Pomarre, & on enquiring into the Cause of it, I find it owing to their having lost their Eldest Daughter Terreenoareah by an Illness called by that name, and which they describe to me by coughing. [marginal note: 'Pomarre is compounded from Po Night & Marre the name of the Disease.'] Whenever a Child dies the Parents or relations take the Name of the disease – if a dozen Children die of different diseases, the Parents have as many different Names, (or give them to their Relations) and may be called by either, but commonly by the last. (Oliver 1988:89)

Bligh encounters examples of closed, or event-specific crowds (Canetti 2000:17), particularly *heiva*s (dance performances) and wrestling displays, which, as in Cook's and other exploration accounts, tremble on the edge of 'riot and confusion' (Bligh 1979:88) only to reaffirm order (see Figure 4). But his more complex responses surface when he himself figures as object of curiosity, rather than honoured viewer, the curious visitor. Though this phenomenon occurs at ceremonies of welcome and prestation, greater affirmation comes with the aggregation of a spontaneous or open crowd. Thus when Bligh perambulates around Matavai Bay he finds that, 'In my walk I had picked up a numerous attendance, for every one I met followed me; so that I had collected such a croud, that the heat was scarce bearable, every one endeavouring to get a look to satisfy their curiosity: they however carefully avoided pressing against me, and welcomed me with chearful countenances, and great good-nature' (Bligh 1979:68). Bligh's Pied Piper magnetism compensates for the discomfort caused by the throng of bodies. At the same time his rather poignant reference to 'chearful countenances, and great good-nature' suggests that he is trying to recuperate some level of intimacy from the encounter, and to emphasize the benign reception that he had received in Tahiti. The avoidance of direct touch in this instance can be attributed to the operation of *tapu*, a local practice of sacred embargo that effectively

---

[21] Howard M. Smith weighs the evidence regarding the European introduction of venereal disease to Tahiti, responsibility for which was repudiated by both the British and the French (H. Smith 1975).

Figure 4. Crowd pleasing: an event-specific crowd in Tonga. 'Onthaal van Kapitein Cook op het Eiland Hapaee', plate 79 in *Reizen rondom de waereld door J. Cook*, 1795–1809.

militates against a complete dissolution of boundaries and distinctions within the crowd. According to Canetti:

It is only in a crowd that Man can become free of [the] fear of being touched ... The crowd he needs is the dense crowd, in which body is pressed to body; a crowd, too, whose physical constitution is also dense, or compact, so that he no longer notices whose body it is that presses against him. As soon as a man has surrendered himself to the crowd, he ceases to fear its touch. Ideally, all are equal there; no distinctions count, not even that of sex. (Canetti 2000:15)

In Tahiti, the laws of *tapu* create currents stronger than the spontaneous pressures of the crowd: invisible barriers that serve precisely to reinstitute distinctions of gender and hierarchy.

Some weeks later Bligh notes the waning of the crowd and explains it in terms of a waning curiosity:

The croud of natives was not so great as hitherto it had been: the curiosity of strangers was satisfied; and, as the weather began to be unsettled and rainy, they had almost all returned to their homes ... our supplies however were abundant; and what I considered as no small addition to our comforts, we ceased to be incommoded, when on shore, by the natives following us, and could take our walks almost unnoticed. (Bligh 1979:84)

There is something slightly peeved in Bligh's response, as though he misses the crowd that incommoded him. That same day he reports putting on a performance that might be regarded as an attempt to solicit the very crowd he repudiates here:

The ship's barber had brought with him from London, a painted head, such as the hair-dressers have in their shops, to shew the different fashions of dressing-hair; and it being made with regular features, and well coloured, I desired him to dress it, which he did with much neatness, and with a stick, and a quantity of cloth, he formed a body. It was then reported to the natives that we had an English woman on board, and the quarter-deck was cleared of the croud, that she might make her appearance. Being handed up the ladder, and carried to the after-part of the deck, there was a general shout of '*Huaheine no Brittanne myty.*' Huaheine signifies woman, and myty, good. Many of them thought it was living, and asked if it was my wife. One old woman ran with presents of cloth and bread-fruit, and laid them at her feet; at last they found out the cheat; but continued all delighted with it, except the old lady, who felt herself mortified, and took back her presents, for which she was laughed at exceedingly. (Bligh 1979:85)

Here Bligh first employs rumour to produce a crowd which he then clears from his decks, reasserting his status as object of interest by creating an object of interest, and carefully working his assembled audience.[22] By creating the spectacle that draws the crowd, Bligh reinitiates and at the same time mocks the local practice of formal gift-giving. Once again we might recall Benjamin's comments on the capacity of the crowd to animate the object. In the city, according to Benjamin, objects derive their charm 'from the crowd that surges around and intoxicates them' (Benjamin 1983:56). In the Tahitian harbour, this process is literalized: only the crowd can animate the painted head, and invite it into the circle of exchange. Yet Bligh's jest also cuts across the very logic of reciprocity upon which his breadfruit mission is dependent. The old woman's act of mortified hospitality, as she retracts the gift she had extended, registers the personal cost of his purportedly crowd-pleasing antics. The published account, however, here departs tellingly from Bligh's log, which makes very clear that the Tahitians are in on the joke from the start: they are figured not as dupes, but as participants in a performance (Bligh 1937: I, 386). More significantly for the current argument, it is only in the published account that Bligh's performance is linked with the waning of the crowd. The incident occurs on 5 November 1788 in both accounts: however, in Bligh's log the reduction of the Tahitian crowd and an attendant sense of the ship's decreased novelty value are only registered on 25 January 1789, when Bligh writes, 'The Novelty of our being here is now wore off, so that we are not crouded with the Natives as at first' (Bligh 1937: II, 23). The reordering of events in the published

---

[22] For a different but not unrelated analysis of this scene, see V. Smith 2004.

version may reflect an editorial awareness of the capacity of the push and pull of the crowd, its role as both impediment and source of affirmation, to drive the narrative of encounter.

The departure of the *Bounty* on 4 April 1789 is again accompanied by crowd scenes. Bligh writes that on the 3rd, 'The ship was crouded the whole day with the natives, and we were loaded with cocoa-nuts, plantains, bread-fruit, hogs, and goats.' As the ship stood off, he writes, 'The outlet of Toahroah harbour being narrow, I could permit only a few of the natives to be on board: many others, however, attended in canoes' (Bligh 1979:140; compare Bligh 1937: II, 68–9). Yet there are two important distinctions between the crowd scenes of arrival and departure, through which Bligh indexes the changed relations between crew members and Tahitians that have developed over the period of the ship's visit. The crowd on board is no longer anonymous. It is a crowd of friends: 'Scarce any man belonging to the ship was without a *tyo*, who brought to him presents, chiefly of provisions for a sea store' (Bligh 1979:139). Where, upon arrival, Bligh scanned the sea of faces around him for individuals made significant by other voyagers' encounters or by rank, here individuals are recognized as significant by virtue of relationships of intimacy. And the crowd is silent. Bligh records that 'In the evening, there was no dancing or mirth on the beach, such as we had been accustomed to, but all was silent' (Bligh 1979:140). The uncanny assembly solemnizes the moment of departure. At the same time, the silent crowd of intimates sets the scene for Bligh's analysis of the mutiny, which he will predicate upon the bonds formed between crew members and Tahitians: 'for to the friendly and endearing behaviour of these people, may be ascribed the motives for that event which effected the ruin of an expedition, that there was every reason to hope, would have been completed in a most fortunate manner' (Bligh 1979:141). Tahitian generosity and hospitality, sustained by a natural abundance that facilitates bounteous gestures, is ultimately adduced as the chief cause of the failure of Bligh's imperial project. (A closer examination of this account of motivation will be the subject of Chapter 6.)

Yet it is the Tahitian crowd that at the same time fissures Bligh's account, undermining the rationale of both his voyage and his explanation of the motives for the mutiny. Because the clamorous crowd brings with it the spectre of insufficiency, of want. Bligh's account of a performance by members of the Arioi sect, an elite troupe exempt from many Tahitian *tapu*s, is followed by an attempt to justify their practice of infanticide, which develops the explanation he has been offered by 'such of the natives as I conversed with . . . that it was necessary, to prevent an over population'. This is in turn dilated into a proto-Malthusian projection:

In countries so limited as the islands in the South Seas ... it is not unnatural that an increasing population should occasion apprehensions of universal distress ... The number of inhabitants at Otaheite have been estimated at above one hundred thousand. The island, however, is not cultivated to the greatest advantage: yet, were they continually to improve in husbandry, their improvement could not, for a length of time, keep pace with an unlimited population. (Bligh 1979:79–80)

This vision of Tahiti has the potential to undermine two arguments crucial to Bligh's account, both of which are founded on a notion of Tahitian natural fecundity, on a thesis of bounty. The first is that the population can easily spare the breadfruit cuttings requested by his mission: that they will create small impact on Tahiti's natural abundance. Bligh claims that, when the gift of breadfruit was proposed, the *ari'i* Tina 'seemed much delighted to find it so easily in his power to send anything that would be well received by King George', and emphasizes his efforts to disguise from his Tahitian hosts the worth to his party of a gift that he feels assured will cost them so little (Bligh 1979:73). The second is that, in returning to Tahiti, the mutineers were returning to a life without labour, in which natural surplus is guaranteed without any need for improved husbandry. Bligh later asserts that the mutineers 'imagined it in their power to fix themselves in the midst of plenty, on one of the finest islands in the world, where they need not labour' (Bligh 1979:162). Labour-free existence cannot be promised in a society threatened by overcrowding.

This passage of speculation, developed from some less coherent musings in Bligh's log (Bligh 1937: II, 78–9), was expanded in the 1792 account into a proposal to ease the burden of potential overpopulation by encouraging Tahitian immigration to New Holland: the work of Bligh's editor, James Burney.[23] Burney had been confronted by the practice of infanticide during his first trip to the Society Islands on Cook's second voyage, and had, like Bligh, posited an explanation that accounted for custom via the crowd:

They have some very barbarous customs, the worst of which is, when a man has as many children as he is able to maintain, all that come after are smothered ... yet notwithstanding all this, these Islands are exceedingly populous – even the Smallest being full of inhabitants & perhaps were it not for the Custom just mentioned, these would be more than the islands could well maintain. (Burney 1975:73)

---

[23] Burney sought approval for his editorial insertions in correspondence with Joseph Banks (Du Rietz 1962:115–25). For a discussion of a proposal in favour of Tahitian emigration to New South Wales received some years earlier by Joseph Banks (SLNSW MITCHELL MSS 1786:7–9), see Smith 2003:126.

Burney's crowd wells up in Bligh's text, converging with Bligh's, so that his further deliberations on the subject become ventriloquized as Bligh's. At the same time, the persistent question of the crowd that Burney's interpolations serve to highlight puts Bligh's project and his defence under question.

Moreover the evocation of another Tahiti – a land of hunger and want – foreshadowed by the crowd, works not only against the terms of Bligh's own narrative, but against the broader discourse of a romanticized Tahitian paradise, a place of easy plenty, launched by Bougainville and disseminated in Britain through popular poetry and theatre.[24] The crowded Tahiti of Bligh's account might thus be said to contest an abiding trope in that exploration literature to which he was nonetheless so keen to make his contribution. There is, indeed, a further retrospective irony to the account's speculation on a proto-Malthusian future for Tahiti. As Catherine Gallagher has argued, the paradox of Malthus's thesis lies in the fact that it is the healthy body, multiplying through 'the very power of its fecundity' (Gallagher 1986:85), that results in the degeneration of the social whole. Healthy bodies reproduce incrementally, competing for diminished resources. In Tahiti, on the other hand, the charged sexual activity that resulted from contact facilitated the transmission of contagious disease, which in turn led to the diminishment of the body of the Tahitian crowd and decreased indigenous pressure upon resources. Where Bligh's and Burney's shared vision of an overpopulated island attests directly to the pressure of bodies that they registered surrounding them in Tahiti – to both the stimulus and constraint of contact – the material consequence of the crowd scene was to be the dwindling of the crowd.

---

[24] For a related discussion of the significance of an unpeopled agricultural landscape to the romanticization of the English countryside, see F. Ferguson 1988.

2 Receiving strangers

People meet me full of friendship; they show me a thousand civilities; they render me services of all sorts. But that is precisely what I am complaining of. How can you become immediately the friend of a man whom you have never seen before?

– Rousseau

When HMB *Endeavour* anchored at Matavai Bay, Tahiti, known to James Cook as Royal Bay, George's Island, for the first time on 13 April 1769, Cook posted a notice to his crew members with the aim of regulating relations with the islanders. It effectively publicized the section of his secret Admiralty Instructions most directly applicable to the scene of contact: the instructions on friendship formation and trade that I discussed in the Introduction.

RULES to be observe'd by every person in or belonging to His Majestys Bark the Endeavour, for the better establishing a regular and uniform Trade for Provisions &ca with the Inhabitants of George's Island.

1st To endeavour by every fair means to cultivate a friendship with the Natives and to treat them with all imaginable humanity.

2d A proper person or persons will be appointed to trade with the Natives for all manner of Provisions, Fruit, and other productions of the earth; and no officer or Seaman, or other person belonging to the Ship, excepting such as are so appointed, shall Trade or offer to Trade for any sort of Provisions, Fruit, or other productions of the earth unless they have my leave to do so.

3d Every person employ'd a Shore on any duty what soever is strictly to attend to the same, and if by neglect he looseth any of his Arms or woorking tools, or suffers them to be stole, the full Value thereof will be charge'd against his pay according to the Custom of the Navy in such cases, and he shall recive such farther punishment as the nature of the offence may deserve.

4th The same penalty will be inflicted on every person who is found to imbezzle, trade or offer to trade with any part of the Ships Stores of what nature soever.

5th No Sort of Iron, or any thing that is made of Iron, or any sort of Cloth or other usefull or necessary articles are to be given in exchange for any thing but provisions. J. C. (Cook 1955:75–6)

Cook advocates here controlled and individuated relations of trade, lubricated by the particularized relations of friendship. The priorities of the Instructions are inverted, and rather than trade figuring as a mode of facilitating friendship, friendship is brought into the service of trade. Yet the interactions his journal describes in Tahiti present a different picture of encounter, of the kind we have noticed in the crowd scene: overwhelming, jostling, confusing and uncontrollable; provoking suspicion, breaches of etiquette, violence and other forms of overreaction in Cook and his crew. In the days that followed the posting of his notice, the crew worked, with some Tahitian assistance, to build a fort and to set up an observatory from which to record the transit of Venus, while cultivating relations with apparently significant individuals. However, thieving also commenced. A man was shot dead for taking a musket. The quadrant necessary to the astronomical observations was stolen. To secure its return, Cook ordered that Tuteha, the man he believed to be 'the Chief man of the Island', and other 'Principle people' (Cook 1955:85, 87) be detained, an action that inevitably soured relations with the local community. On 5 May, Cook, along with the botanists Banks and Solander, paid a conciliatory visit to Tuteha, bearing gifts. It is in his report of this visit that the first Tahitian word (aside from proper nouns) appears in Cook's journal:

As soon as we came to Appara, the place where Tootaha resides, we saw a great number of people at the landing place near his house; one amongst them who had a large Turband about his head and a long white Stick in his hand, drove the others from the landing place by beating them with his stick and throwing stones at them, and at the same time directed us where abouts to land, after we landed he conducted us to the chief but in this there was no order every one crowding upon us calling out *Tyo Tootaha*, that is Tootaha was our friend. (Cook 1955:90)

These two italicized 'texts' – Cook's *RULES* for his crew's conduct and the Tahitian word for friend – seem at first glance to encompass a predictable set of differences. On the one hand, we have a relatively complex literary document, whose explicit linking of humanist sentiment and economic drive conforms to a model of Enlightenment imperial venture that has dominated criticism of sensibility and imperialism and their entanglement in recent years. The injunction to '*endeavour by every fair means to cultivate a friendship*', with its emphasis on singular relationship, is positioned at the head of a list of detailed instructions in which particularity emerges primarily as a mode of controlling trade relations: each has his appointed task, and the modes of exchange that friendship entails are carefully pre-regulated. Friendship claim and economic motive appear obligingly laid out as text and subtext. On the other hand, we have a single, unfamiliar word, linked to a named individual: a verbal enunciation located within a scene characterized by relative spontaneity and prescient disillusionment. The notice and the word map an apparent distinction between mediation and direction; casuistry and confrontation. While both have a clear economic incentive, they betray the lineaments of an inevitably uneven exchange.

Yet it is this book's contention that friendship relations resist any simple denotation. This becomes particularly apparent in cross-cultural friendship, where parties seek to translate friendship terms, only to register that they are in fact always situational and improvised. If Cook and other European voyagers came to Tahiti intending to *'cultivate a friendship'*, what they were asked to enter into was a bond called *taio*, that in some ways lived up to their home cultures' notions of friendship, in some ways exceeded them, and in some ways failed them. The degree to which *taio*'s codes were recorded, misapprehended or invented in European accounts cannot, however, be fully ascertained. Its current obsolescence leaves European records as the most comprehensive sources for speculating what *taio* and cognates might have meant to Oceanians. This speculation has in turn encompassed a broad spectrum of possibilities, from detailed anthropological exposition of the specifics of *taio* practices to the suggestion that the concept never existed, and that the term was simply the result of a misunderstood Tahitian pronunciation of the word 'sailor'. The majority of Tahitians I spoke to did not recognize the term, and it does not appear in the most recent Maohi dictionary. Among anthropologists working in the region it has come to be associated with a highly specific form of bond-friendship, as opposed to the broad friendship terms *hoa* and *tau'a*. Both Ben Finney and Robert I. Levy found survivals of bond-friendship in French Polynesia of the early 1960s that were designated *hoa* or *tau'a* but never *taio* (Finney 1964:431–3; Levy 1973:200). According to Douglas Oliver, *taio* distinguished 'the more formalized friendship relationship founded on a definite contract, that is, on a friendship pact' (Oliver 1974:842). His use here of the word 'contract' is useful for highlighting the institutionalized status *taio* seems to have had for Tahitians: to explore the resonances of the term will be to break down the easy distinction between formality and spontaneity that seemed to be instated in the juxtaposition of Cook's instructions with the welcome shouts of the Tahitians.

A Friendly Word

> The word friend is of a large signification.
>
> – Jeremy Taylor

The notion that *taio* was simply a misheard English word was adumbrated in an article by Pasteur Charles Vernier, 'Les Variations du vocabulaire tahitien avant et après les contacts européens', published in 1948. Vernier argued that, from the earliest European contacts, European vocabulary infiltrated the Tahitian language, citing for example the 'tahitianization' of the word 'captain' as *tapena*: thus *Tapena Uali* (Captain Wallis); *Tapena Tute* (Captain Cook) (Vernier 1948:61). While he did not mention the example of *taio* in the body of his article, he did have '*Taîo!*' in an appended vocabulary list, where he translated it as a 'terme d'amitié' derived from the English word 'Sailor'. In his *Dictionnaire du tahitien nouveau et biblique*, Pierre Montillier expounded the logic behind Vernier's interpretation:

> La réconstitution de l'histoire de ce mot nouveau explique le malentendu dont il a fait l'objet chez les navigateurs européens du XVIIIe siècle: – Lors de l'escale du 'Dolphin' (19 juin–28 juillet 1767), les Tahitiens comprirent que les étranges hommes de l'étonnant navire de Wallis avaient pour nom commun le mot *sailor* qu'ils entendirent et répétèrent *taio*. Quand 'la Boudeuse' et 'l'Étoile' arrivèrent huit mois plus tard, ils reconnurent le même type de navire et la même race d'hommes qu'ils saluèrent donc du même nom *taio* avec enthousiasme.

Montillier suggested that this enthusiasm was in part generated by the thought of the nails that could be procured from the new visitors in exchange for pigs and women. Bougainville, unaware of the English visit that had preceded his own, and thus oblivious to the possibility that the word *taio* could bear relation to 'sailor', took the greeting as an authentic declaration of love from Noble Savages whose natural sympathy had been anticipated by Rousseau. In order to account for the demand for nails and earrings that immediately followed the cry of *taio*, however, 'Bougainville crut et laissa croire à toute l'Europe qu'il s'agissait d'un pacte sacré créant un lien privilégié, une amitié si intime qu'elle était une adoption fraternelle donnant droit réciproque à une communauté des biens, de nom, et même de femme!' According to Montillier's reading, by the time the crowd greeted Cook with '*Tyo Tootaha*', this Chinese whispers effect had reified the initial misunderstanding, and the same misapprehension has continued to dominate both scholarly interpretation and popular fantasy regarding Tahitian friendship and exchange ever since:

> Ce malentendu tint bon et fut même consacré par le comportement des Tahitiens qui se plièrent volontiers à celui des Européens desireux d'être 'adoptés'; de telle sort que, jusqu'à maintenant, historiens, linguistes et ethnologues entretiennent le faux-sens. Il est pourtant révélateur que ce pacte fantaisiste n'ait pas jamais existé nulle part entre deux Polynésiens, mais concerne exclusivement l'alliance entre un Mā'ohi et un Européen. La générosité hospitalière des Tahitiens était certes bien réelle, mais ni le mot *taio* ni la coutume à laquelle il se rattache ne sont authentiquement indigènes. (Montillier 1999:224–5)

Vernier's and Montillier's thesis has one strong element of plausibility: it accounts for the absence of the word *taio* from the *Dolphin* records, and its significant appearance in all subsequent European accounts (French, English and Spanish) of Tahitian contact. Yet Purea performed a ceremony of gifting with Wallis that anthropologists have not hesitated to interpret as binding them as *taio*s (Salmond 2003:48, 50, 55; Gunson 1964:66). Moreover, with words that achieve the level of symbolic significance that I am arguing here for *taio*, silence can be as significant as frequent use. Karl H. Rensch has published the Tahitian vocabulary lists of Joseph Banks and Daniel Solander (compiled on the *Endeavour* voyage) and Domingo de Boenechea and Máximo Rodríguez (compiled during Spanish expeditions of 1772–3 and 1774). While Banks uses 'Tyo' in his journal, and Solander was present at occasions where Banks recorded it, neither includes it in their otherwise comprehensive lists. Nor does Boenechea, who mentions the word a number of times in his account of his 1772–3 visit. Rodríguez's is the only list to include it (Rensch 2003:141), yet his lengthy account of his ten-month stay in Tahiti in 1774 as interpreter to two Franciscan missionaries, which includes numerous Tahitian words, never once mentions *taio*. Vocabulary lists reify language, where journals record its use. As I will suggest in this chapter, *taio* achieves a curious status in early European accounts as a word both utterly transparent and resistant to translation. The fact that it slipped the net of the first written accounts of Tahiti does not mean that it was not heard.

The detailed descriptions of *taio* ceremonies in early ethnographic texts such as *Bounty* mutineer James Morrison's and those of the first missionaries indicate, contra Montillier, that *taio* bonds were indeed cultivated between Tahitians, not just Tahitians and foreigners, and that they were initiated in a complex ceremony. Early visitors perceived the friendship displayed towards them as an attenuated rather than augmented version of local hospitality. Johann Reinhold Forster extrapolated, 'Did they do this to us, who were utter strangers to them; how much more did they exercise hospitality & undertake all the offices of friendship & acts of charity towards their brethren & Fellow Inhabitants' (J. R. Forster 1982:396).

Montillier employs a strict Tahitian academic orthography, acknowledging only 13 idiomatic letters, which do not include the letter 's': however Vernier's vocabulary list, upon which Montillier draws for his explanation of the origin of *taio*, includes a number of words adopted from English beginning with the letter 's', including '*Selo!* (interjection). Sail off (navire en vue)' (Vernier 1948:83). By the internal logic of Vernier's vocabulary it would make more sense for a Tahitian word derived from the English 'sailor' to similarly begin with the letter 's'. Moreover, as I will discuss in more detail later, an exchange of proper names rather than job descriptions is integral to the European understanding of *taio*. Given these numerous objections, I am unconvinced by Montillier's argument. I find more compelling Paul Niva's suggestion that the term and concept of *taio* existed at the time of contact with Europeans but succumbed to pressure from missionary values: that missionary ideology was inherently opposed both to the notion of exchange calibrated to intimacy, and to the inclusion of women among the objects of exchange.[1] Writing from Tahiti in 1824, the missionary William Crook indicated the missionary attitude to the traditional entailments of Tahitian friendship:

> If a native possess many articles of property, he must distribute and cannot withhold; all his friends have a kind of positive claim, and to refuse to give, would be shocking ... The friend was a representative of the person, and partner in everything, the wife not excepted. Our people have of course done away with the sinful part of it, but they are shackled by what [re]mains, and will be many years before they can advance much in civilized life. (Davies 1961:346)

A manuscript holding in the Mitchell Library Sydney confirms a discomfort with the term among the first London Missionary Society missionaries at Tahiti. A missionary is described as working 'with the help of his 'Tyos' with the word 'friends' inscribed next to Tyos as the definition. This has subsequently been crossed out and replaced by the word 'servants' (Haweis papers, vol. 1: compare Lamb, Smith and Thomas 2000:141). If Paul Niva's suggestion is correct, such missionary emendations are illustrative of a broader desire to retranslate the perceived excesses of *taio* obligations from terms of friendship to less benign forms of relation.

Such debates about the provenance and legitimacy of the term arise because *taio*, as one of the first words to translate across the beach, is subject to the ambiguities of gestural communication. It is an initial concept 'understood' in the absence of a shared tongue. Such concepts are vectors for retroactive scepticism, generating their own mythology of misconstrual into which Montillier's analysis seems to fit. Take Johann Reinhold Forster's interpretation of gestural language on Easter Island. He writes that 'the natives told us their *aree*, or *hareekee*, or king was coming towards us. Several men came on before him, and distributed sugar-canes to us all in sign of friendship, at the same time pronouncing the word *heeo*, which signifies friend' (Forster 2000:318). Forster

---

[1] Paul Niva, Musée de Tahiti et des Iles, in conversation.

footnotes the word *heeo*: '*Hòa* at the Society Isles; *Wòa* at the Friendly Isles'. His guess that this alternative Tahitian friendship term slides across island contexts was inaccurate: as Karl Rensch notes, 'Forster ... confounded *hio* with the Tahitian word *hoa* which means "friend". What the natives had actually said when they handed out the sugar cane was "take it" i.e. RAP *hi'* (Rensch 2000:296). However, the debunking of scenes of gestural misconstrual can in turn prove as specious as the original misinterpretation: a retrospective antidote to the imperial confidence that led the Earl of Morton to assume that certain European gestures 'could not possibly' be mistaken. Theoretical debate about gesture has been focused around the question of whether gestural language is universal or culturally particular. In an early article on the question, which cited sources from the archive of Oceanic contact, Gordon Hewes argued that gestural signs were a means by which humans 'transcend the limits of their particular cultural backgrounds and language systems, and exchange information' (Hewes 1974:1). Adam Kendon, on the other hand, has assembled much evidence to argue for the cultural specificity of gestural codes (Kendon 2004: 326–54). The debate is further complicated when the term communicated is itself explicitly acknowledged to be culturally specific, as in the case of *taio*. Where gesture serves as the initial mode for communicating friendship codes in the Pacific, the issue with which this book engages – the recognition on the part of European voyagers that languages of friendship both are highly particular and share a common implication in practices of exchange – becomes increasingly layered.

Joseph Banks gives one of the fuller accounts of the ways in which gestural codes operated to establish the terms of friendship in Tahiti. On 14 April 1769 he reports,

This morn several Canoes came on board among which were two in which were people who by their dress and appearance seemd to be of a rank superior to those who we had seen yesterday. These we invited to come on board and on coming into the Cabbin each singled out his freind, one took the Captn and the other me, they took off a large part of their cloaths and each dress'd his freind with them he took off: in return for this we presented them with each a hatchet and some beads ...

We ... proceeded along shore for about a mile when we were met by a throng of people at the head of whoom appeard another cheif. We had learn'd the ceremony we were to go through which was to receive the green bough which was always brough[t] to us at every fresh meeting and to ratify the peace of which that was the emblem by laying our hands on our breasts and saying Taio, which I imagine signifies freind. The bough was here offerd and accepted and in return every one of us said Taio. (Banks 1962: I, 253–5)

Banks identifies a series of specific gestures and appearances linking status with exchange and exchange with friendship, and then peace with a word that is taken to signify friend.[2] The theatre he records might just as well parse the relationship between exchange, peace and friendship set out in the Admiralty instructions for his voyage. Thus we might wonder whether such gestural language spells out a definition of *taio* or simply impresses a set of connections impelled by wishful thinking, that was already by the time of Cook's second voyage (for instance in the passage from George Forster I quoted in the Introduction) rendered transparent rather than translated.

Whether carefully recorded or misconstrued, it remains clear that Europeans were significantly invested in registering the word *taio* as their first Tahitian exchange. If *taio* is indeed a slip of the tongue or the ear, it becomes available to a mode of reading proposed by Michel de Certeau:

> In the text of the ethnographic project oriented initially toward reduction and preservation, are irreducible details (sounds, 'words', singularities) insinuated as faults in the discourse of comprehension, so that the travel narrative presents the kind of organization that Freud posited in ordinary language: a system in which indices of an unconscious, that other of conscience, emerge in lapses or witticisms. The history of voyages would especially lend itself to this analysis by tolerating or privileging as an 'event' that which makes an exception to the interpretive codes. (Certeau 1991:223; quoted in Sahlins 1995:118)

In Certeau's terms, *taio*, whether it be proto-ethnographic category, misheard word or falsely inflated concept, becomes a privileged term for understanding the ways in which European projections functioned within scenes of contact. *Taio* is always the initial item of vocabulary to be recognized as emerging from the babble of the crowd scene, and in later voyages

---

[2] This locating of gestures of friendship, and their linking with gestures of peace and exchange, occurs throughout the Pacific. The practice of 'nosing' (*hongi*) for instance, is traced on Cook's second voyage from New Zealand through Tonga to Mallicolo (J. Forster 1982:302, 375–7; Cook 1969:466; G. Forster 2000:229; while Georg Heinrich von Langsdorff, naturalist to Kruzenstern's Russian exploring expedition, writes of the Marquesans: 'When two friends meet, they press the points of the noses together; this stands with them in place of a kiss, to the sweet sensation of which they seem entire strangers' (Langsdorff 1968:174). The ways in which islanders use gestures and objects to communicate friendship is repeatedly noted and eagerly mimicked by explorers. For example, George Forster writes of the following exchange at Mallicolo: 'they had waved green boughs, and dipping their hands into salt water, had poured it on their heads. This compliment our officer returned, much to their satisfaction, it being probably a sign of friendship' (G. Forster 2000:480); and at Nukuhiva, Urey Lisiansky, commander of Kruzenstern's consort the *Neva*, records, 'when at a short distance from us, one of the company sounded a large conch, while another waved a piece of white cloth. Thinking these to be tokens of friendship, I ordered, in return, a white handkerchief to be waved, and a white flag hoisted' (Lisiansky 1968:64).

becomes the familiar term, hearing which voyagers know that they have arrived. Greg Dening, who nominates 'taboo' [*tapu*] as the first Polynesian concept to become meaningful to Europeans, concedes that 'perhaps in Tahiti "tayo" – friend – was a word whose meaning was thought to be known before "taboo"', and that both words were 'useful in cross-cultural intercourse' (Dening 1980:51). Certainly, *taio* was heard by Bougainville, and by Cook on his first voyage, whereas *tapu* was not recorded until Cook's second voyage, where it was understood first at Tongataboo and subsequently at Tahiti (Cook 1969:286, 410). Dening's privileging of *tapu*, however, seems influenced by hindsight: taboo has become embedded in European lexicons, and further endowed with a special relationship to the European unconscious in the writings of Freud, whereas *taio* has disappeared from the Maohi language. At the time of early contact, however, it was so eagerly recognized that it was 'heard' throughout Oceania, figuring for instance in reports of Marquesan encounters and understandings of Hawaiian names. Alternative Tahitian friendship terms *hoa* and *tau'a* rarely figure in the same way in these early accounts (George Forster, for instance, glosses *hóa* as friend to the king only (G. Forster 2000:180)). The word that European voyagers believed they heard gave them pause, and the practices they believed they engaged in challenged their assumptions. *Taio* is the unfamiliar embraced. In this sense it is more than another culture's word for friendship: it *is* the principle of cross-cultural friendship.

As I trace *taio* through the archive in this chapter, I will proceed, nonetheless, on the assumption that what is being discussed is more ethnographic fact than European fantasy: that I am compiling a picture of a friendship model that actively engaged and challenged Europeans. Certainly, anthropologists and ethnohistorians do not generally contest the idea that *taio* existed as a friendship model.[3] At this stage, it might be helpful to offer an initial working definition of *taio*, drawn from both anthropological work and the historical sources on which it has drawn. *Taio* is one name given to an Oceanic friendship pact formalized with some degree of ceremony (it seems, for example, to have typically incorporated an exchange of bark cloth (Oliver 1988:60)), and frequently by an exchange of names between two individuals, usually male and of similar social status, that entailed an ongoing exchange of goods and services. I do not wish, however, to present a static anthropological model of *taio*, but rather one that acknowledges its dynamical status. The picture I build of *taio* and cognate Pacific friendships within this chapter has

---

[3] However, the anthropologist Catarina Krizancic has speculated that the term may have evolved from a misunderstanding of the word for classificatory cousin, *taea'a* (email communication).

the stilted animation of a flip-cartoon: by arranging a series of views of the institution in cumulative relation, I seek to create, not merely a composite image, but a sense of its adaptability to the fluctuations of cross-cultural encounter. In the second half of the book, on the other hand, I will focus on more sustained narratives of friendship to suggest something of the development of particular relationships.

Appropriate Friends

> We were seeking each other before we set eyes on each other – ... we embraced each other by repute.
>
> – Montaigne

The *taio* bond is regarded as having been typically forged between males of the same age and class (Oliver 1988:59). Douglas Oliver's analysis of accounts of early contact Tahitian culture yielded 'no specific references to friendship pacts between Tahitian females' (Oliver 1974:843). Ben Finney finds early mention of friendship between men and women and between women and *mahu* (Tahitian third sex), but none between women (Finney 1964:434). His 1960s informants, on the other hand, told him that two men or two women might be bond-friends, but never women and men (Finney 1964:433). In both cases the male/female ratio indicates the close structural relationship of bond-friendship to kinship ties, with the shifting female role reflecting pre- and post-Christian understandings of women's positions within marriage and family. The commitment to exchange a range of goods and services was sustained over the lifetimes of the two friends, and in the event of one party dying heirless, lands and titles were inherited by the *taio* (Oliver 1974:847). *Taio* might also provide one another with heirs through adoption.[4] These aspects of the *taio* friendship correspond immediately to the ancient Greek ritualized bonds of *xenia*, or stranger friendship, which I will describe in detail in the next chapter.[5]

---

[4] Recent discussions of Oceanic adoption interestingly parallel discussions of Oceanic friendship in their tendency to shift focus from an assumed altruism to a purported self-interest. Ivan Brady, for instance, cites Marcel Mauss to argue that 'such transformations in interpersonal relations ... are constrained and regulated in part by institutionalized obligations to give, to receive, and to reciprocate for services rendered, goods transferred and resources shared in various social contexts' (Brady 1976:272; see also Carroll 1970).

[5] Cultivated voyagers were of course fond of drawing comparisons between Tahitians and Greek heroes: Banks and Cook christened Tuteha Hercules and Tupu-raa-tamaiti Lycurgus, while George Forster dilated on the similarities between Tahitian *ari'i* and Homeric heroes (G. Forster 2000:378). I make this equation in a different spirit, in order to illuminate a common tradition of stranger friendship.

Gabriel Herman observes that, through such ritualized friendships, the Greeks 'were not confined within the boundaries of their immediate groups ... but participated in ... alliances outside the groups to which they belonged' (Herman 1987:74). Similarly, Douglas Oliver quotes two early sources suggesting that individual Tahitian friendship bonds cut across group allegiances in battle, legitimating a redisposition of loyalties (Oliver 1974:849).

Though Oceanian ritualized friendship seems to have constituted a less comprehensive set of exogamous alliances than that which networked the ancient Greek world, it was a system that rendered these societies ripe for the coming of visitors. Oceanian bond friendships beyond the immediate social group 'affected their social and economic standing within their own groups: for power and prestige acquired through one system could readily be transferred to the other, and their social status inside the group could be improved by means of resources secured from the outside' (Herman 1987:74). Thus islanders were concerned to establish the status of Europeans before ceremonies of friendship-making sealed the connection. Oliver Berghof has argued that the rise of the Pomare clan in Tahiti was substantially attributable to a politics of friendship with the British:

[The British] preference for the anchoring grounds of Matavai Bay, and their eagerness, born from fear and insecurity, to cultivate friends among the local rulers in effect transferred power to Tu to such an extent that they had unwittingly established the foundation for the rise of his clan ... Where the British thought they saw a monarchy, they had instead created one. (Berghof 2004:85–6; cf. 87–8)

The astronomer William Bayly reported that, when the *Discovery* was at Kaui in the Hawaiian islands in January 1778, gestures of friendship were made towards him that were subsequently retracted when it was realized he was not the highest-ranking officer on the ship: 'having taken me for the Aree de hoi or king of the ship (I having on a red jacket.) I kissed him According to their custom, & he presented me with a curious Yava bowl as captain, but I undeceived him & told him that Capt Clerke was the Aree de hoi or King of the Ship, & consequently gave him the bowl' (Cook 1967:281 n. 2). In the light of such instances, *taio* might be seen to join a number of Oceanic political and social systems adduced in recent years to contradict the 'fatal impact' thesis and highlight the indigenous manipulation of local power relationships through negotiated contact.

The benefits to recognizing status within bond-friendship were not one-sided. The *taio* bond was a dialectical exercise in status reinforcement, from which both parties received endorsement. If the history of the Society Islands during this period could be encapsulated in the rise and fall of partners in friendship with the captains of European voyaging ships, the class relationships on board ship were equally reflected in the friendships that crew members were able to forge on shore. There is an escalating sense, throughout the early voyage accounts, of the significance of exchanges of names and goods, so that, as we saw in Chapter 1, while Wallis is blasé enough to limit significant exchange roles to the *Dolphin*'s gunner and an unnamed Tahitian 'old man', when Bligh is in Tahiti twenty years later he is obsessed with locating significant parties before transacting friendship. Bligh is concerned to establish connections with the figures of authority established during Cook's voyages, while Cook himself, on reaching Tahiti in the *Endeavour*, identified and named the 'old man' of Wallis's voyage and compensated and instated him accordingly:

Amongest those that came off to the Ship was an elderly Man whose name is *Owhaa*, him the Gentlemen that had been here before in the Dolphin knew and had often spoke of him as one that had been of service to them, this man (together with some others) I took on board, and made much of him thinking that he might on some occasion be of use to us. (Cook 1955:75)

Friendohip figureo in European accounto ao a form of record and quotation; *taio* becomes its own archive.

In attempting to establish the local importance of Tahitians and other islanders before forging an exclusive pact, European voyagers identified random signifiers of status. Material wealth could figure equally as the sign of power and as the surface sign that true authority transcends. Joseph Banks, the wealthiest man aboard the *Endeavour* though not the figure of greatest authority on the ship, makes the obvious connection between Tuteha's gifting and wealth, while leaving associations of power implicit: 'Hercules's present is the largest he seems indeed to be the richest man' (Banks 1962: I, 258). Cook, the exemplary self-made man (K. Wilson 2003:58–70), on the other hand, tends to identify status with individual character and to reward perceived virtue with gifts and friendship. At Taha'a in the Society Islands he consciously privileges title over wealth as signifier of status: 'Oo ourou brought a pretty large present as this was his first and only Viset, my present in return was suteable to his title, I say title because I believe he posess'd very little more' (Cook 1969:425). At Tongatabu (Amsterdam Island), Cook confidently forges bond-friendships following his instinct for authority: 'a chief, or man of some note, to whom I had made several presents was in the Boat with us, his name was Hātago by which name he desired I might be called and he by mine (Otootee)' (Cook 1969:249). However, he is confounded to find that greater status is accorded to a chief whose behaviour is far removed from European notions of fine breeding:

I found him seated with so much sullen and stupid gravity that I realy took him for an ideot which the people were ready to worship from some superstitious notions, I salluted him and spoke to him, he answered me not, nor did he take the least notice of me or alter a single feature in his countenance, this confirmed my former opinion and [I was] just going to leave him when one of the natives an intelligent youth under took to undeceive me which he did in such a manner as left me no doubt but that he was the principal man on the Island, accordingly I gave him the present I had intended for the old chief.

Cook is forced to recognize that a man he would not choose as a friend will make the most valuable ally:

I had not been long aboard before word was brought me that a quantity of Provisions was sent me from this chief, a boat was sent to bring it aboard, it consisted of about 20 baskets of containing roasted Bananas, sour bread and yams and a Pig of about twenty pounds weight. Mr Edgcumb with his party was just imbarking when these came down to the Water side, the bearers thereof told him that it was a present from the King of the Island to me, that is the same person as I have been speaking of, after this I was no longer to doubt his dignity. (Cook 1969:257)

In this case nuances of character must be abandoned in favour of the evidentiary weight of gifts. As Johann Reinhold Forster bitterly observed, the impact of wealth over other virtues was also felt by crew members, who found that 'comely Women, very well featured ... coqueted with everybody in order to get some beads or other trifles from them; & those that traded most, & had Iron & beads, them they took for great Men, tho' they were only appointed by the Captain for trading' (J. Forster 1982:327).

Forster meticulously tallied both his own and his Captain's exchanges during the *Resolution*'s August 1773 visit to Tahiti, registering the degree to which they accorded with his frequently troubled sense of the ship's hierarchy. During the visit he was fairly promiscuous in friendship-making, recording three named friends, Oùroe, Wahow and Taunua. He mentions exchanging names with the former, and transacting with Oùroe and Wahow in each other's presence, which doubtless introduced a competitive element to the two Tahitians' gifting (J. Forster 1982:338). Forster also describes the primary and subsidiary gifting surrounding Cook's visit to Otoo (Tu), the ruling Tahitian *ari'i* (see Figure 5), reporting that 'Capt Cook made *Otoò* presents & I to one of the kings Uncles or Relations in the Ascending line ... We distributed

Figure 5. Tu, the most sought-after *taio*: John Hall, after
William Hodges, 'Otoo King of O-Taheite', from James Cook,
A voyage towards the South Pole, 1777, Vol. 1, opposite p. 154.

likewise trifling presents to the kings Sister, Mother, Aunts, etc. for every
body begged & professed Friendship by repeating his *Tāyo*' (J. Forster
1982:339). Forster is aware of an 'Ascending line' of relations in the royal
family, and subtly uses his sense of this to assert his own position within
the chain of command (if Cook exchanges with the paramount chief, he is
the next in line). Arthur Bowes Smyth registers a similarly hierarchy, in
which captain and 'King' become equated at the head of a series of
prestige friendship ties, during the visit of the first fleet convict transport
Lady Penrhyn to Tahiti on its return to England in 1788: 'The name of
Mr Watt's Taio was mona: of mine was Pooetare – of Mr. Anstis's was
Tarta (the King [*sic*] brother) & the Capt's. was Otoo, the King himself'
(Smyth 1979:100). Within European accounts, *taio* is repeatedly the
word that marks a moment of individuation, when focus pulls from crowd
scene to close up, and 'particular' (G. Forster 2000:183) faces and relationships are distinguished. At the same time there is a detectable anxiety
to align this act of discernment and particularization with pre-eminence.

In subsequent visits to the Society Islands it was often, by contrast, only the relic of the friendship-bond that could attest to an individual's former authority. Purea was an individual of significance to British voyagers long after she lost power in the islands because of the importance (or notoriety) she achieved after Wallis's visit and its popular depiction in Hawkesworth's *Voyages* and De Loutherberg's theatrics (Banks 1962: I, 266; G. Forster 2000:369; Oliver 1988:144). Returning to Kealakekua Bay, site of Cook's death, in February 1793 Vancouver acknowledged status as it was previously understood, rather than currently manifested: 'In a very feeble faltering voice [Kanekapolei] said, that we had been formerly acquainted ... I presented her with an assortment of valuables suitable to her former distinguished situation' (Vancouver 1984:830). Friendly exchanges are laden for Vancouver, as he revisits many of the contacts he made during Cook's ill-fated third voyage. He compensates for heavy memories and the repeated scenes of forgetting they induce in himself and others, with an almost fanatical attentiveness to exchange, carefully tallying each gift he gives to the status of the recipient, and consciously erring on the side of generosity: 'It now became necessary that a handsome return be made to the whole group, agreeably to the rank and situation of each individual'; 'In proportion to their rank, and the situations they held, his whole suite were complimented, and all seemed well satisfied with their visit (Vancouver 1984:398, 858).

Exchange Policy

Reciprocal gifts sealed every new connection.

– George Forster

James Burney, Second Lieutenant of the *Adventure* on Cook's second voyage, found friendship an expensive business. Complaining of his experiences in Tahiti, he wrote,

The Custom of getting a Tio, or particular friend is the most comfortable way of proceeding, but the most expensive – Your Tio exchanges Names with you – you are always welcome at his house & whatever you want he'll procure you; ... Some of these Tio's are very interested & when they make any present expect a return that in the common way of trading would purchase treble the worth of theirs – They call me Teparny which unfortunately happening to be the name Mr. Banks went by, induced several to offer me presents & desire to change Names – but my first Tio was so continually begging and hard to satisfy that I commonly declined their civility with as good a grace as I could. – not providing myself with a sufficient Stock of Trade when I left England made me unable to afford it. I parted with every thing that I could in any ways contrive to Spare & with difficulty refrain from selling my Cloaths – had we staid much longer at these Islands, few of the younkers in either ship would have had a Shirt left – (Burney 1975:70)

Burney presents himself as uncovering an economic logic behind a system of prestation: one that he perceives to be *more* exploitative than 'the common way of trading'. Yet if it were true that the *taio* relationship, which, by entangling exchange in a particular personal relationship effectively creates a monopoly, had impeded Burney's ability to trade his stock to best advantage, we might still surmise that part of the swindle that Burney believes he has experienced is about friendship rather than trade. By his account, Tahitian friendship is a scam: the 'most comfortable way of proceeding' is more likely to leave one destitute than equipped. Burney has some difficulty, however, deploying his cynicism. What he has sought here is not primarily friendship, but a convenient trade route. Yet he is affronted to find that, on his side, he cannot trade with insufficient stock; friends in the Pacific will exchange but not supplement. Tahitian friends are 'very interested' only in the commercial sense of expecting a return upon intimate investment. Misrecognized as the wealthy Banks (a further testimony to shallow intimacy), Burney figures himself as the innocent divested by greedy sharks, rather than the stranger fed by local hosts. It is the principles of friendship that appear to have been betrayed.

Burney's discussion of *taio* is perhaps uniquely churlish. Other accounts, for instance that of Arthur Bowes Smyth, emphasize the generosity of gifting under the auspices of *taio*, arriving at a very different understanding of the power dynamics of the relationship: 'These people are extremely docile & it is in the power of their Taio to keep them in as much awe as they please' (Smyth 1979:100). But Burney gives direct expression to a suspicion implicit in many early European discussions of Oceanic friendship. A relationship that Europeans seek to foster in the interests of exchange comes to be read as displaying a more intrinsic cynicism, that is then repudiated with differing degrees of contempt, hurt or philosophy. The two versions of friendship are never allowed to dialogue explicitly. Rather, Europeans disavow or ignore their own motivations in declaring friendship. Yet, as I will argue in depth in the next chapter, the repudiation of a perceived entwining of intimacy and accounting goes deeper within European thinking than the unusual contingencies of early contact. Exchanges such as the following, on Cook's second voyage: 'Many Canoes also came off with Hogs and fruit, the former they even beged us to take from them, calling out, Tyo Boa Atoi which was as much as to say, I am your friend take my Hog and give me an ax' (Cook 1969:229), where the most meagre of vocabularies leaves the concatenation of friendship and exchange unsoftened, affront European sensibilities. Stripped of the forms of etiquette, crude motives are laid bare. In the *taio* relationship, friendship and trade appear to be unapologetically yoked. At the very moment that Europeans are brought to declare friendship, to acknowledge a singular bond, a scepticism emerges that, rather than turn itself upon their own strategic friendship-making, castigates the other as a false friend. *Taio*, in other words, discloses a veritable *mise-en-abyme* of incredulity: cynicism regarding the cynicism of the other party disclosing deeper layers of cynicism in the self.

Mistrust of Tahitian self-interest forms a surprising continuity, more-over, between voyaging accounts and more recent anthropological stud-ies, which draw on these accounts to build up composite sketches of the *taio* bond. Rather than questioning the reflexive linking of reciprocal gifting with disingenuous sentiment, such studies make *taio* a privileged locus for the application of ethno-historical scepticism. Thus Douglas Oliver's brief account of Tahitian friendship speculates that *taio* pacts were initiated by Tahitians 'with their unsuspecting European visitors' from 'cynical self-interest' (Oliver 1974:844). His discussion of codes of reciprocity inherits a particular moralistic inflection, describing Tahitian gifts as 'seemingly sincere' and arguing that 'the fundamental conception of the relationship was one of direct and equivalent exchange, even though each contribution may have been *phrased* as an act of altruism, a nonreciprocal "gift"' (Oliver 1974:848–9). Oliver's undeclared com-mitment to discriminating between prestation and friendship means that he refuses to consider the different ethical register in which gift exchange figured within Tahitian economies of friendship. In the following discus-sion I want to look at both the shifting values that informed the compen-satory logic of *taio*, and the ways in which these were in turn reflected in European apprehensions of genuine or false sentiment informing Oceanic encounters.

The main problem with *taio* for Europeans is that it blurs rather than distinguishes terms of friendship and terms of trade. This confusion is reflected in discussions such as Burney's, where 'Tio' emerges as a sly form of 'civility',[6] exposed as a false name for profiteering, and much less honest than 'the common way of trade'. But if *taio* bruises sentimen-tal expectation, its ambiguities also perform to the letter of Cook's

---

[6] I am adopting Homi Bhabha's expression 'sly civility' with some licence here. See Bhabha 1994:93–101.

notice, quoted at the beginning of this chapter, and the Admiralty Instructions that informed it. Thus commentators find themselves caught between recognition and disavowal, one moment taking pleasure in a profitable, uneven exchange of their own, the next displaying indignation at finding themselves at the mercy of a different system of exchange. 'Trinkets' and 'trifles' are the keywords of the former feeling: words that playfully dilute a canny European politics of uneven exchange. Accusations of withholding, value adding and market manipulation characterize the latter, as for instance when Joseph Banks plays the Tahitian hog market:

> They had one pig with them which they refus'd to sell for nails upon any account but repeatedly offered it for a hatchet; of these we had very few on board so thought it better to let the pig go away than to give one of them in exchange, knowing from the authority of those who had been here before that if we once did it they would never lower their price. (Banks 1962: I, 252)

Wallis, one of 'those who had been here before', had by contrast recognized European responsibility for price fluctuations, as well as the overall generosity of Tahitian reckoning: 'got off Twenty Seven Hogs & Pigs Six fowles & some fruit but pay dearer than usuall on acct of some thieves Onboard who hath stollen Iron & Nails and thereby advanced the price of things very much – tho' all is Cheap enough God knows' (Wallis 1766–8: 20 July 1767). A distinction between basic trade and gifts of friendship emerges most clearly in European accounts when relations with islanders grow strained. When Cook impounded some canoes in an attempt to recover stolen goods during his first visit to Tahiti, Banks experienced little difficulty in registering the food he received as gift rather than merchandise: 15 June, 'Some few presents today but no trade at all'; 16 June, 'Some presents today but no trade'; 24 June, 'The market has been totaly stoppd ever since the boats were seizd, nothing being offerd to sale but a few apples; our freinds however are liberal in presents so that we make a shift to live without expending our bread' (Banks 1962: I, 291, 294). In such cases voyagers feel the value of private connections over public politics, even as their own behaviour strains this distinction.

The fluctuations in European perceptions of exchange as gifting or trade reflect an inherent disequilibrium. Crew members are reliant on islanders for basic subsistence items, and thus ultimately at the mercy of the very whims for trinkets they claim to exploit. Cook attempted to stress the advantages of a system of gifts over trade during his visit to Tahiti on his third voyage,

> It is customary for these people, when they make a present to let us know what they expect in return and we find it necessary to gratify them; so that whatever we

get as presents comes dearer than by barter, but in times of occasional scarcity which will sometimes happen, we can have recourse to our friends for a present, or supply, when we cannot get any by any other method, so that upon the whole this way of traffick is full as advantagous to us as them. (Cook 1967:221)

Nonetheless, his explanation confirms subsistence as the bottom line of European exchange. Resisting the sense of vulnerability this promotes, voyagers adopt various strategies to refigure themselves in a primary role of donor rather than recipient. Thus, whereas *taio*'s exchanges tend to have material or ritual value, Europeans insist on promoting what they regard as useful exchange. Before departing on his third voyage in June 1776, Cook complacently took stock of the useful items he was bringing to Oceania to benefit old friends and captivate new ones:

Took on board a Bull, 2 Cows with their Calves & some sheep to carry to Otaheite ... with a view of stocking Otahiete and the Neighbouring Islands with these usefull animals – nor was this the only attention paid to them; I was furnished by the Admiralty with many other useful articles for those Islands, and both Ships were provided with a proper assortment of Iron tools, trinquets &ca to traffick and cultivate a freindship and an alliance with the Inhabitants of such new Countrys as we might meet with. (Cook 1967:4)

Vancouver prided himself that Hawaiians would distinguish his agenda from that of 'people of the trading vessels' by the character his gifts revealed: 'That my pursuit was of a very different character they must have been well convinced, by the nature of the articles they had received, either as presents from me, or in exchange for the several productions of their country; which were such as were ornamental to their persons, or really instrumental to their welfare' (Vancouver 1984:864). Pressing often unwanted and undervalued seeds or domestic animals on Pacific islanders was seen to mitigate the trade in trinkets, though it often involved a similar swindle. Thus Cook exaggerated the usefulness of pigs to New Caledonians:

I began to expatiate on the merits of the two Pigs, shewing them the distinction of their sex, telling them how many young ones the female would have at a time, in short I multiplyed them to some hundreds in a trice, my only view was to enhance the Value of the present that they might take the more care of them, and I had reason to think I in some measure succeeded. (Cook 1969:538)

Such gifts for the good of the innocent recipient can be weighed against those which equally disguise an imperial agenda, as when Cook leaves at Huahine 'a small plate on which was stamp'd the following Inscription viz. *His Britannick Maj. Ship Endeavour, Lieut^t Cook Commander 16th July 1769. Huaheine*', calculating that it 'would prove as lasting a Testimony of our having first discover'd this Island as any we could leave behind'

(Cook 1955:143),[7] or when, finding Tu engaged in building a war canoe on his 1774 visit to Tahiti, 'captain Cook made him a present of an English jack, a grapnel, and a grapnel-rope, and desired that it might be called Britannia' (G. Forster 2000:369).

Dirty Pretty Things

Which weighs more, a ton of feathers or a ton of iron?

The focus on useful donation among the captains and officers of European ships also counterweighs what emerges as a vulgar tendency to overvalue curiosities among the common sailors. Here the distinction between gifting and trading becomes mapped onto one of class, between discerning officer and indiscriminate marine. Lieutenant Commander Don Thomas Gayangos looks on with amusement as the common sailors are tricked into uneven exchanges during the second voyage of the *Aguila* to Tahiti, indicating his social superiority by his capacity to recognize inferior workmanship even in a novel cultural context: 'We found endless diversion this day in watching the dealings of the Indians, and we were amazed to see the subtlety with which they tricked our men in their exchanges, getting the better of their bargains with old and worn mats and scraps of native cloth, which they sold as new, but were often full of perfectly disguised mends and patches' (Corney 1913–18: II, 127). Harriet Guest has perceptively analysed this tendency as manifested in exchanges at Tonga over the course of Cook's voyages, noting both Cook's and Johann Forster's anxieties 'to distinguish [their] transactions from the impassioned exchanges of the other Europeans' (Guest 2007:111). She argues that European officers were unsettled by the ways in which Tongans appeared to measure, manipulate and mock European desire. She quotes Cook,

it was astonishing to see with what eagerness every one catched at every thing they saw, it even went so far as to become the ridicule of the Natives by offering pieces of sticks stones and what not to exchange, one waggish Boy took a piece of human excrement on the end of a stick and hild it out to every one of our people he met with,

observing that 'when he writes of "the Passion for Curiosities" and the desires that motivate the exchanges he sees as spoiling the market, he suggests that they make Europeans ridiculous and reduce them to a kind of subjection to the islanders' (Cook 1969:255: Guest 2007:110;

---

[7] Oliver Berghof refers to such 'tokens of possession' as playing out 'a futile comedy of inscription' (Berghof 2004:83).

compare Edmond 1997:139). Guest's focus is on the way in which desire operates within trade to enthral and disempower the European voyager. I want further to note how the arbitrariness of value itself is brought to light by the trade in curiosities (not to mention the Tongan boy's proto-Bataillean commentary).[8] Urey Lisiansky finds his entire ship abandoning the principles of use value to become caught up in an accelerated logic of exchange whose focus seems to be not outcome, but pure process: 'In the mean time the general trade had been carried on so briskly, that by noon, not only the officers, but the men, were possessed of a variety of articles, many of which, though pleased with them for the moment, they afterwards threw away as useless and cumbersome' (Lisiansky 1968:102). In earlier voyage accounts, iron is the most valued of commodities, and Tahitian eagerness for nails allows European commentators the double gratification of trading in a technologically superior trinket. Yet the trinket/useful-tool distinction could itself become destabilized in exchange. On his third voyage, Cook steered for Bora Bora with the aim of procuring an anchor lost by Bougainville at Tahiti which had subsequently been gifted to the Bora Boran *ari'i* Puni, 'Not that we were in want of Anchors, but after expending all the Hatchets and other iron tools we had to procure refreshments, we were obliged to make others out of the iron we had on board to continue the trade' (Cook 1967:252).

As Cook's course during the second and third voyages allowed his crew to ply a trade in curiosities *between* islands rather than simply to peddle European goods, journalists were disconcerted to find Oceanic objects valued over the more foreign. Red feathers acquired at Tonga caused a greater sensation then any European object traded or gifted at Tahiti. George Forster reports, 'These feathers produced a great revolution in the connections which the women had formed with our sailors; and happy was he who had laid in a sufficient stock of this useful and precious merchandize at the Friendly Islands; the women crouded about him, and he had the choice of the fairest.' In this context, 'useful' iron tools are merely gifts with purchase: 'We dined heartily on vegetables, and rewarded our host with red feathers to his heart's content; not forgetting to give him some iron-ware, which would be useful to him when the feathers were lost or destroyed' (G. Forster 2000:360, 369).

---

[8] A reciprocal, if less droll, commentary on the excrementality of the European gift was offered by people at Tanna to the crew of the *Resolution*, as Johann Reinhold Forster records: 'We gave them some trifles, but we soon found they were afraid of touching the things they got from us, & if they did they took them between two leaves, as if it were some dirty, poisonous thing' (J. Forster 1982:591–2).

The Tahitian *ari'i* Pohuetea and his wife are 'so greedy after the possession of red parrots feathers' that they are willing to contemplate her prostitution once they have sold all else they can spare, rupturing Johann Reinhold Forster's idealized notions of Tahitian 'amiable innocence' and of Pohuetea's individual nature: 'having received a favourable and great idea of Potatou's character, this transaction made me ashamed of him' (J. Forster 1996:243). Yet desires that Europeans cannot comprehend offer a reflection for their own incomprehensible but urgent enthusiasms, which appear to be treated by local people with an equal, dispassionate indulgence: 'The women [on the beach] sometimes had baskets full of yamboo apples (*eugenia,*) which they sold for trifles, such as small bits of green nephritic stone, black beads, and the like, and, as it seemed, more to shew their good will, than from any value which they set upon those articles' (G. Forster 2000:545). Who is trifling here? The quick shifts of significance in items of exchange pose an allegory of fickleness that has a further psychological register in cultures where exchange is coupled with friendship.

The attempt to manage the vulnerabilities of exchange by revaluing *taio*'s gifts as primarily useful goes the way of many attempts to convince people that they want what is good for them: collapsing into revelations of arbitrary desire. An alternative strategy was to convert virtue to a term of exchange. Voyagers frequently represent their gifts as rewards for good behaviour. Vancouver, returning to Hawaii after the disastrous collapse of relations there on Cook's third voyage, was particularly keen to 'impress on the minds of the royal party and the inhabitants in general, that the liberality they had experienced was wholly to be ascribed to their own civil, orderly, and honest behaviour' (Vancouver 1984:472). However, Cook also rewarded services, and the abstract virtues they illustrated: 'we intend to requite the conf[i]dence this man seems to put in us by treating him with all imaginable kindness'; 'as a reward for his fidillity I gave him a young Dog and a Bitch animals they have not and which they are very fond of' (Cook 1955:82; 1969:451). Such systems of reward wrest control of exchange values from Oceanians, exceeding their expectations:

Although *Tamaahmaah* considered himself to be amply rewarded by the different articles I had from time to time presented him with, yet, the very essential services he had rendered us, his steady friendship, and the attachment he had shewn to our welfare, demanded, I thought, some additional testimony of our general approbation. For this purpose I selected a number of useful as well as ornamental articles... (Vancouver 1984:840)

Despite instigating rewards for fidelity, however, Europeans could not control thieving with strategic gifting. Banks writes, for instance, of a betrayal by his *taio*: 'Toubourai who had slept [with] me as usual was observed by my servant to have an uncommonly large nail under his Cloaths, this I was informd of and knowing that no such had been either given or dispos'd of in trade was obligd to suspect my freind of theft' (Banks 1962: I, 278). Banks runs through a checklist of possible friendly exchanges – gifts, trade – before being forced to acknowledge the possibility of theft. His *taio*'s perfidy leaves friendship itself as Banks's only bargaining point: 'I had resolvd not to restore him either to my freindship or confidence unless he restord the nails' (Banks 1962: I, 280). Cook repeatedly tried to impress upon Oceanians that thieving was incompatible with friendship. On his 1774 visit to Tahiti his *taio* Te To'ofa served as the mouthpiece for this philosophy, as George Forster reports:

> He represented, that though our power was infinitely superior to theirs, yet we neither stole any thing, nor used any violence, but honestly paid a proper price for every thing we received, and frequently gave presents where we expected no return. That we had shown ourselves their best friends, and that to steal from friends was a shameful action, which highly deserved to be punished. (G. Forster 2000:365)

Cook's heavy-handed response to the light fingered could in turn leave him shamed by islanders' generosity. When Tuteha was wrongfully detained for the theft of the *Endeavour*'s quadrant, Cook's notions of just reward led to self-reproach: 'he would not go away untill he had given us two Hoggs notwithstanding we did all in our power to hinder him, for it is very certain that the treatment he had met with from us did not merit such a reward' (Cook 1955:88).

In cases such as this, exchanges themselves become barometers of virtue. The qualities of Oceanians, and their qualities as friends, are purportedly manifested in their gifts. Johann Forster finds exchange with one of his *taio*s unprofitable, and stresses a correspondent discrepancy between his own gentle manner and his friend's insistence:

> I gave him some beads, knives, Nails & a Breakfast cloth, etc. but he wanted still more: I gently put him off & especially told him, if he brought hogs, he should have hatchets, but he grew more & more importune & begged most impudently; at last I was tired of his impudence & left him abruptly & when he wanted to court me I told him I was angry for his promising & bringing nothing... (J. Forster 1982:339)

Forster justifies his growing anger as provoked by the ethics of exchange. Similarly Vancouver damns the Hawaiian *ali'i* Kaiana for his lack of generosity, and modifies his own gifting accordingly:

> During the forenoon we received a visit from *Tianna*, who brought as a present to me about half a dozen small ill-fed hogs, for which we had neither room nor occasion. He was not however dismissed without a farewel present, and such a

one, as in my opinion he ought to have been extremely well contented with; since, on no one of his visits, which had been very frequent, excepting on the first, had he offered us any refreshments; yet he had received from me presents nearly equal to those I had made to other chiefs, who had been instrumental in supplying our wants ... In short, his conversation was in so haughty a stile, and so unlike the general conduct of all the other chiefs of Owhyhee, that I was induced to request that he would return the scarlet cloak, axes, and a variety of other useful articles I had just given him; observing, that as these things were in his opinion so inadequate to his claims, they could not possibly be worthy his acceptance. With this request however *Tianna* did not think proper to comply, but departed, affecting to be perfectly satisfied and contented. (Vancouver 1984:845)

Kaiana's crimes range from outright lack of hospitality to inconsiderate prestation, and provoke the gravest of etiquette breaches: retraction of the gift. Vancouver's insinuation that Kaiana has forfeited his claim to equality with the other *ali'i* through his illiberality implies an acknowledgement that exchange, hospitality and status are carefully calibrated.

Where the calculations of European friendship are, as I will argue in Chapter 3, covert or disavowed, descriptions of *taio* draw attention to its economic equations. The mathematics of *taio* are described by Europeans on the one hand in terms of division of property and on the other as involving multiplying claims, and emerge from different descriptions as either generous or deceptively selfish in spirit. George Hamilton, surgeon of the *Pandora*, employs both models. Reporting his observations of friendships during his brief visit on the ship that rounded up those *Bounty* mutineers who had stayed at Tahiti he writes:

A native of this country divides every thing in common with his friend, and the extent of the word friend, by them, is only bounded by the universe, and was he reduced to his last morsel of bread, he cheerfully halves it with him; the next that comes has the same claim, if he wants it, and so in succession to the last mouthful he has. Rank makes no distinction in hospitality; for the king and the beggar relieve each other in common. (Hamilton 1793:38)

According to Hamilton's paradoxical calculation, the infinitude of Tahitian friendship is demonstrated in a capacity endlessly to divide possessions to accommodate the importunate. Yet elsewhere his account suggests a more cynical attitude to gift-giving among high-ranking Tahitians: 'On the first visit they make it a point of honour of accepting no present; but they make sufficient amends for that, by introducing a numerous train of dependents afterwards, to obtain presents' (Hamilton 1793:26). Here the purported calculation operates in exactly the opposite way: claims are initially repudiated, only to multiply exponentially through the operation of 'numerous ... dependents' who muddle the apparently simple exchanges of initial contact.

This calculation could, in the more synthesizing analysis of Johann Forster, be abstracted into a broader ethics of friendship. In his journal, he posits division of goods against account keeping, as the hallmark of natural hospitality:

> Charity, the main spring of all morality & virtue, is no where more exercised than among these people. If any one has a thing, he immediately communicates it, to every one, who applies for it, as I have frequently seen. A little bread fruit, a Coconut, a couple of bananas go as far as they can, though it should not fill any one's belly. they share their Ahoos & other cloth readily ... How different is this hospitality from carrying a Friend to a Tavern & afterwards let him pay his Share towards the reckoning! (J. Forster 1982:395–6)

This is developed in his *Observations* into one of the pieces of 'stable, consensual knowledge' that Michael Dettelbach has argued Forster derived from his journey (Dettelbach 1996:lxvi). Extrapolating a picture of broader humanity, Forster writes that:

> Men, of different inclinations, ... will soon discover that though there be a strong instinct in their breasts, prompting them to appropriate as much good to themselves as possible, yet the enjoyment of it will soon become more and more imperfect, and unhappiness, in some measure, the consequence; but by transferring acts of benevolence to other men, they soon open to themselves an inexhaustible source of enjoyment, because benefactions of an incredible variety may be bestowed upon an almost infinite number of fellow creatures. (J. Forster 1996:239–40)

In the shift between voyage text and synthesizing observation, goods morph into 'good' as the endlessly disbursable product. Reconciling the paradox of selfishness and generosity that would still confound Hamilton, Forster finds profit in division rather than hoarding and benefit to the self in benevolence to the other. At the same time, his oddly breathless reiteration of the word 'soon' recalls the urgency with which the Forsters raced to translate their voyage into text, and thus to profit in a different way from their observation of the foreign (Dettelbach 1996:lxx–lxxi).

The Genuine Article

> I told him that the English wanted nothing in return for what they had sent them but their Friendship while they were sincere.
> – John McCluer

Like use then, virtue slips out of European control when it encounters foreign ethics of exchange. Generosity reveals shadows of competition;

the distinction between selfishness and restraint proves difficult to manage. What can be done with a notion of friendship so integrally linked to exchange? Rather than acknowledge that the material and sentimental may be co-implicated in this particular form, Europeans subtly misunderstand *taio*, converting it to its opposite: a form of friendship that *disregards* exchange. In Chapter 4 I will look at the complications that Europeans encounter in attempting to locate genuine sentiment among their Oceanian friends. Here I want briefly to consider the ways in which understandings of *taio* are gradually adulterated to incorporate a version of a broader disavowal of the compatibility of canny calculation with true feeling.

Cumulatively, the Pacific voyage accounts of the later eighteenth century work to instate a notion of genuine friendship as indicated by a *failure* of reciprocity. True friendship is identified, not by the exchange of gifts, but by the refusal of exchange. Purea's interactions with Wallis establish a model of friendliness demonstrated by rejection of compensation: '13 july she brought Hogs & fowles & gave some of her Country Dress to & would take nothing in return'; '22 July She brought with her several Hogs & would take nothing in return'; '27 july: I gave her severall usefull presents, & the Officers all did the like but she seemed to take little notice of them, she seemed to be wholly taken up with sorrow' (Wallis 1766–8). Purea's behaviour contrasts with the *Dolphin*'s earlier experience at Tahiti of thieving (a less flattering form of non-reciprocity) and reciprocal violence. It instantiates a distinction between real feeling and exchange, as well as an association of non-reciprocation with high-status behaviour, that persists throughout the voyage accounts. Cook writes of a tussle between representatives of the *ari'i* Tu and Te To'ofa, eager to secure the privilege of his bond-friendship, upon his arrival in Tahiti on his second voyage:

We landed however and were received by a Vast Multitude some under Arms and some not, the cry of the latter was Tiyo no Otoo and the former Tiyo no Towha, this Cheif we soon after learnt was General or Admiral of the fleet. I was met by him presently after we landed, he received me with great Courtsey and then took hold of my right hand. A Cheif whose name was Tee, Uncle to the King and one of his Prime Ministers, had hold of my left, thus I was draged along as it were between two parties, both declaring themselves our friends... (Cook 1969:384)

On subsequent occasions Te To'ofa[9] manages to distinguish himself through a generosity strategically reinforced by evasion of compensation: 'Received a present from Towha consisting of Two Large hogs and some

---

[9] I follow Douglas Oliver's identification of 'Towha' as Te To'ofa (Oliver 1974:1193).

fruit sent me by two of his Servants who had orders to receive nothing in return'; 'After dinner he put a Hog on board the Ship and retired before I had time to make him any return either for this or what I had in the Morning'; 'In the Morning had a very large Supply of Fruit brought us from all parts, some of which came from Towha the Admiral, sent as usual by his Servants with orders to receive nothing in return' (Cook 1969:387, 388, 398). Te To'ofa adapts the logic of competitive gifting to suit the ethics of Europeans, outclassing his rivals by disavowing interest in the returns his gifts can purchase. Vancouver, himself always keen to outdo islanders in generosity, nonetheless recognizes that appearing to lack interest in gifts is a sophisticated manoeuvre: 'I was much pleased with the decorum and general conduct of this royal party. Though it consisted of many, yet not one solicited even the most inconsiderable article; nor did they appear to have any expectation of receiving presents' (Vancouver 1984:808).

This disequilibriating of exchange in the name of friendship involves a crucial redefinition of *taio*. On returning to Matavai Bay in August 1773, Cook greets Tu before a similar crowd to that which christened him *Tyo Tootaha* in May 1769. This time however, while drawing on local practice and terminology, he dictates the principles of exchange:

After the first salutation was over I made him a present of such things as were in most esteem with them with which he seem'd well pleased, I likewise made presents to several of his attendance and was offer'd in return a large quantity of Cloth which I refused giving them to understand that what I had given was for Tiyo (friendship)... (Cook 1969:206)

Between Cook's first and second voyages, *taio* has become subtly transformed in European understanding from a friendship *predicated* on exchange to its very opposite: a friendship *resisting* the pressure to exchange. Both Forsters make much of this distinction in commenting on the friendship between Johann Forster and his *taio* Wahow. George reports that a gift from Wahow 'deserved a compensation, but the generous Taheitian absolutely refused to take any thing, saying that he gave these things as a friend, and without any lucrative view' (G. Forster 2000:184), while Johann provides the details of the encounter in his journal:

There came my Friend *Owàhòw* & brought me a good many Plantains, Breadfruit, some fish, & two or three good *Ahoos* & some fishing hooks; after which I offered him a large knife, & several large Nails, but he refused them, saying he brought them things for friendship. His relation *Māmā* was not under that restriction & took as many Nails, a knife, a Looking Glass etc., which were offered to him. (J. Forster 1982:341)

Johann's less idealized version of the transaction recalls Hamilton's account of the operations of 'numerous ... dependents': the juxtaposition of the *taio*'s gifting with liberality to his relative implies that Wahow has been indirectly compensated for his generosity. Nevertheless, friendship here is understood to compose a 'restriction' – in Polynesian terms a *tapu*, though that word had not yet been recorded – on exchange. This understanding that gifts of friendship are of a higher order than items of exchange accords with a broader mistrust of trade in the Forsters' writing. In Johann Forster's *Observations*, for instance, as Nicholas Thomas points out, Tahitian society is esteemed for its self-subsistence: for the fact that 'most wants were satisfied without engagement in trade' (Thomas 1996:xxxv). Thomas notes that increasing participation in foreign commerce is associated with a corruption akin to that decried by Scottish Enlightenment philosophers concerned with 'the moral ambiguities of commercial society in Europe' (Thomas 1996:xxxvi). (In the next chapter I will touch on the much-debated topic of the relationship between eighteenth-century commerce and sentiment.) *Taio*'s reinscription in European accounts from a friendship manifested in exchange to one manifested by its refusal discloses those metropolitan concerns.

Mistrust of friendly overtures was not simply fostered by the politics of exchange. Voyage accounts record instances where faith in this favourite term is comprehensively breached. By the time Vancouver's expedition was at Tahiti in January 1792, '*Tio*' had been corrupted, in certain contexts, into a term for a drinking buddy. Expostulating in vain with a drunken Pomare 'with a desire to convince him that inebriety was highly pernicious to health', Vancouver was accused 'of being a stingy fellow, and that I was not "*Tio tio*," a phrase lately adopted to signify a jolly companion' (Vancouver 1984:401). At Huahine on 6 September 1773, Anders Sparrman returned to the *Resolution* from a botanizing excursion, as George Forster reports, 'almost stripped naked, and with the marks of several violent blows. He had been accosted on his walk by two of the natives, who had invited him to proceed farther into the country, with many protestations of friendship, and repetitions of the word *tayo*' (G. Forster 2000:208). It was George Forster, of course, who had insisted on the transparency of *taio*, as a term 'which even without the help of vocabularies, we could easily translate into the expression of proffered friendship' (G. Forster 2000:143–4). And incidents such as this suggest that islanders are fully aware of the talismanic appeal the term *taio* has attained for Europeans.

My sense is that this appeal is significantly related to the word's Oceanic provenance. For all George Forster's insistence on the transparency of the concept, its obviation of the work of translation, part of

European investment in *taio* is surely an investment in this work. Europeans did not teach Tahitians and other Pacific islanders their word 'friend': they sought to learn a local term for a level of welcome and hospitality that their own culture's practice of friendship did not seem to attain. And having established the significance of this word, they heard it everywhere in the Pacific. The Tongan greeting 'talamonu' rang like *taio* in George Forster's ears: 'Here we met many of the natives, who were travelling to the beach with loads of provisions, and courteously bowed their heads as they passed by us in sign of friendship, generally pronouncing some monosyllable or other, which seemed to correspond to the Taheitian *tayo*', and the welcome of the Mallicollans sounded friendly to the degree it corresponded to the Tahitian term: 'They now approached the ship in their canoes, waving green plants ... and repeating the word Tomarr or Tomarro continually, which seemed to be an expression equivalent to the Taheitian Tayo (friend)' (Forster 2000:245, 480). At Dusky Bay in New Zealand Cook used the term and its logic of exchange to initiate contact with uncomprehending and frightened Maori:

The Corporal of the Marines *Gibson*, who can talk the Otahaitee Language best, which has an affinity with that of the New Zeelanders ... waved a white cloth to them, calling to them *hārre-māi-Tāyo* i.e. *come Friend*, & promised them beads or as they call it *Pòhe*: but they either did not understand it or did not chose to come for fear.
  We stood in towards the rock & called to him *hāllemāi Tāyo*, come here Friend: but he did not stir ... Capt *Cook* went to the head of the boat, & called him friendly & threw him his handkerchief & I gave him myne likewise. (J. Forster 1982:242, 248)

Lisiansky's officers deployed the term in the Marquesas to initiate orderly trade: 'Mr. Powalishin uttered, repeatedly, the word *teéo* (friend) and made signs that they should come to him, one at a time' (Lisiansky 1968:57–8). Vancouver's friendship with an Hawaiian he calls Taio (Keao) becomes to some degree emblematic of cross-cultural intimacy, I will suggest, precisely because of the resonances of this name. Having identified so fully with the Tahitian term, voyagers are ill-prepared to find it abused in incidents such as the attack on Sparrman, which entail a much more threatening imposition than that obligation to exchange which they have embraced as part of this exotic definition of friendship. By using the word *taio*, Europeans show willing. Homi Bhabha has argued that the indigenous misappropriation of western terms 'inscribes an ambivalence at the very origins of colonial authority': allowing for both the tribute and menace of mimicry (Bhabha 1994:95). But Europeans in Oceania did not experience the uneasy seduction of hearing local people pronounce their word 'friend': they looked to *taio* as not only authentic signifier, but also signifier of authenticity.

If *taio* is betrayed in encounters such as Sparrman's, they also offer the opportunity for its redemption. Cook is ultimately able to retrieve the goods stolen from the botanist because of his *taio* bond with the Huahine *ari'i* Ori. Ori accompanies Cook, first in his boat in an attempt to recover the items, and then on board ship, despite the tearful protestations of the crowd, who fear he will be punished for the theft. Cook pays tribute to both the courage and reason of his friend:

> it shews what great confidence this Brave old Chief put in us, it also in a great degree shews that Friendship is Sacred with these people. Oree and I were profess'd friends in all the forms customary among them and he had no idea that this could be broke by the act of any other person, indeed this seem'd to be the great Argument he made use on to his people when they opposed his going into my boat, his words were to this effect: Oree (for so I was always calld) and I am friends, I have done nothing to forfeit his friendship, why should I not go with him.

Ori's behaviour is taken as a sign not simply of generalized friendship, but of the specific trust engendered by a *taio* bond forged 'in all the forms customary among them'. If *taio* is rehabilitated by Ori's act of good faith, however, Cook does ruefully acknowledge that 'We however may never meet with a nother chief who will act in the same manner on any semiliar occasion' (Cook 1969:220).

Exchange, however, seems ultimately too fraught a mode of conjunction on which to hinge the credibility of friendship. As the archive of encounter develops, memory plays a more fundamental redemptive role. Islanders reveal their genuine fidelity by displaying a capacity to hold their particular friend in mind over the course of several visits and sometimes years. Cook's relationship with Ori on this voyage had developed imperceptibly from the cursorily described interaction of the *Endeavour*'s visit to Huahine, where he was presented with the inscribed plate mentioned earlier, to one of 'old friend': 'I learnt that my old friend Oree was still living and chief of the Island and that he was hastning to this part to see me' (Cook 1969:216). On 4 September 1773, Cook reports,

> I went to pay my first Viset to Oree the Chief who I was told was waiting for me, accompanid by Captain Furneaux and Mr Forster. We were conducted to the place by one of the natives, but we were not permitted to go out of the Boat without going through the following ceremony usual at this Isle on such occasions. The Boat being landed before the chiefs House which was close by the Water side Five young Plantan trees, which are their Emblems of Peace, were brought seperately and with some ceremony into the Boat. Three small Pigs

acompanied the first three and a Dog the fourth, each had its particular name and purpose rather too mysterious for us well to understand, lastly the Chief sent me the Inscription engraved on a small peice of Pewter which I left him when [I saw] him in 1769, it was in the same bag I had made for it together with a peice of counterfeit English coin and a few Beads given him at the same time, this shews how well he had taken care of the whole. After they had done sending the things above mentioned to the Boat, our guide who still remained in the Boat with us desired us to decorate three young Plantan plants with Nails, looking glasses Medals, &ca &ca, which was accordingly done, we landed with these in our hands and walked up towards the Chief a lane being made by the people between us and him for here were a vast crowd. We were made to sit down before we came to the chief, our Plantains were then taken from us one by one and laid down by him, one was for Eatoua or God, the Second for the Arree or King and the third for Tyo or friendship. This being done Oree rose up came and fell upon my neck and embraced me, this was by no means ceremonious, the tears which trinckled plentifully down his Cheeks sufficiently spoke the feelings of his heart. (Cook 1969:216–17)

Ori incorporates the European gift within traditional ceremony, demonstrating that the earlier visit has become enshrined in cultural memory and offers a basis for continued interaction. At the same time, Cook makes a clear distinction between ceremonious and sentimental friendship, the latter manifest in the physical token of 'trinckl[ing]', tears. Moving on to Raiatea, Cook again encounters an *ari'i* he recognizes from the *Endeavour* voyage:

In the Morning we paid a formal Viset to the Chief of this part of the Isle whose name is Oreo, the same as when I was here before. We went through no sort of ceremony at landing but were conducted to the Chief at once who was seated in his House which stands close to the Water side. The Chief and his friends received us with great Cordiallity, express'd much satisfaction at seeing me again, desired that he might be call'd Cook (or Toote) and I Oreo which was accordingly done, he then ask'd after Tupia and several other gentlemen by name who were with me last voyage. (Cook 1969:223)

Here too, Cook focuses on a relationship between ceremony and feeling: a 'formal Viset' is said to involve 'no sort of ceremony', but involves an exchange of names, of which Cook wrote, 'I believe that this is the strongest tie of friendship they can shew to a stranger' (Cook 1969:223 n. 4). The ratification of sentiment for Cook seems once again to be memory: he is pleased to note that Tupaia and other crew members have been held in mind since the earlier voyage. The *Resolution* returns to Huahine and Raiatea in May 1774. With no further visits anticipated, the consolation of finding oneself remembered morphs subtly into fantasies of commemoration. When he farewells Oreo at Raiatea, Cook reports,

Oreo's last request was for me to return and when he found I would not make him the Promise, he asked the name of my *Marai* (burial place) a strange quiston to ask a Seaman, however I hesitated not one moment to tell him Stepney the Parish in which I lived when in London. I was made to repeated [*sic*] it several times over till they could well pronounce it, then Stepney Marai no Tootee was echoed through a hundred mouths at once ... What greater proof could we have of these people Esteeming and loving us as friends whom they wishd to remember, they had been repeatedly told we should see them no more, they then wanted to know the name of the place were our bodies were to return to dust. (Cook 1969:425–6)

It is striking how infrequently, whatever their other self-aggrandizing tendencies, that voyagers attribute the fidelity of Oceanian memory to the singular impact of their own visit. Keen to elicit the tribute of the crowd scene, they nonetheless prefer, once the highly particularized *taio* bond has been forged, to interpret long memory as a token of that friendship, rather than the kinds of unique spectacle that tended to precede it. Where their own recollections fail to match those of islanders, they incur self-reproach. A progress from scepticism to shame regarding the integrity of memory is evident in Vancouver's account of his inter-actions with his Hawaiian friend Keao, whose name he has appositely misunderstood to be Taio. In March 1792 the acting regent at Kauai reminds Vancouver that he gave a lock of hair to Keao when he was there previously with Captain Cook. Vancouver concedes that 'These circum-stances were very likely to have taken place, although at the moment they did not recur to my memory' (Vancouver 1984:469–70). At Maui a year later he encounters Keao who adverts to their former friendship, claiming that 'he still retained a very great regard for me, and hoped we should both remain in the same sentiments towards each other', and mentions 'That, as a proof of the sincerity of his friendship, he had still in his possession a lock of my hair, which I had given him at that period'. Vancouver, who has clearly not tended to his sentiments in the same way, asks where the lock is kept, and 'To this *Taio* replied, that it was on shore, with some other valuable testimonies of friendship, that con-stantly attended him in his travels or campaigns.' The next day he returns with the token, and Vancouver acknowledges that 'The colour corresponding with that of my own, tended to prove its identity' (Vancouver 1984:861–2). His doubt of Keao exposed, Vancouver pays tribute to the better friendship to which his friend's better memory testifies:

On this occasion, I could not help feeling some internal humiliation at the superiority which the steadiness of *Taio*'s friendship had gained over me; by preserving the lock of my hair; by retaining, after an absence of fourteen or fifteen years, a perfect recollection of my name; and by recounting the various incidents, and the several acts of reciprocal kindness and friendship that had taken place in our former acquaintance. All these he seemed to remember with the greatest pleasure; but all these had been long obliterated from my memory. (Vancouver 1984:863)

By cherishing him as both memory and memento, Keao convinces Vancouver not just of his genuine, but of his superior sentiment, fulfilling his allegorical role as the idealized *Taio* of European imagination.

Between Men

> Ori, my brother in the island mode,
> In every tongue and meaning much my friend.
> – Robert Louis Stevenson

I noted earlier that the common understanding in anthropological discussions of *taio* is that it was primarily a form of male bonding, in which women figured more often as objects than subjects of exchange. However, this picture requires some nuancing. Purea performed a *taio* ceremony with Wallis, creating, as Anne Salmond writes, 'a relationship which almost amounted to a partial exchange of social identities' (Salmond 2003:48). The second appearance of the word in Bougainville's published account is vocalized by women: 'The women saluted us, by laying their hands on their breasts, and saying several times *tayo*' (Bougainville 1967:220). Ellis records that a Tahitian woman named Poorahi 'became Captain Clerke's taio, and exchanged names with him' on Cook's third voyage (Ellis 1783:127–8), and George Tobin reported that, when he reached Tahiti on the *Providence* in April 1792, 'the queen ['Itia] ... offered to become my *taio*, or friend, which distinguished honour I most readily accepted' (Tobin 2007:72–3). Voyage accounts mention women becoming the focus of additional exchanges with the male *taio*. Indirectly or with self-conscious manipulation, such women increase the quantity and perceived quality of, rather than themselves figuring as, gifts of friendship: 'I presented *Taow* with a suitable return; and, on including some articles for his wife, who was still living at Morea, he was highly delighted, and the value of the present in his estimation seemed thereby infinitely increased' (Vancouver 1984:404);

Mahine came on board with his bride, who was a very young girl, of a low stature, but not remarkable for beauty. She was very skilled in the art of begging for presents, and went through the whole ship collecting a vast number of beads, nails, shirts, and red feathers, for which she was indebted to the friendship which every body felt for Mahine. (G. Forster 2000:370)

Moreover, the sharing of women within the *taio* relationship was coun-
terbalanced by the polyandry of high-ranking Tahitian females, and on a
much more widespread scale in the Marquesas, through the convention
of *pekio*, which allowed women to have numerous partners (Dening
2004:194–5). As Niel Gunson argued in an important article, the significance of 'great women' in forging friendship bonds and their capacity
to manipulate these 'contract rites' to political advantage cannot be
underestimated (Gunson 1964:53–69). If there is nonetheless a widespread depiction of the relationship as one in which females figured as
objects of exchange, this may be, like the persistent interpretation of *taio*
as a foil for trade, a conception which exposes as much about continu-
ities between eighteenth-century European and recent anthropological
understandings of the role as about Oceanian realities.

Certain sexual licences and prohibitions are widely understood to
accompany the *taio* bond. The *taio* could henceforth have sexual relations with his friend's 'wife', but became prohibited from sexual relations
with his female kin (Finney 1964:434; Oliver 1974:845–7; Ferdon
1981:150, 155). This of course inverted eighteenth-century European
values, which named the former liaisons adulterous and saw the close
female kin of friends as an ideal pool for the selection of marriage
partners.[10] And it was contradicted in some accounts, which report
that the European *taio* was offered both the friend's wife and female
kin. 'It is an indisputable truth,' wrote George Tobin in 1792, 'that
the Tahitian considers it as but a mark of confidence and attention, the
offer of a moiety of his wife, and the entire of his sister or daughter to
him, with whom he has entered on terms of taioship' (Tobin 2007:76).
Although the status of women as property in marriage in eighteenth-
century Europe was implicitly and sometimes explicitly understood,[11]
the idea that women constituted *alienable* property was scandalous. With
the arrival of missionaries, this became the basis of a comprehensive
condemnation of mutually implicated Oceanian friendship and marital
relations, but during the period of exploration it tended to provoke a
worldly comedic rhetoric. The bounds of decency were to some degree
policed, however, by an anecdotal focus on the grotesque corollary of
homosocial partner sharing: the obligation to satisfy geriatric lust.
The depictions of Purea (as Oberea) in satirical poetry, particularly
those focusing on her 'supposed romantic relationship' with the young
Joseph Banks, reflect this bias, converting the 'gracious friend of Wallis

---

[10] Tadmor 2001 offers a detailed account of the imbrication of kinship and friendship
relations in eighteenth-century Britain.
[11] Most famously in Mary Wollstonecraft's *A Vindication of the Rights of Woman* (1792).

and Cook', as Kathleen Wilson writes, into an 'object of much scurrility' (K. Wilson 2003:65).

George Hamilton's account of his efforts to honour his *taio* by copulating with his wife reveals the strains of attempting 'to cultivate a friendship' by what his own culture would have regarded as improper means:

> In becoming the Tyo, or friend of a man, it is expected you pay him a compliment, by cherishing his wife; but, being ignorant of that ceremony, I very innocently gave offence to Matuara, the king of York Island, to whom I was introduced as his friend: a shyness took place on the side of his Majesty, from my neglect to his wife; but, through the medium of Brown the interpreter, he put me in mind of my duty, and on my promising my endeavours, matters were for that time made up. It was to me, however, a very serious inauguration: I was, in the first place, not a young man, and had been on shore a whole week; the lady was woman of rank, being sister to Ottoo, the king of Otaheitee, and had in her youth been beautiful, and named Peggy Ottoo. She is the right hand dancing figure so elegantly delineated in Cook's Voyages. But Peggy had seen much service, and bore away many honourable scars in the fields of Venus. However, his Majesty's service must be done, and Matuara and I were again friends. He was a domesticated man, and passionately fond of his wife and children; but now became pensive and melancholy, dreading the child should be Piebald; though the lady was six months advanced in her pregnancy before we came to the island. (Hamilton 1793:39–40)

Hamilton deploys a self-deprecating gallantry to smooth the numerous varieties of proscribed behaviour nonetheless evident in his account – sex with multiple partners (implied by his euphemistic reference to having been 'on shore a whole week'), between the no longer youthful and (to contradict that impression) with a woman in the third trimester of pregnancy – all of which can be justified it seems, as the duties of a 'friend of a man'. It is in relation to the friend's wife, that most obliging gift of friendship, that the *taio* relationship most unequivocally conforms to Eve Sedgwick's paradigm of homosocial masculinity.[12] Scenes in which the *taio*'s partner figures as an object of sexual exchange replace what in Europe would have been a triangle of erotic rivalry with a triangle of anxious erotic compliance. If, as Sedgwick observes following René Girard, 'in any erotic rivalry, the bond that links the two rivals is as intense and potent as the bond that links either of the rivals to the

---

[12] Sedgwick was careful to dissociate herself from any easy application of this model to 'non-European cultures and people' and to cross-cultural situations (Sedgwick 1985:19). As I stressed in my introduction, I am similarly concerned not to reduce the particularity of the intercultural friendships I discuss to imported models. However, the triangulation of European–Oceanian friendships in relation to exchanged females seems to articulate compellingly with Sedgwick's thesis.

beloved' (Sedgwick 1985:21), this becomes categorical when erotic connection is explicitly understood to take place in the service of the bond between men framed, not as rivals, but as friends. When Hamilton writes, 'However, his Majesty's service must be done, and Matuara and I were again friends', his gallant veiling of the details of the heterosexual liaison leaves only the scene of one man servicing another exposed. The triangle increases exponentially in Hamilton's account with the elision of various masculine figures: the generic male friend, Matuara, 'king of York Island', 'Ottoo' (Tu) of Tahiti (with whose own *taio* his sister would have been prohibited from sexual relations), Tu's inaugural European *taio* Cook (who nonetheless managed a kind of sexualized 'relation' with Peggy between the sheets of his *Voyage* text), and 'his Majesty' (presumably here King George, though equally possibly Matuara or Tu) – who all come together in a virtual group-sex event. The homosocial imperative is highlighted by repetition of the word 'service' to link Peggy's duty, ostensibly to a Tahitian cult of Venus and immediately to her husband's *taio* bond, with Hamilton's duty to his regent, the symbolic pinnacle of British relations between men.

If such scenes shuffle heterosexual sex and homosocial friendship in mutually revealing ways, the corollary of this is that *taio* is also suspected of harbouring sexual possibility. Gunson spells out a sexual subtext to early discussions of Tahitian friendship rites. He argues that formal *taio* relationships, as opposed to more generalized friendships named *taio*, were the prerogative of *ari'i*.[13] Noting that *ari'i* married late, and claiming that 'the concept of continence was unknown' and that 'forms of sexual irregularity were regarded as chiefly prerogatives', Gunson suggests there is reason to believe that sexual relations informed or cemented friendship ties between men (Gunson 1964:66). The existence of a sanctioned Tahitian 'third sex', the *mahu*, might equally confirm or refute Gunson's thesis, suggesting on the one hand that same-sex relations for men were catered to outside the friendship bond, but on the other, that they might as easily be sanctioned within friendship. James Morrison described the Tahitian *mahu* as being 'esteemd Valuable friends' for their abilities to perform traditional 'Womans employment', but, like most early accounts of these ambiguous figures, he at once gestures towards and away from defining their sexual role: 'it is said, tho I never saw an instance of it, that they Converse with Men as familiar as woemen do – this however I do not aver as a fact as I never found any

---

[13] Douglas Oliver contests Gunson's claim that *taio* relationships can be hierarchized, arguing that 'we are concerned here with a more or less continuous series of contractual relationships ... rather than two contrasting types' (Oliver 1974:1148 n. 3).

who did not detest the thought' (Morrison 1935:238). Morrison, else-where capable of making broad and plausible generalizations from limited observation, is here scrupulous in his refusal to confirm the existence of practices he has not witnessed (thus of course disavowing any first-hand involvement with the *mahu*). Lee Wallace and, for other areas of Oceania, Jeannette Mageo and Robert Morris have offered subtle analyses of the ways in which transgendered identities, such as the *mahu*, figure transgressively in both European accounts and Oceanic societies.[14] I want at this point simply to add that if the practices of *mahu* are something that Europeans seek not to name and claim not to witness, *taio*, as the acceptable face of relations between men, becomes as close as they allow themselves to look (I explore these questions in more depth in Chapter 6.)

Whereas Morrison shies away from observing the intimacies of *mahu*, he offers a detailed description of the sanctioned male nuptials of the *taio* ceremony. This is coupled with his discussion of Tahitian marriage ceremonies. Morrison initially represents marriage as simple and formulaic:

Their Marriages are no other than an agreement between the Partys and their Friends, and tho the Young are uncontrouled, they Generally take the Advice of their parents and Friends; which being setled [*sic*], they Join and are Calld Man & Wife without Ceremony, except the Greeting of their Friends who present them with Hogs, Cloth and Sundry Necessary Articles … The Husband then Claims his Wifes Posessions, which are delivered to him without reserve, and they Having Houses on each live where they think Proper (but should they part, then the Wifes property returns to herself). (Morrison 1935:185–6)

Tahitian marriage evidences here a blend of the ad hoc and ritual similar to that which affronted European participants in Tahitian friendship: it appears motivated by expedience rather than passion, and is most expli-citly framed around gifting and property relations. However, Morrison also explains that the ceremonies surrounding the marriage of a virgin are a more complex affair, involving a ritual of *amoa*, or lifting of *tapu* restrictions, which must take place before the males of the bride's family can eat with the groom. As Morrison describes this latter ceremony, the friends of both parties assemble near the *marae*, or sacred ground, where

---

[14] Wallace 2003:15–16; Mageo 1992, 1996; Morris 1990, 1992. Wallace has sought to retrieve ethnographic traces of Oceanic sexual practice that are embedded in European disavowals such as Morrison's. However, ethnographic disputes such as Gunson's and Oliver's over the marital/sexual status of *taio* bonds illustrate the problems involved in a counter-normativization of Oceanic practices, where a reflexive invocation of what was 'sanctioned by custom' can simply facilitate stereotyping of, for instance, Tahitian sexual incontinence.

lengths of cloth have been spread out. The mother of the bride is given pieces of sugar cane and leaves from a sacred tree. She cuts her forehead with a shark's tooth, a gesture also common to ceremonies of mourning, and allows the blood to fall on the sugar cane. She then places the pieces on a leaf, giving two to the father and each uncle and aunt and keeping two for herself:

these they place on the Palms of their hands and holding them up to their Foreheads rise up and proceed slowly along the Cloth till they arrive where the Young Couple sit, keeping their bodys half bent all the way; and having deposited the leaves and Sugar Cane at the feet of the Young Pair they retire without speaking in the same Manner to their Seats.

The priest prays, then takes the leaves and cane and buries them at the *marae*, and makes an offering: 'in the Meantime the Couple rise and go to their Parents and they Embrace them and bestow their blessings on them' (Morrison 1935:188). In the *amoa* ceremony, intimacy is permitted to breach the restrictions of *tapu*'s paradoxically infective sacrality, allowing families to share food.

By Morrison's account, the ceremony that initiates friendship is identical to that which unites the virgin with her husband, 'only placing the Boy in place of the Woman':

When a Man adopts a Friend for his Son the Ceremonie is the same ... the Ceremonie is ratified, and the boy & his friends exchange Names and are ever after lookd as one of the Family, the New Friend becoming the adopted son of the Boys Father – this Friendship is most religiously kept, and never disolves till Death, tho they may separate, and make temporary Friends while absent, but when they meet they should always acknowledge each other.

The ceremony that unites friends, then, resembles not the more casual type of marriage, but rather the more formal ceremony that initiates the virgin bride. Furthermore, it appears to be indissoluble in a way that marriage is not, binding the partners in a lifelong commitment to support one another and their families in times of need:

And should a Brother or one who is an adopted friend become poor or loose his land in War, he has nothing more to do but go to his Brother, or Friend, and live with him partaking of all he posesses as long as he lives & his wife and Family with him if he has any – or if any relation or Friend, tho not in immediate want, comes to the House of his Friend, he is always fed while he Stays and is Not only welcome to take away what he pleases but is loaded with presents. (Morrison 1935:189)

To this extent, bonds of marriage are subordinate to unions of friendship: support of the friend's wife and family can constitute one of the potential entailments of friendship. Through the *taio* bond, friendship between men is given a potentially regenerative, patriarchal status.

Children, however, like women, trouble the depiction of *taio*'s economies. Again, it is often unclear whether they are objects or agents of exchange. George Forster makes a beguiling child the focus of his gifting in Tanna:

A little girl, about eight years old, of very agreeable features, peeped at us between the heads of the people who were seated on the ground … I beckoned the child to come back, and shewed her a piece of Taheitee cloth, but I could not prevail on her to come and fetch it. Her father got up, and with some entreaty persuaded her to come to me. I took hold of her hand, and gave her the cloth, and a number of little ornaments. But I was overpaid by the pleasure of the father, the joy, the fondness which sparkled in his eyes, and lighted up his whole countenance. (G. Forster 2000:538)

An image of benevolent paternalism more than compensates Forster for his gift. However, Europeans are also capable of fantasizing monstrous exchanges that project fears of savagery into images of craven maternity and paternity. 'A woman would very readily have given a child at her breast, which had been asked by us in jest, in exchange for a piece of iron,' wrote Langsdorff of the Marquesans at Nukuhiva (Langsdorff 1968:140).[15] In New Zealand on his second voyage Cook contradicts rumours of a barter in children:

it was even said that some of them offered their Children to sale but this certainly had no foundation in truth, the report took rise on board the Adventure where they were utter strangers to their Language and Customs: It was not uncommon for them to bring their children with them aboard and present them to us in expectation of our making them presents, this happened to me yesterday morning a Man brought his Son a boy about 10 years of age and presented him to me and as the report was then currant I thought he wanted to sell him, but at last I found out that he wanted me to give him a Shirt which I accordingly did… (Cook 1969:170)

Cook equates the monstering of islanders with ethnographic ignorance, but the slippage between child as gift-magnet and child as gift is commensurate with the more sophisticated scepticism that inflected European accounts of *taio*. Both ignorant fears and informed doubts articulate a perceived mismatch between sentiment and exchange. I will return to the relationship between images of bad parenting and disingenuity in Chapter 4.

---

[15] Marquesan codes of adoption allowed for a relatively free exchange of children, based around a concept of extended family, rather than the simple commodification of the child that Langsdorff comprehends. As Greg Dening expresses it, Marquesans 'exchanged their children as other men might gifts' (Dening 1980:68).

Exchanging Names

> An exchange of names is equivalent to a ratification of good will and amity among these simple people; and as we were aware of this fact, we were delighted that it had taken place on the present occasion.
>
> – Herman Melville

One of the words that recurs most strongly in discussions of *taio* within early voyage accounts is 'particular': a word with all the associations of specialness, singularity and privacy that give frisson to any new friendship. The suspicions that are set off by *taio*'s potential to serve economic and social advancement are soothed by a sense that exchange can only be instantiated by an initial recognition of affinity – one so powerful that it in turn allows exchange to figure as sentimental. As John Marra put it in his account of Cook's second voyage,

[They show] fidelity to those who condescended to place confidence in them as particular friends. To such there is no service that they will not readily submit, nor any good office they will not willingly perform; they will range the island through to procure what they want, and when encouraged by kindness and some small presents and tokens of esteem, no promises or rewards will influence them to break their attachments. (Marra 1775:43)

In this description 'small presents and tokens' are indicative, not of a European capacity to profit by uneven exchange, but of the immateriality of such exchanges once 'particular' attachment has been forged. I will look at examples of particularized friendship in Part II, but to conclude this chapter I want to think about the oddly compromised relationship between this sense of particularity and a ceremonial practice of name exchange.

The exchange that enabled all subsequent exchanges of goods and services between *taio*s was the preliminary exchange of names. Although the first actual description of such an exchange in the voyage texts comes with Cook's first meeting with Ori in Huahine on 16 July 1769, it is a ceremony always understood to be customary practice. The European understanding of the relationship that name exchange entails is one that puts an end to generalized trade by initiating a highly particularized gifting. On his return to Huahine in April 1774, towards the end of Cook's second voyage, George Forster observed that all gifting and trade had become the prerogative of individual relationships established on previous visits: 'We received presents of hogs and targets from different chiefs, who came on purpose to visit their old acquaintance, and would not sell or part with their goods, till they saw their friend for whom they were destined' (Forster 2000:384). Name exchange invites a trade of identities. Arthur Bowes Smyth reports

Every Chief upon his first coming on board selected his Taio, wt. whom he exchanges names & ever after his attachment & friendship to him was unalienable, & scarcely a day pass'd but they came on board loaded wt. presents of Hogs, Otaheitean Cloth, Fowls, Bananas, Cocoa Nuts, Bread fruit & all the Catalogue of things wh. their Islands produces each for his Taio... (Smyth 1979:100)

Bowes Smyth's account succinctly marshals the contradictions encapsulated by *taio*. An exchange of alienable property is predicated on an 'unalienable' bond forged through a ceremony at once arbitrary (the selection of the friend takes place 'upon . . . first coming on board', in the absence of personal knowledge) and unique. Name exchange, in other words, crystallizes all of those elements of *taio* that I have been emphasizing throughout this chapter: status anxiety, the politics of exchange, notions of generalized versus specific friendship-making, concerns with fidelity, recognition and memory.

The inaugural name exchange recorded by Cook is clearly a form of status recognition: Cook writes, 'among those who came was the King of the Island whose Name is *Oree* he had not been long on board before he and I exchange'd Names and we afterwards address'd each other accordingly' (Cook 1955:140–1). At Tonga on his second voyage, he reports that 'a chief, or man of some note, to whom I had made several presents was in the Boat with us, his name was Hātago by which name he desired I might be called and he by mine (Otootee)' (Cook 1969:249). The relationship between status and name exchange is mutually reinforcing: Cook desires to exchange names because he figures the man to be 'of some note', though his lack of clarity about this also suggests that his sense of the chief's status is in part informed by his desire to exchange names. The highly status-conscious Johann Forster spelled out the hierarchies that name exchange in Tonga expressed: 'The Chief commonly changed names with Capt *Cook*, consequently all the other Chiefs became related to him & to all the Officers, & the Girls used to call them *Tuana*, elder brother' (J. Forster 1982:400). Langsdorff likened name exchange, which he encountered in the Marquesas, to the formalities of a christening: 'With this man he claimed relationship, although he had only changed names with him; a ceremony, which here, and in many other of the South-Sea islands, creates a sort of relationship, or rather religious compact, somewhat resembling the tie created among us by standing as sponsor for any one at their baptism' (Langsdorff 1968:98–9). While Langsdorff intends through this analogy to create a sense of arbitrary, rather than essential, relation, it incorporates a notion of rebirth that could be implicit in such exchanges (especially in relation to figures such as the beachcomber he discusses here, Jean Cabri, who used the exchange to enhance rather than confirm his status).

But like the material exchanges it inaugurated, name exchange could be made to reflect values other than status. Oreo, *ari'i* of Raiatea, who waited until Cook's second visit to the island in September 1773 to request the same ceremony initiated by Ori at Huahine some months earlier: 'The Chief and his friends received us with great Cordiallity, express'd much satisfaction at seeing me again, desired that he might be call'd Cook (or Toote) and I Oreo which was accordingly done' (Cook 1969:223), seems to gain credence from having held his bid for friendship. In one version of his journal Cook added the observation, regarding name exchange, 'I believe that this is the strongest tie of friendship they can shew to a stranger' (Cook 1969:223 n. 4). George Forster, invested in the notion that *taio* was a transparent, immediately legible term, initially figured the relationship as anti-ceremonial, writing early in his time in Tahiti of 'taking our leave, without any troublesome ceremony, only pronouncing a hearty *tayo*, (friend), which had more meaning in it than many studied speech' (G. Forster 2000:171). However, because in Forster's lexicon *taio*, as Tahitian practice, is essentially natural rather than cultural, its very ceremonies can eventually be endorsed for their affective immediacy. After re-encountering the practice of name exchange in Tanna, Forster writes

This custom of making friendship, by a reciprocal exchange of names, is common in all the southern islands which we had hitherto visited, and in reality has something in it very engaging and affectionate. After having been in this manner adopted among the natives, we continued upon the best terms imaginable, and collected great supplements to the vocabulary. (G. Forster 2000:519)

Yet this very question, of transparency versus cultural specificity, and its clearly stated relationship here to a project of translation, signals a paradox that seems to encompass all the provisionality of *taio*'s lost relationship. For even as name exchange offered the possibility of a change of identities with a completely foreign other, this exchange always created, in the early days of cross-cultural contact, not a swapping of identities but two completely new identities, invented between subjects. In Chapter 1 I observed Bligh's confusion at finding that 'Almost every individual of any consequence has several names, which makes it frequently perplexing, when the same person is spoken of, to know who is meant' (Bligh 1979:82). This multiple identity formation is the product of multiple name exchanges, formed primarily in the name of friendship, though entangled with complex issues of status and *tapu*. As Alfred Gell puts it, describing the dissemination of identity through naming in the Marquesan context (where naming practices were comparable to, if more extreme than, those of the Society Islands), 'identity was extra-ordinarily labile; a man with an extended network of name-exchange partners was, in effect, a multiple person: in Edinburgh he was Angus; in Birmingham, Neville; in London, Albert' (Gell 1993:176). My suggestion is that, in name exchanges with Europeans, this division of identity cut two ways. The identities that both Europeans and islanders took on in the name of friendship were not exactly those traded to them. On 27 April 1769, Joseph Banks, who had enjoyed giving Tahitians the names of Greek heroes, wrote that

This day we found that our freinds had names and they were not a little pleasd to discover that we had them likewise; for the future Lycurgus will be calld *Tubourai tamaide* and his wife *Tomio* and the three women who commonly come with him *Terapo*, *Teraru* and *Omie*.

Relatively confident of a transliteration that does not always match the eventual spellings of these names,[16] Banks bemoans that 'As for our names they make so poor a hand of pronouncing them that I fear we shall be obligd to take each of us a new one for the occasion' (Banks 1962: I, 265). And on 10 May he confirms,

As for our own names the Indians find so much dificulty in pronouncing them that we are forcd to indulge them in calling us what they please, or rather what they say when they attempt to pronounce them. I give here the List: Captn Cooke *Toote*, Dr Solander *Torano*, Mr Hicks *Hete*, Mr Gore *Toarro*, Mr Molineux *Boba* from his Christian name Robert, Mr Monkhouse *Mato*, and myself *Tapane*. In this manner they have names for almost every man in the ship. (Banks 1962: I, 274–5)

Ignorant of his own hashing of Tahitian, Banks is alert to slips of the Tahitian tongue. Yet he willingly embraces the new roles they create for the *Endeavour*'s officers. Unlike the copper plaques with which Europeans staked their island claims, these exchanged names offer a flexible model of cross-cultural interaction, at once playing with and memorializing identities. They, like the lost concept of *taio* and other gestures of friendship, can never be simple signs of goodwill, but are rather co-inventions of its possibility.

---

[16] While *Terapo* and *Teraru* are believed by Banks's editor J. C. Beaglehole to be correct, *Omie* was probably Omae, *Tubourai tamaide* became Tepau i Ahurai Tamaiti, and *Tomio*, Tomaio.

3   Calculated affection

Marcel Mauss's influential essay *The Gift* begins by quoting some stanzas
from the Hamaval, one of the poems of the Scandinavian Edda that
Mauss suggests 'may serve as an epigraph for this study, so powerfully do
they plunge the reader into the immediate atmosphere of ideas and facts
in which our exposition will unfold' (Mauss 1990:1). I want to take the
same text as this chapter's point of departure.

I have never found a man so generous
And so liberal in feeding his guests
'That 'to receive would not be received',
Nor a man so ... [the adjective is missing]
Of his goods
That to receive in return was disagreeable to Him

With weapons and clothes
Friends must give pleasure to one another;
Everyone knows that for himself [through his Own experience].
Those who exchange presents with one another
Remain friends the longest
If things turn out successfully.

One must be a friend
To one's friend,
And give present for present;
One must have
Laughter for laughter
And sorrow for lies

You know, if you have a friend
In whom you have confidence
And if you wish to get good results
Your soul must blend in with his
And you must exchange presents
And frequently pay him visits.

But if you have another person
Whom you mistrust
And if you wish to get good results,
You must speak fine words to him
But your thoughts must be false
And you must lament in lies.

This is the way with him
In whom you have no trust
And whose sentiments you suspect,
You must smile at him
And speak in spite of yourself:
Presents given in return must be similar to those received.

Noble and valiant men
Have the best life;
They have no fear at all
But a coward fears everything:
The miser always fears presents.

It is better not to beg [ask for something]
Than to sacrifice too much [to the gods]:
A present given always expects one in return.
It is better not to bring any offering
Than to spend too much on it ...   (Mauss 1990:1–2)

Of these lines, Mauss tells us, 'The subject is clear. In Scandinavian civilization, and in a good number of others, exchanges and contracts take place in the form of presents; in theory these are voluntary, in reality they are given and reciprocated obligatorily' (Mauss 1990:3). Yet in pointing his thesis through this text, Mauss ignores many of its resonances. For the verse is as much about friendship as it is about gifts. It is as much about ambiguous or performed sentiment as it is about practical obligation. Indeed, I would suggest that these stanzas are first and foremost about friendship: about how to know and be and play the friend, and about the place of gifts within what is primarily an affective economy. Within the logic of these stanzas, the friend precedes the gift. And the gift does not solve the question of true and false friendship. Rather the same rules of gifting must proceed in both cases: 'To one's friend' one must 'give present for present', and 'with him / In whom you have no trust', still 'Presents given in return must be similar to those received'. The scrupulous reciprocation of present with present in each case conflates true and false friendship, allowing the relationship of mistrust to be the perfect copy of the relationship of confidence. If there is a qualitative difference between the two, it lies in an ineffable blending of souls in true friendship, which somehow serves to smooth the process of gift-giving so that it becomes simple 'exchange', rather than a punctilious weighing and evaluation.

Where studies of exchange such as Mauss's typically avoid the territory of friendship in favour of more clearly structured relationships of kinship or social hierarchy, western ethical philosophy has evidenced an equivalent disavowal of the imbrication of friendship with exchange. In the European philosophical tradition, exchange is the mode of relationship that true friendship transcends. Take, for example, Montaigne's expression of what I argue in this chapter is a historically persistent understanding of ideal friendship:

> The union of such friends, being truly perfect, leads them to lose any awareness of such services, to hate and drive out from between them all terms of division and difference, such as good turn, duty, gratitude, request, thanks and the like. Everything is genuinely common to them both: their wills, goods, wives, children, honour and lives; their correspondence is that of one soul in bodies twain ... (Montaigne 1991:214)

Montaigne here follows a logic that I find repeated in philosophical writing from Plato onwards: deploying an equation that converts the two to one and formulates the integer as sign of integrity, while in the same process repudiating vulgar accountancy. Friendship is again and again a merger that transcends base reciprocity: ineffable and inscrutable. Yet this very incalculability can only be expressed as a calculation. It is the balancing of two ideally matched subjects; it is measured in terms of the gifts it takes for granted. And perhaps for this reason, Montaigne's representation of the naturalized exchanges that true friendship entails – where 'wills, goods, wives, children, honour and lives' become understood as the common property of the friend – sounds very much like a description of *taio*. The desire to hold calculation at bay while at the same time formulating a mathematics of ideal friendship is something I will trace throughout this chapter, as a way of illuminating the particular challenges that Oceanic friendship posed for the European imagination.

Questions of social calculation agitated the eighteenth century in new ways. With the consolidation of commercial society through the combined force of utilitarian and sentimental discourses, attempts to reconcile intimacy with self-interest became pressingly explicit. As Allan Silver has argued across a trio of important articles, Scottish Enlightenment philosophers played a particularly significant role in attempting to free personal relationships from instrumental motivations, by relegating calculated exchanges to 'the newly distinct domain of the market' (Silver 1990:1484, 1487; also Silver 1989, 1997). Friendships thus liberated from associations of personal interest came to be conceived of as motivated more uncompromisingly by pulses of sympathy and affection. Where Silver builds this analysis into an argument that 'the normative abhorrence of instrumentality in personal relations ... was seminally formulated by the Scottish Enlightenment' (Silver 1990:1479), this chapter contends that such antipathy has a deeper tradition in European thought, and that its eighteenth-century articulations were symptomatic, rather than conclusive, formulations of an ongoing disavowal. The exploration of the Pacific and, in particular, encounters with Oceanian gift-giving practices, reflected this disavowal back to eighteenth-century European voyagers, necessitating confrontation with a model of exchange in which intimacy and calculation were held in productive tension rather than relegated to separate spheres.

I am interested in this chapter, then, in two connected aspects of western philosophies of friendship: the repudiation of calculation and its relationship to the identification of true friendship, understood as both virtuous and genuine. These are, of course, not the only themes to be found in an evaluation of traditions of thinking on friendship. I focus on the transhistorical development of certain topics of discussion and denial, rather than particular contextual nuances. I do not detail the development of Greek democracy or early-modern courtly ritual in order to illuminate my readings of Aristotle or Montaigne. And there are other aspects of friendship that have been pursued with great subtlety in recent early-modern and eighteenth-century scholarship, particularly friendship's role in marking the shifting boundary between the lives designated private and public, and its complex relationship to other modes of intimacy, that I do not touch upon here.[1] But those studies have focused on specific cultural milieus, whereas I am concerned with the issues cross-cultural contact throws into relief. The repressed question of friendship's accountancy seems to me exactly that which *taio* discloses. Even as a western ethics of friendship repudiates any notion of debt, a tallying takes place. Receipts can be thrown away only once terms have been balanced.

Mauss's *The Gift*, so stringent in its recognition of the obligations that gift-giving entails, nonetheless recognizes one ostensibly free gift. 'Our much regretted friend Hertz', Mauss writes,

had perceived the importance of these facts. With *touching disinterestedness* he had noted down 'for Davy and Mauss', on the card recording the following fact. Colenso says: 'They [the Maori] had a kind of exchange system, or rather one of giving presents that must ultimately either be reciprocated or given back.' For example, dried fish is exchanged for jellied birds or matting. All these are exchanged between tribes or 'friendly families without any kind of stipulation.' (Mauss 1990:10; my italics)

---

[1] Hutson 1994, Bray 2003, O'Donnell and O'Rourke 2003, Schachter 2008.

Mauss exempts one European gift of friendship from the logic of exchange that he so carefully delineates. In doing so, he repeats the ellipsis that is the subject of this book. Mauss's co-national, fellow-ethnologist, mourned predecessor (he had died in World War I) and friend Robert Hertz becomes, by virtue of all these circumstances, and above all by virtue of his capacity to *touch* the feelings of the recipient, a lone representative of *disinterested* donation in a world of mutual obligation.[2] That world is in turn enshrined in the gift Hertz gives, the record on the card, which documents a very different relationship between friendship and exchange in the Maori society of their joint study. For the Maori, the logic of reciprocity has become so systematized as to require no explicit *stipulation*. The European archives of early contact in Oceanic societies betray a comparable understanding of an essential gap between Oceanic and European notions of the relationship between friendship and exchange: an understanding that is nevertheless troubled by a submerged recognition of the complicities of cross-cultural friendship-formation with the imperatives of exchange. In this chapter I will examine some western traditions of theorizing the gift and friendship, to isolate the persistent hold that a notion of antipathy between intimacy and self-interest has exercised upon European thought. My aim is not only to provide a two-way trajectory for thinking about friendship during the late eighteenth century, but to register some deeply embedded assumptions that may affect our ability to recognize the ambivalences of European thinking at that time and their practical implications for Oceanic contact. I also seek to tackle an implicit, persistent division between cultures whose friendships are understood as affective or sentimental and those understood as gifting: a division that to some degree parallels that between cultures that have been understood, respectively, as historical and anthropological. On the contrary, questions of gifting and friendship are inextricably entwined in both European and Oceanic thinking. My selective analysis aims to illustrate the emergence of a pattern of disavowal, or outright ethical repudiation, of calculation within key texts on gift exchange and friendship.

---

[2] The obligations of 'armchair' anthropology, of which Mauss's essay is one of the later great examples, are a reflexive subtext of his analysis of exchange. Among other sources, Mauss draws heavily on Malinowski's account of *kula* exchange in the Trobriand Islands, *Argonauts of the Western Pacific* (1922), published two years prior to Mauss's essay. Malinowski's promulgation of fieldwork ethnography marked a moment at which synthesizing anthropological texts such as Mauss's were seen to lose some of their value, precisely because their insights were perceived to be disembodied, abstracted from experience and indebted to the labours of others.

Theories of Exchange and the Problem of Intimacy

We have during our lifetime become so much indebted to one another
we can no longer compute how our credit and debit stand.

– Goethe

Mauss's discussion of the gift is informed by an anti-calculative ethics.
In value-laden terms he exposes the self-interest of archaic forms of
prestation and appraises residual modes of exchange in modern societies.
His essay encompasses a spectrum of potentially contradictory positions,
from deep scepticism to a kind of magical thinking. The sceptical position
is encapsulated in Mauss's recognition that gifts are forms of entailment,
always comprehending the expectation of a return. Thus he describes the
gift as 'the present generously given even when, in the gesture accompanying the transaction, there is only a polite fiction, formalism, and
social deceit, and when really there is obligation and economic self-
interest' (Mauss 1990:3). Yet he also represents the gift as so socially
embedded as to be, effectively, embodied and animate. Thus the precious
items exchanged in the potlatch of Native America or the *kula* of the
Trobriand Islands are 'living beings'. 'Everything speaks', objects
'are animate things' (Mauss 1990:44). Similarly among the Maori, 'the
thing itself possesses a soul, is of the soul. Hence it follows that to make a
gift of something to someone is to make a present of part of oneself'
(Mauss 1990:12). Traces of this thinking remain in modern societies,
where, Mauss suggests, 'things sold still have a soul' (Mauss 1990:66).

What unites these somewhat contradictory attitudes to prestation is a
resistance to the logic of accountancy, particularly in its utilitarian
formulation.[3] Mauss exposes the motive of 'economic self-interest' in
archaic forms of exchange: speaking of the obligation to give and receive
in 'primitive' societies he writes of the commitment to 'balancing
accounts', of 'reciprocal creditors and debtors', of 'presents ... reciprocated with interest' and that 'the gift necessarily entails the notion of
credit' (Mauss 1990:14, 20, 36). Of course, Mauss is in part making an
analogy in order to isolate similarities between archaic and modern
exchange that have been repressed in understandings of the gift as free
and unconstrained. Yet the implication in the first part of his argument is
that the cultures he analyses are complicit in a kind of disingenuousness
regarding the gift: that he is exposing a reality of self-interest behind a
false representation of disinterest: 'The aim of all this is to display

---

[3] The conflation of utilitarianism with calculation in Mauss and his successors is a
significant aspect of their repudiation of accountancy, and one that my own analysis
cannot avoid inheriting to some extent.

generosity, freedom, and autonomous action, as well as greatness. Yet, all in all, it is mechanisms of obligation, and even of obligation through things, that are called into play' (Mauss 1990:23). On the other hand, the second part of his argument goes on to make favourable comparisons between the embodied and socially constituted transactions of gift cultures and the distanciated economics of western societies. Reversing the terms of Lévi-Strauss's celebrated social metaphors, he contrasts the heated and lively exchanges of the former with the 'cold' calculations of the latter. Gift cultures 'are in a perpetual state of economic ferment and this state of excitement is very far from being materialistic' (Mauss 1990:72); 'If some equivalent reason animates the Trobriand or American Indian chiefs, the Adaman clan etc., or once motivated generous Hindus, and Germanic or Celtic nobles, as regards their gifts and expenditure, it is not the cold reasoning of the merchant, the banker, and the capitalist' (Mauss 1990:75). To the extent that western societies 'are still somewhat removed from this constant, icy, utilitarian calculation', they remain in tune with a form of exchange that is, by virtue of its embodiment, its living heat, inherently more communal and virtuous. Mauss expresses this nostalgically: 'For a very long time man was something different, and he has not been a machine for very long, made complicated by a calculating machine' (Mauss 1990.76). He then forges a link between increasingly disembodied exchange and calculation, which he implicitly links to social disintegration. The suggestion is that genuine community and calculation are inimical. Yet he also exposes a mathematical logic behind gift transactions. The gift is reciprocated, he argues, 'to prove one is not unequal' (Mauss 1990:41). The motivating principle is to balance an equation: to make an equal or greater return for what is given. The simultaneous repudiation and suppressed recognition of a connection between communal sociability and a type of accounting that we find in Mauss's essay is also central to philosophical thinking about friendship.

Questions of calculation have not gone unnoticed in philosophical responses to Mauss's thesis. Georges Bataille's ecstatic meditation on gift exchange, and particularly its manifestation in the rivalries of potlatch, tries to counter the type of 'reasoning that balances *accounts*'; 'a sinister calculation' that he equates with bourgeois meanness, with a celebration of agonistic waste and loss (Bataille 1997:176). Bataille divides human activity into the productive, or useful, and the unproductive – that is, luxurious or perverse. Only this second set of activities deserves to be characterized as expenditure, since it 'constitute[s] a group characterized by the fact that in each case the accent is placed on a loss that must be as great as possible in order for that activity to take on its true meaning'. The 'principle of loss' is valorized by Bataille precisely because of its anti-calculative ethos, its contrariety 'to the economic principle of balanced accounts (expenditure regularly compensated for by acquisition)' (Bataille 1997:169). Like Mauss, he equates systems, such as potlatch, that eschew conservation, with both a heated excitation and inherently aristocratic 'unproductive values', which contrast with the cold calculations of bourgeois accountancy: 'In their intensified form, the *states of excitation*, which are comparable to toxic states, can be defined as the illogical and irresistible impulse to reject material or moral goods that it would have been impossible to utilize rationally (in conformity with the balancing of accounts)' (Bataille 1997:180). But more than Mauss he seems seduced by the oxymoronic possibilities of 'ostentatious loss', 'spectacular destruction', 'ruinous ceremony', and the paradoxes to which they point: profit through loss, 'waste [as] itself an object of acquisition' (Bataille 1997:174, 172, 201, 205). His celebration and sacralization of *la parte maudite*, however, remains an attempt to formulate an economy removed from 'the profane utilitarian sphere' and the (far greater than excremental) shame that 'petty calculation' sustains – 'the shame of man', bourgeois existence: 'A certain evolution of wealth, whose symptoms indicate sickness and exhaustion, leads to shame in oneself accompanied by petty hypocrisy' (Bataille 1997:206, 208, 176, 175). Bataille celebrates an excremental abandon that is in the end less soiling than the grubby work of reckoning.

Despite this, and despite his explicit claim that gift exchange is 'far removed from present commercial practices' (Bataille 1997:201), there remains a model of reckoning in Bataille's account of the gift. He still recognizes the principle of reciprocity, emphasizing, however, the agonistic impulse to exceed the gift one has received: 'The exchange value of the gift results from the fact that the donee, in order to efface the humiliation and respond to the challenge, must satisfy the obligation (incurred by him at the time of acceptance) to respond later with a more valuable gift, in other words, to return with interest' (Bataille 1997:172). He acknowledges a capacity for usury in potlatch, and indeed that 'wealth is multiplied in *potlatch* civilizations in a way that recalls the inflation of credit in banking civilizations' (Bataille 1997:173). Models of accountancy, then, apply where they balloon into excess, where they are at once threatened and sustained by a different selfish or aggressive calculation that paradoxically amounts to 'squandering' (Bataille 1997:192). And what is calculated on is ultimately a gain in what Pierre Bourdieu will term 'symbolic capital'; in 'prestige, glory and rank' (Bataille 1997:204).

Bourdieu's recognition that the symbolic representation of wealth is not exempt from a calculative rationale extends what I have referred to as the sceptical aspect of Mauss's critique. Like Mauss, Bourdieu exposes what he calls 'the sincere fiction of disinterested exchange'. He suggests that the archaic societies discussed by Mauss were actively engaged in the disavowal of the economic ends to which their exchanges were nonetheless 'objectively oriented' (Bourdieu 1993:171). That gift exchange is itself 'a system governed by the laws of interested calculation, competition, or exploitation' is a 'misrecognized or, one might say, socially repressed, objective truth' (Bourdieu 1993:172). In what Bourdieu refers to as 'good-faith' economies, gifts and celebrations function to attract capital, yet are regarded as exempt from accountancy: as gestural and '*symbolic*, i.e., in a sense the word sometimes receives, as lacking concrete or material effect, in short, *gratuitous*, i.e. disinterested but also useless' (Bourdieu 1993:176–7). The logics of capitalist and good-faith economies have equally conspired in the production of a fiction of non-economic archaic exchange: the former by indulging the fantasy of 'a "sacred" island miraculously spared by "the icy water of egotistical calculation" and left as a sanctuary for the priceless or worthless things it cannot assess', and the latter by seeking to disguise 'the cost of operating an economy which, by its refusal to acknowledge and confess itself as such, is forced to devote as much time to concealing the reality of economic acts as it expends in carrying them out' (Bourdieu 1993:178, 172). Once again the language is morally inflected: Bourdieu takes up Mauss's metaphors of cold calculation, and introduces further weighted terminology of dissimulation and absolution. At the heart of his critique is a consistent ethical position from which calculation constitutes the base reality of exchange: unsoftened, but also unblurred, by affect. His radical solution to the comprehensive disavowal he identifies is a comprehensive accountancy, that would incorporate rather than exempt symbolic exchanges:

> to extend economic calculation to *all* the goods, material and symbolic, without distinction, that present themselves as *rare* and worthy of being sought after in a particular social formation – which may be 'fair words' or smiles, handshakes or shrugs, compliments or attention, challenges or insults, honour or honours, powers or pleasures, gossip or scientific information, distinction or distinctions, etc. (Bourdieu 1993:178)

The social formation Bourdieu alludes to and the examples he adduces, while explicitly referencing archaic societies, might equally epitomize the languages and transactions of friendship. Like friendship, the practices whose 'symbolic interest' Bourdieu seeks to calculate can be dismissed as 'the irrationality of feeling or passion' (Bourdieu 1993:177), precisely because they are perceived to be exempt from capitalist economic analysis or calculation. As we will see, theories of friendship share an investment in a discourse of non-utility and non-profitability. It is this discourse in its application to the gift that Bourdieu seeks to expose as fictive, proposing in place of its apparent obfuscations 'a *general science of the economy of practices*, capable of treating all practices, including those purporting to be disinterested or gratuitous, and hence non-economic, as economic practices directed toward the maximizing of material or symbolic profit' (Bourdieu 1993:183).

Jacques Derrida takes Mauss's thesis to its logical extreme, arguing that the very fact that exchange is predicated on a structure of reciprocity and hence of calculation renders gifting an impossibility. The gift is 'annulled each time there is restitution or countergift'. A true gift could only be one that somehow managed to free itself, by an instantaneous and radical forgetting, from the circle of exchange:

> For there to be a gift, there must be no reciprocity, return, exchange, countergift, or debt. If the other *gives* me *back* or *owes* me or has to give me back what I give him or her, there will not have been a gift, whether this restitution is immediate or whether it is programmed by a complex calculation of long-term deferral or difference. (Derrida 1994:12)

The heaviest implications of Derrida's ethical position are for gift-exchange cultures: indeed, Derrida reproaches Mauss with failing to 'worry enough' about the inherent incompatibility 'between gift and exchange or about the fact that an exchanged gift is only a tit for tat, that is, an annulment of the gift' (Derrida 1994:37). While acknowledging that his critique is specific to an understanding of the word gift 'in our language or a few familiar languages' (Derrida 1994:12), Derrida does not thus fully account for the ethnocentrism, or indeed the paranoid Christian conscience, that seems to inform a meditation anxious to apply the letter of the Gospel injunction not to let the right hand know what the left does. Derrida's gift must *on no account register*:

> The simple intention to give, insofar as it carries the intentional meaning of the gift, suffices to make a return payment to oneself. The simple consciousness of the gift right away sends itself back the gratifying message of goodness or generosity, of the giving-being who, knowing itself to be such, recognizes itself in a circular, specular fashion, in a sort of auto-recognition, self-approval, and narcissistic gratitude. (Derrida 1994:23)

Of course his discussion of the gift must be contextualized, as John Frow points out in his deft and comprehensive account of theories of gift and commodity, within an ongoing engagement with philosophy's 'denial of economy, of debt, of mundane temporality and the difference of exchange' (Frow 1997:109). Derrida's reading of gift exchange demonstrates the end point of ethical engagement with a suppressed accountancy. It is my argument in this book that the eighteenth-century encounter with Oceanic societies and the literature it produced rendered the European philosophical denial of economy and debt highlighted by Frow aporetic and even, to some degree, explicit. Oceanic exchange provided Europeans, from the moment of initial contact well into the recent ethnographic past, with encounters with the resistances, assumptions and silences inherent in their own ethics of intimacy.

Bourdieu's discernment of the interest accrued from symbolic capital is attentive to Mauss's tenet that gift exchange constitutes a 'total social fact'. As I suggested earlier, notions of the gift as socially embedded morph, in Mauss's argument, into suggestions that the gift is embodied. Yet the notion of the gift as 'total social fact', glossed by Lévi-Strauss as 'an event which has a significance that is at once social and religious, magic and economic, utilitarian and sentimental, jural and moral' (Lévi-Strauss 1969:52), also allows for an explicit dialogue with philosophies and practices of friendship. (Indeed, Lévi-Strauss's pairing of 'utilitarian and sentimental' invokes the two main discourses framing eighteenth-century literary-philosophical discussions of friendship.) Anthropologists writing on gift exchange tend to develop this aspect of Mauss's critique. An inevitable tension arises in these studies between the impulse to lay bare the social structures within which exchange practices are embedded, and an investment in, or desire to respect, the inscrutability of other cultural systems. Such studies, nonetheless, open up a space for the examination of friendship within exchange. Thus Lévi-Strauss recognizes 'the idea that a mysterious advantage is attached to the acquisition of commodities, or at least certain commodities, by means of reciprocal gifts, rather than by individual production or acquisition' (Lévi-Strauss 1969:55), but also names the kinds of symbolic interest into which this 'mysterious advantage' translates: 'power, influence, sympathy, status and emotion'. Although his main focus will be the identical structure of exchange with kinship relations, specifically the incest taboo, Lévi-Strauss also adduces examples from the realm of friendship. He draws attention to Radcliffe-Brown's observation on gift exchange among the Adaman Islanders, that 'the purpose that it did serve was a moral one. The object of the exchange was to produce a friendly feeling between the two persons concerned' (Lévi-Strauss 1969:55). He looks at western gifting, particularly at Christmas, as a preserve of excessive and prestigious exchange (a subject that has more recently been examined in detail by James Carrier (1995)). And he discusses the ways in which rituals of hospitality and their etiquettes of exchange function to transition strangers into cordial relations.

Post-Maussian analyses of gift-giving that focus on Oceanic societies have redirected attention towards the bodies involved in exchange and the singular embodiment of objects caught up in gifting. Interventions in the theorization of Oceanic exchange such as Marshall Sahlins's *Stone Age Economics*, with its debunking of global in favour of local models, and rethinking of economic rationalism as a socially embedded logic, or Marilyn Strathern's use, in *The Gender of the Gift*, of a combination of Melanesian and feminist paradigms to interrogate accepted wisdom on gendered exchange relations, have extended Mauss's thesis, succinctly summarized by Frow: that 'gifts are precisely not *objects* at all, but transactions and social relations' (Frow 1997:124). It is within this corpus that we might expect to find some engagement with the relationship between gift-giving and friendship-making. The inauguration, in many Oceanic societies, of friendship relations in an act of name exchange that in turn instigates the exchange of material goods, would seem paradigmatically to co-implicate bodies and exchange. Yet attention to the transactions of friendship, rather than kinship or group hierarchical relations, is a striking omission in this literature. Cross-cultural transactions are also generally subsidiary: with the exception of Nicholas Thomas's groundbreaking *Entangled Objects*, which recognizes that 'the problem of . . . unitary conceptions of indigenous economies is that they suppress the entanglement with other systems such as capitalist trade' (Thomas 1991:4), these studies focus on and to some degree reify endogamous systems of exchange. According to Chris Gregory's *Gifts and Commodities*, based on research in Papua New Guinea, absolute distinctions characterize gift and commodity systems. His tabulation of inherent divisions between archaic gift and capitalist commodity cultures is focused around notions of private property. As Gregory argues, using terminology that inadvertently characterizes members of gift societies as more human than those of commodity economies, and thus echoes Mauss's, Bataille's and Bourdieu's insistent metaphors of heated and icy exchange, 'The material basis of society not only determines the social status of the transactors, it also determines the social status of the object being transacted: commodities are *alienable* objects transacted by aliens; gifts are *inalienable* objects transacted by non-aliens' (Gregory 1982:43).

Annette Weiner takes up the concept of inalienability in challenging Lévi-Strauss's thesis that women are reduced to the status of objects within gift exchange. In *Inalienable Possessions: The Paradox of Keeping-While-Giving*, she argues against Bataille and others that gift exchange is motivated not by a primary logic of circulation and loss, but rather by the desire to enshrine and exempt certain treasured objects from that very logic. 'Whereas other alienable properties are exchanges against each other, inalienable possessions are symbolic repositories of genealogies and historical events, their unique, subjective identity gives them absolute value placing them above the exchangeability of one thing for another' (Weiner 1992:33). While Weiner extends the prevailing understanding of gifts as primarily relational rather than material, she inverts the priority given by scholars since Bronislaw Malinowski to a model of uninterrupted circulation, and focuses instead on the relationship between value and exemption from circulation. She returns to Mauss's Maori and Trobriand examples to argue that certain objects attain, often through the activities of women who 'produce, guard and authenticate' them, the status of 'transcendent treasures to be guarded against all the exigencies that might force their loss' (Weiner 1992:19, 33). In pursuing her thesis, Weiner asserts that 'convictions about the morality and sanctity of reciprocity' (Weiner 1992:31) are western impositions upon gift ethics. Yet the counter-notion espoused by Weiner of value as inhering in exemption from circulation belongs to an equally influential discursive tradition. Furthermore, Weiner's equation of feminine production with embodied value participates in the broader tendency I have observed, to conflate inalienability and embodiment. Her study joins other discussions of the gift in reiterating certain unexamined associations between calculation and mechanism, gifting and cultural embeddedness. By placing this repudiation of calculation within a European tradition of thinking about both exchange and intimacy, I seek to explore rather than reproduce eighteenth-century voyagers' disavowals of grubby trade and mixed motives in those Oceanic societies that were later to become so integral to the formulation of gift-exchange theory.

Theories of Intimacy and the Problem of Exchange

1.   *Philia, Amicitia and Calculation*

> They Lov'd each other with a love,
> That did all things in equal prove
>
> – Theocritus

In her fine study of the exchange practices entailed by *philia*, or classical Greek friendship, Lynette Mitchell draws attention to the tension between affect and reciprocity in both Greek and Roman friendship.

She favours a commonsense resolution of this perceived ambivalence: 'the fact of the matter is that some friendships were more affectionate and some less so, and that friendships worked on a sliding scale of affection and utility with some inclining more towards the affective (and altruistic?) end, and some towards the side of simple advantage' (Mitchell 1997:8). Yet her own language, with its tentative equation of altruism and affection, and its simplification of self-interested motives, is indicative of the implicit value judgements that tend to inform discussion of friendship in the classical world. Compare David Konstan, writing of the Roman concept of *amicitia*. After noting that, unlike the Greek notion of *philia*, *amicitia* has conventionally been understood to have a primarily political significance, so that political allies were *amici*, forging alliances 'of practical affiliation having nothing to do with real and lasting affection', Konstan elaborates,

The evacuation of emotional content from the concept of friendship was facilitated by the Roman concern with reciprocity. Like the Greek *kharis*, the Latin term *gratia* refers both to the return that is due for a service (*officium* or *beneficium*) one has received, and to the sense of debt or gratitude that is morally incumbent on the beneficiary ... This ethic of obligation was assumed to be associated particularly with relations between friends. (Konstan 1997:123)

Against this received wisdom, Konstan references Peter Brunt's expanded allocation of Roman friendship: 'the range of *amicitia* is vast. From the constant intimacy and goodwill of virtuous or at least like-minded men to the courtesy that etiquette normally enjoined on gentlemen, it covers every degree of genuinely or overtly amicable relation' (Konstan 1997:124). Konstan opposes 'practical affiliation' to 'real and lasting affection', while Brunt redeems *amicitia* for 'genuinely' as well as 'overtly' amicable relations. For both scholars, the idea that calculated and genuine friendship are inherently incompatible remains unproblematic. The reading of the key classical texts on friendship that follows suggests that these inaugurate rather than resolve the term's ethical ambiguity.[4]

In Plato's *Lysis* (*c.* 380 BC), Socrates encounters Hippothales, who has a crush on the boy Lysis. Socrates is dismayed to find that Hippothales is confessing his devotion in poetry and song, and offers to demonstrate the superior effect of uncompromising argument in attracting young minds. He engages Lysis and his friend Menexus in conversation on the subject of friendship, raising and then disposing of propositions until

---

[4] For Graeco-Roman thinking on friendship, see Herman 1987, Konstan 1997, Mitchell 1997, Hutter 1978, Fraisse 1974, Fitzgerald 1997. For analysis of Plato's and Aristotle's philosophies of friendship, see Bolotin 1979, Pangle 2003, Cooper 1977, Penner and Rowe 2005, Price 1989, Kenny 1992: 45–55, Stern-Gillet 1995.

he is forced to admit he is lost for words and has failed to define friendship. For Socrates, the principle of value is a given in friendship: 'friends they cannot be, unless they value one another' (Plato 1892:64). It is the way in which value may be calculated that poses a problem. Socrates' propositions circle around the issue of reciprocity: 'which is the friend of which? Is the lover the friend of the beloved, whether he be loved in return or hated; or is the beloved the friend; or is there no friendship at all on either side, unless they both love one another?' (Plato 1892:60) He attempts to balance various similar terms: are the like and the like friends? Or do unlike types attract one another, by a compensatory logic? Does the union of virtue with virtue make for perfect friendship? Is it a question of mutual congeniality? Yet Socrates and his interlocutors are confounded by the sufficiency of positive terms to themselves. Like can add nothing to like; goodness is a kind of wholeness. Such putative friends require nothing else for their completion; they obviate equation. In the light of these observations, Socrates concludes that 'If neither the beloved, nor the lover, nor the like, nor the unlike, nor the good, nor the congenial, nor any other of whom we spoke – for there were such a number of them I cannot remember all – if none of these are friends, I know not what remains to be said . . . as yet we have not been able to discover what is a friend' (Plato 1892:74–5). Socrates draws attention to the limitations of his rational and argumentative powers in defining friendship. Friendship becomes, by default, that which exceeds his powers of calculation. The performative quality of this conclusion is reinforced if we recall that the dialogue is framed as a form of tease, a flirtation designed to remind the boys of their own limitations, as a mode of facilitating intimacy. By explicitly exhausting the available calculations of intimacy, Socrates is effectively drawing the boys into intimacy: he is allowing them to feel the limits of their powers.

This inconclusive dialogue implicitly raises a question that I want, for the sake of argument, to formulate mathematically: does the self relate intimately to another as integer or as fraction; as complement or supplement? The content and form of the dialogue answer this question in different ways, for while Sophocles argues that the integrity of the self renders friendship unnecessary, the dialogue form might be said to illustrate that philosophical completeness is only attained between two reflecting and sparring selves. The paradox of friendship, as both occurring between equals, and enabling a completion of the self, is further probed in books VIII and IX of Aristotle's *Nicomachean Ethics* (c. 350 BC). As is well known, Aristotle divides friendship into three types: the pleasurable, the useful and the good, and goes on to argue that *philia*, the friendship between equals in virtue, incorporates and subsumes those lesser friendships based around pleasure and use. *Philia* constitutes a perfectly balanced equation: 'exactly the same and similar results accrue to each party from the other; which ought to be the case between friends' (Aristotle 1998:142). As Ronna Burger has elegantly argued, however, Aristotle's thesis shifts in book IX, where the friend becomes necessary to the self not as reflection, but as the other voice in a dialogic relationship:

> The friend was originally designated an *allos autos*, suggesting the replication of myself as an other; as a partner in dialogue he becomes *heteros autos*, forming a pair with me precisely because of the difference that makes him genuinely other. Sharing speeches and thoughts is motivated by and in turn produces an awareness of one's partial perspective or incompleteness: it introduces into friendship the possibility of some kind of longing, which the friendship of the good seemed to preclude. (Burger 2003:50)

Aristotle spells out the algorithm that Socrates enacted, linking dialogue with the desiring aspect of intimacy while stressing the sufficiency of the virtuous self unto itself. Focusing on the same passage as Burger, Giorgio Agamben suggests a further nuance to the paradox of the friend as *heteros autos*, or *alter ego*: 'At the point at which I perceive my existence as pleasant, my perception is traversed by a concurrent perception that dislocates it and deports it towards the friend, towards the other self. Friendship is this de-subjectivization at the very heart of the most intimate perception of self' (Agamben 2004:5). In his exegesis, intimacy is *at once* fractional and integral. The friend is that part of self that makes self aware of its integrity. And equally, the friend is the reflection that troubles the sense of self-integrity.

Burger's recognition that friendships of pleasure are privileged over those of utility in Aristotle's anatomy of friendship brings us to another critical factor: the disavowal of accounting. As I have suggested, the desire to repudiate calculation in the baser sense is as strong in Graeco-Roman thinking on friendship as the desire to balance the friendship equation. For Aristotle the disavowal takes the form of a depreciation of the value of friendships based in 'motives of profit' (Aristotle 1998:143). Such friendships are underpinned by self-interest and competition, leading to fault-finding and blame:

> Friendship because of advantage is very liable to fault-finding; because, as the parties use one another with a view to advantage, the requirements are continually enlarging, and they think they have less than of right belongs to them, and find fault because though justly entitled they do not get as much as they want: while those who do the kindnesses can never come up to the requirements of those to whom they are being done. (Aristotle 1998:155)

By Aristotle's truistical calculation, such friendships do not add up. Profits reveal their finitude even as they swell, and each party seeks to appropriate for itself and concomitantly underrates the partner. Yet Aristotle's discussion of virtuous friendship also incorporates, both explicitly and in unacknowledged ways, a language of utility. Thus, in a formula not so far removed from European representations of *taio*, Aristotle argues that all friendship rests upon communion: that 'brothers and intimate companions have all in common, but other people have their property separate' (Aristotle 1998:149). And where intimacy is not immediately assessed as a partnership of equals, he represents friendship as a complex system of valuation, in which inherent worth is calculated against the degree of feeling:

The feeling of Friendship should be in due proportion in all Friendships which are between superior and inferior; I mean, the better man, or the more profitable, and so forth, should be the object of a stronger feeling than he himself entertains, because when the feeling of Friendship comes to be after a certain rate then equality in a certain sense is produced, which is thought to be a requisite in friendship. (Aristotle 1998:147)

The friendship of the inferior must make up in intensity of feeling what it lacks in superiority or profitability. At this point, Aristotle appears to equate instrumentality with virtue. If his argument is that the better or more profitable friend naturally inspires a greater force of feeling, what he more strongly implies here is that feeling is the compensatory labour of the friend who has less to bring to the table.

I quoted David Konstan's observation that Roman *amicitia* was understood as inherently more of a political relationship than *philia*. However, an ambivalence about the relationship between politics and friendship informs Cicero's meditation on friendship, which has been explored by Jacques Derrida in his *Politics of Friendship*. I want here to draw both Cicero's rhetoric and Derrida's commentary into my developing analysis of friendship's disavowal of calculation. Framed as a dialogue in which Laelius speaks of his relationship with the recently deceased Scipio Africanus, Cicero's *Laelius de Amicitia Liber* (*c.* 44 BC) again weighs the role of self-interest in friendship. In the great friendships with which Laelius's and Scipio's bond hopes to join ranks, need is eschewed. Discussing the motivations of friendship, Cicero writes,

Anyone of the opinion that this feeling emanates from mere inadequacy and is entirely concerned with getting hold of someone who will provide us with things that we should like to get is surely assigning friendship altogether too humble and ignoble an origin ... Indeed, the contrary is true: the *more* confidence a person feels in himself, the stronger his equipment of moral and intellectual gifts will be.

And although these are qualities that relieve him of dependence upon others and make him feel completely self-sufficient, they will actually strengthen his capacity for making and keeping friends. (Cicero 1971:193)

In Cicero's formulation, worthy individuals do not seek in friendship to gain from the other: however, their friendships nonetheless effectively complete them, by making manifest their self-sufficiency. While Cicero marks a distinction between 'things that we should like to get' and less tangible 'moral and intellectual gifts', the language of profit threads his discussion even as it is repudiated:

When a man shows kindness and generosity, his motive in doing so is not just to exact repayment. We do not hire out our favours, and charge interest for them: we behave kindly because that is the natural thing to do. The reason why we count friendship as a blessing is not because we are hoping for a material return. It is because the union is quite enough profit in itself.

Cicero is a subtle exegete, turning the tendency of discussions of intimacy to slip into the language of calculation to illustrate the paradox of friendship: that profit arises where it is least sought. Yet his understanding of friendship is inflected with implicit hierarchy. The man who needs nothing, the worthy friend, is the natural aristocrat, transcendent in those material gifts for which his moral and intellectual advantages are to some degree ciphers. Reformulating his equation later in the dialogue, Cicero allows this to become explicit:

It is quite untrue to say that people only form friendships because there is some deficiency in themselves. On the contrary, the most generous and liberal friends are those who have the very least need of anyone else, because they themselves already possess wealth and power and, above all, goodness, which is the strongest resource a man can command. (Cicero 1971:204)

Moral and material gifts are connected here by an emphasis on moral qualities whose display is facilitated by material wealth. This allows Cicero, in a more slippery fashion, effectively to conflate wealth and power with virtue: while ostensibly equating goodness with generosity and liberality, he has already indicated that these are predicated on the wealth and power that he now suggests they simply illustrate.

Cicero goes on to argue, however, that friendship exceeds the value of material benefits:

When a man is overflowing with wealth and goods and all kinds of abundance, and has got hold of everything that money can buy – horses, slaves, splendid clothes, expensive plate – he will be very foolish if he fails to add friends to that list, since *they* are the finest equipment that life can offer ... For possessions of this kind get passed on – they go to the next man whose turn it is to rise to the top. Friendship, on the other hand, remains a firm and durable asset. Indeed, even if a man does manage to keep his hands on fortune's transitory gifts, his life will still remain unhappy if it is empty and devoid of friends. (Cicero 1971:205)

Friendship, then, is not immeasurable, but rather a 'firm and durable asset', worthy of greater investment than material wealth. If wealth here turns out to belong inevitably to a capricious economy of gift exchange, friendship is valuable because it is, by contrast, inalienable.

Cicero then raises and dismisses the idea of setting restrictions on friendship, by proposing what amounts to a series of false equations:

The first opinion is that our feeling for our friends should be identical with our feeling for our own selves. The second is that our goodwill towards friends should correspond in every respect to their own attitude towards us. The third point of view is that the value we attach to our friends should be exactly the same as the value they attach to themselves. (Cicero 1971:205–6)

Cicero suggests that attempts to balance the friendship equation are inevitably reductive, since they leave out incalculable human factors, such as the capacity to be more active on a friend's behalf than our own or the self-deprecation of the friend. He is particularly dismissive of 'the second attitude, which restricts friendship to an equal interchange of services and feelings, reduces it to a too mean and narrow calculation of payments and receipts meticulously balanced' (Cicero 1971:206), yet calculation and balancing are the principle of each of his three options and the basis of their repudiation. Rather Cicero proposes that the 'two men of sound character' who form appropriate friendship should 'unreservedly share' (Cicero 1971:207). He has earlier described friendship as a form of mirroring: 'When a man thinks of a true friend, he is looking at himself in the mirror' (Cicero 1971:189). The two subjects in the ideal friendship are identical: not only do fellow citizens have stronger ties than foreigners, and relatives than strangers, but the best friendships are forged through identity of feeling: 'Friendship may be defined as a complete identity of feeling about all things in heaven and earth: an identity which is strengthened by mutual goodwill and affection' (Cicero 1971:187). If then, he now proposes to do away with the calculation implicit in attempts to restrict friendship to a balanced equation, it is because he has already proposed his own, more stable equation. For Cicero the advantages that accrue from friendship are flow-on effects from the identity of the participants in friendship. The material benefits of friendship are disavowed, and the careful calculation that he nonetheless espouses is represented as a natural balancing of character and principle.

Jacques Derrida has drawn attention to a different kind of '*arithmetical twist*' that informs Cicero's discussion of the rare exemplary friendship. Derrida formulates this quantitatively:

How many friends? How many of us are there? Determining a nomination and a quotation (*pauci nominantur*: those who are named or whose name is quoted are few and far between when true and perfect friendship is named), the distinction expresses rarity or the small in number. ... Are friends rare? Must they remain rare? How many are there? What account must be taken of rarity? (Derrida 1997:3)

Derrida here parses Laelius's confession of his

hope that my friendship with Scipio will go down to posterity. This is a hope which I cherish all the more keenly because, throughout the whole course of history, the pairs of friends who have been lastingly remembered only amount to barely three, or four at the very most. It is my greatest desire that future generations will add the friendship of Scipio and Laelius to this small number. (Cicero 1971:184)

This rare, unique pairing figures not just as exemplary, but as (therefore) exempt from history itself. Ideal friendships evade the losses that come with time: both lapses from memory and the tarnishing effects of hindsight. There are echoes once again of Weiner's inalienable possessions, whose value is inherently related to their status outside the flow of circulation. Alternatively, Derrida probes the exemplarity that Laelius seeks for its resonance, not simply as ideal, but also as 'the duplicate, the reproduction, the copy as well as the original, the type, the model' (Derrida 1997:4). The friendship is singular because the friends are copies: mirror images of one another, as Cicero claimed.[5]

Where friendship is, as Aristotle argues, ideally a pairing of the virtuously like-minded, or as Cicero suggests, a form of mirroring, this in turn leaves open the possibility of flattery: friendship's false copy. In 'How to tell a Flatterer from a Friend' (AD *c.* 100), from the *Moralia*, Plutarch compares friends to true and flatterers to false coin, suggesting that 'we should try our friend, as we do our money, whether or not he be passable and current, before we need him'. The flatterer, 'as counterfeit

---

[5] Derrida links this to enduring questions in his own ethical project about survival. Each friendship is predicated on mourning; one friend will always survive, and thus frequently testify to, the other. The eulogies collected in *The Work of Mourning* are informed by this sense of friendship (Derrida 2001). The idea that survivor guilt may be inherent to friendship itself is significant for my examination of issues of cross-cultural friendship, intersecting compellingly with questions of survival and witnessing in encounter. Both written testimony and physical survival are weighted in favour of the European side of Oceanic exchanges.

gold imitates the brightness and lustre of the true, always puts on the easiness and freedom of a friend, is always pleasant and obliging, and ready to comply with the humor of his company' (Plutarch 1878:2). Plutarch acknowledges the trickiness of distinguishing false from true friend. He proposes that this is best achieved by pretending in one's turn to a fickleness of opinion, and watching the flatterer, whose policy is always agreement, swerve course to match one's feigned changes of heart. Of course, this means that the flatterer effectively makes the true friend false: in order to distinguish himself from the flatterer the individual must be untrue to himself. Flattery renders explicit the calculative impulse at the heart of an insistence upon equality in friendship: of what Leela Gandhi has referred to as the homophilic impulse in Aristotelian *philia*. She argues that *philia*, formulated in the ideological service of a vulnerable Greek city-state, 'borrows heavily, if wishfully, from the sparse vocabulary of filiation: "a friend is another self"; "The basis of affection is equality and similarity"; "like is friend to like"; and so on' (Gandhi 2006:28). The counterfeit friend makes a mockery of the drive towards duplication in the ethics of *philia* and *amicitia*, and forces the mathematics of friendship to declare itself as a form of account keeping.

If classical models of *philia* and *amicitia* seed later European notions of appropriate friendship, they were preceded by, and possibly also a response to, a different ideal. In his fascinating study *Ritualised Friendship and the Greek City*, Gabriel Herman reconstructs the nuances of Attic friendship bonds to recover an account of ritualized friendship between strangers, or *xenia*. Herman locates the pre-eminence of *xenia* in the eighth and seventh centuries BC, prior to the establishment of the *polis* and the attendant development of notions of community obligation and its enforcement through legal institutions. Rather than co-citizens, *xenoi* were strangers, whose friendship was often forged in the face of an equal pressure towards hostility. Herman writes, 'A *xenos*, says Hesychius, is a friend (*philos*) from abroad. Indeed, the idea of strangeness combined with friendship is built into the assumptions of the actors' (Herman 1987:12). This paradox offers a broad framework of comparison between early Oceanic–European contact and *xenia*. The details of the latter practice cement the comparison. Herman defines Greek ritualized friendship as 'a bond of solidarity manifesting itself in an exchange of goods and services between individuals originating from separate social units' (Herman 1987:10). Between *xenoi*, 'intimacy was established not through a lengthy interaction, but abruptly, as in marriage, through a ritual act' (Herman 1987:29–30). 'The partners involved in ritualised friendship', writes Herman, 'were presumed to be bound by mutual affection. This affection, however, imitated the outward manifestations but not the inward spirit of kinship: ritualised friends were not supposed to love each other, but to behave as if they did' (Herman 1987:17). The immediate establishment of a bond with entailments equivalent to those of European kinship, proceeding not from a welling up of feeling but from material or political necessity, and proceeding towards possible genuine feeling simply by virtue of its enactment, mirrors the expectations that burdened the *taio* pact. For eighteenth-century Europeans *taio* represented a reversal of the principles of friendship formation: homophilic principles that had in turn been formulated against the very model of friendship that *xenia* represented.

In ancient Greece, the bond thus abruptly forged entailed a total commitment to provide and care for the friend: as Herman writes, 'This was no ordinary hospitality, ancient style or modern. Besides shelter and food, the host undertook to take care of the welfare of his partner, material and spiritual – to feed him at his table and maintain him in his household' (Herman 1987:28). Greek ritualized friendship often involved subsidiary customs of naming and of fostering. These practices were trans-generational, rather than the immediate name exchange or adoption rituals that took place between Pacific islanders and Europeans, but they similarly constituted symbolic practices of integration. If there was an impulse akin to the one we have isolated in later Greek philosophy – to seek an equal in friendship – the principle of equality was defined within *xenia* by need rather than social status: 'What mattered most was the possession of a quality which the other needed, and that is why, in fact, a bond of ritualised friendship did not necessarily involve exact social equals' (Herman 1987:37). We have observed a similarly incongruous understanding of equality in European voyagers' attempts on the one hand to locate the Tahitian of highest perceived status before forging a *taio* bond, while on the other remaining aware that exigencies limited their capacity to prolong this assessment of rank.

Xenia was forged typically through the performance of a service or the offering of a gift. Herman's discussion of this initiative focuses on its distinction from a later anti-calculative ethos:

unlike in Judaeo-Christian morality, the good deed was not an end in itself, an act of uncalculated, altruistic generosity for which perhaps heavenly, but never earthly, rewards were expected. On the contrary, *euergesia* was unabashedly recognised as a secular strategy in the conduct of interpersonal relations. The benefactor put the beneficiary in a state of indebtedness, from which state the beneficiary could only redeem himself by a display of submission and loyalty – and that was all there was to it. (Herman 1987:48–49)

Here friendship is bound up in the complex logic of gift return. Herman's slightly combative declaration 'that was all there was to it' anticipates the foreignness of this system of thought to contemporary readers more familiar with subsequent ethics of charity and obligation. His choice of the term 'unabashed' is indicative, recognizing as it does the complex sense of shame that inflects our understandings of altruism. European discussions of *taio* are in part, I have suggested, informed by unacknowledged shame: by a sense of the simple need that compels voyagers, at the periphery of their world, to participate in friendships whose ethics they would also seek to repudiate.

Although he doesn't directly cite Mauss or other theories of the gift that I have discussed here, Herman's discussion of *xenia* fits the Maussian model of archaic exchange, raising attendant questions concerning motivation. Indeed Herman departs from his otherwise scrupulous relativism when discussing motive, suggesting that 'the courteous language of ritualised friendship could conveniently be harnessed to disguise real motivations' (Herman 1987:109). In this sense his study aligns itself with a later philosophical tradition he is otherwise careful to historicize, that figures materialism as both inherently inimical to friendship and the most likely motive for its profession. As he explains, 'there was in the Greek language no vocabulary of bribery distinct from that of gift-exchange itself, the same set of words served to denote both practices' (Herman 1987:75). According to the logic of ritualized friendship, gifts placed their recipients under obligation. Both parties were bound to give and give in return, to serve and serve in return. Herman's study shows that this structure of obligation only became problematic when the pre-political world of individual noble heroism gave way to the communal society of the city-state. At that point, personal fidelity to an individually forged bond became less important than obedience to the interests of the community. 'Thus, while lavish gift-givings had been the mark of heroes and kings, abstinence from gift-exchange became the mark of the good citizen' (Herman 1987:78). It is in relation to this historical development that we can best consider the philosophical tracts I have discussed. Their simultaneous repudiation of materialist motivations for friendship and emphasis on relationships of social equality addresses the ethos of the *polis* through the ethics of friendship. Hence the retention of an ambivalent utilitarianism that I have been foregrounding: classical Greece developed an ethics of friendship that was designed to further, not the interests of the individual, but 'utility to the *polis* as a whole' (Herman 1987:79). In considering Oceanic models of ritualized friendship we might reanimate the opposition between periphery and metropole by contemplating the parallels between, on the one hand, archaic Greek and Oceanic societies and, on the other, European city culture and its acknowledged roots in democratic Athens and Roman law. This is not to attempt to 'classicize' the encounters of eighteenth-century Oceanians and Europeans, but rather to recognize the deep history of specific friendship practices that informed European voyaging. By focusing on *xenia* rather than *philia* as a model for Oceanic friendship I seek to avoid Paul Lyons's charge that 'reading Islander–Anglo friendships in terms of a conjunction of differing concepts of *philia* [can] too easily slip into overdetermined models of rigid Native *custom* vs. flexible Euroamerican *practical reason*'. Lyons argues that 'classical friendship theory . . ., in comparative contexts, appears as a severely restricted framework' (Lyons 2006:102). My point is rather that Oceanic models of friendship can make visible ambivalences within and counter-traditions to classical friendship theory.[6]

Herman notes that when the two partners in the *xenia* bond first come together, 'the prospect of violent exchange looms over the encounter'. Part of what is difficult to stomach about such relationships is the immediacy with which the potential for violence is converted to one for friendship:

> Violence is averted . . . mostly against common expectations, by some generous gesture. This gesture, together with certain rituals, serves as a kind of triggering event which brings about a reversal: strangeness and enmity are replaced at a stroke by warm intimacy. And, if we are to believe the ancient authors, the friendship that results from this consists not only of external formalities, but of genuine sentimental attachment and large-scale co-operation. (Herman 1987:43)

Early encounters between Oceanians and European voyagers also involve the establishment of sudden intimacy in situations fraught with violence. I have tried to reconstruct a sense of this precarious balance of possibilities in my opening discussion of the crowd scene. Focusing on the capacity of contact to develop towards violence or intimacy, I have suggested that neither is finally subsumed in the outcome: moments of recognition can emerge during scenes of violence, and equally sudden friendships retain seeds of animosity, even as they gesture towards genuine sentimental attachment. At the same time, it remains important to recognize, as Herman has succeeded in doing, the capacity of what

---

[6] Alternatively, Leela Gandhi elegantly reconciles *xenia* with 'classical friendship theory' by focusing on the representation of *philoxenia* in the fragments of Epicurus. She suggests that an Epicurean 'ethic of fidelity to strange friends is predicated upon a principled distaste for the racial exclusivity of the *polis*' (Gandhi 2006:29).

appear to be contradictory feelings to coexist in other cultural and historical contexts. Violence is not the reality which instantaneous and ritualized friendship bonds must disclose, but rather a significant factor in their formation.

2.   *Economies of Sensibility*

> Friendship is a disinterested commerce between equals; love, an abject intercourse between tyrants and slaves.
>
> – Oliver Goldsmith

I have proposed, in my discussion of classical philosophies of friendship, that a 'low' accountancy, repudiated in relationship to the ethics of friendship, was nonetheless smuggled into discourses structured according to a 'high' mathematics of intimacy, and that these two modes of calculation remain impossible to disentangle. Their imbrication emerged particularly explicitly in the Enlightenment, when ethical deduction became figured as mathematical, even as economic reasoning claimed to achieve the severance of the realms of feeling and finance in the wake of a more explicit co-implication of friendship with exchanges of gifts and services during the early modern period. On the one hand, Louis Bredvold has depicted eighteenth-century philosophical thought as consolidating a seventeenth-century 'invention of the ethical calculus'. He refers to 'the mathematical ground-tone of the age', analysing the post-Cartesian belief that the nature of man could be computed and ethical problems resolved through calculation. He suggests that this moral accountancy achieved its ludicrous apotheosis in the deductions of Locke and Hutcheson, and quotes at length from the algebraically formulated section of Hutcheson's *Inquiry into the Original of Our Ideas of Beauty and Virtue* (1725) devoted to 'an attempt to introduce a Mathematical Calculation in subjects of Morality' (Bredvold 1965:173).[7] As I will go on to show, this spirit of calculation informs eighteenth-century discussion of friendship. On the other hand, according to Allan Silver, the development of theories of economic liberalism in the eighteenth century effected a relegation of friendship from the realm of exchange to that of the private. Silver writes,

As the network of bureaucracy and market exchange spread, distaste mounted for the practical reciprocities that had marked personal bonds in earlier times ... Friendship emerges as one of a variety of benevolent social bonds, like family,

---

[7] Hutcheson omitted these algorithms from the fourth edition, noting that they 'appear'd useless, and were disagreeable to some readers' (Hutcheson 2004:xvii).

neighbourhood, and the intercourse of citizens in civil society, understood as shaped by propinquity and elective affinities more decisively than by station, corporate group and political imperatives ... The early liberals were concerned to define friendship as intrinsically private. At the conceptual level, they sought to show how personal relations, such as friendship, could not be governed by any formal code, such as provided by religion or honour – nor, indeed by exchange relations similar to that of the market. (Silver 1989:289)

If Silver seems confident that Enlightenment theories of sensibility performed what they desired: effecting a sharp break from traditions that co-implicated friendship and calculation, and consigning social and economic behavior to separate spheres, I want to suggest that eighteenth-century thinking was less certain. Discourse on friendship in this period remains alive to questions of false and calculating motivation, to the entanglement of fellow feeling with possibilities of exploitation and to the disavowals that accompany the invention of separate public and private spheres. Its doubts, as well as its assurance, were carried by voyagers to the Pacific, and became manifest in initial Oceanic encounters.

My selective reading of eighteenth-century thinking on friendship here, designed to highlight the kinds of preconceptions with which Europeans travelled in Oceania, complements the approach of other scholars who have focused on texts of exploration and encounter to rethink Enlightenment formulations of sympathy. Jonathan Lamb and Anna Neill have both recently turned to the interweaving of commercial and political selfhood in Enlightenment philosophy, and exposed its unravelling in extreme scenarios of voyaging. Both critics discuss a philosophical tradition, derived from Shaftesbury and Locke and encompassing Montesquieu, Hume, Henry Home (Lord Kames) and Adam Smith, in which the recognition of property and the development of the spirit of commerce are seen to foster and instantiate evolved social relations. Each situates this tradition against an alternative: for Neill discourses of deregulated or luxurious commerce in the 'mercantilist' tradition (a term she complicates), and for Lamb a Hobbesian/Mandevillean evocation of more divided and ambivalent civic selfhood. Each of these counter-traditions threatens to articulate the eruption of the 'savage' or uncontrolled at the heart of the civil, to isolate an atavistic potential even within discourses of progress. And for both Lamb and Neill voyaging has the potential to unearth this contradiction within civic identity, by transporting European subjectivity outside the metropole and exposing it to the logic of repudiation and reflection inherent in confrontations with cultural difference. Thus both critics focus on voyaging as an encounter for the European with self as well as other, and one in which distinctions between the two become blurred.

If the following excursus into eighteenth-century philosophy performs something of a similar manoeuvre, the focus on friendship marks a significant difference to my approach. For both Lamb's and Neill's explorations of the permutations of European subjectivity in the Pacific, it makes little difference whether the self is reflected back through cultural encounter or extreme isolation. Desert and inhabited islands throw up versions of the same question for European civic identity (Lamb 2001:12; Neill 2002:4). My readings instead focus on sociability as, precisely, constituted by social contexts and thrown under scrutiny by perceived difference between familiar and foreign modes of affinity and hospitality.

Anthony Ashley Cooper, Third Earl of Shaftesbury, sees friendship as a virtue that escapes the charge of self-interest by eluding Christianity's logic of future reward. In *Characteristics of Men, Manners, Opinions, Times* (1711), he notes the paradox that Christians 'have made virtue so mercenary a thing and have talked so much of its rewards that one can hardly tell what there is in it, after all, which can be worth rewarding' (Shaftesbury 1999:46). For Shaftesbury, private friendship is one such value:

Private friendship and zeal for the public and our country are virtues purely voluntary in a Christian. They are no essential parts of his charity. He is not so tied to the affairs of this life, nor is he obliged to enter into such engagements with this lower world as are of no help to him in acquiring a better. His conversation is in heaven. Nor has he any occasion for such supernumerary cares or embarrassments here on earth as may obstruct his way hither or retard him in the careful task of working out his own salvation. If nevertheless any portion of reward be reserved hereafter for the generous part of a patriot, or that of a thorough friend, this is still behind the curtain and happily concealed from us that we may be the more deserving of it when it comes. (Shaftesbury 1999:46–7; cf. 271)

Friendship, in its 'private' or particularized, rather than broadly charitable, form, serves as a prime example of that which cannot be valued according to a system of compensation. Shaftesbury turns the purported disinterestedness of Christian friendship into its opposite: a calculation on the future. Private friendship, in turn, is figured as excess: fostered in a spirit of generosity rather than calculation, its rewards remain undeclared.

In equating private friendship with public 'zeal', however, Shaftesbury makes a different computation, designed to reconcile particular to general, and whose rhetorical equivalent is synecdoche. Friendship with an individual becomes representative of, or sufficient for, broader sociability. In his 'Moralists' conversation, he asserts that 'he who justly proves himself a friend is man enough nor is he wanting to society. A single friendship may acquit him. He has deserved a friend and is man's friend, though not in strictness or according to your high moral sense, the friend of mankind' (Shaftesbury 1999:255). By making private friendship representative of national and social allegiance, Shaftesbury avoids E. M. Forster's famous dichotomy: 'if I had to choose between betraying my country and betraying my friend I hope I should have the guts to betray my country' (Forster 1951:66).[8] To choose the friend *is* to choose the country. And Shaftesbury justifies this as the only natural mode of fellow feeling: 'As for a plain natural love of one single person in either sex, I could compass it, I thought, well enough, but this complex, universal sort was beyond my reach. I could love the individual but not the species' (Shaftesbury 1999:256). He delivers friendship from the theological dilemma posed by its uneven distribution (a subject I will return to in Chapter 7), by claiming that its very singularity both absolves it from compensatory dynamics and renders it representative of a social ethics.

Francis Hutcheson's philosophical project might be described as an expanded attempt, not merely to calculate ethics, as Bredvold observes, but to prevent the positive calculation of qualities such as benevolence, virtue and friendship from becoming confounded with the mercenary computation of self-interest. Algebra must not be blurred into accountancy. Thus Hutcheson defends 'the applying a mathematical Calculation to moral subjects' by highlighting the corollary that 'how small soever the Moment of publick Good be, which any one can accomplish, yet if his Abilitys are proportionably small, the Quotient, which expresses the Degree of Virtue, may be as great as any whatsoever'. His algorithm enables the 'honest Trader, the kind Friend ... the charitable and hospitable Neighbour' to attain equality with the prince, statesman or general (Hutcheson 2004:134). In other words, it nuances the simple quantitative calculation of wealth and prestige as gauges of worth. Yet the attempt to hold ethical and material calculation apart is repeatedly stymied in Hutcheson's writing by their co-implication. Illustrating the relationship between good to the self and to the social body through a comparison with gift-giving between people of differing degrees of wealth, he writes:

The Moment of Good to any Person, in any given Case, is in a compound Ratio of the Quantity of the Good it self, and the Indigence of the Person. Hence it

---

[8] Leela Gandhi's *Affective Communities* (2006) is in part an extended exegesis of Forster's position and its implications for the politics of cross-cultural friendship.

appears, that a Gift may make a much greater Addition to the happiness of the Receiver, than the Diminution it occasions in the happiness of the Giver: And that the most useful and important Gifts are those from the Wealthy to the Indigent. Gifts from Equals are not useless neither, since they often increase the Happiness of both, as they are strong Evidences of mutual Love: but Gifts from the Poor to the Wealthy are really foolish, unless they be only little Expressions of Gratitude, which are also fruitful of Joy on both Sides ... (Hutcheson 2004:123–4)

If Hutcheson seeks to factor wealth and status into ethical calculation precisely to diminish their force, his depiction of this algorithm in terms of gift-giving nonetheless reinstates the priority of wealth. The mathematics of virtue, as we also found in Aristotle and Cicero, cannot be dissociated from calculations of interest.

In his *Treatise of Human Nature* (1739–40), David Hume suggests that one's degree of feeling for others can be calculated in relation to their degree of proximity to self:

The relation of blood produces the strongest tie the mind is capable of in the love of parents to their children, and a lesser degree of the same affection, as the relation lessens. Nor has consanguinity alone this effect, but any other relation without exception. We love our country-men, our neighbours, those of the same trade, profession, and even name with ourselves. Every one of these relations is esteem'd some tie, and gives a title to our share of affection.

There is another phaenomenon, which is parallel to this, *viz.* that *acquaintance*, without any kind of relation, gives rise to love and kindness. When we have contracted a habitude and intimacy with any person; tho' in frequenting his company we have not been able to discover any very valuable quality, of which he is possess'd; yet we cannot forebear preferring him to strangers, of whose superior merit we are fully convinc'd. (Hume 1985:401)

The principle of association privileges contiguity over 'valuable qualit[ies]'. Hume also acknowledges the role of resemblance in cultivating a sense of relationship:

'Tis obvious, that people associate together according to their particular tempers and dispositions, and that men of gay tempers naturally love the gay; as the serious bear an affection to the serious. This not only happens, where they remark this resemblance betwixt themselves and others, but also by the natural course of the disposition, and by a certain sympathy, which always arises betwixt similar characters. Where they remark the resemblance, it operates after the manner of a relation, by producing a connexion of ideas ... The idea of ourselves is always intimately present to us, and conveys a sensible degree of vivacity to the idea of any other object, to which we are related. (Hume 1985:403)

In both these senses, friendship personifies a relationship to the self that manifests as a relation to the other. This in turn can agitate those questions of self-interest and disingenuity that I have argued are intrinsic to western thinking on friendship. As Hume notes, 'whoever can find the means either by his services, his beauty, or his flattery, to render himself useful or agreeable to us, is sure of our affections' (Hume 1985:397). This of course reiterates Aristotle's lesser forms of friendship, based on use or beauty, as well as Plutarch's concern with the insinuations of flattery. Yet a clear division between self-interest and interest in the other is further complicated in Hume's analysis.

Hume argues that, whereas pride and humility are self-engendered emotions, love and hatred 'are always directed to some sensible being external to us; and when we talk of *self-love*, 'tis not in a proper sense, nor has the sensation it produces any thing in common with that tender emotion, which is excited by a friend or mistress' (Hume 1985:379). He devises thought experiments to show the play of these four passions in a situation where 'let us suppose I am in company with a person, whom I formerly regarded without any sentiments either of friendship or enmity' (Hume 1985:382). In such situations, feelings follow a simple grid pattern: virtue in the self leads to feelings of pride, and in others to feelings of love; vice in the self leads to feelings of humility and in others to feelings of hatred. Yet this alters when 'the person, along with whom I make all these experiments, is closely connected with me either by blood or friendship. He is, we shall suppose, my son or brother, or is united to me by a long and familiar acquaintance.' Such kinship or friendship ties instantiate what Hume calls 'a double relation' (Hume 1985:387) of knowledge as well as feeling: the behaviour of the other is now a source of pride or humility, not simply love or hatred.

In this sense, friendship can be seen inherently to add value. As Hume expounds, in terms that echo Cicero's discussion of *amicitia* (Cicero 1971:205),

In all creatures, that prey not upon others, and are not agitated with violent passions, there appears a remarkable desire of company, which associates them together, without any advantages they can ever propose to reap from their union. This is still more conspicuous in man, as being the creature of the universe, who has the most ardent desire of society, and is fitted for it by the most advantages. We can form no wish, which has not a reference to society. A perfect solitude is, perhaps, the greatest punishment we can suffer. Every pleasure languishes when enjoy'd a-part from company, and every pain becomes more cruel and intolerable. Whatever other passions we may be actuated by; pride, ambition, avarice, curiosity, revenge or lust; the soul or animating principle of them all is sympathy; nor wou'd they have any force, were we to abstract entirely from the thoughts and sentiments of others. Let all the powers and elements of nature conspire to serve and obey one man: Let the sun rise and set at his command: The sea and rivers roll as he pleases, and the earth furnish spontaneously whatever may be useful and agreeable to him: He will still be miserable, till you give him some one person at least, with whom he may share his happiness, and whose esteem and friendship he may enjoy. (Hume 1985:412)

Hume presents an Adamic scenario, in which a world created for the pleasure of one lacks what the mate or friend can bring. Yet friendship, by Hume's calculation, does not always represent this simple positive: rather, it complicates feeling because clear distinctions between self and other are broken down. The friend belongs to the self as well as being separate from the self. Hume acknowledges that the flow of feeling from other to self is more straightforward than in the opposite direction: 'The passage is smooth and open from the consideration of any person related to us to that of ourself, of whom we are every moment conscious. But when the affections are once directed to ourself, the fancy passes not with the same facility from that object to any other person, how closely so ever connected with us' (Hume 1985:389–90). Yet if feeling tends to begin with the self and moves outward, the 'double relation' of kin and friends to self stymies this clear trajectory, complicating even as it instantiates solipsism. Friendship's ideal contiguity renders its claims difficult to divorce from self-interest. The 'double relation' its ties promote raises the spectre of a potential disingenuousness.

When his discussion turns to the broader pressure of sympathy, a subtle shift occurs in Hume's discussion of the influence of association. Sympathy, he argues, is not only aroused directly by those close to us, but channelled towards other objects through our associates. The friend thus becomes in this case, not simply the object but the conductor of affective response:

No quality of human nature is more remarkable, both in itself and in its consequences, than that propensity we have to sympathize with others, and to receive by communication their inclinations and sentiments, however different from, or even contrary to our own. This is not only conspicuous in children, who implicitly embrace every opinion propos'd to them; but also in men of the greatest judgment and understanding, who find it very difficult to follow their own reason or inclination, in opposition to that of their friends or daily companions. To this principle we ought to ascribe the great uniformity we may observe in the humours and turn of thinking of those of the same nation; and 'tis much more probable, that this resemblance arises from sympathy, than from any influence of the soil and climate, which, tho' they continue invariably the same, are not able to preserve the character of a nation the same for a century together. A good natur'd man finds himself in an instant of the same humour with his company; and even the proudest and most surly take a tincture from their countrymen and acquaintance. (Hume 1985:367)

Adela Pinch has superbly analysed the operations of what she terms 'vagrant emotion' in Hume's and subsequent texts, arguing that

'For Hume, sympathy is the mechanism by which people can catch the feelings of others.' Pinch notes the implications this interpretation has for understanding social behaviour: 'People's ability to feel other people's feelings is the sign of humankind's essentially social nature. People are fundamentally linked through their common feelings, and what allows those feelings to be shared is sympathy' (Pinch 1996:24). But Hume's version of society is a shifting one, and its inconsistencies have implications for any argument that addresses feeling in cross-cultural contexts. Society is, once again, both those we are contiguous to and those we resemble. In this latter sense, friends are the like-minded who reduce all else to likeness; difference is, by implication, what lies outside the field of friendship, and its capacity to subsume the contrary within 'the great uniformity'. The friend plays a pivotal role in the centre of a circle of causality, whose principle is not simply the ludic vagrancy Pinch ascribes, but rather a centrifugal pull towards consensus.

Adam Smith's *The Wealth of Nations* (1776) advocated a reckoning of the body – as labour and in terms of subsistence – into the calculation of profit. However, the work has long been associated with laissez-faire principles of exchange. *The Theory of Moral Sentiments* (1759) equally seems both to point the ludicrousness of ethical calculation and to exemplify a form of such calculation. Smith is an important figure for Allan Silver in arguing that eighteenth-century economic liberalism enabled the dissociation of friendship from self-interest. Silver quotes at length Smith's discussion of the debts of friendship, noting his rejection 'of a model of exchange theory, drawn from the impersonal market, as applicable to personal relations' (Silver 1989:290). Certainly, Smith points out the absurdity of a literal or pedantic adherence to the rules of exchange in the realm of human intimacy:

That as soon as we can we should make a return of equal, and if possible of superior value to the services we have received, would seem to be a pretty plain rule, and one which admitted of scarce any exceptions. Upon the most superficial examination, however, this rule will appear to be in the highest degree loose and inaccurate, and to admit of ten thousand exceptions ... If your friend lent you money in your distress, ought you to lend him money in his? How much ought you to lend him? When ought you to lend him? Now, or to-morrow, or next month? And for how long a time? It is evident that no general rule can be laid down, by which a precise answer can, in all cases, be given to any of these questions. (A. Smith 2002:203)

Smith demonstrates his own lack of investment in such calculation by displaying an uncharacteristically loose grip on figures; allowing for 'ten thousand exceptions'. Contra Silver I would read this repudiation, not primarily in terms of the economic telos of Smith's *oeuvre*, but rather within the extended philosophical tradition I have described in this chapter, that prohibits accountancy. If Smith here seems to reject co-implicating friendship with the pettiness of weighed accounts, the spirit of calculation is once again reinvigorated in relation to friendship by a focus on equality and balance in the formation of friendship bonds. Thus Smith advises, in Aristotelian fashion, that the only 'natural and proper' attachment is 'among men of virtue'. Likeness in virtue offers a stability in intimacy that 'slight' similarities of taste cannot. Virtuous friendship is an investment, 'permanent and secure', promoting 'entire confidence'. As such, it is worth capitalizing upon, rather than enshrining:

Such friendships need not be confined to a single person, but may safely embrace all the wise and virtuous, with whom we have been long and intimately acquainted, and upon whose wisdom and virtue we can, upon that account, entirely depend. They who would confine friendship to two persons, seem to confound the wise security of friendship with the jealousy and folly of love. (A. Smith 2002: 264)

Prudent intimacy between equals in virtue constitutes a safe investment, to be extended towards the many, rather than reserved for Shaftesbury's excessive one.

If for Hume like-minded friends promote a community of sympathy, for Adam Smith what best regulates conduct is, effectively, a society composed not of friends but of strangers:

Are you in adversity? Do not mourn in the darkness of solitude, do not regulate your sorrow according to the indulgent sympathy of your intimate friends; return, as soon as possible, to the day-light of the world and of society. Live with strangers, with those who know nothing, or care nothing about your misfortune; do not even shun the company of enemies . . .

Are you in prosperity? Do not confine the enjoyment of your good fortune to your own house, to the company of your own friends, perhaps of your flatterers, of those who build upon your fortune the hopes of mending their own; frequent those who are independent of you, who can value you only for your character and conduct, and not for your fortune. (A. Smith 2002:178–9)

There are again echoes here of Plutarch's concerns regarding the capacity of the flatterer to tincture friendship with falsity. But this model of society – one antithetical to intimacy as much as to solitude – in turn provides an ideal for a relationship to the self: one of impartial spectatorship.[9] Only thus self-alienated, unbiased by the hot pulse of individual

[9] Wendy Matooka has examined Adam Smith's impartial spectator as mediating 'the disparity between particular feeling and general moral principles' (Matooka 1998:198). She suggests that in the figure of the impartial spectator Smith embodies the limits of empathy.

passion, can subjects attain an ideal objectivity that in turn allows them fairly to weigh and calculate the claims of others. The stranger is in this sense a better friend than the friend: 'The conversation of a friend brings us to a better, that of a stranger to a still better temper' (A. Smith 2002:178).

Smith's stranger here is one found within the parameters of a shared culture and society. He still operates within a framework of consensual values: his detached gaze moderates rather than disconcerts. This stranger must be distinguished, then, from the deep strangeness of the foreigner, who turns a different kind of gaze back onto the civically constituted European subject. But if Enlightenment formulations of the civic subject depended on both the oppositions and universalisms made available by the library of travellers' tales of barbarous alterity (Hulme and Jordanova 1990:7), it is also when eighteenth-century philosophies of friendship turn to the spectacle of the remote, when they imagine reconciling domestic versions of intimacy with the encounter with cultural difference, that discourses of sympathy show the strain of consolidation. This, I would suggest, is not merely another example of the relativization of discourse through real or imagined travel adumbrated by Lamb and Neill, though it is in part that. Rather, it manifests the crucial intersection between the practice of foreign contact and the evolving western philosophical imagining of friendship, as comparable but also potentially disjunctive models of two-sided encounter.

In his *Inquiry*, Hutcheson takes a swipe at the tendency to focus on monstrous antipathy over quotidian bonds in accounts of other cultures. He notes that Shaftesbury

justly observ'd the Absurdity of the monstrous Taste, which has possess'd both the Readers and Writers of Travels. They scarce give us any Account of the natural Affections, the Familys, Associations, Friendships, Clans, of the Indians; and as rarely do they mention their Abhorrence of Treachery among themselves; their proneness to mutual Aid, and to the Defence of their several States; their Contempt of Death in defence of their Country, or upon points of Honour. 'These are but common Storys. – No need to travel to the Indies for what we see in Europe every Day.' The Entertainment therefore in these ingenious Studys consists chiefly in exciting Horror, and making Men Stare. The ordinary Employment of the Bulk of the Indians in support of their Wives and Offspring, or Relations, has nothing of the Prodigious. But a Human Sacrifice, a feast upon Enemys Carcases, can raise an Horror and Admiration of the wondrous Barbarity of Indians, in Nations no strangers to the Massacre at Paris, the Irish Rebellion, or the Journals of the Inquisition. (Hutcheson 2004:139)

Objections to fabulation in travel narrative resounded across eighteenth-century moral philosophy and criticism, but Hutcheson's elaborations point particularly to the incompatibility between their uncanny emphases and the simple and recognizable domesticity of human relationship. Friendship and kinship ties are uninteresting, Hutcheson assumes, because they are the same everywhere: they are precisely not among the observable differences of travel. The figuration of the other as inherently the same by virtue of friendship, of friendship as the bond that renders the traveller always at home, is one this book will continue to explore, particularly in the final chapter. But it is counterpointed by another tendency that emerges strongly in a tradition of Enlightenment thinking that informed Pacific voyaging: to suspect that the other is, on the contrary, different by virtue of being a *better* friend.

In his *Essay on the History of Civil Society* (1767), published in the year that Wallis reached Tahiti, Adam Ferguson offered a reflexive analysis of the operation of calculation. Philosophers account for social motivation as calculated, he suggested, when they are in what might be termed calculative mode: 'we assign as the motives of conduct with men, those considerations which occur in the hours of retirement and cold reflection'. In this state of cool-headed judgement, the warmth of feeling, of stimulated sentiment, is set aside. But in a further twist to his argument, Ferguson goes on to suggest that these active and reflective, or warm and cold, modes of conceiving and enacting social relation are not simply the properties of times of activity as opposed to reflection, but also of simple versus complex societies.[10] He adduces travellers' accounts of Native American friendship: 'the ardent affection with which he selects and embraces his friend; with which he clings to his side in every season of peril; and with which he invokes his spirit from a distance, when dangers surprise him alone': implying that the very extremes of primitive life refine the bonds of friendship. Against this he posits 'the spirit which reigns in a commercial state', concluding that

It is here indeed, if ever, that man is sometimes found a detached and a solitary being: he has found an object which sets him in competition with his fellow-creatures, and he deals with them as he does with his cattle and his soil, for the sake of the profits they bring. The mighty engine which we suppose to have formed society, only tends to set its members at variance, or to continue their intercourse after the bands of affection are broken. (A. Ferguson 1999:22, 23, 24)

Paradoxically, civil society is antipathetic to friendship, diluting its embodied ardour or falsifying it into a form of profit. For true examples of feeling, moralists must travel away from the civic centre, for 'Whatever

---

[10] Ferguson's association of cool and warmth with developed and primitive societies respectively comes close to Mauss's, and was inverted in Lévi-Strauss's later formulation of the 'hot' and 'cold' social distinction (Lévi-Strauss 1989:233–4).

proofs we may have of the social disposition of man in familiar and contiguous scenes, it is possibly of importance, to draw our observations from the examples of men who live in the simplest condition, and who have not learned to affect what they do not actually feel' (A. Ferguson 1999:23). Contrary to Hutcheson, then, Ferguson reconciles friendship and exoticism, consigning calculation to the metropole, and genuine feeling to the periphery. True friendship is not the all too familiar, but the geographically and historically remote.

Ferguson's situating of the exemplary friend in pre-capitalist societies is the most Rosseauist gesture in Scottish Enlightenment thinking on friendship. But in his *Discourse on the Origin of Inequality* (1754), Rousseau had little to say directly to friendship, seeing it as one of the many ramifications of compassion: a virtue he argued was stronger in 'uncivilized man', whose reason did not intercept response. 'Even benevolence and friendship are, if we judge rightly, only the effects of compassion, constantly set upon a particular object,' wrote Rousseau, arguing that intimacy and pity are linked by the testimony they give to a capacity for fellow feeling (Rousseau 1973:75). In the next chapter I will discuss both compassion and Rousseau further, attempting to establish prevailing Enlightenment notions of sentiment and savagery that seemed to be betrayed in the theatre of contact. In scenes of mourning rather than friendship-making we will encounter the same question: how to distinguish the calculated from the true? As we saw in Chapter 2, travellers, in part beguiled by Ferguson's compelling vision of a stronger savage capacity for friendship, nonetheless compulsively uncovered evidence of calculated friendship in the purportedly simple society of Tahiti. In the case of mourning too, intense concern with the emotional sincerity of Oceanians accords an affective indigenous agency that is incommensurate with contact's potential imbalances of power.

You received gifts from me; they were accepted.
But you don't understand how to think about the dead.

– Czeslaw Milosz

On Saturday 6 December 1788 William Bligh, anchored in Matavai Bay on the *Bounty*, 'experienced a scene ... of Wind and Weather which I never supposed could have been met with in this place'. A 'very high breaking Sea' increased after sunset; all hands were on deck all night, with 'the Sea foaming all around us so as to threaten instant destruction'. 'In this situation,' wrote Bligh in his journal, 'my Friends on shore became very anxious for my safety.' Tina, his wife 'Itia and Moana, one of the *ari'i* of Matavai, assisted in paddling a canoe, and 'came through it all to see me', bearing provisions: 'each of these Kind people came and embraced me with a flood of tears, said they had prayed to the Eatua for my safety, but that they feared the Ship would be lost'. While Bligh managed to reassure Tina and his wife, Moana was inconsolable: 'He remained still not to be comforted, or [*sic*] could I get this good old Man to resume a natural chearfullness which from the first moment I saw him he never lost before' (Bligh 1937: I, 414).

Further canoes come on Sunday 7 December, bringing supplies to other crew members, for as Bligh explains:

As it is the custom among these people whenever a Ship comes here, to have their separate Friend or Tyo as he is called so it has been the case among my people and Officers. Great friendship and disinterestedness from the Natives have been the result of this connection, for those who could not get a Cannoe to come off in, swam to the Ship with bunches of Cocoanutts without any view of reward.

On Monday 8 December 'Itia returned to the ship from shore with a hog, breadfruit and coconuts. Bligh writes, 'I expected this present, on account of which it was that she had quitted the Ship last Evening, and I would fain have recompensed her trouble with a return of other Valuable things if she would have allowed me, but they insisted that I should not, as the present was out of friendship and not from view of any reward' (Bligh 1937: I, 415). Immediately after this he was visited by his other significant Tahitian friends:

These kind people had no sooner left me than Poeeno and his wife came of[f] with another supply of fruit. This Woman has on many occasions shown that she is possessed of great Sympathy, and now marked it with such excess of Greif for the danger the Ship had been in, that would have affected the most dispassionate creature existing. The strongest and only established proof among these people of their sincerity on those occasions is the Wounding of themselves on the Top of the Head with a Sharks tooth untill they bring on a vast profusion of blood, and having a knowledge of this I was prepared to prevent this Woman from doing it; but I had no sooner come to her than the Operation was performed before I was aware of it, and her face was covered with blood in an instant. This circumstance however frequently happens upon trifling occasions, and with the drying up the Blood all feelings of the mind subsides it is allways a proof of great joy as well as excess of greif, but at this last time it was a lasting token of the latter, and this affectionate creature could not be brought to resume any kind of chearfullness for two hours that she remained on board. (Bligh 1937: I, 416)

I want to focus here on the notion of a 'proof of sincerity', which becomes explicit in Bligh's discussion of the grieving practices of Tahitians, but threads through his entire discussion of the pitching emotions attending this crisis. In Bligh's account, the storm at sea figures as an overarching test of sincerity: a natural disaster through which the friendships he has made are tried and proven true. Bligh's Tahitian friends place themselves at physical risk to come to him in the storm, abandoning protocols of rank to participate in propelling their craft: 'They were no useless passengers on board the Cannoe in which they came, each had their Paddle and the Sea was such as required them to be used with much Skill and dexterity' (Bligh 1937: I, 414). The 'Flood of Rain' that threatens the ship is mirrored by the 'flood of tears' with which they betray their overwhelming emotion: Moana exceeding his fellows in his refusal to be consoled. The tears of the Tahitians are tokens for Bligh of genuine sentiment: as numerous commentators have observed, they were sensibility's crucial signifier in the popular literature of the period.[1]

If tears are a Tahitian gift framed to the English emotional calculus, Bligh shows a reciprocal understanding of Tahitian economies of friend-ship. Thus he points to the ways in which assistance in the crisis is predicated on individual relationships: that the gifts which the Tahitians bear to members of the crew are the products of particular *taio* bonds, rather than generalized charitable impulses. Yet while Bligh is prepared to operate within a logic of reciprocity and compensate 'Itia with

---

[1] Vincent-Buffault 1991; M. Ellis 1996:19.

'a return of other Valuable things', he insists that the generosity precipitated by the crisis is 'not from view of any reward'. He thus repeats the rhetorical manouevre that I highlighted in Chapter 2, converting *taio* from a relationship manifest through practices of exchange into a bond whose genuine sentiment reveals itself by abjuring recompense. Bligh, as we have noted, generally sought to present his Oceanic encounters as echoing events in the voyages of Cook: this particular scene, however, resonates most compellingly with the foundational encounter of Samuel Wallis and Purea just over ten years earlier. Wallis's account of his interactions stressed Purea's embodiment of a heartfelt sentiment, which he implicitly equated with her elevated social status: 'we took our leave of the Inhabitants who parted with us with much seming [*sic*] regret, Particularly the better sort amongst them, the Queen followed us longer than any and Cryed much as she had done for three days before on my first making signs to her of my departure' (Wallis 1766–8: II, 1). Both status and sentiment are in turn authenticated by a refusal of exchange. Purea is repeatedly referred to as resisting any return upon her gifts (Wallis 1766–8: I, 20, 29), and upon the *Dolphin*'s departure is distinguished by her lack of interest in receiving any: 'the Queen kept in her Canoe at the Gunroom Port & wept very much – I gave her severall usefull presents, & the Officers all did the like but she seemed to take little notice of them, she seemed to be wholly taken up with sorrow' (Wallis 1766–8: I, 34). 'Itia figures in Bligh's account as a latter-day Purea: an authentically disconsolate 'queen'.

Bligh's grieving queen is upstaged, however, by Poeno's wife. Like 'Itia, she shows the hallmarks of a sentimental heroine – 'possessed of great Sympathy' that threatens to teeter into excess. But where for the sentimental heroine tears are the 'incontrovertible markers of sensibility' (M. Ellis 1996:97), for Poeno's wife tears will not suffice. And although the language of eighteenth-century sensibility relied also on 'the sanguinary indices of the pulse and the blush' (M. Ellis 1996:19), the Tahitians require more explicit sanguinary evidence: 'Wounding' and bringing on 'a vast profusion of blood' is the only real index of sincerity. Bligh claims he was a moment too late to prevent the self-mutilation, but he in some ways seems as intent on the production of this visible sign as Poeno's wife, desiring as well as abhorring this final proof of friendship. Although the expression 'resume . . . chearfullness' echoes between the descriptions of Moana's and her perseverant mournfulness, she represents a whole new level of distress, both in terms of intensity and foreignness. The Tahitian wounding of the forehead was matched by equivalent rituals of self-mutilation in other areas of the Pacific: the knocking out of the front teeth in Hawaii or the cutting off of a joint of the little finger in Tonga. Yet Bligh's ethnographic extrapolations complicate the picture of emotional release. If, as he says, self-mutilation is as often a sign of joy as of grief, and if the drying of the blood signifies the relatively swift dismissal of mental distress, then the very extremity of the act may in fact be testimony, not to deeply visceral, but to shallow and ambiguous emotion.

This book is concerned with ways in which calculation shadows intimacy. I have argued that the entangled relationship between friendship-formation and exchange in early contact between Oceanians and Europeans becomes articulated through *taio* bonds, which expose a disavowal of self-interest in European thinking on friendship. Displays of feeling such as that of Poeno's wife, however, raise more specific doubts about calculated *effects*. Was Ferguson wrong: have people 'who live in the simplest condition' still 'learned to affect what they do not feel?' (A. Ferguson 1999:23; see Chapter 3). To what extent can grief and joy be put on and off like masks, performed like theatre, or merge vaporously, like symptoms of nervous disorder? This chapter pursues the problematic of the genuine in early European accounts of Oceanians, probing the confusing search for sincerity that impels certain kinds of encounter and their narration.

Emotional Propriety

> The man whose sympathy keeps time to my grief, cannot but admit the reasonableness of my sorrow.
>
> – Adam Smith

The signs of emotion displayed by the Tahitians present Bligh with a problem of affective interpretation. They differ from those signs that are culturally familiar to him, and while the difference is identified as excess, it remains unclear whether such excess is to be equated with deeper or shallower emotion. The question of the universality of sentiment was one that occupied eighteenth-century moralists. In Chapter XV of *Elements of Criticism* (1762), Lord Kames discusses the 'External Signs of Emotions and Passions'. He argues that emotions comprise a universal semiotics, promoting instant intelligibility even in the absence of shared language or culture:

The natural signs of emotions, voluntary and involuntary, being nearly the same in all men, form an universal language; which no distance of place, no difference of tribe, no diversity of tongue, can darken or render doubtful: even education, tho' of mighty influence, hath not power to vary nor sophisticate, far less to destroy, their signification. This is a wise appointment of Providence: for if these signs were, like words, arbitrary and variable, the thoughts and volitions of strangers would be entirely hid from us; which would prove a great or rather invincible obstruction to the formation of societies: but as matters are ordered, the external appearances of joy, grief, anger, fear, shame, and of the other passions, forming an universal language, open a direct avenue to the heart. As the arbitrary signs vary in every country, there could be no communication of thoughts among different nations, were it not for the natural signs, in which all agree: and as the discovering passions instantly at their birth, is essential to our well-being, and often necessary for self-preservation, the author of our nature, attentive to our wants, hath provided a passage to the heart, which can never be obstructed while eye-sight remains. (Home 1972: I, 434–5)

For Kames, emotional language is innate and direct, bypassing linguistic communication and registering on the features. Actions, he continues, 'must not be overlooked: for tho' they singly afford no clear light, they are upon the whole the best interpreters of the heart' (Home 1972: I, 437). While actions do not themselves constitute a universal language, he argues, 'it is a language, however, which every one can decipher in some measure; and which, joined with the other external signs, affords sufficient means for the direction of our conduct with regard to others' (Home 1972: I, 436). In Kames's emotional hermeneutic then, actions spell out those feelings that are more immediately legible on the features: there is a consistency between appearance and action (a premise which, as we saw earlier, impelled the formulation of Morton's Hints, with their gestural lexicon of 'amicable signs'). Yet Bligh and other Pacific voyagers who describe encountering displays of intense emotion within actual scenarios of culture contact do not show confidence in their ability to read the 'universal language' of affect. Instead Bligh moves nervously back and forth between action and the emotion of which it is said to be the proof, in an attempt to reconcile what he perceives as excessive grief with what he is prepared to recognize as genuine emotion. The self-mutilation that opens, quite literally, 'a passage to the heart', in Bligh's account retains the status of 'arbitrary sign'. He seeks, behind the blood which covers Poeno's wife's face, alternative 'natural signs' of a feeling that persists beyond performance, that cannot be dissimulated.

Bligh's concern with what he regards as the excessive elements of the Tahitian woman's display of grief chimes with the philosophy of sympathy expounded by Adam Smith in *The Theory of Moral Sentiments* (1759). In Part I of his treatise, Smith argues that a specific type of fellow feeling motivates sympathy. We identify with the emotions of another not by replicating them, but by entering into their circumstances. However loudly another's misfortunes are lamented, Smith suggests, they will not affect us in the same way unless we can 'bring the case home to ourselves'. On the contrary, loud lamentations will produce the opposite of their intended effects, leading to shock and charges of 'pusillanimity and weakness' in the sufferer, if they cannot be 'entered into' by the spectator (A. Smith 2002:19–20). In Chapter III of Part I, 'Of the manner in which we judge of the propriety or impropriety of the affections of other men, by their concord or dissonance with our own', Adam Smith risks truism to establish his point about emotional identification:

> When the original passions of the person concerned are in perfect concord with the sympathetic emotions of the spectator, they necessarily appear to this last just and proper, and suitable to their objects; and, on the contrary, when, upon bringing the case home to himself, he finds they do not coincide with what he feels, they necessarily appear to him unjust and improper, and unsuitable to the causes which excite him. To approve of the passions of another, therefore, as suitable to their objects, is the same thing as to observe that we entirely sympathize with them; and not to approve of them as such, is the same thing as to observe that we do not entirely sympathize with them. (A. Smith 2002:20–1)

Smith's final statement circumvents simple repetition by foregrounding the role of observation. The individual seeking to identify with another's feelings avoids total incorporation due to the simultaneous distancing effect of the observing role. Yet for Adam Smith, the roles of observation and identification are also the same. Only by 'bringing the case home' to the self can one occupy the position of observer, and paradoxically find the distance to judge whether or not one can identify fellow feeling. This position differs markedly from Kames's confident universalism. Although Smith's sentimental adjudications reflect his own cultural biases, his delineation of the roles of identification and observation within sympathy is particularly resonant for situations of cross-cultural contact. To return to Bligh's discussion of Tahitian emotion, it is indeed by 'bringing the case' of their expressions of grief *home* – by comparing these with the customs of his home culture, that Bligh seeks to identify their elements of excess. But as a proto-ethnographic observer, he also wishes to acknowledge a cultural particularity to this expression of emotion that he necessarily cannot bridge. And it is this simultaneous delight, in difference and equally in the forms of tribute it seems to offer him, that stimulates another hinted response in Bligh's account: one of titillation. Cross-cultural contact complicates late eighteenth-century sympathy by testing the limits of identification between subjects who are not universal, but insistently culturally specific.

I noted in Chapter 3 that for Smith, strangers in some ways make the best friends, precisely because their degree of identification does not outweigh their capacity for detached observation. In his discussion of 'reflected passion' (A. Smith 2002:28), Smith raises the issue of proximity, in describing the emotional dialectic whereby the spectator seeks to identify with the sufferings of another, while the other struggles to moderate their emotion to accord with the spectator's capacity to identify. Smith suggests that, within the hierarchy of friend/acquaintance/ stranger, it is the stranger who best helps the individual to moderate emotion: we compose ourselves best before those with whom we are least intimate. He goes on to elaborate a disgust for excessive grief and to fetishize self-command in ways that themselves seem particular to his own British cultural heritage:

What noble propriety and grace do we feel in the conduct of those who, in their own case, exert that recollection and self-command which constitute the dignity of every passion, and which bring it down to what others can enter into! We are disgusted with the clamorous grief, which, without any delicacy, calls upon our compassion with sighs and tears and importunate lamentations. But we reverence that reserved, that silent and majestic sorrow, which discovers itself only in the swelling of the eyes, in the quivering of the lips and cheeks, and in the distant, but affecting, coldness of the whole behaviour. It imposes the like silence upon us. We regard it with respectful attention, and watch with anxious concern over our whole behaviour, lest by any impropriety we should disturb that concerted tranquility, which it requires so great an effort to support. (A. Smith 2002:29–30)

For Smith, the appropriate 'marks', or physical manifestations of grief, are precisely those that indicate its restraint: the 'swelling of the eyes' and 'quivering of the lips and cheeks' that testify not, as they might, to any self-brutalization, but to an equally brutal self-possession.

By Smith's account, the most legible signs of emotion are those that indicate restraint. This paradox only resolves itself if we recognize the elision of cultural specificity in his account. Even as he spells out the process of identification that characterizes sensibility, he accommodates social and gender-inflected understandings of emotional propriety (the 'silent and majestic' version of sorrow he espouses has an aristocratic bearing; Julie Ellison argues that such Stoicism is repeatedly invoked in a complex tension with masculine sentiment during the eighteenth century (Ellison 1999:70)). An anatomization of emotion resorts in the end to a cultural consensus between writer and reader. Yet in situations of cross-cultural encounter such as Bligh's, complacency regarding shared values is troubled by the apprehension that performativity and sincerity may not be reconcilable; that neither restraint nor effusion may be fully legible.

As Douglas Oliver has observed, the European archive of contact with Tahitians evidences numerous examples of visitors' concerns over apparently contradictory displays of emotion. On the one hand, grief seems excessively violent, and on the other, overly dramatic. The Tahitian lexicon supports this confusion, containing 'numerous words connoting (and implicitly censuring) the dissimulation of emotion'. Oliver cites the following terms from the London Missionary Society Dictionary of 1851:

'arufa'ahema, deception by fair words, while a plot of destruction has been planned.
'arufa'aīpaea, words of conciliation, without sincerity.
aureva, to impose upon a person under the appearance of friendship. (Oliver 1974:591)

The implicit censure that Oliver notes may easily be an effect of either missionary teaching or missionary translation: however, it seems valid to conclude that Tahitian culture allowed for an ambiguity of response that Europeans found ethically and interpersonally confounding, and tended to attribute to conscious dissimulation. The second clause of each English translation cited, moreover, specifies a set of concerns that I have identified as integral to European anxieties regarding cross-cultural friendship: fear of malign intent, of insincerity and of false friendship.

In Bligh's account of the Tahitian response to his ship's vulnerability, bodily fluids – tears and blood – become on the one hand the index and on the other the potential threshold of fellow feeling. His anecdote displays one response to the emotional confusion such scenes produce in European observers: the incommensurability of grief with object creating a moment of light comedy that in part reflects the ultimately bathetic nature of the incident described. It fits into a category that we might term 'grief without a corpse'. James Morrison cites a number of apparently minor occasions for expression of grief:

When they meet each other, after but a short absence, they embrace each other as we do but instead of kissing each other they Join Noses and Draw in each others breath through the Nostrils; sometimes in token of great love they almost suffocate each other by their long Continuance of their embrace – this Method is common to both Sexes, but if they have been long absent the Weomen Weep and Cut their heads with a sharks tooth till the blood flows copiously, which is always the Case in either excess whether of Grief or Joy to show their love. They always perform this Ceremony on the slightest accident happening to their Children and evry Woman is provided with one or two as soon as she is Married, as they never Cut their heads before and have them wrappd in Cloth, and fastened with the Pitch of the Bread fruit, so that the points stick out about a quarter of an inch like lancets. (Morrison 1935:189)

Morrison's account recognizes a number of comic ironies: a relatively short absence provides the occasion for an embrace so over-extended as potentially to be the cause of a final and complete separation through suffocation; 'the slightest accident' becomes the impetus for a copious flow of blood. The notion that this display of emotion is attendant on the woman reaching marriageable age and is dependent on props contributes to the sense of its unspontaneity. Just as Bligh notes that self-mutilation is 'allways a proof of great joy as well as excess of greif', so Morrison observes that the same physical sign is used to denote opposite emotions. However, Morrison's less polished syntax – 'always the Case in either excess whether of Grief or Joy to show their love' – works more explicitly both to register and to resolve the confusion of emotions, with love ultimately introduced as the synthesizing term that motivates both grief and joy.

In his account of the brief 1814 visit of the British naval frigates *Briton* and *Tagus* to annex Nukuhiva in the Marquesas islands, John Shillibeer relates an anecdote concerning a woman whose husband expresses an interest in travelling back to England with his British *taio*. Here the claims of friendship and marital bonds and of extraneous and internal cultural ties explicitly compete. As Shillibeer recounts, the woman

came up to us in the most frantic and wild manner, talking with unequalled rapidity, but not a word could we distinguish but 'Vahana Picatanee' or husband to England. She cried and laughed alternately, tore her hair – beat her breast – lay down on the ground – danced, – sang, – and at length in a paroxysm of despair, cut herself in several places with a shark's tooth, which until then she had concealed; nor could we disarm her before she had done herself considerable injury.

She is reassured that her husband will not be taken away, and Shillibeer continues, 'This had the desired effect, and she soon became as placid and cheerful as ever; nor did she appear to notice the wounds she had inflicted. There were several spectators to this affecting scene, which clearly proved that the natives of this remote region, although in a perfect state of nature, are neither destitute of feelings or affection' (Shillibeer 1817:43–4). Like Bligh, Shillibeer displays a conflicting impulse at once to pay tribute to and to dismiss the islander's emotions: to depict them as both superlative and excessive sentimental subjects. Once again here, feeling is figured as equally, potentially, its opposite: tears become laughter, desperation is expressed as song. The failure to disarm women of the means of self-harm until the display of grief has been witnessed is a concomitant feature of this tragicomic set piece. While Shillibeer's claim is that the calming of the woman is 'the desired effect', his anecdote evinces a more palpable desire for the special effect of an apparently excessive marking of grief.

There is, of course, a European tradition for understanding slippery or disassociated feeling as a form of genuine sentiment. In the previous chapter I discussed Hume's recognition of the effects of contiguity and contagion in the transmission of feeling. The notion of emotion as a labile, transitive phenomenon had earlier been expressed via the analogy of the humours. Commenting on 'How we weep and laugh at the same thing', Montaigne observes that

while it is true that most of our actions are but mask and cosmetic ... nevertheless we ought to consider when judging such events how our souls are often shaken by conflicting emotions. Even as there is said to be a variety of humours assembled in our bodies, the dominant one being that which normally prevails according to our complexion, so too in our souls: although diverse emotions may shake them, there is one which must remain in possession of the field; nevertheless its victory is not so complete but that the weaker ones do not sometimes regain lost ground because of the pliancy and mutability of our soul and make a brief sally in their turn. (Montaigne 1991:263)

Montaigne registers that dominant emotions can be shadowed by conflicting feelings. Alternatively, they may be stymied or misdirected. In his essay 'On sadness', he recognizes the paradoxical tendency for extreme emotion, such as grief, to express itself by leaving the subject apparently unmoved, describing 'that sad, deaf, speechless stupor which seizes us when we are overwhelmed by tragedies beyond endurance' (Montaigne 1991:8). In 'Our emotions get carried away beyond us', he observes that emotions characterized by anticipation, such as fear, desire or hope, 'impel us towards the future; they rob us of feelings and concern for what now is' (Montaigne 1991:11). In analysing 'How the soul discharges its emotions against false objects', he even offers a way of understanding self-mutilation as an expression of genuine, if perverted, emotional discharge: 'It is not those blond maiden tresses which you are tearing, nor the whiteness of that bosom which you are beating so cruelly in your distress, which killed your beloved brother with an unlucky musket-ball' (Montaigne 1991:20). Yet despite his flexible model of emotion as often mobile, contradictory and self-deluding, Montaigne ultimately singles out rituals of self-mutilation as irreconcilable with genuine grief. He objects to what he calls the 'lying veneration' of the Spartan populace: 'On the death of their kings all their allies and neighbours and all the helots – men and women indiscriminately – slashed their foreheads in token of their grief, declaring in their cries and lamentations that the dead king was the best they had ever had, thus attributing to rank the praise which belongs to merit' (Montaigne 1991:13). For Montaigne, the performativity of such ceremonies confirms their evacuation of genuine, merited sentiment.

Self-mutilation pushes the question of cultural differences of response into new territory. Unlike the slippery play of facial features or the familiar physical indexes of blush and tears, self-mutilation is neither clearly fakeable nor genuine, not simply calculated nor involuntary. It is at once mechanical and dramatic, automatic and excessive: a thing that one might make oneself perform, yet that one could not bring oneself to do. The exemplary discussion of such 'marks of grief' takes place in European voyaging accounts in relation to Oceanic rituals of death, burial and mourning.

Loud Lamentations and Silent Sorrow

> I will not pretend to say whether it was real or feigned greif they shewed on this occasion, perhaps it was a mixture of both, but was I to abide by my own opinion only I should believe it was real.
>
> – James Cook

Joseph Banks regarded the Tahitian disposal of the dead and ceremonies of mourning as 'so remarkable that they deserve a very particular description'. He wrote, in his *Endeavour* journal:

As soon as any one is dead the House is immediately filld with their relations who bewail their Loss with Loud lamentations, especially those who are the farthest removd in blood from or who profess the least greif for the deceasd; the nearer relations and those who are really affected spend their time in more silent sorrow, while the rest join in Chorus's of Greif at certain intervals between which they laugh, talk and gossip as if totaly unconcernd (Banks 1962: I, 376).

Banks's account inaugurates a more dismissive trend in European writing on Oceanian emotion than we saw in Bligh and Shillibeer, in which an excess of grief is instantly refigured as false grief. His diction echoes directly Adam Smith's contrast between 'the clamorous grief, which, without any delicacy, calls upon our compassion with sighs and tears and importunate lamentations' and 'that silent and majestic sorrow, which discovers itself ... in the distant, but affecting, coldness of the whole behaviour' (A. Smith 2002:29–30). Banks's confidence that he can adjudicate between real and false emotion in the Tahitian funeral scene is underpinned by contradiction: his claim that those who lament loudest also profess least grief disregards the fact that these lamentations are themselves a form of profession. In the philosophical tradition of his home culture he reflexively precludes any equation of public, theatricalized expression with genuine sentiment, even as he appeals to local knowledge – apparently alluding to sources of private information regarding kinship ties, and so drawing on his authority as the most connected and participant of the *Endeavour*'s Tahitian observers.

After discussing the laying out of the dead, Banks dilates on the subject of displayed grief:

No sooner is the corpse fixd up within the House or *ewhatta* as they call it than the ceremony of mourning begins again. The women (for the men seem to think lamentations below their dignity) assemble Led on by the nearest relation, who walking up to the door of the House swimming almost in tears strikes a sharks tooth several times into the crown of her head, on which a large effusion of blood flows, which is carefully caught in their linnen and thrown under the Bier. Her example is imitated by the rest of the women and this ceremony is repeated at the interval of 2 or 3 days as long as the women chuse or can keep it up, the nearest relation thinking it her duty to Continue it longer than any one else. Besides the blood which they beleive to be an acceptable present to the deceasd, whose soule they beleive to exist and hover about the place where the body lays observing the actions of the survivors, they throw in Cloths wet with tears, of which all that are shed are carefully preservd for that purpose, and the younger people cut off their hair either all or in part and throw that also under the Bier. (Banks 1962: I, 377–8)

Banks probes the authenticity of the grief exhibited here by determining particular roles. He isolates lamentation as a feminine prerogative, and, contradicting his earlier claim that those 'farthest removd in blood' display the most grief, identifies the nearest relation as the chief female mourner. The shift from a metonymic use of the word 'blood' in association with private, less expressive emotion, to the figuration of the 'nearest relation' as sacrificial victim, letting a blood whose abject materiality is rendered even more explicit by its 'careful' collection in pieces of linen, might be seen to enact the shifting perceptions of an observer, keen to associate genuine emotion with restraint, but confronted by all too material evidence of grief. Traces of scepticism persist in the reference to the nearest relation leading 'on', rather than simply leading, the other mourners, and subsequently 'thinking it her duty to Continue it longer than anyone else'. Yet these are relatively ineffectual against the overwhelmingly evidentiary impact of caught tears and blood and hacked hair.

Tom Lutz, in his comprehensive and engaging study *Crying: The Natural and Cultural History of Tears*, devotes a chapter to cultures of mourning. He notes the suspicion aroused in European observers by what is perceived as the ability of mourners from a wide variety of other cultures 'to turn their tears on and off', arguing that 'their very fluency in the languages of grief, is exactly what made them suspect to outsiders' (Lutz 2001:203). In early accounts of Oceanic grief the question is, as we have seen, not simply one of tears turned on and off, but of emotion that slips equally into its opposite: that may as easily signify joy as grief.

Lutz's cultural relativist account of mourning practices locates the very advent of cultural relativism in European discoveries of alternative emotional responses: 'Whatever cultural blinders they might have worn ... early anthropologists, travelers and missionaries discovering new emotional styles succeeded in showing an emotion to be a piece of culture rather than simply a natural reaction' (Lutz 2001:198). While some degree of relativism may have been one of the outcomes of European contact with Oceanic cultures of feeling, on an interpersonal level, early travellers were more often confounded, injured or aggressively amused by unfamiliar emotional responses. The recognition of alternative modes of expression was not easily synthesized, but led instead to concerns about the potential for false and deceptive displays that might leave the observer shamed in his sincerity, or alternatively for acknowledgements so earnest that they might show up the observer's sentiments as insincere.

Lutz includes rituals of self-mutilation in his discussion of mourning, and through them turns to Freud's paper on 'Mourning and Melancholia'. Developing Freud's notion of melancholia as pathological mourning, Lutz initially suggests that self-mutilation is the expression of unresolved loss. He then seeks to extricate himself from the implication that such mourning rituals are, in Freudian terms, 'mourning gone bad', by arguing that the desire to resolve loss through 'normal' mourning is in turn particular to western cultures.[2] His representation of self-mutilation as a form of culturally inflected melancholia, however, blurs the specificity of both Freud's argument and the self-mutilation ritual. Lutz writes, 'Melancholia includes refusing to give up the dead, and the only way to do this, Freud suggests, is by some form of self-denial or masochism' (Lutz 2001:216). Yet Freud does not use the term masochism in his paper, focusing instead on types of verbal 'self-beratement' (Butler 1997:140) that seem in excess of or mismatched to their subject, and which he argues disclose the transformation of object-loss to ego-loss (Freud 1984:257–8). The flow of shameless verbiage Freud associates with this type of self-indictment is far removed from the loud lamentations described by Banks, through which Tahitian women directly 'bewail their Loss', or from their practice of blood-letting. Furthermore, by figuring their mourning rituals as inherently melancholic, Lutz fails to allow members of the various cultures he examines

---

[2] A more benign reading of the psychology and ritual of self-mutilation is offered by Armando Favazza, who describes the psychiatric presentation of such practices as 'a morbid form of self-help', and distinguishes this from 'culturally sanctioned mutilative rituals' which have significant medical, religious or social functions (Favazza 1996:286).

the capacity equally to maintain a distinction between mourning and its more aggravated, melancholic manifestation. Yet this more nuanced understanding is present in Banks's account, where he writes that, after five nights 'the mourning then ceases unless some of the women who find themselves more than commonly afflicted by the Loss repeat the ceremony of *Poopooing* or bleeding themselves in the head, which they do at any time or in any place where they happen to be when the whim takes them' (Banks 1962: I, 378). For Banks this persistent, melancholic version of mourning remains ambivalent: is it a genuine sign of uncommon affliction or simply 'whim'?

The destabilization of Banks's confidence in assessing the authenticity of the mourning rituals may also be accounted for by what lies between these two discussions of female lamentation: the putrefied corpse. While the priest performs his offices, a house is erected: 'In the center of this house are posts set up for the supporting of the bier which as soon as the ceremonies are finishd is brought here and set upon then, where the Corps is to remain and putrifie in state to the no small disgust of every one whose business requires them to pass near it' (Banks 1962: I, 376–7). Hawkesworth terms these funeral platforms 'houses of corruption' (Hawkesworth 1773: II, 235), adding a resonance of the brothel to the sense of their illicit strangeness. Compared with the performances and traces of grief, the corpse has a salient irrefutability, producing an immediate and identical reaction in 'every one'. Yet this object of universal disgust is also to some extent an object of prestige. Although there is some discrepancy in the sources, it seems that only the wealthy could afford to display the corpse for any length of time: its very state of public abjection was testimony to the status of the deceased (see Figure 6). While Banks claims that all corpses are displayed in the house of corruption for five nights, Johann Reinhold Forster describes a mourning ceremony identical to that witnessed by Banks, but states that such were 'usually performed on the demise of persons of rank' (J. Forster 1996:333). The missionary William Ellis suggests that wealth influenced the length of time for which the corpse was kept before the public eye:

However great the attachment between the deceased and the survivors might have been, and however they might desire to prolong the melancholy satisfaction resulting from the presence of the lifeless body, on which they still felt it some alleviation to gaze, the heat of the climate was such, as to require that it should be speedily removed, unless methods were employed for its preservation, and these were generally too expensive for the poor and middle ranks. They were therefore usually obliged to inter the corpse sometimes on the first, and seldom later than the second day after death. (Ellis 1967: I, 519)

Figure 6. Status and funerary display: John Webber, 'Waheiadooa, chief of Oheitepeha, lying in state', 1789.

While Ellis is sensitive to a potential for emotional ambivalence in grieving ('melancholy satisfaction') and tolerant of its apparently perverse manifestations ('alleviation to gaze'), he stresses the prerogatives of wealth over attachment in keeping the putrefying corpse above ground. Historical-anthropological studies remain perplexed by the question of which classes of bodies were exposed and which buried directly. John Gascoigne adduces burial arrangements to a broader argument that 'In Polynesian society . . . death, like all other aspects of society, was marked by hierarchy', arguing that 'a chief's passing required greater time for society to adjust than the death of a commoner, so the mourning ceremonies were often more prolonged' (Gascoigne 2007:209). On the other hand, while Douglas Oliver acknowledges that it is logical to assume that wealth and status played a part, he also notes evidence in Bligh's account 'of relatively unimportant persons as well having been accorded this treatment', and concludes by assuming that strongly motivated kinship and friendship ties – presumably the very bonds of 'great . . . attachment' whose significance Ellis de-emphasized – led to arrangements being made 'for the body to remain in view to receive further expressions of grief' (Oliver 1974: I, 496).

Figure 7. The house of corruption: William Byrne, after John Webber, 'The Body of Tee, a Chief, as preserved after Death, in Otaheite', from James Cook and James King, *Voyage to the Pacific Ocean*, 1785.

The apodictic corpse, then, turns out to be as contentious as the emotions displayed around it. Julia Kristeva has argued that corpses confront the survivor with the threshold of their own animation. 'As in true theatre, without makeup or masks,' writes Kristeva, 'refuse and corpses *show me* what I permanently thrust aside in order to live' (Kristeva 1982:3). However, if Oliver's interpretation is correct, the staging of the corpse in Tahiti is testimony to a continuation beyond death of lived, affective relationships. Like the blood of the mourning women, the corpse appears in this context to be a visible, visceral sign of sustained feeling. Yet European observers such as Banks, by maintaining their scepticism, represent such displays as false theatrics rather than 'true theatre'. Generically, they are always gothic rather than sentimental. Abjection becomes, not a sign of emotional interiority, but perversely its opposite: a sign of the surface nature of Tahitian sentiment.

The putrefaction of the corpse made it both impossible to ignore and difficult to approach (see Figure 7). Máximo Rodríguez, interpreter to the Spanish mission at Tahiti, reports, upon passing some funerary platforms, 'the corpse in one of these was so recent that we could not go near it, because of the stench it gave off' (Corney 1913–18: III, 14). The corpse thus simultaneously invites and precludes both ethnographic inspection of the kind to which Europeans seek to subject Tahitian death and continued affective engagement by local relatives and friends. The gut wrenching caused by the decaying body manifests at what, for Tahitians, constituted the primary site of emotion. Douglas Oliver cites the LMS Dictionary definition of the Maohi word *'ā'au*, as 'the bowels or intestines – *fig.* the heart or mind; the affections; the conscience; courage or spirit', in support of his recognition that for Tahitians 'the more important internal states – thinking, feeling, and so on' were centred in the bowels (Oliver 1974:1134 n. 7; 590). Robert Levy suggests that the conflation of bowel and heart was in turn a Tahitian concession to the perception that Christian missionaries accorded the heart with representing the primary physical site of feeling (Levy 1973:271). His argument implies the predominance of cultural over visceral response: through religious indoctrination, the very perception of the locus of feeling within the Tahitian body shifted. On the other hand, although Levy acknowledges that the Tahitian heart may retrospectively have come to register emotional response, this appears to have remained supplementary to gut feelings. Recent work on the enteric nervous system supports the idea of a thinking, feeling digestive tract. Elizabeth Wilson has analysed research into the workings of the gut that suggests that 'distal parts of the body (such as the stomach) have the capacity for psychological action', and are vulnerable to the same pathologies as the central nervous system (E. Wilson 2004:34, 35). The corpse's displayed putrefaction, which hits the nose and turns the gut (provoking 'disgust'), may perform a parallel work to the ritual cutting practised by Tahitian women, enacting a transformation of abstracted feeling into visceral response.

'The rage inspird by his sorrow'

> Tell me now, Can one pass and repass in this way from one deep feeling to another, from sorrow to anger, from anger to sorrow?
>
> – Diderot

Banks concludes his comments on death and mourning by remarking on the male ceremony of mourning that succeeds the female ritual of self-mutilation:

When these ceremonies have been performd for two or three days the men, who till now seemd to be intirely insensible of their loss, begin their part which the Nearest relations take in turns. They dress themselves in a dress so extraordinary that I question whether words can give a tolerable Idea of it, I therefore refer intirely to the annexd figure. In this dress they patrole the woods early in the morn and late at night, preceded by 2 or 3 boys who have nothing upon them but a small peice of Cloth round their wrists and are smutted all over with Charcoal; these sable emissaries run about their principal in all directions as if in pursuit of people on whoom he may vent the rage inspird by his sorrow, which

Figure 8. 'A dress so extraordinary that I question whether words can give a tolerable Idea of it': William Woollett, 'A view in the Island of Otaheite; with the house or shed called Tupapow, under which the dead are deposited, and a representation of the person who performs the principal part in the funeral ceremony in his peculiar dress; with a man climbing the bread-fruit tree to get out of his way', from John Hawkesworth, *An account of the voyages undertaken by the order of His present Majesty*, 1773.

he does most unmercifully if he catches any body, cutting them with his stick the edge of which is set with sharks teeth, but this rarely or never happens for no sooner does this figure appear than every one who see either him or his emissaries fly inspird with a sort of religious awe, fly with the utmost speed, hiding wherever they think themselves the most safe but by all means quitting their Houses if they lie even near the path of this dreadfull apparition. (Banks 1962: I, 378; see Figure 8)

Like the feminine shifts between laughter and self-mutilation, these masculine ceremonies enact a similar transition from insensibility to a kind of performative excess, betraying a familiar slipperiness of affect, as sorrow inspires rage. As the 'sable emissaries' assume the mantle of mourning from the women, grief turns outward: the shark's tooth employed against the self is now used to threaten others, and a kind of incorporation is replaced by venting.

Banks's claim that his words are insufficient to describe the costume of the male mourners belies the fact that he has an intimate knowledge of this ceremony, having played the role of 'sable emissary' himself. On

Figure 9. Chief mourner and his 'sable emissary', mourners and funeral platform: William Woollett, 'A toupapow with a corpse on it, attended by the Chief Mourner in his habit of ceremony', from James Cook, *A voyage towards the south pole*, 1777.

9 June 1769, he witnessed for the first time the male mourning ceremony, and was inspired to request if he might participate:

Yesterday and today the *Heiva no Meduah* or funeral ceremony walkd. My curiosity was raisd by his most singular dress. I was desirous of knowing what he did during his walk; I askd Tubourai, at the same time desird leave to atend him tomorrow which upon my consenting to perform a character was readily granted. Tomorrow therefore I am to be smutted from head to foot and to do whatever they desire me to do. (Banks 1962: I, 288)

Banks's willingness to play the submissive boy here paradoxically contributes to his authority, reflecting the breadth of his enthusiastic participant-observation during the course of the *Endeavour* voyage. The image of himself 'smutted' dominates his subsequent description of the activities of these mourners:

Tubourai was the *Heiva*, the three others and myself were to *Nineveh*. He put on his dress, most Fantastical tho not unbecoming, the figure annexd will explain it far better than words can. I was next prepard by stripping off my European cloths and putting me on a small strip of cloth round my waist, the only garment I was allowd to have, but I had no pretensions to be ashamd of my nakedness for neither of the women were a bit more coverd than myself. They then began to smut me and themselves with charcoal and water, the Indian boy was compleatly black, the women and myself as low as our shoulders . . . To the fort then we went to the surprize of our freinds and affright of the Indians who were there, for they every where fly before the *Heiva* like sheep before a wolf. [. . . Having scattered any Tahitians we could find,] we the *Ninevehs* then came to the *Heiva* and said *imatata*, there are no people; after which we repair home, the *Heiva* undressd and we went into the river and scrubbd one another till it was dark before the blacking would come off. (Banks 1962: I, 288–9)

The act of mimicry in which Banks engages as participant-observer is a particularly complex one, which claims a unique authority from a display of utter unself-consciousness. Although he disowns shame, confining its potential to the heterosexual politics of self-display (however naked he feels he is less exposed than the women), a sense of illicitness pervades a scene in which the aristocratic Englishman dresses down to play with native women and boys.[3] The repetition of the word 'smut', which in Banks's day as now denoted indecent or obscene language as well as sooty matter, vulgarity as well as the possibility of a chameleon change of skin, reinforces the illicit aspect of his research. So too does Banks's transliteration of his role (*neneva*) as Nineveh, invoking the biblical city that narrowly avoided being punished for its corruption by divine destruction (Jonah 1:2). Banks's narrative entangles the acts of stripping and putting-on in ways that further complicate the act of mimicry. He 'strip[s] off' in order to put 'me on a small strip' of material; he smuts himself black, but so do the Tahitians, so that any essential distinction between his white and their darker skin becomes equally obscured. Then, when stripping themselves of the disguise to which they had stripped, Banks's jumbled phrasing – 'scrubbd one another till it was dark before the blacking would come off' – ambiguously implies that the party becomes darker through the very act of ablution: an inadvertent acknowledgement, perhaps, that he has become nativised at a more than superficial level through his participation in the mourning ritual.

While eighteenth-century etiquette accorded mimicry a vulgar status, social versatility, and the capacity to accommodate to different cultural contexts, was the prerogative of a gentleman. In Philip Stanhope's vocabulary, low mimicry segues smoothly into worldly adaptability. The Fourth Earl of Chesterfield's letter to his son of 19 October 1748 advises that:

Mimicry, which is the common and favourite amusement of little, low minds, is in the utmost contempt with great ones. It is the lowest and most illiberal of all buffoonery. Pray, neither practise it yourself, nor applaud it in others. Besides that the person mimicked is insulted; and as I have often observed to you before, an insult is never forgiven.

---

[3] Robert Levy describes the male mourning ritual as 'inverse behavior' (Levy 1973:291).

I need not (I believe) advise you to adapt your conversation to the people you are conversing with: for I suppose you would not, without this caution, have talked upon the same subject, and in the same manner, to a Minister of state, a Bishop, a philosopher, a Captain, and a woman. A man of the world must, like the Chameleon, be able to take every different hue; which is by no means a criminal or abject, but a necessary complaisance; for it relates only to manners, and not to morals. (Stanhope 1998:106)

Stanhope's confidence that he can maintain the distinction between low and high mimicry is undermined by the juxtaposition of the two in his writing. Similarly, Banks's impersonation is precariously poised between vulgar theatrics and a display of consummate cross-cultural flexibility. The latter aspect of his engagement with Tahitian cultural practices tends to be ignored in favour of analysis of Banks as sentimental imperialist. Lee Wallace argues that Banks's 'energetic combining of botanical and social pursuits among the Tahitians' epitomizes the 'sentimental agent of imperialism', who throws himself into culture, 'never holding himself back' (Wallace 2003:11; Pratt 1992:78). But the notion of Banks as something between a mimic and a chameleon complicates this picture by allowing for an element of self-reflexivity in what is generally seen as his scientistic buffoonery. I will return to this set of questions when I look at Banks's friendships in Chapter 5. Here I want simply to suggest that the complexities of his cross-cultural performances in turn allow him compellingly to illuminate an equivalent entanglement of affective involvement with cool calculation in Tahitian responses.

Homi Bhabha's frequently cited work on mimicry seems once again relevant here. His essay 'Of Mimicry and Man' has been criticized by eminent Pacific scholars for its reliance on universalized psychoanalytic terminology (Thomas 1994a:47; Edmond 1997:127), and its elision of 'the agency of native subjects' (Edmond 1997:123; cf. Thomas 1994a:56–7). While these comments are well taken, they seem to miss some of the nuance and flexibility of what remains for me a particularly useful theoretical paradigm for discussing Oceanic encounter (compare V. Smith 1998:54). The threat of mimicry to the 'desired ends' of imperial enterprise in the Pacific was explicitly acknowledged. We earlier witnessed Cook's disconcertion at the jest of one 'waggish boy' who mocked sailors' enthusiasms by proffering excrement on a stick. Manuel de Amat, viceroy of Peru, in his instructions to the *padres* bound for Tahiti, anticipated the capacity of mimicry to interfere with the control of communication by the Spanish:

No doubt one of the means of bringing about the desired ends, and fulfilling the Instructions in the manner we hope earnestly for, will be to so conduct the questioning when the natives are giving their words to our people as to preclude them from imagining they are being made sport of, lest they, on their part, retaliate and beguile us by substituting one word for another. You should therefore put aside such buffoons or waggish persons as mock these and other serious transactions by giving vent to expressions they deem smart ... (Corney 1913–18: I, 281–2)

The disruptive potential of mimicry anticipated here is two-way: the sailors may also be responsible for its instigation and effects. While both Bhabha and his detractors have focused on the part comic, part menacing ambivalence of indigenous mimicry, Europeans have less commonly been looked at as the mimics in scenes of culture contact.[4] Yet it is illuminating to contemplate agency as it operates in Banks's engaged demonstration of the ways 'in which to be [Tahitianized] is *emphatically* not to be [Tahitian]'.[5] Bhabha's recognition of the pliancy of humour seems lost on his critics. Thus he writes that 'mimicry represents an *ironic* compromise'; that it is 'the sign of the inappropriate', and that it is 'in this comic turn from the high ideals of the colonial imagination to its low mimetic literary effects [that] mimicry emerges as one of the most elusive and effective strategies of colonial power and knowledge' (Bhabha 1994:84, 85). In my reading of Banks's mimicry of Tahitian mourning, the practice of 'smutting' the body – ostensibly 'the sign of the inappropriate' – is ambivalently foregrounded, as a camouflage that primarily serves to obscure the differences between *uncamouflaged* Indigenous and European skins. Moreover, Banks's self-depiction demonstrates the European's willingness to risk comedy in pursuit of seriousness and to tread a fine line between distanciation and a kind of performative catharsis.

Yet Banks's very participation in the mourning ceremony aggravates rather than assuages those issues of sincerity that later trouble his and other European accounts of Tahitian grief. It embodies that 'partial presence' which Bhabha calls 'the basis of mimicry' (Bhabha 1994:88). If the theatre of death in Tahiti can incorporate such ill-rehearsed and disingenuous players as Banks, allowing him to supplant those 'nearest relations' who, he has established, should play such roles and whose interests apparently become subordinate to a desire to impress and include the European visitor, then how genuine can Tahitian rage or sorrow or friendship be? Banks's flagrant participation in cross-cultural

---

[4] Anne Salmond's account of the mock court-martial and execution of a New Zealand dog for cannibalism on the *Discovery* during Cook's third circumnavigation is a shining exception here (Salmond 2003:1–9).

[5] This is to adapt Bhabha, who writes of 'a flawed colonial mimesis in which to be Anglicized is *emphatically* not to be English' (Bhabha 1994:87).

theatrics highlights a more general phenomenon, where the presence of the participant-observer in the arena of sentiment casts doubt on the validity of the emotion expressed, raising the spectre of mimicry.[6]

Affective Theatre: 'the outward signs of feeling'

> The actor finally reaches such a point that even in the deepest sorrow he cannot cease from thinking about the impression made by his own person and the general scenic effect; for instance, even at the funeral of his child, he will weep over his own sorrow and its expression like one of his own audience.
>
> – Nietzsche

Banks's involvement in the funeral scene brings the European suspicion of Tahitian emotion full circle: exposing the theatrics of Tahitian grief by engaging in an inherently superficial performance. The relationship between acting and genuine feeling was extensively debated in Britain and France in the years preceding the first European voyages to Tahiti.[7] In England, John Hill's *The Actor: A Treatise on the Art of Playing* (1750) dilated on the 'laws [for] the French stage' of Rémond de Sainte-Albine[8] in promoting the notion of an essential link between theatrical and genuine emotion. Hill argued that:

The performer, who does not himself feel the several emotions he is to express to the audience, will give but a lifeless and insipid representation of them. All the art in the world can never supply the want of Sensibility in the player; if he is defective in this essential quality, all the advantages of nature, all the accomplishments he may have acquired by study, are thrown away upon him; he will never make others feel what he does not feel himself, and will always be as different from the thing he is to represent, as a mask from a face. (J. Hill 1750:16)

---

[6] Jonathan Lamb has argued that metropolitan sympathy was subject to a pressure akin to the one I'm suggesting skewed perceptions of peripheral grief: it could quickly appear mechanical or theatrical. Lamb contends that, for the European sympathetic subject, 'the consistent transformation of an egoistic into a social impulse ran the danger of losing its self-evidence and becoming a performance' (Lamb 2001:253).

[7] Detailed analysis of a more comprehensive selection of acting treatises than could be covered in the scope of this chapter can be found in Goring 2005. Goring contends that via such treatises the bodies of actors 'became invested with the potential to symbolize politeness and to propagate its modes of expression, and consequently they were enlisted as civilizing tools in both the legitimization of the theatres and the nurturing of polite culture more broadly' (Goring 2005:9). Goring skilfully argues that such texts were instruments of legitimation in metropolitan Britain: however, I am concerned here to emphasize the potential they also had to foster incredulity in the arena of the emotions.

[8] The author of *Le Comédien* (1747), who was to become a target of Diderot's essay on acting (Diderot 1957:58).

Hill sets up a distinction between art and embodied feeling: without the invigorating essence of real sentiment, both natural and achieved accomplishments serve as the mere decoration of a corpse. The thesis was expressed in verse by Robert Lloyd, whose *The Actor: A Poetic Epistle* urges that

> The Play'r's Profession (tho' I hate the Phrase,
> 'Tis so *mechanic* in these modern Days)
> Lies not in Trick, or Attitude, or Start,
> Nature's true Knowledge is his only Art.
> The strong-felt Passion bolts into the Face,
> The Mind untouch'd, what is it but Grimace?
> To this one Standard make your just Appeal
> Here lies the golden Secret; learn to FEEL. (Lloyd 1760:3–4)

In both texts, the face figures as the site of emotion: true and false feeling register immediately to the eye as the difference between mask and face, felt passion and a corpse-like grimace. If John Hill's comments suggest a natural relationship between heartfelt sympathy and the ability to represent it, however, this is complicated by an understanding of sensibility as epitomized by emotional flexibility: 'The sense of this term is very extensive; it takes in not only the natural turn of mind in the player, but that pliantness of disposition by means of which the different passions are made easily to succeed one another in his soul' (J. Hill 1750:15). Emotional agility rather than simple emotional intensity characterizes the theatrical embodiment of feeling subjectivity.

The notion that genuine sensibility was best represented by a quick succession of highly reflexive emotions led in turn to the development of gestural codes and exercises for stage actors. Aaron Hill's 'Essay on the Art of Acting' identifies ten dramatic passions: Joy, Grief, Fear, Anger, Pity, Scorn, Hatred, Jealousy, Wonder and Love, and proposes facial exercises that will enable the actor best to convey these emotions individually and in succession. For the purposes of this chapter's argument, I will quote from his instructions on performing Grief:

A speaker, who would distress his imagination, into a complete assumption of . . . sorrow . . ., will first consider, that *grief* being a passion the most opposite in nature to joy, his look, that before was enliven'd, must, now, in a moment, take a mournful and declin'd impression. His muscles must fall loose, and be unbrac'd into the habit of languor. – And, then, no sooner shall his nerves have form'd themselves to this lax disposition, for complying with the melancholy demand of the sentiments, than his voice also will associate its sound to the plaintive resignation of his gesture, and the result, both in the air, and in accent, will be the most moving resemblance of a heartfelt and passionate sorrow. (A. Hill 1754b:348)

In eighteenth-century acting theory the language of emotion is figured as one of flux. Emotions are defined interrelationally, in terms of the subtle expressive differences that belie highly contradictory emotional states.[9] The consolidation of a language of gesture was not intended, in texts such as Aaron Hill's, to call into question the genuineness of the emotion portrayed: elsewhere he asserted that acting constitutes a type of embodiment: 'Rightly to *seem*, is transiently, to *be*' (A. Hill 1754a:392). Yet if texts such as the 'Essay on the Art of Acting' seek to define the essential lineaments of human emotion, they also imply a lack of definition between emotions – their capacity to slip into one another. They also, of course, reveal techniques by which expression can be artfully manipulated, so that, as William Worthen elucidates, 'if the actor's use of the natural language of gesture epitomizes the principles of social interaction, his ability to depict the signs of passion disingenuously – to become a kind of sincere hypocrite – profoundly threatens the necessary spontaneity of expression that makes gesture so crucial to the benevolent society' (Worthen 1984:84).

Worthen has argued that texts such as Hill's can be placed alongside social theoretical writings of the same period, such as Kames's discourse on the 'External Signs of Emotions and Passions' which I cited earlier: both argue for an expressive language that is universally intelligible (Worthen 1984:78, 4). The facial communication of expression appears capable of transcending particularities of language and culture. But if theories of acting and social emotion in this sense combined to create a climate of confidence for the assessment of cross-cultural representations of emotion such as those represented by Tahitian mourning, they equally undermined that confidence by suggesting that faces might be put on, not in the recognizably stylized mode of masks, but through careful manipulation of tissue and muscle, creating not a static but a 'moving resemblance' of heartfelt and passionate emotion. Take Edward Robarts's description of the apparently quickly shifting emotions of Marquesan women in mourning. Robarts writes:

Numbers of women allways comes to weep over the deceased. Their tears are allways very handy. I have seen women weep with so much appearent sorrow that I thought their hearts would break, and at the same breath would get up, wipe her eyes and go sing in another part of the house, or tell those around her what a fine schole of fish had been caught that day. This sudden change I could not let pass unnoticed to see the difference between real and false sorrow. (Dening 1974:56)

---

[9] In this sense, acting theory differs from artistic treatises such as Charles Le Brun's posthumously published *Méthode pour apprendre à dessiner les passions* (1698), translated into English as *The Passions of the Human Mind* (c. 1760). Le Brun also propounded a universally recognizable facial lexicon. His treatise illustrated the typical expressions of emotions such as Hope, Dejection and Love; however, such static visual codification did not allow for the representation of mutable emotion.

Robarts's variant 'appearent' highlights the notion of deceptive appearances, which is supported by a range of references that suggest a confusion of gestural language. 'Handy' tears spring to the 'hand' rather than the eye, presumably by a kind of sleight of hand; the same breath breaks hearts and invigorates; rooms of the house, rather like those of the body's temple, are devoted to apparently contradictory behaviours. Robarts's affront that such contradictions can be accommodated without self-fragmentation leads to an attempt to deduce from what he sees a typology of expression, with the shifts of emotion in the Marquesan women figuring as allegories of 'real and false sorrow'.

In France, two of the most didactic treatises on theatricality were produced by authors who also romanticized 'savage' over 'civilized' society. Jean-Jacques Rousseau is credited with having invented the concept of the 'Noble Savage', although, as Ter Ellingson has exhaustively demonstrated, he neither coined nor indeed ever used the expression (Ellingson 2001:81–2). Rather, Rousseau promulgated a distinction between natural and social behaviours, arguing that progress rendered natural feeling egocentric and attenuated. In his *Discourse on Inequality* (1754), which I looked at briefly at the end of Chapter 3, he writes of 'the pure emotion of nature, prior to all kinds of reflection', and uses the example of the theatre to epitomize the distanciation and ultimate falsification of emotion that arises with increasing cultural sophistication:

we daily find at our theatres men affected, nay shedding tears at the sufferings of a wretch who, were he in the tyrant's place, would probably even add to the torments of his enemies; like the bloodthirsty Sulla, who was so sensitive to ills he had not caused, or that Alexander of Pheros who did not dare to go and see any tragedy acted, for fear of being seen weeping with Andromache and Priam, though he could listen without emotion to the cries of all the citizens who were daily strangled at his command. (Rousseau 1973:74)

Rousseau invokes 'the sanguinary Sulla [who] cried at the accounts of evils he had not himself committed' again in his *Letter to d'Alembert Concerning Spectacles* (1758), a response to d'Alembert's suggestion in his *Encyclopédie* entry on Geneva, that the city would be improved as a civilized centre by the construction of a theatre.[10] Rousseau figures the theatre as a microcosm of urban society, and as such a space of disingenuous feeling:

---

[10] Jonas Barish has linked Rousseau's *Discourse* to his *Letter to d'Alembert*, though surprisingly he does not discuss the reference to theatre common to both texts (Barish 1981:257–8).

I hear it said that tragedy leads to pity through fear. So it does; but what is this pity? A fleeting and vain emotion which lasts no longer than the illusion which produced it; a vestige of natural sentiment soon stifled by the passions; a sterile pity which feeds on a few tears and which has never produced the slightest act of humanity. (Rousseau 2004:268)

Rousseau recognizes the capacity of emotions to suggest or morph into one another: thus tragedy exploits the imbrication of pity and fear in the human psyche. However, he is concerned with the social effects of feeling. To this end, he recognizes that theatrical catharsis constitutes a closed emotional circuit: sentiment expends itself within the theatre, rather than producing moral outcomes in the world beyond its walls:

If, according to the observation of Diogenes Laertius, the heart is more readily touched by feigned ills than real ones, if theatrical imitations draw forth more tears than would the presence of the objects imitated, it is less because the emotions are feebler and do not reach the level of pain ... than because they are pure and without mixture of anxiety for ourselves. In giving our tears to these fictions, we have satisfied all the rights of humanity without having to give anything more of ourselves. (Rousseau 2004:268–9)

In Rousseau's ideological syntax the theatre is to 'natural' sentiment as civilized is to 'natural' man. Tears sustain the 'sterile' theatrical version of pity, and are caught up in its economy of fabrication, flowing more readily in contexts of manufactured sentiment than in situations where they might lead to charitable impulses.

Like Rousseau, Denis Diderot, in his 'Supplement to Bougainville's Voyage' (1771), opposes a genuine 'savage' sentiment to metropolitan false feeling, albeit in far more sceptical mode. Diderot sketches a Tahitian society in which mutual care is a byproduct of the supreme valuation of fertility. His Tahitian priest Orou claims that only within this reproductively oriented and sexually enacted economy can genuine sentiment flourish: 'It is among such that a child's sickbed is watered with tears; where a mother is nursed tenderly through illness; where a fertile woman, a marriageable girl, an adolescent boy are highly prized and every care is lavished on their upbringing, because their survival is an increase of riches and their loss is an impoverishment' (Diderot 1993:98). Diderot's essay *The Paradox of Acting*, a text finished in 1778 but not published until 1830 (Sennett 1977:113), evinces a more particular scepticism about urban sensibility.[11] Where John Hill saw the actor as drawing on genuine feeling and Rousseau bemoaned theatre's

---

[11] Greg Dening examined Diderot's essay and a tradition of anti-theatrical writing in thinking about the relationship between theatre and 'going native' (Dening 1996:121–5).

engagement of a false or vestigial sentimentality, for Diderot, the actor in the theatre must *ideally* be emotionally disengaged: 'an unmoved and disinterested onlooker', with 'penetration and no sensibility' (Diderot 1957:14). He elaborates at length on the particular art behind the actor's emotional deception:

> The actor has listened over and over again to his own voice. At the very moment when he touches your heart he is listening to his own voice; his talent depends not, as you think, upon feeling, but upon rendering so exactly the outwards signs of feeling, that you fall into the trap. He has rehearsed to himself every note of his passion. He has learnt before a mirror every particle of his despair. He knows exactly when he must produce his handkerchief and shed tears; and you will see him weep at the word, at the syllable, he has chosen, not a second sooner or later. The broken voice, the half-uttered words, the stifled or prolonged notes of agony, the trembling limbs, the faintings, the bursts of fury – all this is pure mimicry, lessons carefully learned; the grimacing of sorrow, the magnificent aping which the actor remembers long after his first study of it, of which he was perfectly conscious when he first put it before the public. (Diderot 1957:19)

In the figure of the actor, Diderot makes a virtue of a phenomenon that posed a threat to so many eighteenth-century commentators: the possibility of standing aloof from and falsely representing genuine sentiment. He manages this by maintaining a complete separation of spheres between the world of the stage and the world at large: 'the actor says nothing and does nothing in private life in the same way as on the stage: it is a different world' (Diderot 1957:57). False sentiment becomes culurally contained: relegated only to the profession of the actor.

There are, however, traces of an ongoing ambiguity about the status of performed emotion in Diderot's discourse, which surfaces in the slippage between a notion of the actor as on the one hand lacking sensibility, and on the other embodying emotional self-restraint. Although Diderot takes as exemplary female actors such as Clairon and Dumesnil, his ideal of the detached actor is always a masculine type. Like Adam Smith's restrained griever, both Diderot's actor and dramatist exert 'that recollection and self-command which constitute the dignity of every passion' (A. Smith 2002:29). Diderot privileges a dramatic poetry that is created 'in moments of stillness and self-command', claiming that 'the extravagant creature who loses his self-control has no hold on us; this is gained by the man who is self-controlled' (Diderot 1957:17). The contrast between 'extravagant creature' and 'the man who is self-controlled' is inherently gendered, and Diderot soon makes this explicit, arguing that, 'If a man who is really manly drops a tear, it touches us more nearly than a storm from a weeping woman' (Diderot 1957:18). Behind this dichotomy of sentiment lies a distaste for and fear of their opposites: the effeminate man and, more particularly, the cold woman. Diderot initially praises Clairon for her performative detachment: 'she has herself well in hand, she repeats her efforts without emotion ... As she lies careless and still on a sofa with folded arms and closed eyes she can, following her memory's dream, hear herself, see herself, judge herself, and judge also the effects she will produce' (Diderot 1957:16). Yet from this image of a feminine abandonment that is perfectly calculated develops a more unsettling vision of a false maternal sentiment:

This is all very well, you may reply; but what of these touching and sorrowful accents that are drawn from the very depths of a mother's heart and that shake her whole being? Are these not the result of true feeling? are these not the very inspiration of despair? Most certainly not. The proof is that they are all planned; that they are part of a system of declamation; that, raised or lowered by the twentieth part of a quarter of a tone, they would ring false; ... Look you, before he cries 'Zaïre vous pleurez,' or 'Vous y serez ma fille,' the actor has listened over and over again to his own voice. (Diderot 1957:19)

Natural sentiment turns out, once again, to be the product of a very careful 'system' calculated to the smallest fraction. And with this realization, the actor as falsely grieving mother morphs into the male actor addressing a daughter: as though even Diderot must shy away from his own harsh contemplation of disingenuous maternity. Against this he in turn sets the pathetic spectacle of genuine grief which cannot communicate, but rather, by failing to embody coldly the ideal image of emotion, provokes contradictory responses of indifference, amusement or dislike:

An unhappy, a really unhappy woman, may weep and fail to touch you; worse than that, some trivial disfigurement in her may incline you to laughter; the accent which is apt to her is to your ears dissonant and vexatious; a movement which is habitual to her makes her grief show ignobly and sulkily to you; almost all the violent passions lend themselves to grimaces which a tasteless artist will copy but too faithfully, and which a great actor will avoid. (Diderot 1957:23)

Diderot's model of the genuinely sensitive but theatrically untalented actress is Madame Riccoboni, of whom he tells: 'There was an incident in her life which led her to the brink of the tomb. After an interval of twenty years she has not ceased to weep; the source of her tears is not yet dry' (Diderot 1957:58–9). Still welling with tears of genuine grief, Madame Riccoboni is nonetheless and indeed therefore 'one of the worst actresses that ever appeared on the stage' (Diderot 1957:59).

The shifting pronouns of Diderot's sophisticated discourse on acting are illuminating for thinking about European responses to Oceanic sentiment, and particularly to the sentiment of grief. As I noted earlier in this chapter, Europeans observe Tahitian mourning rituals to be significantly gendered, and are careful to distinguish female and male roles. It is, however, consistently the female mourner who is seen to embody false feeling. When Cook returned to Raiatea in late May 1774 during his second circumnavigation, he figured mourning women as a chorus of hags who threaten sailors with a bloody embrace:

> I went on Shore accompanied by Mr F. &c[a] to make the Chief the Customary present. At our first entering his house we were met by 4 or 5 old Women, Weeping and lamenting, as it were, most bitterly and at the same time cuting their heads with Instruments made of Sharks teeth so that blood ran p[l]entifully down their faces and on their Shoulders, and what was still worse we were obliged to submit to the Embraces of these old Hags and by that means got all besmear'd with Blood: this ceremony (for it was meerly such) being over, these women went and Washed themselves and immidiately after appear'd as Cheerfull as any of the Company. (Cook 1969:419)

In contrast to this female embodiment of simultaneous horror and insincerity, the *ari'i* Oreo's inquiry after the location of Cook's future burial platform, which I quoted in Chapter 2, is cited as token of both natural delicacy and genuine friendship: 'What greater proof could we have of these people Esteeming and loving us as friends whom they wishd to remember, they had been repeatedly told we should see them no more, they then wanted to know the name of the place were our bodies were to return to dust' (Cook 1969:426).[12]

Máximo Rodríguez interrupts numerous mourning ceremonies during his time in Tahiti, yet each description in his account reads like a first encounter. The shifts from violence to equanimity in the female mourners appear always to strike him afresh: 'his sisters were weeping and scarifying their heads, and smearing themselves over, face and body, with the blood. I was much puzzled at this, but when the said Pautu saw me again he ordered them to stop their wailing; which they promptly did, and washed off the blood'; 'On the ceremony being brought to a close they withdrew in order to wash their upper parts, which were besmeared with blood; and after that they engaged in gossip with the Chiefs'; 'on approaching the head of the bier on which the body lay the two who had scarified themselves all over their faces and heads, and were besmeared with blood, threw down the wraps and remained seated and weeping ... The wailing then ceased and a general conversation ensued' (Corney 1913–18: III, 14, 17, 32). The repeated evocation of female insensibility in turn seems to

---

[12] In *Memoirs of Arii Taimai*, Henry Adams reconciles the horror and apparent calculation of acts of female self-mutilation by claiming that powerful women employed such gestures politically, to signify 'revenge as well as grief' (Adams 1976:44).

legitimate a negligence of feminine feeling. Seeking herbs to relieve the chronic flatulence of one of the Spanish *padres*, Màximo neglects the tears of a bereaved mother at the behest of a less sentimental father:

Seeing my eagerness for it . . . he said he would bring it; but, as soon as his wife knew about it, and that her husband was going to pull up the purslane, she gave vent to an immeasurable flood of tears because, it seems, the said purslane was growing inside their *marae* or cemetery, which had been built by a son of hers who lay buried within the cemetery in question. I procured the purslane and withdrew, leaving the woman still weeping. (Corney 1913–18: III, 100–1)

Maximo's doubting phrases – 'it seems', 'the said purslane' – suggest that even in this scenario it is the mother's sentiment, rather than the father's indifference, that remains suspect and potentially calculated.

William Bligh felt free to doubt the sincerity of a mourning mother:

I was suddenly surprized at a violent degree of distress by some one at a little distance off . . . As I expressed a desire to see the distressed person, Tynah took me to the place, but we no sooner came in sight than the Mourner burst into a fit of laughter at seeing me. This person was a Mother of a Young female Child that lay dead. Several Young Women were with her, but they all resumed a degree of chearfullness, and the tears were immediatly dryed up. I told Tynah the Woman had no sorrow for her Child, as her grief could not so easily have subsided if it was the case that she regretted the loss of it. When with some humour, he told her to cry again; however we left her without any visible marks of its return. (Bligh 1937: II, 18)

However, Bligh respected paternal grief. Encountering the bereaved parents of a young man who died of consumption, both overwhelmed by sorrow and engaged in complementary rituals of self-mutilation, he singled out the father as exemplary:

I may state the above instance as an example of Parental tenderness and sorrow at the loss of a Child, equal to what it would have been in the most civilized society. We see the Father in the height of sorrow and distress assisting his beloved Son in his last moments, and when life no longer remained, effecting such offices, manfully Struggling against the weight of Sorrow that would carry everything before it, but for that intuitive principal of duty, which nothing can get the better of among these people. (Bligh 1937: II, 51)

The father's resistance to his own distress creates a space for that distress to be recognized as genuine. The mother's grief, on the other hand, in its lack of containment and labile expressivity, becomes suspect. Its very visibility renders it fit for disregard. Yet it is Bligh's own voyeuristic detachment that stands out in the earlier passage. Motivated by a 'desire to see the distressed', Bligh rushes to a scene of mourning, whose tenor shifts once he himself is 'in sight'. The mother responds to his sudden arrival with laughter that might threaten to expose the inappropriateness of Bligh's own prurient enthusiasm for others' grief, but for his ability to refer it instead to her want of feeling.

Tina maintains the mode of levity by 'with some humour', and presumably recognizable irony, directing the mother to cry on cue, yet Bligh finds confirmation of her lack of feeling in the fact that 'visible marks' of sorrow do not at this stage reappear. He factors out the effect of his own dominant emotion, curiosity, upon the emotions of the female mourners he is keen to observe. The intrusion of two high-status males, one of them a foreigner to the rituals through which grief is being managed, makes the scene of bereavement an explicit performance space, and the emotion which Bligh had conceded was surprisingly 'violent' when private becomes self-conscious and abashed. In Diderot's terms, this very inability to hold a pose, to become emblematic of grief like the bereaved father, rather than a messy participant in the mixed emotions with which encounter confuses ritual, would signify genuineness of feeling. Like Madame Riccoboni, the mother cannot act. Bligh's assumption that therefore she does not feel leads to his enjoyment of Tina's humour, which has something of the punitive relish of a male child affronted by the very possibility of a callous maternity.

Thomas J. Scheff has linked theories of ritual, theatre and emotional catharsis. Deploying Freud's and Breuer's notion of catharsis as allowing the resolution of trauma through appropriately distanced recurrence, Scheff suggests that ritual in traditional societies and theatre in modern societies both serve to allow subjects to discharge distress by creating an 'esthetic distance' from trauma. Where Rousseau argued that this very discharge depleted the capacity of theatrical audiences to feel genuinely or effectively, Scheff contends that experiencing emotion at aesthetic distance allows the subject to avoid either underdistanced or overdistanced emotional states: that is, in the instance of grief, to become either overburdened to the point of experiencing depression or experiencing 'emotionlessness and/or distraction in [a] situation of loss' (Scheff 1977:487). If Oceanic mourners such as the grieving mother seem typically incomprehensible to European observers, it is perhaps, in Scheff's terms, because their grieving ritual is poised so explicitly between extremes of under- and overdistanced emotion: between excess and absence of grief.

The unnatural mother and the feeling father seem to invert the conventional gendering of sensibility. Bligh's portrait of restrained and therefore eloquent masculine emotion exemplifies that union of stoicism with feeling that Julie Ellison shows to complicate discourses of sensibility, and which was exemplified by Adam Smith's endorsement of 'reserved, ... silent and majestic sorrow'.[13] On the other hand, if

---

[13] Ellison has convincingly argued that the assumption that sensibility is gendered feminine is overdue for revision: 'the relationship between gender and sensibility is not symmetrical or transitive' (Ellison 1999:20).

curiosity is associated primarily in the late eighteenth century with masculine authority – with the burgeoning world of exploration and collecting – it also connotes a lax acquisitiveness and morally dubious intrusiveness that tend towards feminine gendering. As Nicholas Thomas has argued, during the period of European exploration in the Pacific, 'though the idea of legitimate inquisitiveness is often encountered, there are many forceful statements in a variety of genres to the effect that curiosity is feminine, unstable, somehow tarnished, and licensed in the sense of licentiousness rather than in that of authorization' (Thomas 1994b:123). Bligh's over-enthusiastic coffin-chasing during his Tahitian sojourn (compare Bligh 1937: II, 18, 35, 43–4, 50, 57) risks participating in this version of curiosity. Instead he passes the burden of emotional indignity to the grieving mother, and then retrieves true sensibility for masculine subjectivity through the figure of the appropriately restrained grieving father.

The Tahitian scene of mourning, then, opens up for European voyagers not simply differences between cultural rituals or questions about the authenticity of others', and therefore also their own, sentiments, but also the question of how both ritual and sentiment are gendered and reassigned within and across cultural boundaries. I want, in conclusion, to return to that most compelling figure of masculine mourning in the early voyage accounts: not the restrained father, but the Chief Mourner. We may recall that Banks acted out his eager pursuit of this curious figure by participating in the mourning ceremony as one of his 'smutted' assistants. It would be difficult to find a more theatrical manifestation of Nicholas Thomas's thesis that 'licentiousness was an ambivalence internal to curiosity rather than merely an external deprecation of it' (Thomas 1994b:133) than Banks, his 'curiosity . . . raisd', agreeing 'to be smutted from head to foot and to do whatever they desire me to do'. Yet although Banks was thus allowed to approach the mourner's costume through theatre, he was unable to purchase one. On Cook's second voyage, however, as George Forster reports, 'A number of complete mourning dresses, not less than ten, were purchased by different persons on board, and brought to England' (G. Forster 2000:361–2). Forster marks the change in the terms of trade from the earlier voyage, noting how 'surprising . . . was their offering for sale these curious and singular mourning dresses, which are mentioned in captain Cook's first voyage, and which they would not part with on any account at that time' (G. Forster 2000:361). He attributes this to the circulation of highly valued red feathers, of which the sailors had picked up a supply in Tonga in late 1773. Forster focuses on the 'general and irresistible longing' the red feathers create among the Tahitians, and in particular their capacity to purchase sexual favours for the sailors. Yet he notes that profit is to be made from overwheening desire back in the metropole as well: 'In England the curiosity has been so great, that a Taheitian mourning-dress, which a sailor brought over, has been sold for five and twenty guineas' (G. Forster 2000:363). On the other hand, Cook, reporting the exchange around the dress, makes a distinction between the evaluative capacities of the crew and the Tahitian who is simply randomly desirous: '[Otou's father] made me a present of a compleat Mourning dress, curiosities we most valued, in return I gave him whatever he desired' (Cook 1969:392). Cook and Johann Reinhold Forster are in turn exempted in George Forster's account from the frenzy of desirous accumulation he describes among the crew members, with the former reported as donating the mourning dress he acquires to the British Museum and the latter to the Ashmolean. Both thus participate in what Nicholas Thomas has perceptively formulated as a 'struggle to licence collecting – and particular collectors – by abstracting the objects of their desire from licentious associations, from desire itself' (Thomas 1994b:130).

For George Forster, the mutual curiosity of cultures facilitates a particular version of civility, commercial rather than aristocratic, enabling a continuous circulation unimpeded by discernment:

But in this respect the Taheitians are no way inferior to civilized nations ... The chiefs continually importuned us to give them curiosities from Tonga-Tabboo, Waïhoo, and Waitahoo, instead of English goods, in exchange for their provisions and curiosities. The feathered head-dresses of the two last islands, and the baskets, clubs, and painted cloth of the former, pleased them excessively; nay, they were eager to possess the mats of Tonga-Tabboo, though in general they perfectly resembled their own manufacture. Our sailors therefore frequently took advantage of their disposition, and gave them the same mats under another name, which they had formerly purchased in their own island, or in the Society Islands. Thus there is a similarity in the general inclinations of human nature, and particularly in the desires of all nations who are not in a state of savage barbarism, but have the advantage of civilization. (G. Forster 2000:363)

Forster's discourse on the civilized commensurability of Tahitian and European curiosity teeters into a comparison of base impulses of gullibility and duplicity. If the islanders are dupes who can't ultimately distinguish home wares from foreign manufacture,[14] and if the sailors

---

[14] In fact the eagerness to trade local objects may not have reflected a failure of recognition so much as expedience. As Brigitta Hauser-Schäublin notes, feathers and mats belonged to a category of articles that 'already had an established cultural value': thus that could easily enter circulation (Hauser-Schaüblin 1998:17). John Gascoigne has suggested that red feathers may have been appreciated as items of trade throughout Oceania because of their sacred associations (Gascoigne 2007:212).

take advantage of this ignorance, these roles might easily be switched, as we saw when the Tongan boy with excrement on a stick mocked British acquisitive credulousness. And ignorance persists higher in the ranks of European exploration. Despite Cook's and J. R. Forster's commendable gestures in offering the dresses to museums as objects of public knowledge, these artifacts remain inscrutable. Banks had insisted on his inability to describe the mourner's costume, directing his readers twice, instead, to an illustration. Perhaps because his party has gained possession of several of the dresses and he thus has them to hand, Forster by contrast describes them in great detail. Yet ultimately possession brings him no closer to understanding the rituals of death in Tahiti: as he acknowledges, his party 'could never obtain any intelligence from the natives on the subject; they gave us an account of the ceremony, and of the dress, telling us the names of every part; but it was impossible for us to make ourselves understood, as soon as we wanted to know why was it so?' (G. Forster 2000:363). Exemplarily unenlightening yet hugely valuable, the dresses resist the attempt Thomas recognized to abstract them from licentious desire, and become instead trophies of desire divorced from empathy or explanation.

Diderot's *The Paradox of Acting* concludes with a compelling invocation of the way in which the actor inhabits emotion. Diderot writes:

the great actor . . . shuts himself up inside a great basket-work figure of which he is the soul. He moves this figure so as to terrify even the poet, who no longer recognises himself; and he terrifies us . . . just as children frighten each other by tucking up their little skirts and putting them over their heads, shaking themselves about, and imitating as best they can the croaking lugubrious accents of the spectre they counterfeit . . . Have you not observed an urchin coming forward under a hideous old man's mask, which hides him from head to foot? Behind this mask he laughs at his little companions, who fly in terror before him. This urchin is the true symbol of the actor . . . And if he is endowed with extreme sensibility what will come of it? – What will come of it? (Diderot 1957:67–8)

Diderot's actor bears an uncanny resemblance to the Tahitian mourner in his 'whimsical dress', with its basket-like structure of board and string and mask of shells, in one of which 'there is a small hole cut, through which the wearer must look in order to find his way' (G. Forster 2000:363, 362). Forster too makes an association with the terrors of the nursery, writing of the 'fantastical dress' that 'has so much of that strange and terrifying shape which our nurses attribute to ghosts and goblins' (G. Forster 2000:363). Diderot's question, 'extreme sensibility

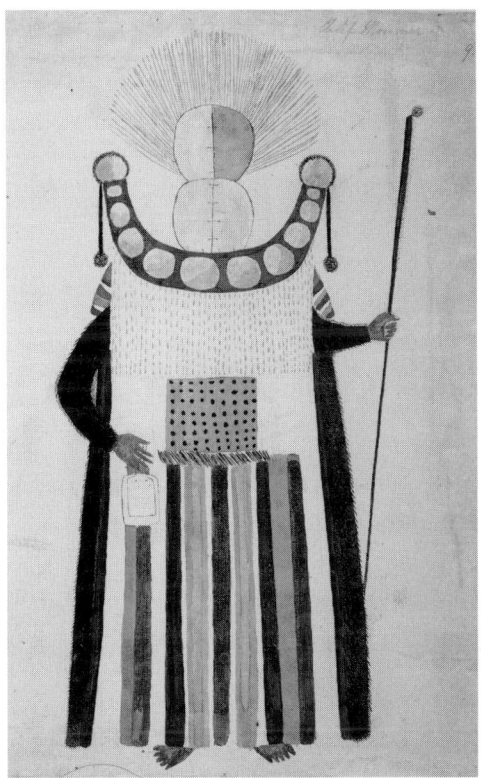

Figure 10. The chief mourner as represented by Tupaia: Artist of the Chief Mourner, 'Chief Mourner', from 'Dancing Girl and Chief Mourner, Otaheite'. Drawings illustrative of Captain Cook's First Voyage, 1768–1771. Pencil and watercolour, June–August 1769.

what will come of it?', chimes with Forster's collapse of inquiry, 'why was it so?' Both the mourner's costume and Diderot's image of the actor figure forth emotion epitomized, but of doubtful interiority. The question of what feeling lies behind Oceanic rituals of grief is one that Forster and his fellow voyagers, scientists and avid collectors remained ill-equipped, despite their haul, to answer.

Part II

Particular friendships

5   Fellow travelling

> It is true that, even between people who are foreign and strange to one another, nature encourages the development of a friendly feeling. But in such cases the sentiment lacks a solid basis.
>
> – Cicero

On 12 July 1769, Joseph Banks recorded with delight in his journal that the high-ranking Society Islander Tupaia had resolved to travel to England in the *Endeavour*:

> This morn Tupia came on board, he had renewed his resolves of going with us to England, a circumstance which gives me much satisfaction. He is certainly a most proper man, well born, cheif *Tahowa* or preist of this Island, consequently skilld in the mysteries of their religion; but what makes him more than any thing else desireable is his experience in the navigation of these people and knowledge of the Islands in these seas; he has told us the names of above 70, the most of which he has himself been at. The Cap[tm] refuses to take him on his own account, in my opinion sensibly enough, the goverment will never in all human probability take any notice of him; I therefore have resolvd to take him. Thank heaven I have a sufficiency and I do not know why I may not keep him as a curiosity, as well as some of my neighbours do lions and tygers at a larger expence than he will probably ever put me to; the amusement I shall have in his future conversation and the benefit he will be to this ship, as well as what he may be if another should be sent into these seas, will I think fully repay me. (Banks 1962: I, 312–13)

Banks's response has itself come to function as a kind of critical show-piece. Once seen to advertise the imperialist disregard that informs Banks's ethnographic curiosity – as Harriet Guest writes, to 'emphasize the extent to which that curiosity thrives on the isolation of its exotic object, on the colonizing displacement or dislocation of its object from any signs of the personal estate or cultural content that might produce legible or potent significance' (Guest 2007:70; first published in Guest 1992:104), it has lately been acknowledged to affirm the authority and curiosity of the Oceanic traveller. Thus Nicholas Thomas, who previously read Banks's comments as simply 'dilettantish' (Thomas 1997:1), has more recently recognized that while his 'characterization of Tupaia

179

as "a curiosity" in the same class as a tiger has rightly become notorious', Banks primarily views Tupaia as 'a man of rank and social eminence', a worthy companion, and an explorer in his own right (Thomas 2003:81). However, the shift in Banks's journal entry, from regarding Tupaia as curious to viewing him as curiosity, is, I think, less bipolar than has been assumed. Banks's scepticism here is not so much a manifestation of the worldly disregard of the British imperial connoisseur, as an exposé of that disregard. He anticipates a lack of curiosity on the part of government in the exotic visitor that must be compensated for by the compromised curiosity of the privately wealthy. This in turn creates a particular context for the potential reception of the Oceanic traveller: he can *only* be understood in British terms as something collected on the whim of a wealthy gentleman. But such a perception constrains Banks as well as Tupaia. Always caught between the identities of serious scientist and wealthy dilettante, Banks is relegated, in a society that can only see the curious exotic as exotic curiosity, to the role of undiscriminating aristocratic collector.[1] Tupaia's and Banks's authority as voyaging subjects are, in other words, co-dependent. If Tupaia is to be disregarded, Banks knows he will equally find himself reduced, from man of science to showman. For the space of the voyage, however, this diminished prospect is deferred. Instead Banks envisages improving and interesting conversation, mutual respect and admiration, real amusement. He imagines the respite of friendship.

In the late eighteenth century a number of Oceanians came aboard European voyaging ships, either reaching Europe and its salons, or helping to guide explorers through the Pacific. This chapter looks at four of them. Ahutoru sailed with Bougainville from Tahiti in 1768, and was the first Polynesian to visit Europe. He was in France for approximately a year, from March 1769 to March 1770, when he sailed for Mauritius, arriving in October. He departed for Tahiti in Marion de Fresne's ship the *Mascarin* on 18 October 1771; however, he died en route of smallpox on 6 November. Tupaia (and his twelve-year-old 'servant' Taiata) sailed with the *Endeavour* when Cook left Tahiti, and

---

[1] Banks was of course clearly tempted by the luxurious aspects of collecting: he eventually disengaged from Cook's second expedition after his attempts to redesign the *Resolution* to accommodate 'all kind of curious things, for use, amusement and pleasure', modifications for which he 'had put himself to very great expence', led to the ship being declared top-heavy, and restored to its original form (Elliot and Pickersgill 1984:7). John Gascoigne has comprehensively examined the co-implication of Banks's identities as aristocrat and scientist, reading his later career as head of the Royal Society as a consolidation of a tradition of aristocratic virtuosity with a new model of scientific workmanship (Gascoigne 1994: esp. 57–118).

voyaged throughout the Pacific, facilitating contacts in the Society Islands, New Zealand and Australia before succumbing to disease in Batavia (Jakarta) in December 1770. Cook admitted Mai and Hitihiti on board the *Adventure* and *Resolution*, respectively, during his second voyage. Hitihiti travelled the Pacific but ultimately decided against continuing to Europe. He resurfaces as a significant figure in the *Bounty* literature. Mai, on whom I will concentrate, continued aboard the *Adventure*, reaching London on 14 July 1774. He returned to the Society Islands on Cook's third voyage, arriving back in Tahiti, to great but short-lived excitement, in August 1777 (Rickman 1967:132–53). Lebuu was taken to England from the Koror islands in Palau in 1783. He spent five months in London before he contracted smallpox and died on 27 December 1784.[2] The focus this chapter inaugurates, on individual stories and sets of relationships, which is sustained throughout the remainder of the book, represents an attempt to recognize that aspect of particularity – calculation's antidote – that I noted in Chapter 2 was so necessary to the cross-cultural understanding of *taio*.

Each of the travellers I discuss was asked to play a different and conflicting role once they entered the societies of ship and metropole: local informant, generic Oceanian, island prince, noble savage, savage savage, sentimental subject. Recent scholarship, reviewing their stories, has discussed the contradictions these roles entailed, introducing further identities for consideration: the curious foreigner, the ambitious parvenu, the self-fashioner.[3] Yet it has remained notably silent on the identity of the friend. In this chapter, I address this collusion between early accounts and their recent critics, regarding the intimacies that may

---

[2] Other Oceanic travellers of this period include the Tahitians Tipitipia, Heiao, Pautu and Tetuanui, who were taken to Lima by the Spanish captain Domingo de Boenechea in 1772. Pautu and Tetuanui survived to spend the next two years as guests of the Spanish viceroy, Manuel de Amat y Junyent, before returning to Tahiti in 1774 with the Spanish mission. The party that brought news of Lebuu's death back to Koror in the *Panther* took three Palauans – a boy known as Kockywack and two girls – to China. A different boy, called by the British Phymoo, and three Palauan girls accompanied the British on an exploratory voyage to the coast of New Guinea and on to Ambon in the Moluccas (Maluku), where one girl, known as Kathelbly, succumbed to disease. Phymoo died at the British trading base of Bengkulu in Sumatra (McCluer 1790–2). A Tahitian, Hara Va'e, deserted the *Duff* at the time William Pascoe Crook was left at Tahuata in the Marquesas. He and two Marquesans, Timuateitei and Hiko Nekai, accompanied Crook back to England in 1799. They died from illnesses induced by the change of climate.

[3] See for instance Chappell 1997; Salmond 2003, 2005; Rennie 1995:109–25; Gascoigne 2007; Le Fur 2001; Turnbull 1998; Carter 1998; Williams 2003; McCormick 1977; Alexander 1977; Guest 2007; Russell 2004; Hackforth-Jones 2007; Nero 2002; Thomas 2002; Lamb 2001:250–80.

have been forged between Oceanic travellers and their shipboard or metropolitan companions. This mutual silence testifies, I will suggest, to a shared, persistent embarrassment about what such friendships might have been. I investigate the possibility that Oceanians and Europeans were in these contexts fellow travellers, by which I mean not that they shared an equally viable set of vested interests in their explorations, that it is the task of criticism on the one hand to foreground and on the other hand to expose, but rather that their knowledge and authority became inevitably conjoined. I try to stare down the embarrassment of admitting friendship to the lexicon of cross-cultural contact, and so allow the things that friendship knows to challenge the worldliness of both discourse and its critics. This chapter examines the fortuitous friendships of Oceanic travellers as they test the complacencies of connoisseurship, collecting, curiosity and criticism.

Ahutoru in Paris: The Point Venus Scene

> 'tis evident, that if a person full-grown, and of the same nature with ourselves, were on a sudden transported into our world, he wou'd be very much embarrass'd with every object, and wou'd not readily find what degree of love or hatred, pride or humility, or any other passion he ought to attribute to it.
>
> – Hume

In April 1769 two savants came to observe the Tahitian traveller Ahutoru in Louis de Bougainville's apartments in Paris (Liebersohn 2006:146). The first was Jacob-Rodrigue Pereire, the royal interpreter and celebrated teacher of the deaf and dumb (Bougainville 1967:272). The second was the traveller and *philosophe* Charles-Marie de La Condamine, who left an unpublished account of the meeting:

> J'ai vu notre insulaire [faire des signes très énergiques] qui n'avoient rien d'équivoque à l'aspect d'un tableau qui représentoit une Vénus presque nue; il fit semblant d'abord d'écarter le linge qui la couvroit très légèrement. Ici je me trouve embarrassé à décrire les autres signes que fit le jeune sauvage ... [4]

The energetic signs the savage makes are classic signs of savagery: hyperliteral and shameless. As Neil Rennie summarizes, La Condamine details 'an elaborate mime of smelling, tasting, grimacing and smiling' performed by the Tahitian in front of the painting, which he then interprets, not to signify sexual relish so much as 'Aotourou's prodigious ability to diagnose female venereal infection by smell and taste' (Rennie 1995:110).

---

[4] La Condamine, 'Observations', MS, quoted in Rennie 1995:110. My description of this scene follows Rennie's.

The mimicry of connoisseurship Ahutoru performs in front of the image of the semi-naked Venus is clearly understood to rend the veil of his own recently assumed civility and expose the naked primitive within. Ahutoru displays a very different version of 'taste' from that to which the salon commonly plays host, and equally a far from noble savagery. La Condamine's embarrassment is in turn far removed from the sentiments of a Rousseau, who in his *Discourse on the Sciences and Arts* (1750) juxtaposed savagery and connoisseurship in order to expose the superficiality and moral laxity of the Arts. Rousseau, on the contrary, thought an encounter with 'the perfection of our Arts' would reveal to 'an Inhabitant of some distant lands seeking to form an idea of European morals' their bankruptcy, claiming that galleries of painted images 'carefully culled from ancient Mythology' were themselves likely to corrupt, rather than expose the innate corruption of the viewer (Rousseau 1997:9, 23). Uncannily reminiscent of La Condamine's anecdote is a passage in Darwin's correspondence, to which Gillian Beer has drawn attention. Here Darwin reminisces about various English cultural excursions, expressing a particular desire to stand before Titian's Venus in the Fitzwilliam Museum. Just prior to this, he has described his 'first sight of a Savage':

It was a naked Fuegian his long hair blowing about, his face besmeared with paint. There is in their countenances, an expression, which I believe to those who have not seen it must be inconceivably wild. Standing on a rock he uttered tones & made gesticulations then which, the crys of domestic animals are far more intelligible.

Beer suggests that for Darwin 'the dismay of seeing his own male body figured in so dissimilar a guise, given back to him through observation, estranged, immediately produces ... a counter-image of the naked body. This time it is one from Western culture. And it is that of a woman' (Beer 1996:23, 26).

Beer then alerts us to the compensatory aspect of the pleasure the reclining Venus offers the viewer: 'the tactile is aroused. Touching is embargoed and experienced at once'. Her appreciation retrospectively legitimates Ahutoru's confusedly sensuous response to the invitation offered by the erotic image. But the response may equally have seemed legitimated by European reactions to women that Ahutoru would have witnessed on his home shores. Bougainville's French crew members were particularly fond of identifying Tahitian women as Venus figures. Charles-Félix-Pierre Fesche retails the following story of Venus disrobed:

Soon the veil that hid the charms which a regrettable modesty no doubt requires to be hidden, this veil I say, is soon lifted ... What brush could depict the marvels we discover when that troublesome veil happily falls, a retreat reserved for Love alone, none other could rest within it, an enchanting grove planted no doubt by that god himself. We fall into a state of ecstasy, a lively and gentle warmth spreads over our senses, we burn, but decency, that monster which so often fights against the will of men, comes and opposes our vehement desires and makes us plead in vain to the god who presides over pleasure to render us invisible for a moment or merely to fascinate for an instant the eyes of all those present. This new Venus, after a long wait, seeing that neither the invitations of her fellow citizens and especially of her elderly mentors, nor the eagerness she was herself displaying to offer a sacrifice to Venus with one of us whichever he might be, could make us cross the boundaries of decency and of the prejudices built up for us, a sentiment she may have interpreted to our disadvantage, left us with an offended look and ran away in her canoe. (Dunmore 2002:255–6)

While Fesche describes the living Tahitian Venus as beyond the scope of art, he also regrets the civilized prohibitions that prevent the sailors from interacting with her. Their refusal to touch becomes a source of disappointment: an indication of the European's unnatural relationship to physical beauty. In the Parisian drawing room, on the other hand, Ahutoru's attempt to push through art to the body it enshrines is equally inappropriate.

In Bougainville's apartment, Ahutoru exposes himself by trying to expose the Venus. Yet the embarrassment the encounter produces is ultimately less sexual than social. Applying the touchstone of culture, La Condamine reveals what Bougainville, as host, cannot admit: that his guest doesn't suit the salon; that while he is fascinating as curiosity, he is unsuitable as friend. Ahutoru's appearance in the drawing room provokes exactly the response in the worldly La Condamine that I have suggested Banks's comments on Tupaia anticipate. In a metropolitan setting the Oceanic traveller figures as spectacle rather than spectator, his expertise rendered ludicrous when brought to bear on the high-cultural artifact. Ahutoru is simply not allowed, in La Condamine's prose, to figure as subject of his own observations: he is consistently relegated to object of La Condamine's superior observation. The anecdote thus becomes a parable of the mode of relationship that emerges when Indigènes are given the opportunity to display their specialized knowledge at an imperial centre, where their role is always understood to be performative and their contribution assessed through a comparativist framework. However, once again, I would argue, the authority of the Oceanic traveller is crucially hinged with the authority of the European who invites him home. Ahutoru is, precisely, understood to be oblivious to the shame La Condamine highlights, which must instead redound to Bougainville: the person ultimately responsible for this inappropriate tableau.

Bougainville's discussion of Ahutoru's metropolitan sojourn in the published account of his voyage reveals a correspondent susceptibility to projections of shame. He writes:

The desire of seeing him has been very violent; idle curiosity, which has served only to give false ideas to men whose constant practice is to traduce others, who never went beyond the capital, never examine any thing, and who being influenced by errors of all sorts, never cast an impartial eye upon any object, and yet pretend to decide with magisterial severity, and without appeal! How, said some of them to me, in this man's country the people speak neither French, nor English, nor Spanish? What could I answer them? I was struck dumb; however, it was not on account of the surprize at hearing such a question asked. I was used to them, because I knew that at my arrival, many of those who even pass for people of abilities, maintained that I had not made the voyage round the world, because I had not been in China ... But it is common in a capital to meet with people who ask questions, not from an impulse of curiosity, or from a desire of acquiring knowledge, but as judges who are preparing to pronounce their judgment; and whether they hear the answer or no, it does not prevent them from giving their decision. (Bougainville 1967:263, 265)

Bougainville's defence of Ahutoru registers a circuitry between percep-tions of the Tahitian and of his own authority as traveller. The pair is, we might say, held in the same regard. The exotic traveller and the Euro-pean traveller to exotic places are together misconstrued as fabricators by people who themselves have never travelled. The repetition of the word 'capital' in this passage reinforces a sense that Bougainville identi-fies himself with the periphery against the metropole, the former here signifying experiential, as opposed to specious, authority. When Ahutoru's purported linguistic ineptitude is questioned, Bougainville finds himself concomitantly dumbstruck. Ventriloquizing his guest has produced a state of complete identification.

Among the questions with which he is importuned about his guest, Bougainville singles out for ridicule the insularity of those pertaining to Ahutoru's language acquisition. 'Some other sharp critics conceived and propagated a very mean idea of the poor islander,' he writes, 'because, after a stay of two years amongst Frenchmen, he could hardly speak a few words of the language' (Bougainville 1967:263–4). The Frenchmen ask Ahutoru to speak in their own terms before according him hospitality.[5]

---

[5] Thus enacting the paradox of foreignness expounded by Jacques Derrida, who asks, 'That is where the question of hospitality begins: must we ask the foreigner to understand us, to speak our language, in all the senses of this term, in all its possible extensions, before being able and so as to be able to welcome him into our country?' (Derrida 2000:15).

Bougainville justifies this perceived deficit in his guest in terms of the paucity of Tahitian vocabulary, for which he offers two, potentially contradictory explanations. The first is that 'the Taiti-man [has only] a small number of ideas, relative ... to a most simple and most limited society' (Bougainville 1967:264). The second is mnemonic:

Upon the whole, the language of this island is abundant enough; I think so, because Aotourou, during the course of the voyage, pronounced every thing that struck him in rhythmic stanzas. It was a kind of blank verse, which he spoke extempore. These were his annals; and it seems as if his language furnished him with expressions sufficient to describe a number of objects unknown to him. We further heard him pronounce every day such words as we were not yet acquainted with; and he likewise spoke a long prayer, which he calls the prayer of the kings, and of all the words that compose it, I do not understand ten. (Bougainville 1967:273)[6]

These two explanations divide along the same lines of interpretation that I have suggested pertain in recent critical discussion of Tupaia's travels. The first denigratingly compares indigenous capacities for conceptualization to the European, while the second posits the sufficiency of indigenous discourse to agendas that are not compassed by foreign observers. By shifting the emphasis from what the Tahitian cannot say to what the European cannot hear, Bougainville allows the possibility of an elite Tahitian discourse, a cryptic poetry, to emerge. Again, however, the tenuous dynamics of co-authorization are played out. By narrowly conceiving the experience of the Tahitian and his particular relationship to language, purportedly 'sharp critics' betray the limitations of their own capacity to think beyond their own sphere. By contrast Bougainville and Ahutoru are united in conceptual exploration. Reciprocally, they test the limits of their cultural vocabularies.

Bougainville's burgeoning understanding of Ahutoru's language is in part attributed to Pereire, who, as I noted earlier, had accompanied La Condamine on his visit to Bougainville's rooms. Given that he acknowledges Pereire's presence, the absence of any reference to La Condamine becomes a telling silence in Bougainville's text. He is consigned, by implication, to the anonymous ranks of 'sharp critics' whose sharpness is clearly of the cutting rather than astute kind. Other aspects of Bougainville's account might be read as further refutations of

---

[6] British redactions of Bougainville tend to exclude the references to Ahutoru's particular poetry and reiterate the more denigrating explanation for his slow language acquisition: for instance, *New Discoveries concerning the World and its Inhabitants* (Anon 1778:150).

the savant. If the sting of La Condamine's anecdote lies in its unmasking of Ahutoru's attempt to pass in the salon, Bougainville is adamant that his guest can pass in broader Parisian society:[7]

Though Aotourou could hardly blabber out some words of our language, yet he went out by himself every day, and passed through the whole town without once missing or losing his way. He often made some purchases, and hardly ever paid for things beyond their real value. The only shew which pleased him, was the opera, for he was excessively fond of dancing. He knew perfectly well upon what days this kind of entertainment was played; he went thither by himself, paid at the door the same as everybody else, and his favourite place was in the galleries behind the boxes. (Bougainville 1967:265–6)

Ahutoru's metropolitan knowledge is sufficient to his needs, and his needs are grounded in his personal tastes. Bougainville posits Ahutoru's choices – his sense of discrimination – against the cultural discrimination that cannot hear where the Society Islander is coming from. Indeed, according to the logic of Bougainville's account, Pereire, 'celebrated for his art of teaching people, who are born deaf and dumb', is the appropriate instructor of the metropolitan ear, rather than Ahutoru (Bougainville 1967:272). Where others hear only blabber, Bougainville, who has been taught to distinguish unfamiliar language as poetry or prayer, can recognize the clearly directed utility of the terms Ahutoru employs.

La Condamine is not the only figure competing to authorize himself at the expense of the Oceanic visitor. Bougainville's English translator, Johann Reinhold Forster, annotates his text with numerous swipes at Ahutoru's intelligence. His footnote to the above comment of Bougainville's, for instance, repeats La Condamine's gesture, converting Ahutoru's expertise to voyeurism. He notes that: 'in the French theatre there is, in the door of each box, a small window or hole, where people may peep through, which made it possible to Aotourou to enjoy even in the galleries the sight of the dancers', recasting Ahutoru's acquisition of salient knowledge as secret sexualized knowledge. He attributes the lack of consonants Bougainville registers in Tahitian speech to his having 'picked up his vocabulary of words from Aotourou, who had an impediment in his speech', and questions his intellect:

Though our author has strongly pleaded in this paragraph in behalf of Aotourou, it cannot, however, be denied that he was one of the most stupid fellows; which not only has been found by Englishmen who saw him at Paris, during his stay there, and whose testimony would be decisive with the public, were I at liberty to

---

[7] I have discussed the representation of Ahutoru's passing at greater length in V. Smith 2004a.

name them; but the countrymen of Aotourou were, without exception, all of the same opinion, that he had very moderate parts, if any at all. (Bougainville 1967:266, 272, 265)

Subtly and insistently Forster attempts to undermine 'our author's' authority by querying the specimen he has collected. Yet in order to combat the conjoined expertise of French explorer and islander he can only assert the equally conjoined authority of unnamable Englishmen and innumerable Tahitians. His counterevidence is specious precisely because it lacks the authorizing *conversation* that is at the heart of Bougainville's championing of Ahutoru. Forster attacks a specimen, but Bougainville defends a relationship. His partisanship understands that mutual curiosity between Indigenous and European subjects may not simply be a juggling and trading of the roles of investigator and specimen, but rather a mode of co-invested exploration.

Bougainville's discussion of Ahutoru is framed as self-exculpation since, he claims, 'people oblige me to use this word, for having profited of the good will of Aotourou, and taken him on a voyage, which he certainly did not expect to be of such a length'. Effectively, he must defend himself against a charge of kidnapping, by demonstrating the genuineness of feeling on both sides – European and Tahitian, peripheral and metropolitan – of Ahutoru's voyage. Thus Bougainville asserts that 'The zeal of this islander to follow us was unfeigned. The very first day of our arrival at Taiti, he manifested it to us in the most expressive manner', while in turn 'I have spared neither money no trouble to make his stay at Paris agreeable and useful to him. He has been there eleven months, during which he has not given any mark at all of being tired of his stay' (Bougainville 1967:262, 263). Bougainville and Ahutoru make together a perfect complement of generous host and enthusiastic guest. In Aristotelian terms, they are not only 'agreeable and useful' to each other, but equal in their capacity to enhance one another. Ahutoru's noted 'zeal' is matched by 'the zeal which inspired us' (Bougainville 1967:263); Ahutoru provides the French with 'information . . . concerning his country', while they intend to return him to Tahiti 'enriched [with] useful knowledge' (Bougainville 1967:262, 263).

In Bougainville's account, ultimately, the fashionable tastes of Frenchmen are less significant to the reception of Ahutoru than formal relationships of patronage. Ahutoru figures as a sentimental touchstone, whose natural gravitation towards the generous and friendly allows him to illuminate metropolitan acts of virtue:

Among the great number of persons who have been desirous of seeing him, he always distinguished those who were obliging towards him, and his grateful heart never forgot them. He was particularly attached to the duchess of Choiseul, who has loaded him with favours, and especially shewed marks of concern and friendship for him, to which he was infinitely more sensible than to presents. Therefore, he would, of his own accord, go to visit this generous benefactress as often as he heard that she was come to town. (Bougainville 1967:266)

In this circle of friendly obligation, Ahutoru's gratitude towards the 'generous benefactress' enables both parties to transcend the logic of reciprocity, so potentially confounding to European accounts of Tahitian friendship: to achieve a bond of sentiment rather than 'presents'. Yet if Ahutoru is figured as singling out the Duchess among the undiscerning Paris crowd, this is in turn sleight of hand on Bougainville's part. Through Ahutoru's acknowledgement of her, Bougainville is able, indirectly, to pay tribute to the wife of his own patron, the Duke de Choiseul.[8] In yet another friendly return of favours, it becomes Ahutoru's role to ventriloquize Bougainville's gratitude. Where the reciprocity of metropolitan patronage is obfuscated in Bougainville's account, however, another relationship of friendly patronage frames Bougainville's account of Ahutoru's visit to Paris. Recounting his departure from Tahiti, Bougainville writes:

At day-break, when they perceived us setting sail, Ereti leaped alone into the first periagua he could find on shore, and came on board. There he embraced all of us, held us some moments in his arms, shedding tears, and appearing much affected at our departure ... Ereti took [an islander] by the hand, and, presenting him to me, gave me to understand, that this man, whose name was Aotourou, desired to go with us, and begged that I would consent to it. He then presented him to each of the officers in particular; telling them that it was one of his friends, whom he entrusted with those who were likewise his friends, and recommending him to us with the greatest signs of concern. (Bougainville 1967:241)

If Ahutoru's relationship with Bougainville and his status as guest in Bougainville's home city are ultimately substitutive of any particular friendship, it is that forged with the *ari'i* Bougainville acknowledges as his *taio* and Tahitian host, Reti. Playing host to Ahutoru Bougainville repays a debt of friendship, translating the politics of exchange into the rhetoric of sensibility.

By Means of Tupaia

I next, by means of Tupia, explained ... that we were come to set up a mark upon the Island ...

– James Cook

---

[8] Choiseul had granted Bougainville his captaincy immediately prior to his circumnavigation. Bougainville named one of the Solomon Islands Choiseul after his patron (the largest of the group he named for himself).

Tupaia came from Raiatea, where he was a high priest of the dominant war god Oro. When Raiatea was invaded by Borabora around 1760 he was driven to Tahiti, and was instrumental in promoting the cult of Oro under Purea (Henry 1928:190–5; Davies 1961:xxvi). During Purea's ascendancy, at the time of the *Dolphin's* visit in 1767, Tupaia was involved in building a great *marae* at Papara in Tahiti. By the time of Cook's visit in 1769, Purea, and hence Tupaia, had lost favour (Cook 1955:563; Turnbull 1998:127; Williams 2003:40–1; Salmond 2003:47, 66). However, Tupaia was a man whose authority both Cook and Banks continued explicitly to acknowledge. Only Banks, though, considered him a friend. I want to suggest that this made a difference both to how they travelled together and shared their knowledge and to the ways in which they were each authorized by that exchange. The framework of the distinction I am drawing between Tupaia's interactions with Banks and with Cook was suggested by David Turnbull's interesting essay on Cook and Tupaia (Turnbull 1998:117). Turnbull fixes on Cook and Tupaia as the potential fellow travellers of the *Endeavour* because of their proximity in age (both were in their mid-forties at the time they met) and status and the unrecognized similarities between their projects of knowledge. Yet Cook and Tupaia emerge in Cook's writings as epistemological competitors rather than co explorers.[9] Indeed it is interesting, in recognizing the intellectual tenor of this competitiveness, to note the degree to which Cook's expressions of irritation with Tupaia are echoed in his later resentment towards Johann Reinhold Forster, botanist on the second of his voyages. We might see Tupaia and Forster as equivalent figures for Cook, against whose expertise he chafed. Banks, on the other hand, who at twenty-five was just young enough to have been Tupaia's, or indeed Cook's son, seems to have embraced a friendship with Tupaia that included aspects of mentoring. Banks was able to acknowledge the Raiatean as senior not just in age, but in knowledge. He was clearly proud of the friendship. Turnbull reconciles the journeys of Cook and Tupaia by suggesting that both embraced a model of anthropological reflexivity, represented in the figure of the trickster (Turnbull 1998:126, 131). However, it was surely Banks, the man we last encountered dancing semi-naked and 'smutted' in a Tahitian mourning ceremony, who better embodied such a proto-anthropological trickster. His exchanges with Tupaia were characterized precisely by an enabling perception of similarities that in turn allowed them to recognize each other not simply as informants but as friends.

---

[9] Glyndwr Williams notes that J. C. Beaglehole, the most Cook-identified of Pacific scholars, accuses Tupaia of intellectual arrogance (Williams 2003:43).

Banks seems at significant junctures to have emulated Tupaia's version of authority rather than Cook's. Two days before Tupaia communicated his willingness to sail, two marines had deserted, and Cook detained a number of *ari'i*, including Purea, in an attempt to orchestrate their return. He also sent midshipman Jonathan Monkhouse and a Corporal of Marines to find the deserters, who were in turn captured. Tupaia acted, in Banks's words, as a 'voluntary prisoner' in negotiations with the Tahitians, and the next morning the crew members were returned to the *Endeavour*. This was the first in a long and notorious series of instances in which Cook took hostages to punish or influence Pacific islanders, and that culminated in the events leading up to his death (see Chapter 1). Where Cook orchestrated a trade of bodies, however, Banks claims he placed himself in the fray:

We were intirely without defences so I made the best I could of it by going out among them. They wer[e] very civil and shewd much fear as they have done of me upon all occasions, probably because I never shewd the least of them but have upon all our quarrels gone immediately into the thickest of them. (Banks 1962: I, 311–12)

Immediately after he has referenced Tupaia's voluntary hostage role, then, Banks depicts himself as equally able to trust himself in the hands of a foreign party. Implicitly he aligns his own behaviour with the bodily engagement of Tupaia rather than the detached strategizing of Cook. And Tupaia's decision to leave Tahiti is further figured as part of this respectful responsiveness between the two men. When Tupaia decided the following morning to sail on the *Endeavour*, Robert Molyneux recorded in his journal: 'He has conceiv'd so strong a Freindship for M[r] Banks that he is Determind to Visit Britannia' (Cook 1955:564).

This characterization of his voyage as one to 'Visit Britannia' rather than King George, if it indeed records Tupaia's formulation, seems significant.[10] He was Purea's erstwhile lover as well as her chief adviser, and must therefore have been used to associating authority with female pre-eminence. Banks in his turn became Purea's lover while in Tahiti, a relationship that, once it was intimated in Hawkesworth's *Voyages*, scandalized British society. Tupaia and Banks, then, were both Purea's men. Tupaia's example invested this liaison with gravitas. Banks records Tupaia's legitimating presence and fidelity, for instance, in a subsequently notorious scene in which his clothes and pistol were stolen while

---

[10] In Loutherberg and O'Keeffe's pantomime *Omai, or, A Trip Round the World*, as we shall see, the visit of Mai to London is said to be motivated by his desire to woo Londina, daughter of Britannia.

he slept in a canoe with Purea: 'Tupia was the first man I saw, atending with my Musquet and the remainder of my cloaths, his faith had often been tried, on this occasion it shone very much' (Banks 1962: I, 282). In Tupaia's case, the role of Purea's lover had been one of personal advancement and power. Tupaia seems in turn to have shepherded the union between Banks and his own former consort, while the pre-eminent woman implicitly ratified the bond between the two men. In Chapter 2 I noted the way in which the obligation to a male friend was used as a way of framing and excusing sexual relations with older Tahitian women. On the other hand, the absence of the legitimating friend, Tupaia, upon Banks's return to England contributes to the reduction of his Tahitian encounters to sexual scandal.

The subsequent identity of Banks and Tupaia in the British imagination is apparent in the cycle of satirical poems that followed the publication of Hawkesworth's *Account of the Voyages* in 1773. I have commented on the ways in which mishearing and mispronunciation on both sides of the Tahitian beach led to the invention of new identities through name exchange. A common example was the appending of an 'O' (which in Tahitian signifies 'it is') to the proper noun: hence 'Otaheite' for Tahiti, or 'Oberea' for Purea (Henry 1928:11). Hawkesworth brought several of these misconstrued characters to public attention. Thus the figures 'Opano' (Banks, via Hawkesworth) and Omai (Mai) were effectively a twin birth in the British imagination, and became coupled in a variety of texts: diary entries, newspaper notices, poetic satires and pantomime. In John Scott's *Epistle from Oberea, Queen of Tahiti, to Joseph Banks* (1773), Purea is portrayed in 'wise debate' with her 'faithful senate', formulating policy regarding the arrival of British ships. By opting for gift exchange over war she is said to have 'sooth'd the terrors of Tupia's mind'. A footnote suggests that Tupaia himself represents a gift of friendship, and the greatest token of her intimacy with Banks: 'Tupia was Prime Minister to Oberea. She consented that he should come to England with Mr. Banks, and thereby gave the strongest proof of her attachment to that gentleman. Unfortunately this great politician and philosopher died on the voyage' ([Scott] 1774:7). The rest of the poem unfolds as a catalogue of sexual highlights of Banks's voyage, cribbed from Hawkesworth. Implicitly, the death of Tupaia thus represents the death of the possibility of authorization through friendship within the poem, and its substitution with the scandalous figure of an excessively libidinized Banks. The poem plays with the notion of the tongue as both locus of specialized knowledge and sexual play: the 'Editor' claims of his 'translation' that 'He is sensible that it is impossible in English, to convey any Idea of the Beauties of the Otaheite Tongue' ([Scott] 1774:3). In the feeble satirical response *An Epistle from Mr. Banks, voyager, monster-hunter, and amoroso, to Oberea, Queen of Otaheite* (1773), the 'Editor' in turn defends 'the English tongue' ([A. B. C. Esq.] 1773:3) as 'more noble' than the Tahitian. However, the Banks satires also offer a more subtle play on the notion of corruption of tongue, in the creation of a counter-Banks to the scientific explorer, denoted by the pseudo-Tahitianized name 'Opano'. Banks's Tahitian alliances and dalliances produce, for the audience of these poems, the character Opano, licentious buffoon, the bastardized child of Banks's eager friendships with Tahitians.

Once the *Endeavour* set sail from Tahiti, Tupaia's authority emerged as both immediate and comprehensive. He had, as Banks mentions in his journal entry, mapped numerous Oceanic islands on paper: although these do not appear in cartographic perspective, the voyage accounts acknowledge that he accurately nominated the number of days required to sail between different islands (Lewthwaite 1970:1–19). He was able to communicate with other Polynesians: to negotiate the consonantal shifts that distinguish dialects between different regions of Oceania. William Monkhouse, the *Endeavour*'s surgeon, recorded in his journal at Poverty Bay in New Zealand that 'Topia's name was now ecchoed incessantly – he talked with them – ' (Cook 1955:570). As interpreter he was sole negotiator of knowledge transfer between different island communities and the British. Moreover, he was clearly a conscious cultural comparativist, who registered similarities and subtle distinctions between Society Islands practices and those further afield. The authority that attended his navigational, linguistic and ethnographic authority communicated itself to the islanders the *Endeavour* visited, so that he was frequently believed to be directing the voyage. Greg Dening notes that 'among the Maori he was remembered for generations longer than Cook' (Dening 2004:174). Perhaps their disparate investments in this contest for perceived captaincy is at the heart of Cook's and Banks's commensurately resentful and appreciative perceptions of Tupaia.

Both Cook and Banks were equally aware of Tupaia's value to the expedition, but their sense of this value is linked to alternative perceptions of personal relationship. Cook consistently stresses Tupaia's role as functionary: the ways in which his capacities as translator, navigator and informant serve the greater purpose of the British expedition. Thus he announces Tupaia's decision to voyage in the *Endeavour* in very different terms from Banks:

For some time before we left this Island several of the natives were daily offering themselves to go away with us, and as it was thought that they must be of use to us in our future discoveries, we resolved to bring away one whose name is *Tupia*, a Cheif and a Priest: This man had been with us the most part of the time we had been upon the Island which gave us an oppertunity to know some thing of him: we found him to be a very intelligent person and to know more of the Geography of the Islands situated in these seas, their produce and the religion laws and customs of the inhabitants then any one we had met with and was the likeliest person to answer our purpose ... (Cook 1955:117)

Cook presents himself as the head of a selection committee, assessing numerous applicants for a travelling fellowship. He acknowledges Tupaia's superior qualifications, but these are in turn immediately linked to his own project of exploration. There is none of Banks's enthusiastic anticipation of reciprocity. As the account of the voyage progresses, Cook, while recording Tupaia's initiatives in directing the ship's course and parleying with local people, continues to stress his supplementary and functional role: 'Tupia always accompanies us in every excursion we make and proves of infinate service' (Cook 1955:240).

Cook's attitude is encapsulated in a phrase that recurs in his journal, 'by means of Tupia'. On 31 January, at Queen Charlotte's Sound, he records: 'I next, by means of Tupia, explained to the old man and several others that we were come to set up a mark upon the Island in order to shew to any ship that might put into this place that we had been here before' (Cook 1955:242). And upon leaving New Zealand, projecting further voyages of Pacific exploration, he refers to the advantage Tupaia would give the British, primarily in his ability to serve as an ambassador in promoting friendly relations:

> But, should it be thought proper to send a ship out upon this service while *Tupia* lieves and he to come out in her, in that case she would have a prodigious advantage over every ship that have been upon discoveries in those seas before; for by means of Tupia, supposeing he did not accompany you himself, you would always get people to direct you from Island to Island and would be sure of meeting with a friendly reseption and refreshments at every Island you came to... (Cook 1955:291)[11]

Tupaia's role for Cook, as it is defined by this recurrent phrase, seems to spell out the classic text and subtext of imperial encounter. In the first instance, he enables the appropriation of territory, while in the second, he is nominated as the friendly face of imperialism. But such an analysis only pertains if we, as critics, agree to share Cook's instrumentalist perspective on relationships between Oceanians and Europeans. In the process we allow ourselves to imagine that Tupaia was unaware either of European agendas or his own: something that Banks, by contrast, never suggests.

Banks always acknowledges Tupaia's initiative. There is no sense that orders are issued which Tupaia carries out effectively: rather, Banks records

---

[11] Williams takes the first section of this quotation as an indication that 'Cook left readers of his journal in no doubt about Tupaia's importance' (Williams 2003:43). However in my reading the second part of Cook's comment aligns it rhetorically with a tendency to figure Tupaia's role as instrumental rather than authoritative.

Tupaia's practices and strategies of cross-cultural interaction, which appear, in the absence of any alternative source of command, to be self-motivated. Thus, in New Zealand, interchange with the Maori is represented not as an act of translation via Tupaia as interpreter, but as a conversation between Maori and Tupaia that is later translated to include the British: 'they came tolerably near and answerd all the questions *Tupia askd them* very civily'; 'After they had done this for some time they came nearer and *Tupia talkd with them* from the stern; they came into better temper and answerd *his* questions'; 'Just then Tupia came upon deck, they ran *to him immediately, he assurd them* that their freind would not be killd' (Banks 1962: I, 410, 411, 437; my italics). Banks asks, not what the British achieve 'by means of Tupia', so much as what Tupaia seems to manage by way of the British. And this impression is augmented by his tendency to figure Tupaia as in every way capable: alone equipped to 'comfort' and 'make easy' (Banks 1962: I, 403–4) two Maori boys taken on board the *Endeavour*, able to cure himself of scurvy, or to find a way of roasting coconuts that 'made them lose intirely their acridity' (Banks 1962: II, 85). Banks boasts of his friend's religious authority: 'he however seemd to be much better vers'd in such legends than any of them, for whenever he began to preach as we calld it he was sure of a numerous audience who attended with most profound silence to his doctrines' (Banks 1962: II, 34), and proudly showcases his innate philosophic reasoning:

Tupia who I beleive guessd that they were coming to attack us immediately went upon the poop and talkd to them a good deal, telling them what if they provokd us we should do ... They answerd him in their usual cant 'come ashore only and we will kill you all'. Well, said Tupia, but while we are at sea you have no manner of Business with us, the Sea is our property as much as yours. Such reasoning from an Indian who had not had the smallest hint from any of us surprizd me much and the more as these were sentiments I never had before heard him give a hint about in his own case. (Banks 1962: I, 434–5; compare 447)

Tupaia's picture of Banks bartering with a Maori is emblematic of this respectful exchange between the two fellow travellers (see Figure 11).[12] The image memorializes Banks's and Tupiaia's co-expedition into foreign

[12] Harold B. Carter confirmed the identity of the European figure in the image as Banks with reference to a manuscript letter of Banks's of 12 December 1812, in which he writes 'Tupia the Indian who came with me from Otaheite Learnd to draw in a way not Quite unintelligible The genius for Caricature which all wild people Possess Led him to Caricature me and he drew me with a nail in my hand delivering it to an Indian who sold me a Lobster but with my other hand I had a firm fist on the Lobster determind not to Quit the nail till I had Livery and Seizin of the article purchasd.' As Carter concludes, 'if we make reasonable allowance for the approximation of Banks's *ex tempore* recall of the incident and the actual detail of the drawing ... it follows that the European figure is Mr Joseph Banks FRS' (Carter 1998:133–4).

Figure 11. A gift for friendship: Artist of the Chief Mourner [Tupaia], 'A Maori bartering a crayfish with an English naval officer'. Drawings illustrative of Captain Cook's First Voyage, 1768–1771. Pencil and watercolour, June–August 1769.

territory. Like the generic friend in a snapshot of a holiday fishing expedition, Banks appears alongside an authentically dressed local figure with hypertrophied crayfish. He allows himself to become the object of one Society Islander's take on exchange between Europeans and Oceanians. The gift Banks proffers, misremembered later as a nail, might be a handkerchief or neckerchief, consistent with his own European costume, but is more likely an item of value from Tupaia's own culture: white tapa cloth (Salmond 1991: note to image interleaved 208–9). The splayed fingers of the two participants in exchange mirror the shape of the crayfish, emphasizing the focus on the gift as the medium of cross-cultural outreach.

Everything I have pointed to as indicative of a friendly respect in Banks for Tupaia – his ethnographer's accreditation of Tupaia's learning, his recognition of his sensibility and reason, their sharing of women, his non-instrumentalism in comparison with Cook – can be seen as naive, or even retrograde: as glossing over the complicities between ostensibly appreciative discourses of ethnography, noble savagery or sexuality and the agendas of empire. In *Sexual Encounters: Pacific Texts, Modern*

Sexualities Lee Wallace also attends to the differences between Cook and Banks, but concludes that they represent corollaries rather than alternatives: 'agents of the same project of imperial expansion, they also map between them the outer limits of disciplinary and affective masculinity that such a project allows'. She finds Mary Louise Pratt's thesis that 'scientific and sentimental discourses came together in the expansionist project of the Enlightenment' to be:

> particularly applicable to the Pacific voyages of discovery, wherein the concern with the control of territory and colonization of indigenous populations is frequently muted or disguised beneath the production of incremental knowledges, navigational and botanical, that seemingly hold imperial interest at arm's length.

Wallace characterizes Banks as 'the palpitating male type' against 'the coolly distant Cook', concluding that they embody 'the tough and soft cops necessary for a successful expedition' (Wallace 2003:9, 11, 12).[13]

Wallace focuses primarily on representations of Cook and Banks by recent scholars and biographers, rather than on their journals: she looks at where history has taken these figures, in order to gauge their complicity with historical outcomes. But if we focus only on knowledge produced in hindsight, we obscure modes of interaction that produced less concrete or comprehensive results. Like Cook, we see Tupaia only in terms of his functionality for the voyage. We rule out the very possibility of friendship between Indigenous and European subjects, and its fortuitous, fine-grained hierarchies and equalities. Intimacy, particularly intimacy with an Oceanian who died before he could fulfil all the 'means' envisaged for him, becomes irrelevant to our narrative. But Banks seems nonetheless to have forged a friendship with Tupaia: one whose particular lineaments are perhaps better described by the concept of *taio* than by European versions of 'affective masculinity' and 'sentimental immersion' (Wallace 2003:11).

Indeed Banks, by the time he leaves Tahiti, appears to have elided a European notion of sensibility with the version of particular friendship enshrined in the concept of *taio*. Like Bougainville redeeming Ahutoru from the scorn of the savants, and as we shall see again in Keate's more literary portrait of Lebuu, Banks emblematizes signs of feeling and

---

[13] The anachronism of Wallace's last metaphor is, I think, telling. While it is right that scholarship recognizes the ways in which modern disciplinary institutions are nested in seemingly historically detached enterprises, issues of policing applied to a later phase of colonial settlement and their value as analogies for Enlightenment investigation is doubtful.

friendship in Tupaia. He attributes these in turn to the structures of bond friendship. Immediately after Tupaia's announcement of his decision to sail, Banks writes that 'he took [ashore] with him a miniature picture of mine to shew his freinds and several little things to give them as parting presents' (Banks 1962: I, 313). Here the gifting of miniatures, which was a significant form of affective exchange in Europe, lends itself to the ritual of Tahitian gift exchange.[14] Banks also makes a point of distinguishing the parting tears of the *taio* from those of the unparticularized crowd:

Some of them at least I realy beleive personaly sorry for our departure ... We had Oborea, Otheothea, Tayoa, Nuna, Tuanna Matte, Potattou, Polotheara &c. on board when the anchor was weighd; they took their leaves tenderly enough, not without plenty of tears tho intirely without that clamourous weeping made use of by the other Indians, several boats of whoom were about the ship shouting out their lamentations, as vyeing with each other not who should cry most but who should cry loudest – a custom we had often condemnd in conversation with our particular freinds as savouring more of affected than real greif. (Banks 1962: I, 313)

The named friends, each of whom has made a formal bond with a particular crew member, are marked by a restraint that registers, in terms we have observed in previous chapters, as unfeigned. Yet this is also, potentially, role playing: a performance of affect learned 'in conversation' with Europeans. It is the *taio* relationship that resolves this ambivalence, allowing cultural mimicry to register primarily as respectful exchange. And Tupaia's mode of departure confirms the completeness of this achieved reciprocity: 'Tupia who after all his struggles stood firm at last in his resolution of accompanying us parted with a few heartfelt tears, so I judge them to have been by the Efforts I saw him make use of to hide them' (Banks 1962: I, 313–14). Tupaia farewells not the Europeans but his homeland, with a perfect blend of fortitude and feeling, the epitome of Adam Smith's 'reserved, ... silent and majestic sorrow' (A. Smith 2002:29). Once again he seems to offer Banks a masculine role model: one that Banks may have borne in mind not long after this, when he lost his friend at Batavia. Certainly, restrained grief recurs in Banks's account of Tupaia's death, through which the muted refrain 'Poor Tupia' echoes with a similar regularity to Cook's instrumentalist 'by means of Tupia'.

[14] Eger 2009 offers a subtle discussion of an eighteenth-century 'friendship box' comprised of four miniature portraits.

Mai in London: A Proper Sample

too great a novelty to be soon forsaken . . .

– John McCluer

It wasn't until July 1774, when the *Adventure* returned from playing its part in Cook's second circumnavigation, that Banks got his proxy 'Tahitian' friend: Mai. Like Tupaia, Mai was a Raiatean refugee who had been living in Tahiti since the early 1760s. Unlike Tupaia he made it to Britain, and unlike Ahutoru and Lebuu he subsequently returned to Tahiti. Anne Salmond's assessment of the relationship between Banks and Mai foregrounds the latter's role as replacement exotic: 'Mai's arrival in London was reported by the British press, who delighted in this exotic visitor. For Banks, who had hoped to bring Tupaia to Britain, his advent was a godsend. He carried Mai off and lodged him in his townhouse' (Salmond 2003:296). Mai figures here as both substitute and trophy, offered strategic hospitality. But the course of Banks's friendship with Mai might equally be said, like many ostensible answers to prayer, to illustrate the limits of the original wish. If Mai represented the Oceanian as specimen (Rüdiger Joppien calls him 'a curiosity, a visually striking personality, and a living experiment' (Joppien 1979:82)), then, as Banks's comments on keeping Tupaia as curiosity had presciently satirized, the corollary of such a public perception was both to find him to be a poor one and to de-credentialize those who collected him.

Cook's comments on Mai exemplify this:

I at first rather wondered that Captain Furneaux would encumber himself with this man, who, in my opinion, was not a proper sample of the inhabitants of these happy islands, not having any advantage of birth, or acquired rank; not being eminent in shape, figure or complexion. For their people of the first rank are much fairer, and usually better behaved, and more intelligent than the middling class of people, among whom Omai is to be ranked. (Cook 1777:169–70; quoted in McCormick 1977:182)

Mai, as improper sample rather than acknowledged authority, is regarded as unfit to represent Tahiti. Cook's comments make clear the ways in which issues of rank and status intertwined with perceptions of intelligence. Bougainville's defence of Ahutoru's intellect had been formulated to combat the same set of instinctive hierarchies:

The inhabitants of Taiti consist of two races of men, very different from each other, but speaking the same language, having the same customs, and seemingly mixing without distinction. The first, which is the most numerous one, produces men of the greatest size; it is very common to see them measure six (Paris) feet and upwards in height. I never saw men better

Figure 12. Francesco Bartolozzi, after Nathaniel Dance, 'Omai,
a native of Ulaietea, brought into England in the year 1774
by Tobias Furneaux', 1774.

made, and whose limbs were more proportionate: in order to paint a
Hercules or a Mars, one could no where find such beautiful models.
Nothing distinguishes their features from those of Europeans: and if they
were cloathed; if they lived less in the open air, and were less exposed to the
sun at noon, they would be as white as ourselves: their hair in general is
black. The second race are of a middle size, have frizzled hair as hard as
bristles, and both in colour and features they differ but little from mulattoes.
The Taiti man who embarked with us, is of this second race, though his

father is chief of a district: but he possesses in understanding what he wants in beauty. (Bougainville 1967: 249)[15]

Like Mai, Ahutoru, as a perceived member of the 'second race' in Tahiti, raises the kinds of European anxieties that I have established, as to whether appropriate friends have been identified. Added to this, once the 'curious' Oceanian is taken to the metropole, is the concern that these second-rate ('second race') products may be veritable cultural imposters, who have taken advantage of friendly attachment to misrepresent themselves within society. Oceanic hierarchies map too easily onto British class politics. Surely Society Island visitors cannot be the genuine article if they are not high-ranking? The inherent structure of this supposition persists in recuperative projects such as the 'Between Worlds' exhibition in 2007 at London's National Portrait Gallery. Discussing Joshua Reynolds's portrait of Mai in Oriental-styled white tapa cloth (compare Figure 13), Jocelyn Hackforth-Jones writes that 'in Tahiti, white tapa was reserved for those of highest or chiefly status, ari'i. Thus Mai may have been using the process of sitting for this portrait as part of a strategy to (mis)represent himself as belonging to a higher class' (Hackforth-Jones 2007:49). Such analysis leaves the premise of status anxiety – which seems primarily to reflect eighteenth-century English concerns – intact. The downward momentum of Mai's Oceanic descent is simply countered by the upward thrust of his metropolitan aspirations. Like folds of tapa, Tahitian hierarchies and British class tiers enclose Mai in what is consistently understood to be a reciprocal project of self-advancement.

The notion of a hierarchy, ostensibly intellectual but implicitly in rank, between Banks's two friends, is played out in relation to the politics of gift exchange. In the preface to his *A Voyage Round the World*, George Forster figured Mai as the sensual child to Tupaia's self-regulating adult:

He was not able to form a general comprehensive view of our whole civilized system, and to abstract from thence what appeared most strikingly useful and applicable to the improvement of his country. His senses were charmed by beauty, symmetry, harmony, and magnificence; they called aloud for gratification, and he was accustomed to obey their voice. The continued round of enjoyments left him no time to think of his future life; and being destitute of the genius of Tupaïa, whose superior abilities would have enabled him to form a plan for his own conduct, his understanding remained unimproved. (G. Forster 2000:11)

---

[15] I have discussed the slippage between issues of race and social hierarchy in this passage in V. Smith 2004.

Figure 13. Johann Jacobe, 'Omai, a native of the
island of Utietea, painted by Sir Joshua Reynolds,
engraved by John Jacobi', 1 Sept. 1780.

Mai, the unrepentant sensualist without a vision of the hereafter, has
learned nothing from the worldly evangelism of Britons whose only gifts
have been items of exchange rather than use-value:

He carried with him an infinite variety of dresses, ornaments, and other trifles,
which are daily invented in order to supply our artificial wants. His judgment was
in its infant state, and therefore, like a child, he coveted almost every thing he
saw, and particularly that which had amused him by some unexpected effect. To
gratify his childish inclinations, as it should seem, rather than from any other
motive, he was indulged with a portable organ, an electrical machine, a coat of
mail, and a suit of armour. Perhaps my readers expect to be told of his taking on

board some articles of real use to his country; I expected it likewise, but was disappointed. (G. Forster 2000:11–12)

Weighed down with useless trinkets, Mai is ill-equipped for adulthood or the afterlife: the two futures for which an encounter with civilization should precisely have prepared the child heathen. And this is in turn figured as a failure of friendship: 'It can hardly be supposed that he never formed a wish to obtain some knowledge of our agriculture, arts, and manufactures; but no friendly Mentor ever attempted to cherish and gratify this wish, much less to improve his moral character, to teach him our exalted ideas of virtue, and the sublime principles of revealed religion' (G. Forster 2000:11). The bad-faith friendship Forster describes here in turn bears a striking resemblance to those Oceanic friendships whose emphasis on what appeared to be self-perpetuating exchanges both perplexed and engaged Europeans. Such exchanges were incomprehensible in terms of use-value, wresting the weary sense of control from European dispersal of 'trinkets' and mirroring it back as excrement on a stick: that most improper of samples. And just as sailors going mad for trinkets in Tonga are repudiated by Cook and Johann Reinhold Forster as unflattering reflections of European scientific curiosity (see Chapter 2), so Mai, apparently unable to distinguish between civilized knowledge and metropolitan trinketry, threatens to collapse cultural superiority into legerdemain.

Harriet Guest has perceptively argued that the Oceanic traveller reflects British imperial masculinity back to metropolitan society. For Guest 'Mai's possessions ... , in their curious assortment of the functional or useful and the frivolous or ornamental, indicate the ambivalence with which English metropolitan society conceived of its own modernity' (Guest 2007:158). Guest further notes that once he returned to the Society Islands, it was his European goods that appear to have retained their prestige, while that of their owner was not commensurately accorded (Guest 2007:160). But Mai returning with his sample bag of civilized trinkets – neither clearly metonyms of advanced society nor false copies – and himself neither clearly proper sample nor corrupted natural man, is equally a reflection of proto-ethnographers such as Banks and George Forster, and the figures they may have cut while pursuing curiosity on their own terms in Tahiti. And one of the ways this reciprocity is expressed is through the default friendship between Mai and Banks. Between the death of Tupaia and the forging of his fortuitous allegiance with Mai, Banks had achieved a two-sided reputation. As Gillian Russell has noted, 'In the early 1770s Banks was variously the libertine dilettante motivated by licentious curiosity, the man of science and agent of empire, and the macaroni man of fashion' (Russell 2004:53).

After his return from the Pacific he was accorded much of the credit for the *Endeavour* voyage, and in the process validated by fellow scientists and academic institutions (Salmond 2003:167–8). On the other hand, his popular legend grew as much from reports of his relationships with women as with botany.[16] The imbrication of Banks's scientific reputation with sexual notoriety is illustrative of a phenomenon noticed by Barbara Benedict, whereby 'Curious spectators become simultaneously subjects and objects of inquiry' (Benedict 2001:9). A similar phenomenon was manifest in relation to Mai: his metropolitan explorations were reported in double entendre, a mode that we registered earlier in Johann Forster's recasting of Ahutoru's opera-going as peep show.

In this respect Banks and Mai seem to have become interchangeable. They form, precisely, a likely friendship: they are paired in the public imagination by perceived resemblance. I mentioned earlier the cycle of satires that pursued Banks after the publication of Hawkesworth's *Voyages* exposed his Tahitian encounters to public ridicule. In poems penned after the arrival of Mai in Britain, Mai replaces Tupaia as Banks's Oceanic reflection. These satires tease out the meaning of the association between two men understood to be united by a dubious similarity rather than enduring contact. Indeed, the capacity to refigure the affinities that we might imagine to be grounds of friendship as instead points of sharp comparison is the special provenance of satire. In *An heroic epistle, from Omiah to the Queen of Otaheite* (1775), London is depicted as a city:

> Where Macaronies, *Sçavoir vivres* rife,
> And varied whims of puppyhood surprise:
> Whose only care is in ambiguous dress
> To veil their sex, that wiser folks may guess … ([Omiah] 1775:2)

Banks, famously caricatured in 1772 as both the 'fly catching' and 'botanic' macaroni (see Figures 14 and 15), and depicted in variously 'ambiguous' states of cross-cultural dress and undress during his time in Tahiti, is a shadow presence in the epistle.[17] Mai as commentator stands aloof from a declining metropolitan civilization, criticizing its arts and sciences, including the transactions of the Royal Society, into which Banks had been inducted after the *Endeavour* voyage.[18] Yet the

---

[16] The conflation of the two terms in satirical poetry has been the subject of much critical discussion. See in particular, Bewell 1996, Browne 1996 and Stern 1993.

[17] For discussion of 'The Fly-Catching Macaroni', see Rauser 2004:101–17 and Coleman 2006.

[18] A more extreme, later example of this poetics of disparagement as manifest in relation to Banks's Royal Society career is *Sir Joseph Banks and the Emperor of Morocco* ([Wolcot], 1789).

Figure 14. Whipcord, 'The fly catching Macaroni', 12 July 1772.

interdependence of the two figures remains implicit in such poems. Banks and Mai are embodiments of the new state of reciprocity that exists between Britain and Oceania. Their union is the sociable manifestation of what is otherwise perceived to be a primarily sexual exchange between the two cultures that is seen to infect both ways, spreading disease to the islands, and offering a whole new vocabulary of concupiscence to metropolitan society. In William Preston's *Seventeen hundred and seventy-seven* (1777), fashionable London women are depicted as

Figure 15. 'The botanic Macaroni', 14 Nov. 1772.

enflamed by reports of Tahitian sexual freedom. Classical traditions of
female love and maternity have been deposed:

> Some statue thus, the garden's ancient boast,
> Of naked Venus, smirking at the frost,
> Or bounteous Ceres, with her wheaten crown,
> Defac'd by truants, or by time cast down;
> Not exil'd wholly from the pleasure ground,
> (Tho' noseless now, and somewhat batter'd found)
> O'er stable-gate, or kennel-door presides,
> Or bashful guest to squalid temple guides. (Preston 1777:12)

The noseless Venus signals not just the English garden turned brothel, but the Tahitian Eden, where women have become disfigured by sexual contact. The poem concludes with a call for sexual exchange (a concept rendered synonymous, via the popular image of Banks, with scientific exchange) between London and Tahiti:

> In pleasure's sources, what a gainful trade!
> Of mutual science, what exchanges made! (Preston 1777:25)

Within this compromised context of exchange, Mai and Banks are depicted as both passive and active: swapping roles of overweening carnality and curious effeminacy; their co-implicated authority undermined even as it is acknowledged. Preston's image of the noseless, battered Venus, symptomatic of the mutually infective transaction between metropolitan salons and Tahitian beaches, takes us back to Ahutoru, diagnosing the traces of venereal infection in Bougainville's picture of the reclining Venus. Like Bougainville, Banks struggled to authorize himself in relation to popular understandings of his Tahitian encounters, which appeared to be given substance by his relationships with Oceanic friends.

Probably the most influential metropolitan representation of Mai, however, emerged over a decade after his visit to London, with Philippe Jacques de Loutherbourg and John O'Keeffe's feted pantomime *OMAI: Or, A Trip Round the World*, first performed in 1785. Like the Banks satires, the pantomime has become the focus of much astute critical analysis in recent years. Greg Dening, Iain McCalman and Kathleen Wilson have drawn attention to the ways in which *Omai* brought new ethnographic information to the metropolitan stage (Dening 2001; McCalman 2001; K. Wilson 2003:63–70), while Christa Knellwolf, Daniel O'Quinn, Vanessa Agnew and Matthew Goldie have looked at the politics of *Omai*'s theatre (Knellwolf 2001; O'Quinn 2005:74–114; Agnew 2008:130–5; Goldie 2009:109–20). Nothing, however, has been said about the significance of Banks and Mai's friendship for this cultural artifact. The pantomime was originally conceived following a suggestion of the celebrated actor David Garrick that the pantomime *Arlequin Sauvage* be revived with Mai as hero. As Christa Knellwolf explains, the original *Arlequin Sauvage* had figured an Indigenous Harlequin who satirizes 'the follies and depraved customs of a civilized nation'. However, *Omai* is evacuated of satire, portraying instead 'an idealised encounter between the British Empire and the Tahitians', with Mai's visit to London motivated by his desire to woo Londina (daughter of Britannia) (Knellwolf 2001:17). Any satiric remnant seems to have been reserved for the character of Don Struttolando, Mai's rival for Londina. Agnew follows Dening in interpreting the Spanish Don

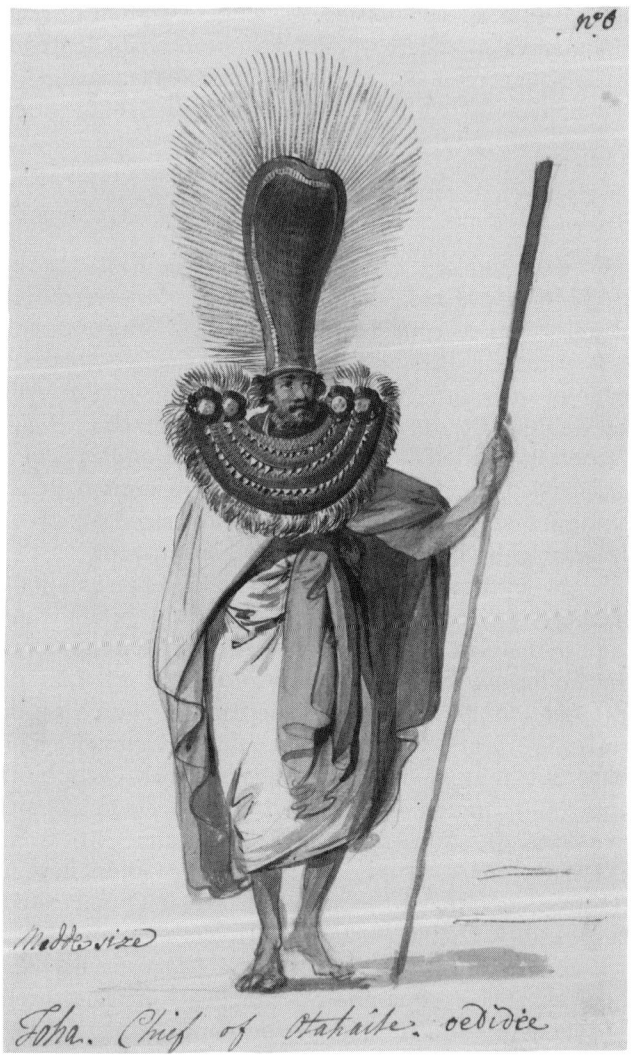

Figure 16.   Philippe Jacques de Loutherbourg, 'Toha, Chief of Otahaite, Oedidee', costume design for the pantomime *Omai*, 1785.

Struttolando as a commentary on Spanish/English rivalries in Tahiti, but equally compelling is O'Quinn's suggestion that the Don is an *amoroso* of the kind evoked in the satirical poem *An Epistle from Mr. Banks, voyager, monster-hunter, and amoroso, to Oberea, Queen of Otaheite*

Figure 17. Philippe Jacques de Loutherbourg, 'Toha', costume design
for the pantomime *Omai*, 1785.

([A. B. C. Esq.] 1773).[19] O'Quinn argues that, whereas Don Struttolando is 'an idealized figure for Banks', his servant, the Clown, 'carries

[19] O'Quinn's characterization of Don Struttolando as 'an Italian *amoroso*' however seems a
wilful misreading: he is referred to in a song which O'Quinn himself quotes as 'Spanish
Struttolando' (O'Quinn 2005:105, 110).

Figure 18. Philippe Jacques de Loutherbourg, 'Chief mourner
Otahaite', costume design for the pantomime *Omai*, 1785.

the negative qualities associated with his supposed libertinism'
(O'Quinn 2005:109).

I am going to cite O'Quinn's reading of the descriptions of the pantomime at some length, since it illustrates both the subtle insights offered
by attention to the imbrication of imperial power with Enlightenment

knowledge and the modes of relation that such a critical perspective neglects. As O'Quinn points out, Omai, Londina and Struttolando are each shadowed by their servants Harlequin, Columbine and the Clown. He suggests that

The potential union of Londina with Omai or Struttolando involves the threat of transculturation or interracial sexual practice. This internal circuit, therefore, carries with it the combined signification of the sexual and racial degeneration of the aristocracy. However, the sexual and racial signs associated with the internal triangle have been separated from Omai, Londina, and Struttolando and projected onto their servants. (O'Quinn 2005:105)

The difference between Omai's blacked Harlequin and Struttolando's libertine, foppish Clown is one of a number of techniques of 'hygienic' containment by which, O'Quinn argues, the cultural mixing pot, produced in the pantomime, and much commented upon by other scholars, is re-hierarchized. As respective sidekicks, Harlequin spells out Omai's racialized and the Clown Struttolando's simply continental, libertine Otherness. O'Quinn suggests that this delegation would have been ultimately soothing to an audience potentially profoundly disturbed at the layered prospect of miscegenation raised by Omai's union with Londina.

What light might the recognition of a popularly accepted friendship between Mai and Banks cast on the conception and reception of the pantomime? In Chapter 2 I drew on Eve Sedgwick's analysis of the intense bonds of erotic rivalry to think about how the *taio* bond, with its understood injunction to share partners, enabled a European pursuit of libertinism in the Society Islands under the aegis of friendship. In Omai and Struttolando we may again find an erotic rivalry that attests more persistently to affinity than hygienic compartmentalization. Indeed, imperial rivalry seems more effectively sublimated into the representation of competition between Omai and Oediddee (Hitihiti: see Figure 16), which tends to be neglected in critical analyses of the pantomime. Where Omai is figured as Otoo's (Tu's) favourite, Oberea (Purea) supports Oediddee. Before Omai can woo Londina he must be reconciled with his rival:

> Ere, lov'd youth, you quit your native shore,
> Your rival Oediddee shall restore
> The Royal Ensigns, Britain to convince
> That in Omai she receives a Prince. (O'Keeffe 1785:5)

As we have seen, the battle to 'convince' metropolitan Europeans of their status was a fraught one for Oceanic travellers, with implications for the British and French travellers who sought to befriend them. Here, friendship resolves such issues before Omai leaves Tahitian shores, allowing his courtship of Londina to proceed unburdened by questions of status. Yet the friend remains incorporated into a projected erotic triangle: as Oediddee sings, 'Double joys to him and me, / Ever such let friendship be' (O'Keeffe 1785:6).

Like Omai and Oediddee, Omai and Struttolando are as similar as they are rivalrous. But perhaps they are linked in another way to which the pantomime makes reference. Don Struttolando is clearly an emblematic performer: not just a vain man – a strutter – but one who struts the boards. And as such he may again reference that consummate cross-cultural performer, Joseph Banks. Banks's performance as 'smutted' strutter alongside the Tahitian Chief Mourner had long been familiar to the British public from Hawkesworth (Hawkesworth 1773: II, 146–7).[20] In the pantomime, Otoo solicits the blessing of the high priest (Towha) (see Figure 17) on Omai's journey. At this stage Towha appears in the guise of the Chief Mourner. Loutherburg's design for the Chief Mourner's costume (see Figure 18) is notable for its verisimilitude: the pantomime brings to life a figure that Banks, we recall, repeatedly found beyond his powers of description. Omai thus sails to England under the protection of the Chief Mourner/god, accompanied by his own smutted assistant, Harlequin, to outbid his rival the libertine Don Struttolando, secure the hand of Londina and the applause of London. The complexities with which allusions to Banks and Mai intersect throughout the pantomime, in alternatively authorizing and de-authorizing configurations, confound attempts to reduce the British perception of their relationship, over ten years after they befriended each other in London, to any straightforward articulation of imperial relations.

Lebuu: The Speaking Heart

They are assailable under the smile of dissembled friendship . . .
– George Keate

Banks, once again like Bougainville, was forced to defend himself against charges of false friendship to his Oceanic visitor. Lord Sandwich reprimanded him for neglecting Mai during his time in London: 'I should think we were highly blameable if we did not make use of all the sagacity and knowledge of the world which our experience has given us, to do every thing we can to prove ourselves his real friends' (quoted in Salmond 2003:298), while George Forster, as we saw, felt Mai had been poorly served in the selection of gifts with which he returned to the Society Islands. Such responses testify to a growing sense of what was

---

[20] Hawkesworth uses the terms 'blacked' and 'smeared' rather than Banks's 'smutted' in his account of the mourning ceremony.

owed to the foreign visitor, and of the capacity of such visitors to expose the fault lines in metropolitan claims to friendship. This efflorescence of metropolitan 'friendship conscience' is the corollary of those European concerns we have been tracing with determining the genuineness of emotion in Oceanians. The most comprehensive manifestation of the phenomenon is to be found in accounts of Lebuu.

On 10 August 1783, the British East India packet *Antelope* was wrecked on a reef near the uninhabited island of Ulong in Palau. The Captain Henry Wilson and crew spent thirteen weeks on the island building a boat in which they were eventually able to make their way to Canton. The island upon which they found themselves was under the jurisdiction of Ibedul of Koror, with whom the English formed a strategic allegiance. Ibedul sent his son Lebuu to England with Wilson, and he spent five months in London, based in Rotherhithe at the captain's home, but died of smallpox in December 1784. During his time in London he made the acquaintance of George Keate, a literary figure who subsequently published *An Account of the Pelew Islands*, memorializing both the contact with the people of Koror and the life of Lebuu.[21] Keate's generically sentimental account of the reciprocal encounters of the English with the Palauans and Lebuu with London life offers a revision of the sceptical or satirical modes of representing friendship between the European man of science and the Oceanian traveller. This is achieved by the elevation of sympathetic intuition over scientific observation as the true mode of intercultural understanding. Friendship, in Keate's *Account*, becomes the new science.

Keate concludes the longer section of his *Account*, set on the beaches of Palau, with a familiar ethnographic turn. With the British crew safely back in Macao and the exigencies of the narrative relaxed, he begins an 'account of the Government, Customs, Manners, and Arts, of the Natives of Pelew, as far as I have been able to collect them, from the different reports of the Captain, and such of his officers who have favoured me with their communications' (Keate 2002:224). He prefaces this section of his work with this disclaimer:

The reader will bear in mind that the ANTELOPE was not a ship particularly sent out to explore undiscovered regions, or prepared to investigate the manners of mankind; it had not on board philosophers, botanists, draughtsmen, or gentlemen experienced in such scientific pursuits as might enable them to examine with judgment objects which presented themselves, or trace nature through all her labyrinths. – Distress threw them on these islands, and when there, every thought was solely occupied on the means of getting away . . . (Keate 2002:225)

---

[21] For George Keate's biographical and literary background, see Dapp 1939.

As Keate recapitulates here, the voyage of the *Antelope* had not been conceived as part of any enlightened project of knowledge: the crew's sojourn in Palau was a detour, motivated by extreme necessity. But something nonetheless operated to give this account a singular ethnographic authority. Keate continues:

All the varied courtesies offered to the English by the natives, from whom a very different line of conduct had been apprehended, operated forcibly on their minds; and their misfortune happening at a moment when their assistance was very material for Abba Thulle's service against his enemies, this circumstance soon formed a connection, and produced an unreserved intercourse and steady friendship between the natives and our countrymen, which, during the thirteen weeks they remained there, afforded them opportunity of observing the manners and dispositions of the inhabitants, and thereby to form some notion of their government and customs. (Keate 2002:225–7)

Something other than familiar appeals to primacy or eyewitness operates to authorize the ensuing ethnographic excursus. As Keate marshals together those facts that might be said to constitute the English crew's communal cultural knowledge of Palau, he invokes the authority, not of science, but of friendship. His ethnography may be piecemeal rather than comprehensive, assembled experientially rather than experimentally, but it has its own kind of uncontestable inclusivity, based upon its foundation in 'unreserved intercourse'. This sounds like a version of free exchange, but of course there are no free gifts: as Keate makes clear, the connection to which 'steady friendship' testifies is a reciprocal contract. Free communication is achieved in return for 'very material . . . service' given in battle by the crew members of the *Antelope* to Ibedul, which in turn reciprocates those 'varied courtesies' shown by the people of Koror to the distressed crew. Yet, typically, this passage does not wish to dwell on instrumentality. Instead, Keate emphasizes the special knowledge that friendship has brought the English. Intimacy is a valid substitute for expertise, and a gift for friendship is presented as equal if not superior to a training in science, in promoting insight into the manners and customs of a foreign society.

By situating his ethnographic commentary within a context of friendly relations, Keate challenges the distinction between sentimental and scientific knowledge of foreign societies. His sentimental narrative of unfolding relations with Palau desires an Oceanic subject recognizable at heart as the same. However, his account of Palau also requires those traces of difference that constitute the three ethnographic chapters of the *Account*. If Keate predicates his analysis of cultural difference on the recognition of similarity that is testified in friendship, equally, his recognition of similarity is predicated on the acknowledgement of a difference to be displaced by intimacy. The dynamics of a conflicted attempt at authorization are made explicit in Keate's recurrent disquisitions on the co-implication of curiosity and friendship. He repeatedly asserts that curiosity and hospitality are incompatible in Palauan eyes. The hesitancy of the Palauans to disturb their stranded guests is a sign of their natural delicacy. Keate claims that 'At all times they seemed so cautious of intruding, that on many occasions they sacrificed their natural curiosity to that respect, which natural good manners appeared to them to exact' (Keate 2002:250). Equally, the English hesitate to overwhelm the Palauans with curious questions: 'they would probably have entertained doubts of our people, had the English surrounded them to gratify curiosity, they might, from their apprehensions, have hastily departed' (Keate 2002:77). And the shared understanding that curiosity is an impediment to friendship extends to scientific, as well as idle, curiosity. Attending the funeral of Ibedul's nephew, the surgeon of the *Antelope* rejects the temptations of ethnographic observation in favour of sentimental sympathy. Keate writes,

Mr. Sharp and his companion, observing [a woman] go towards the young man's grave, their curiosity would have induced them to follow her, in order to have observed the conclusion of this ceremony; but peculiarly circumstanced as the distressed father then was, they felt an unwillingness to trespass on his feelings, by testifying any desire after further information. (Keate 2002:155)

While once again the sympathy lies with masculine grief, whose non-demonstrativeness is compensated with sympathetic recognition, we might nonetheless contrast this response with both William Bligh's dismissal of feeling in the grieving mother and Banks's proto-ethnographic forays into Tahitian mourning rituals discussed in Chapter 4. The surgeon, effectively the 'man of science' among the ship's crew, elects to read the funeral scene in terms of what is perceived to be its common or universal aspect – the emotion of distress – rather than in its cultural particularity.

Keate, then, performs a recurrent rhetorical manoeuvre, which eschews curiosity in favour of friendship and ethnographic observation in favour of sympathy. Commentators have tended to regard this as the product of his position as man of letters rather than man of science (Thomas 2002:28). It follows that Keate is not required, in the manner of Banks, to depict affective relationships as a form of specimen collection in order to authorize his *Account*. But rather than setting up sensibility against science, Keate argues that these discourses are mutually reinforcing. The physician is right to refuse participation in the mourning scene, but Keate is nonetheless able later to include a discussion of funerary practices, based on the observations of another crew member at the funeral of a young man less intimately connected with the *Antelope*. The cultural sensitivity of the English is calibrated to a perception of levels of affective engagement in their encounters. And Keate suggests that this attunement to the emotions of subjects perceived as friends in turn produces a fuller account of Palauan lifeways than brutal investigation: one free, furthermore, from those recurrent suspicions that sentiment is being dissimulated. For Keate, friendship has its own hermeneutic and constitutes an ultimately more effective key to another culture than distanciated observation.

Repeatedly Keate invites the reader to participate in adjudicating the claims of curiosity and friendship by carefully tallying the debts of reciprocal obligation. Key scenes revolve around misunderstandings that are resolved by peeling back perceived difference to register sympathetic similarity. When Captain Wilson experiences an unexpected cooling of relations with Ibedul, 'far unlike, indeed, that undisguised openness which marked the interview of the preceding day', Keate invites the reader to participate in the captain's experience of rejection:

And I doubt not but by this time the reader will have shared a portion of that concern, for his unfortunate countrymen, which was awakened in their bosoms by this unexpected alteration in the behaviour of the natives. What will he think of the hearts of these yet unknown inhabitants of Pelew? – He will have already loaded them with reproach, and judged, too hardly judged them to be an inconsistent, faithless people, on whom no reliance could be placed, whom no profession could bind. – His imagination may have started a multitude of conjectures, yet at last will probably suppose any thing sooner than the real cause which spread this visible dejection over their true character.

Keate then asks his readers to shift their focus of identification from 'his unfortunate countrymen' to the Pelauans. This is in turn effected by eschewing perceptions of difference in favour of a notion of universal sympathy. Explanation will be found, not in cultural particularity – by uncovering some local peculiarity of custom or practice that accounts for the sudden illegibility of affect – but in the universally intelligible, if sentimentally conflicted, operations of the human heart. Keate continues,

Never perhaps was exhibited a nobler struggle of native delicacy; their hearts burnt within them to ask a favour, which the generosity of their feelings would not allow them to mention ... Thus was harmony restored between our people and the natives; interrupted only for a few hours, from no other cause than that extreme delicacy of sentiment which no one would have expected to have found in regions so disjoined from the rest of the world. (Keate 2002:103–4)

The reader is privy here to an 'exhibition' of the 'native' as similar rather than different. Cultural particularity is a necessary preliminary, but appears easily sloughed off: what remains to be assessed is the quality of the Palauan heart. This desire to expose the human heart within the superficially different body can be read as a kind of violence, but it too is reciprocal. The native is equally able to eviscerate the metropolitan reader. Noting the crew members' persisting reserve even on the point of departure, Ibedul poignantly asks, '*can you not confide in me at the last?*' Keate in turn inquires:

When the foregoing pages are attentively considered, the hospitality with which our people had been treated, both by Abba Thulle and the natives, from the first friendly interview to the present moment . . . – is there a reader who, recalling all these circumstances, can wonder they affected the sensibility of Abba Thulle? – Or rather, is there a reader who will not be ready with myself to ask, Under what sun was ever tempered the steel that could cut such a passage to the heart as this just reproach of the King's – Every individual . . . felt how much his mind had injured the virtues of this excellent man. (Keate 2002:203–4)

The violence of sentimental recognition becomes explicit here, impacting on all the subjects of Keate's *Account*. The 'just reproach' of the king slips into the self-reproach of the crew, and the reader is identified with both, as transcendent sympathizer.

Scenes like this one readily offer themselves to sceptical interpretation. They seem exemplary of an attempt to convert relations of power to relations of sympathy, which is in turn exposed through the irrepressible lexicon of violence. Jonathan Lamb is critical of the ways in which post-colonial criticism has simply inverted claims of sympathy, exposing kindness as the flip side of cruelty (Lamb 2001:253). Instead he proposes a slippery sympathy: 'Wearing the same Janus face as self-interest, . . . sympathy is willing to gesture at the good of others while being good for itself, and it offers no easy way of proving the truth of its claims.' This can leave sympathy at times disconcerted by the reflection of the other: 'sympathy finds in the blurred divisions between noble and ignoble savagery a mirror that reflects and complicates its own unsteady position between values associated with self-preservation and those attached to sociability' (Lamb 2001:255). Lamb joins a number of recent scholars of the *Account of the Pelew Islands* in seeking the local agendas that motivated Palauan friendship. Nicholas Thomas, for instance, argues that Keate's

presentation of friendly equality between the British and the people of Koror is likely to have been quite inconsistent with the Palauan view. All evidence suggests that Ibedul and his people regarded Wilson and his crew as Ibedul's subordinates; the chief protected them and feasted them, but the English in turn were required to surrender their valuables and provide their armed service. (Lamb, Smith and Thomas 2000:113)[22]

Such approaches testify to a particular idea of what critical hindsight can achieve. In suggesting motivations for Palauan sympathy, Lamb shifts the violence of Ibedul's eviscerating speech out of the realm of metaphor and into a differently veiled language of threat, claiming that 'Abba Thulle's cutting speech, if thoroughly examined, is not a plea made by a weaker party to a stronger, or by a more innocent to a more knowing. It opens a passage to the heart because of the threat strongly implicit in it, which he soon makes explicit' (Lamb 2001:274). He takes the characteristic observation that the Palauans recruited the English and their weapons for their own political purposes one step further, pointing out that the English were, by virtue of their distressed circumstances, at the mercy of the Palauans, and that the Palauans knew of and exploited this advantage. His approach unites critical endeavour with an ethics of reparation. The more comprehensive the exegesis ('if thoroughly examined'), the more justice is done to the reconstituted native subject. The reinvigoration of hidden Indigenous agendas thus simultaneously accords a new level of agency to Palauan and critic. In choosing instead to follow Keate's lead and assume that in Palauan interactions distrust gave way to a recognition of sympathy, I propose a more direct method of respecting Palauan agency. It seems unnecessary to recast friendship as false friendship in order to recognize the complexities of affective claims in the *Account*.[23]

Keate makes these very questions of how to read friendship explicit via the figure of the translator. As Keate explains, 'both the English and the inhabitants of Pelew had each an interpreter who could converse freely together in the Malay tongue' (Keate 2002:78). Keate reserves particular vitriol for the purportedly unreliable interpreter Soogle, a Malay in the employ of Ibedul, who he claims came to be known by the Pelauans as 'worthless Malay' (Keate 2002:187). Malay was the lingua franca of Pacific trade, and Keate's depiction of uncalculated exchange in Palau depends on literally disowning, in the figure of

---

[22] Criticism that aims to redress imperialist discursive assumptions by locating evidence of local agency typically instates equality in the face of claims to superiority; however, both Lamb's and Thomas's analyses of Keate's *Account* serve to introduce a sense of hierarchy where the authorial claim has been for a putative equality. See also Thomas 2002.

[23] My approach here finds affinities with Sharon Marcus's 'just reading', mentioned in my introduction: 'I do not claim to plumb hidden depths but to account more fully for what texts present on their surface but critics have failed to notice' (Marcus 2007:75).

Soogle, the language and imperatives of trade that in fact informed the *Antelope*'s East India Company voyage. Lamb focuses on Soogle as bearing the brunt of a shared European/Palauan investment in presenting communication across the beach as naturalized (Lamb 2001:273–4). But Soogle does not take up the translator's task alone. His role is shared with Tom Rose, a Malay-speaking 'native of Bengal calling himself a Portuguese': a man whose very self-identity is itself a free translation. Keate continues:

TOM ROSE speaking English, an easy intercourse was immediately opened on both sides, and all those impediments removed at once, which would have arisen among people who had no means of conveying their thoughts to one another by language, but must have trusted to signs and gestures, which, to those born in climates so remotely separated, might have given rise to a thousand misconceptions. (Keate 2002:78)

This complexly mediated process, then, is the reality behind Keate's echoing appeal to 'easy intercourse'. The direct speech that renders Ibedul's voice so immediately interlocutory, allowing it to cut to the heart of the reader, occurs in the parenthesis of a *double* act of interpretation. Soogle's purportedly unworthy translations are hinged to the virtuous renditions of Tom Rose. And the relative merits of the two translations are measured in circuitous relation to an understanding of their relative talents for friendship.

Tom Rose is the ideal cross-cultural translator because he is the ideal friend. Returning from a battle in which the English have assisted Ibedul against his nearby enemies, the Palauans break into a song. Keate reports that:

Though Mr. SHARP could not understand the whole sense of it, yet he readily comprehended that the English were the subject, by the frequent repetition of the words *Englees – Weel a Trecoy* – and *Tom Rose*. – This man going with the English upon every expedition, as interpreter, and possessing a great fund of pleasantry and humour, hit the fancy of all the natives, with whom he became a wonderful favourite. – So singular were the talents of this truly faithful fellow, that wherever he went he made himself not only useful, but beloved ... (Keate 2002:180–1)

By Keate's account, Tom Rose has effectively become synonymous in the Palauan mind with the English. In their song he is rendered the object rather than subject of translation, functioning as the familiar term that bridges linguistic differences. Equally, Rose's service is seen to transcend instrumentality. His status as favourite and his role as translator are synonymous. Soogle by contrast comes to represent a pure instrumentality: all his actions are attributed to self-seeking motives, and he can only therefore translate falsely. Translation as embodied by the figure of Tom Rose is grounded in conscious and reciprocal efforts of positive interpretation: in a mode of friendship from which Soogle is understood to be excluded by his tendency to foreground negative motivations. Yet despite Keate's efforts to distinguish the characters and therefore the roles of the two translators, all the interactions he reports testify to their combined efforts. In the two translators, then, we might locate a figure for Oceanic friendship as we have traced it in the European imagination: calculation and sympathy conjoined.

Despite the inclusion of a brief vocabulary as appendix, there are actually very few Palauan terms in Keate's account. Apart from the phrase 'weel-a-trecoy', translated as 'very good', which is invoked at various times to register Palauan receptiveness or stoicism, the only native words in Keate's text are those describing rank. The exception, however, is the frequently repeated word *sucalic*, or friend. Just as the friendly Tom Rose becomes the figure of cross-cultural translation, so the word friend comes to represent, literally, the act of translation within the text. If Keate situates the ethnographic sections of his narrative within the authorizing context of 'steady friendship', so knowledge of the other culture's terms and practices becomes embodied in his text in the word for friendship. In this sense, the word *sucalic* works in Keate's text in the same way that I have argued *taio* works in European voyaging accounts. It is a double sign of authenticity. But while friendship may be the bond that links two societies sentimentally and ethnographically, Keate also acknowledges it as a term of cultural difference. During a presentation of gifts that marks the introductory stage of relations between the English and the Palauans, he writes,

our people observed, by the gestures and looks of the natives, that each chief fixed his attention upon some particular person: this at the time alarmed them, apprehending that the individual each chief had particularly noticed, was singled out as his devoted prisoner; but they soon afterwards found the meaning to be quite contrary, and that the individual so selected was to be that chief's particular friend or guest. (Keate 2002:95)

Once again, this tableau enacts misrecognition and its displacement. Instead of the unequal devotion of the captor to his charge, the singular attention of the Palauan chief signals the equal devotion of the friend to potential friend. What comes to light here, however, is not a universal, but a highly specific idea of friendship: akin in its reflexive emphasis on particularity, again, to *taio*.

The friendship term *sucalic* is the link between translatability and recalcitrant cultural particularity: it is the word that redeems the speaking heart from the forked tongue. The complex bridging work performed by the notion of friendship emerges even more explicitly in the account of a subsequent visitor to Palau, Amasa Delano. Delano was an American who shipped from Macao in April 1791 aboard the *Panther*, the ship commissioned to bring the news of Lebuu's death back to Palau.[24] In his subsequent account of this and other voyages, Delano relegates his own discussion of Palauan friendship traditions to a set of ethnographic remarks, situated between paragraphs on religion and marriage practices. He portrays the Palauans as hyper-literal readers of the obligations of friendship, writing, 'They carried their ideas of the sacredness of this virtue to a very great extent, and doubted whether it were proper to make a profession of it, in the first degree, to two persons at the same time. In this they were probably too scrupulous.' Like the crew of the *Antelope*, Delano is bemused by the emphasis on particularity intrinsic to the Palauan notion of friendship:

On our arrival, the king proposed to us, that we should each chose a friend. We answered, that we intended to be friends to them all, and hoped that they would be our friends in return. This however did not meet the sentiments of the king. He spoke to us of the pleasure, the peace, and the mutual safety, which would arise from the kind of confidence required by their laws of particular and inviolable friendship. (Delano 1817:72)

A friendship that on the one hand appears to be explicitly instrumental, motivated by desires for 'the pleasure, the peace, and the mutual safety', on the other hand invokes what would to Delano and the crew have been a familiar rhetoric of intimacy, emphasizing a unique bond. Thus, if the response of the crew members – their offer of a pluralized, non-specific friendship – does not 'meet [the king's] sentiments', equally it does not, in this latter respect, match his sentimentality. For the Palauans instrumentality and intimacy do not appear mutually exclusive. The serviceable and the personal friendship are, as we have seen elsewhere in Oceania, one and the same. In his defence of Palauan friendship, Delano employs reasoning worthy of Hume:

Should it be thought by any reader, that the terms of friendship, as here described, must have rendered it mercenary, because the reciprocity led each of the parties to expect a reward for every office of kindness, I would answer, that such an objection carries with it its own refutation. The very idea of a perfect

---

[24] Other narratives of this voyage are McCluer 1790–2, and Hockin, in Keate 2002.

reciprocity removes the motive of selfishness, and makes the good, which results from united efforts, a social possession.

But he segues from this abstract speculation to personal anecdote:

But besides this, the fact deserves a place in my narrative, that when I was about to leave the Pelew islands for the last time, and forever, I found it difficult to persuade the friend, whom I had chosen, to accept of the presents, which I had purchased for him during my absence, and which I knew were particularly agreeable to his taste. (Delano 1817:73)

While he initially defends calculation in local terms – its 'perfect reciprocity' cancels out any possibility of acquisitiveness – Delano, once again in a familiar manoeuvre, nonetheless persists in exonerating his own friend's sentiment by exempting him from such logistics. In his captain's account, on the other hand, the sentiment and calculation that Delano has so carefully distinguished become re-entangled. McCluer's journal entry for 27 June 1791 describes the Palauans as 'a deep compassionate people, who felt our departure from them, with great affliction, and I have reason to believe it was not feigned but real, having in general felt the value of our friendship and acquaintance –'. McCluer's underlining emphasizes debt even as he writes of pure sentiment.

The story that lies between the voyages to Pelau that Keate and Delano narrate may account for their different levels of engagement with Palauan sentiment: the brief history of another particular friend, 'Prince Lee Boo'. Lebuu was the second son of Ibedul, sent to England by his father aboard the boat that the English crew constructed at Ulong. His was not a friendship struck on the beach; he makes his initial appearance in Keate's account just as the crew prepares to depart Palau. At this point, he effectively takes the baton from Tom Rose as representative of cross-cultural friendship. Where Tom Rose mediated between British and Pelauans on the beach, Lebuu mediates between the two cultures at the metropole, most significantly through his friendship with George Keate. Tom Rose translates between tongues, Keate translates speech to print, while Lebuu ultimately transcends the logic of mediation to represent the self-declarative heart.[25]

The final, lengthy chapter of Keate's book is subtitled '*Anecdotes of* Lee Boo, *second Son of* Abba Thulle, *from the time of leaving* Canton *to his Death*'. An 'anecdote' suggests a context of conversation, redolent of

---

[25] Lebuu's 'curious and friendly' legacy is perpetuated into the nineteenth and twentieth centuries through redactions of his story such as [Anon] 1790; [Anon] 1810 (which maintains the tension between curiosity and sentiment in the title *The Interesting and Affecting History of Prince Lee Boo*); [Anon] 1820; [Anon] 1841; Palau Community Action Agency 1976; Peacock 1987.

friendly feeling, but also a partial, fragmentary text. Lebuu's brief life is a conversation cut short, and each anecdote therefore carries a heavy burden of interpretation. The structure is ethnographic, in the sense that each interaction is regarded as evidential, yet once again, what is sought is less evidence of cultural difference than of common humanity. What Keate anxiously adduces and rhetorically privileges is confirmation of Lebuu's heart. He writes, 'As the anecdotes of this singular youth are but scanty, being all unfortunately limited to a very short period, I would unwillingly, in this place, withhold one, where his own heart described itself' (Keate 2002:263). The corroborating anecdote in which the heart is gently prompted to speak for itself is the tentative, civilized epilogue to that brutal moment of recognition on the beach at Ulong, where Ibedul's words cut to the heart of the English claim to friendship. In Jonathan Lamb's analysis, Lebuu remains in Keate's anecdotal chapter imprisoned forever between roles of curious foreigner and savvy mimic. Yet this final chapter of Keate's account, and the subsequent literature of 'Lee Boo', remains embarrassed by simple questions: Did we care for him? Did he care for us? Were we friends?

Ibedul has entrusted Captain Wilson with a double and contradictory commission: '*I would wish you to inform* Lee Boo *of all things which he ought to know, and make him an Englishman*' (Keate 2002:205). Wilson is charged both to instruct and to reform: to draw attention to cultural difference and to eradicate it. This double significance is held in tension in the appellation 'new man' (Keate 2002:259), given to Lebuu by a Portuguese official at Macao and taken up by Keate: he is at once cultural novelty and product of a cultural makeover; son of and visitor to new worlds. There are some fairly obvious ironies to Lebuu's cultural self-transformation, that play themselves out neatly in Keate's account in a pair of mirror scenes. On a visit to a fine house in Macao, Keate narrates, 'Amongst the things that solicited his notice, was a large mirror at the upper end of the hall, which reflected almost his whole person. Here Lee Boo stood in perfect amazement at seeing himself; – he laughed – he drew back, and returned to look again, quite absorbed in wonder' (Keate 2002:218). This innocent delight in the technology of a new culture is reappraised in a later scene in which Lebuu, now familiar with the mirror's function, uses it to gauge the real effects of his cultural transformation: 'On the Thursday before his death, walking across the room, he looked at himself in the glass (his face being then much swelled and disfigured); he shook his head, and turned away, as if disgusted at his own appearance' (Keate 2002:265). The native who would make himself over in civilization's image is instead destroyed by civilization's degenerate shadow, contagious disease.

It seems to me that Keate is all too aware of these ironies, and is better able to address them by casting Lebuu as Noble Savage than he is the more private claims that Lebuu makes. His death marks the failure of a duty of care warranted by the friendship forged between England and Palau, and it is a failure in which Keate seems conscious of being implicated. Describing his own first meeting with Lebuu he writes, with some ambiguity, 'I might tire the reader were I to enumerate the trivial occurrences of a few hours, rendered only of consequence from the singularity of this young man's situation' (Keate 2002:259). Keate reassesses the encounter with hindsight: what had felt perhaps like the beginnings of a friendship must now be read as the last evidence of a curious stranger. Lebuu's story is of consequence because of the 'singularity' of his 'situation': an allusion to his cultural difference. But the 'few hours' of his conversation with Keate are of consequence because they were so few: they have been made significant by Lebuu's death. His exoticism and his death seem mutually implicated here, and equally responsible for the pressure of interest that has produced Keate's text.

Yet the *Account of the Pelew Islands* also highlights an alternative model of recordation. Keate reports that, to assist him in recalling the sights of his voyage, Lebuu 'took a piece of line, which he had brought with him for the purpose of making remarks, and tied a knot thereon, as a remembrance of the circumstance' (Keate 2002:216). Lebuu was adapting the Palauan mnemonic aid of *teliakl*, or knotted twine, generally employed to indicate lapses of time (McKnight 1961:8; Nero 2002:9[26]). The practice of knotting was registered by the crew members with whom he travelled as a form of writing: as Keate recounts, 'The officers ... when they saw him thus busied with his Line, used to say he was reading his journal' (Keate 2002:257). Keate's account concludes by imagining a scenario in which Ibedul employs the knotted cord to register the length of Lebuu's absence and the abandonment of his hope of his son's return. Keate invites the reader to picture Ibedul gradually undoing the thirty knots he made to mark the time of Lebuu's absence:

the Reader's imagination will figure the anxious parent, resorting to this cherished remembrancer, and with joy untying the earlier records of each elapsing period; – as he sees him advancing on his Line, he will conceive that joy redoubled; – and, when nearly approaching to the thirtieth knot, almost accusing the planet of the night for passing so tardily away. (Keate 2002:269)

---

[26] Nero explores the metaphoric implications of *teliakl* as a way of thinking about cultural difference and mnemonics (Nero 2002:9–11).

The reader of Keate's text is here identified and elided with Ibedul, reader of the 'cherished remembrancer', that, rather than building towards a happy ending, unravels to poignant inconclusion. No simple conversion of cultural object to sentimental signifier, the chosen symbol here is an Oceanic mode of narration undone as it is constructed, in which curiosity and friendship are reconciled.

6   Ruinous friendships

> for to the friendly and endearing behaviour of these people, may be
> ascribed the motives for that event which effected the ruin of an
> expedition . . .
>
> – William Bligh

William Bligh published two accounts of the *Bounty* mutiny.[1] Viewed in
relation to one another, they can acquire the status of hasty and reflective
responses, of part and whole, or on the other hand, of eyewitness and
modified text. The *Narrative of the Mutiny, on board his Britannic
Majesty's ship* Bounty; *and the subsequent voyage of part of the crew, in the
ship's boat, from Tofoa, one of the Friendly Islands, to Timor, a Dutch
Settlement in the East-Indies*, published in 1790, begins almost exactly
where his *Bounty* log breaks off, with Bligh's departure from Tahiti, and
takes the reader immediately into the events of the mutiny. After
recording his own good conscience and hence good spirits upon being
consigned to the ship's boat, Bligh addresses the question of motivation:

It will very naturally be asked, what could be the reason for such a revolt? in
answer to which, I can only conjecture that the mutineers had assured
themselves of a more happy life among the Otaheitans, than they could
possibly have in England; which, joined to some female connections, have
most probably been the principle cause of the whole transaction.

As Bligh immediately elaborates:

The women at Otaheite are handsome, mild and cheerful in their manners and
conversation, possessed of great sensibility, and have sufficient delicacy to make
them admired and beloved. The chiefs were so much attached to our people, that
they rather encouraged their stay among them than otherwise, and even made
them promises of large possessions. Under these, and many other attendant
circumstances equally desirable, it is now perhaps not so much to be wondered
at, though scarcely possible to have been foreseen, that a set of sailors, most of
them void of connections, should be led away; especially when, in addition to

---

[1] Indeed, as Philip Edwards points out, the publication afterlife of the *Bounty* mutiny was
initially dominated by Bligh (P. Edwards 1994:131).

such powerful inducements, they imagined it in their power to fix themselves in the midst of plenty, on the finest island in the world, where they need not labour, and where the allurements of dissipation are beyond anything that can be conceived. (Bligh 1977:9)

A Voyage to the South Sea, undertaken by command of His Majesty, for the purpose of conveying the bread-fruit tree to the West Indies, in His Majesty's ship the Bounty, *commanded by Lieutenant William Bligh. Including an account of the mutiny on board the said ship, and the subsequent voyage of part of the crew, in the ship's boat, from Tofoa, one of the Friendly Islands, to Timor, a Dutch Settlement in the East-Indies,* published in 1792 while Bligh was away on his second breadfruit voyage, with editorial intervention by James Burney and Joseph Banks, draws on the logbook to flesh out the earlier part of the *Bounty* voyage and the five-month stay at Tahiti that preceded the mutiny. This account incorporates, with occasional significant emendation, the 1790 narrative of events immediately leading up to and following the mutiny, repeating Bligh's explanation quoted above almost word for word. However, in the 1792 volume that explanation is effectively prefaced by a subtly different account of motivation, embedded in the description of the crew's departure from Tahiti:

We made sail, bidding farewell to Otaheite, where for twenty-three weeks we had been treated with the utmost affection and regard, and which seemed to increase in proportion to our stay. That we were not insensible to their kindness, the events which followed more than sufficiently proves: for to the friendly and endearing behaviour of these people, may be ascribed the motives for that event which effected the ruin of an expedition, that there was every reason to hope, would have been completed in the most fortunate manner. (Bligh 1979:141)

Bligh's two speculations on motive, considered side by side, illustrate the hermeneutic alternatives that I raised in the Introduction. The first sets up an unstable relationship between a number of terms: plenty, 'female connections', the 'attach[ment]' of the *ari'i*, and dissipation. Bligh segues from an ostensibly sympathetic understanding of the desire for such female and male attachment among men conspicuously 'void of connections', to insinuations of the lure of degeneracy, via the ambivalent appeal of a life without labour. The word 'allurements' plays a significant role in this process of insinuation, implicitly linking the qualities of the Tahitian women with unspoken, indeed inconceivable, debauchery. As Bligh's careful account of motivation unfolds, then, a text and subtext appear to emerge. Beneath broad notions of intimacy in the absence of existing attachments, we can spell out a hinted licentiousness. The 1792 version on the other hand simply offers synonyms for intimacy as additional motives for the mutiny: 'affection and regard', 'not insensible', 'kindness', 'friendly and endearing behaviour'. Exegesis and innuendo are eschewed.

In the 1790 text friendship seems to invite speculation; in the 1792 text it resists it. In the earlier version, friendship is the term that conceals a fuller story, of sexuality, of class and its relationship to labour. However, the composition sequence of the 1792 text suggests that friendship and its subtexts are held in tension, rather than understood to embody a clear order of understanding. The explanation that comes first in this fuller version was also, in effect, a second thought: part of a text that was elaborated later. Its relatively unparsed formulation of friendship as motive for the mutiny is thus simultaneously reinstated and displaced by the chronologically subsequent reiteration of the 1790 explanation. Both accounts of motivation are at once primary and secondary. And they have, as I noted, other types of competing authority that it is difficult to weigh: the effect of raw impression versus editorial intervention, partiality versus completion.[2] The hierarchy of the two explanations of the mutiny as text and subtext, then, cannot be demarcated. Rather they constitute sustained alternatives, whose relevance depends upon and highlights our inclination to read denotatively or connotatively.

Other friendship alternatives emerge between these two accounts. Less than a page before he writes of complicated male and female friendship and its influence on sailors 'void of connections' in the 1790 text, Bligh states:

Notwithstanding the roughness with which I was treated, the remembrance of past kindnesses produced some signs of remorse in Christian. When they were forcing me out of the ship, I asked him, if this treatment was a proper return for the many instances he had received of my friendship? he appeared disturbed at my question, and answered, with much emotion, 'That, – captain Bligh, that is the thing; – I am in hell – I am in hell.' (Bligh 1977:8)

Bligh's reproach reiterates the keynotes of eighteenth-century friendship discourse. Christian has on the one hand broken the reciprocal contract of friendship, offering no 'proper return' to his mentor. But the friendship claim is also seen as the vector of true emotion in a situation of otherwise confused and false feeling. To inquire of the mutineer's capacity for friendship constitutes a moment of truth, that strips away the potential legitimacy or illegitimacy of other claims about abuses of power, and returns the protagonists to a world of absolute judgement:

---

[2] Scholars have complicated even the terms of these oppositions, focusing for instance on Bligh's open boat voyage as itself a period of intense editing of his story for Bligh. See in particular P. Edwards 1994:125–40, and Reimann 1996:198–218.

to hell. Above all, friendship is the question that can momentarily slow the inevitable course of events. Within Bligh's 'hasty' narrative it represents a pause for thought.

When Bligh explicitly reinstates friendship as a cause of the mutiny in his 1792 account, it seems to me that he too has been forced to dwell on friendship. And two pages before he cites 'the friendly and endearing behaviour of these people' as 'motives for that event which effected the ruin of an expedition', he again offers a further insight into friendship, this time from the beach rather than on deck:

I now made my last presents to several of my friends, with whom I had been most intimate ... Several people expressed great desire to go with us to England. Oedidee, who was always very much attached to us, said, he considered it as his right, having formerly left his native place, to sail with Captain Cook. Scarce any man belonging to the ship was without a *tyo*, who brought him presents, chiefly of provisions for a sea store. (Bligh 1979:139)

As Anna Neill has noted, this reference to the particular friendship bonds of crew members is missing from Bligh's logbook account of the departure from Tahiti. Neill interprets Bligh's remarks as 'the concerned observation that within a short time such an intimacy grew between the crew members and the natives' (Neill 2002:173), but I think Bligh is concerned rather, in this retrospective insertion, to highlight an understanding of friendship as reciprocal obligation. The passage references a series of transactions that translate acknowledged sentiment into an understanding of what is owed. The give and take of Bligh's prestation and the *taios*' provisioning frames the more explicit assertion by Hitihiti ('Oedidee') of a chain of obligation that links Bligh's voyage back to Cook's. However, what Bligh seems to want to highlight here is the fit between his understanding of the obligations of friendship and that of the people with whom he has been interacting. As preface to his further comments on friendship in the 1792 text, these recollections show Bligh giving the ethnographic measure of those friendships that, he soon after reiterates, were the mutiny's cause. Precisely unlike Christian, the Tahitians through the *taio* pact recognize the logic of 'proper return'.

The story of the *Bounty* mutiny has fallen prey to the 'for or against' logic that it enacted. The first two voices commenting on the events of the mutiny were those of Bligh and of Edward Christian, and were both texts of exculpation. But *Bounty* scholarship seems particularly and enduringly partisan: arguments are framed as further trials of crew and captain, and historians continue to identify as friend or foe of Christian or Bligh. In the process of disclosing the particular ingredients of naval and class stratification, masculine narcissism or suppressed sexual tension that produced this extreme rupture between men of the same country of origin, scholars have weighed the degree to which Tahitian connections, and particularly those with women, could have indeed been instrumental to the mutiny.[3] But the concern has been with unravelling the mutiny's compelling plot. In this chapter I consider the events and archive of the mutiny primarily in terms of account keeping rather than narrative. I suggest that the question of 'proper return' was integral to the framing of the voyage and the mutiny, and that the British crew members' thinking on this subject was crystallized by their Tahitian friendships and exchanges.

Account keeping

> Where Captain Bligh have wrote single he should have wrote plurel –
> – John Fryer

Bligh was the keeper of accounts on the *Bounty* in more than one sense. As Greg Dening has elucidated, the dual role he assumed on the voyage, of purser as well as captain, involved inherent conflicts of interest:

Pursers were objects of almost universal suspicion because they distributed provisions, accounted for every ounce of food and every farthing of expense. Pursers were the brokers of every transaction on a ship and had to find a profit in these transactions if they were to win back the surety they had laid down . . . Any man who became purser had to have some genius for knowing what would adversely affect him and had to labour instantly to record whatever he counted and measured. A mean spirit and calculating shrewdness were his chief defences. The altruism expected of a captain glimmered lowly behind the parsimony anticipated from a purser. (Dening 1992:23)

The conflict between altruism and calculation Dening highlights in Bligh's divided role echoes that within friendship discourse. And it inflects all the first-hand reports of the voyage, rendering each of them an 'account' in both the primary and secondary senses. The most compelling alternative version to Bligh's is James Morrison's *Journal . . . describing the mutiny and subsequent misfortunes of the mutineers, together with an account of the island of Tahiti*. Discussing the semiotics of Morrison's text, Dening isolates two recurrent 'yarns': food and bad language. The obsessive quantification of food in the early pages of the journal,

---

[3] Rutter n.d., Fullerton n.d., Darby 1965, Nicolson 1965, Barrow 1989, Christian 1999. Owen Rutter prefaces his *True Story of the Mutiny*: 'many books have been written on that melodrama of the sea, both fact and fiction . . . Moreover, most writers have shown a bias against Bligh, since sympathy is always bound to be with the underdog, who was Fletcher Christian' (Rutter n.d.: 13).

and the sense of affront that is registered when weights appear to be short or inadequate substitutes are made to serve for the staples of bread and meat – 'pumpions' (pumpkins) in place of loaves, oil and sugar in place of butter and cheese – is contrasted with the plenty that greets the sailors at Tahiti.

Philip Edwards and K. A. Reimann have both examined the subtle variations in account keeping between the different primary texts of the *Bounty* mutiny, focusing on scenes that highlight the significance of terms of exchange and equality (P. Edwards 1994:125–40; Reimann 1996). One important prequel to the immediate events of the mutiny that is excluded from Bligh's *Narrative*, and is filled in by both John Fryer and James Morrison, regards the flare up of Bligh's temper over what he believed to be a depletion in the store of coconuts he had reserved on board the *Bounty*'s deck. In both Fryer's and Morrison's accounts, this is *the* event that precipitates the mutiny. And its narration involves a shifting language of exchange, with the alternating terms gifting, trade and theft coding labile interpersonal relations. So, to quote Morrison's version,

In the Afternoon of the 27th Mr. Bligh Came up, and taking a turn about the Quarter Deck when he missed some of the Cocoa Nuts which were piled up between the Guns upon which he said that they were stolen and Could not go without the knowledge of the Officers, who were all Calld and declared that they had not seen a Man toutch them, to which Mr. Bligh replied 'then you must have taken them yourselves', and ordered Mr. Elphinstone to go and fetch evry Cocoa nut in the Ship aft, which He obeyd. He then questioned evry Officer in turn concerning the Number they had bought, & Coming to Mr. Christian askd Him, Mr. Christian answerd 'I do not know Sir, but I hope you dont think me so mean as to be Guilty of Stealing yours'. Mr. Bligh replied 'Yes you dam'd Hound I do – You must have stolen them from me or you could give a better account of them – God dam you, you Scoundrels, you are all thieves alike, and combine with the men to rob me – I suppose you'll Steal my Yams next, but I'll sweat you for it, you rascals. (Morrison 1935:40–41; compare Fryer 1934:55–6)

As accusations of theft rendered objects of exchange items of suspicion, the randomly piled coconuts were systematically counted. The term 'accounting' shifts from the nebulous realm of story to the literal realm of 'the Number': if Christian cannot 'give a better account of them' – cannot tell a self-exonerating tale – then the bald account of figures will be left to tell the tale in his place. But what in turn inflects this intense affective charge around the notion of accountability?

The *Bounty* had just departed Annamooka in the Tonga islands, which, as Morrison points out, 'was likely to be the last Island where Iron Currency was the Most valuable'. That is, it was the last time that the crew would be able to trade really effectively between cultures: to take advantage of their ironware to accumulate both local crafts – 'Matts, Spears & many Curiositys' that would have a continued exchange value when they returned to England – and food items 'for Private Store'. Thus, after 'two Hours liberty was given to the people to expend their trade', Morrison recalls, 'the ship was fairly lumbered that there was scarcely room to stir in any part' (Morrison 1935:39). He reports that at this stage Bligh detained some Tongan chiefs. Bligh accounts for this action in his 1792 text as an attempt to get a stolen grapnel returned. He was following Cook's repeated but ultimately disastrous policy here, but claims that once he realized that it was unlikely to be successful, he freed the chiefs, gave them unexpected gifts, of which 'they were unbounded in their acknowledgements; and I have little doubt but that we parted better friends than if the affair had never happened' (Bligh 1979:153). In Morrison's version, the chiefs were simply, inexplicably detained: moreover, in a way that breached etiquettes of hospitality and rank. Morrison comments,

At this the Chiefs seemd much displeased, on which they were ordered down to the Mess room where Mr. Bligh followed them and set them to peel Cocoa Nuts for His Dinner. He then came up and dismissd all the Men but two, that were under arms, but not till he had passd the Compliment on officers & Men to tell them that they were a parcel of lubberly rascals ... (Morrison 1935:39)

Again the coconuts become symbolic here of Bligh's perceived tendency to disrespect the status of others. There is little basis for thinking that Bligh would have asked the chiefs to prepare his food. As noted earlier, the word *tapu* in its various spellings appears almost as frequently in European accounts of Oceanic contact as does *taio*, and the common example given of its broad-ranging and hierarchical injunctions is the exclusion of high-ranking individuals from the preparation of food. Bligh, who was already on his second voyage to the Pacific and seems to have borne his predecessors' examples constantly in mind, would have been fully aware of the offence such a demand would provoke. However, Morrison adduces Bligh's purported action, after the crew's months in Oceania, as a shocking act of cultural misreading. Breaching status and infringing *tapu*, it provides further evidence of what Morrison represents as the commensurate disrespect – the false 'Compliment' – of mislabelling Officers and Men as rascals, all of a 'parcel'. How could men as disparate in rank and culpability as the *Bounty*'s crew not find themselves united against a commander who bundles them together like coconuts?

But there are more coconuts to count. When Morrison writes of the *Bounty*'s departure from Tahiti, he figures coconuts not as items of trade, but as gifts of friendship: 'the Natives to show the last token of their Freindship loaded us with presents, & the Ship became lumbered with Hogs Cocoa Nuts & Green Plantains for Sea store'. Morrison gives an example of a particular farewell exchange, where Bligh and the carpenter, Purcell, a figure deeply at odds with the captain, proffer parting gifts:

Mr. Bligh gave Matte a Musquet two pistols some powder & Ball flints &c. and a Chest to keep his trade & Amunition in, the Chest being also filld with the Presents Mr. Bligh had made him; the Carpenter also Gave him an Amercian Musquet with all which he seemd highly Pleased, but was at quite a loss how to express himself on the occasion and when they landed loaded the Boat with Cocoa Nuts when she returned & was hoisted in. (Morrison 1935:35)

It is unclear whether the gifts of captain and carpenter are mutually reinforcing or competitive, but their effect is apparently to flummox the recipient. They cannot be accommodated; the return load of coconuts becomes a sign of destabilized, rather than achieved, reciprocity. Once again, the ground of contention is friendship and its locally coded relationship to practices of exchange, negotiations of status and perform-ances of sentiment.

Bligh was afraid of alternative accounts. As K. A. Reimann points out, he had felt the injustice of a single official voyage account, having been accorded little recognition in that of Cook's final voyage,[4] although he had 'made a substantial contribution to those aspects of the voyage that proved a success' (the charting of the Sandwich Islands and the north-west Pacific) (Reimann 1996:201). Yet when it came to his own cap-taincy, it seems Bligh felt that writing had the potential to imply an act of sedition. Lieutenant Francis Godolphin Bond, First Lieutenant of the *Providence*, reported to his brother from St Helena, towards the end of the second breadfruit voyage, Bligh's paranoia regarding the existence of other reports:

Among many circumstances of envy and jealousy he used to deride my keeping a private journal, and would often ironically say he supposed I meant to publish ... Every officer who has nautical information, a knowledge of natural history, a taste for drawing, or anything to constitute him proper for circumnavigating, becomes odious; for great as he is in his own good opinion, he must have entertained fears some of his ship's company meant to [submit] a spurious Narrative to the judgment and perusal of the publick. (Mackaness 1953:71)

As Bond is fully aware, Bligh is afraid that his position of command remains unstable: that his capacity to control the voyage account is his

---

[4] *A Voyage to the Pacific Ocean* (1784), a text completed by Lieutenant James King.

only distinction. He is unable to realize or even to recognize the potential of a ship's crew for mutually reinforcing endeavour. What might be aid becomes threat. Yet with the use of the word 'spurious' Bond also ventriloquizes Bligh and de-authorizes his own report, indicating that a belief in the relationship between captaincy and control of accounts is on another level a matter of broad consensus rather than paranoid delusion. Bligh's attack on Bond's writing has involved setting up an opposition between work and writing, coded as public and private duties. He admonishes Bond: 'No person can do the duty of a 1st Lieut. who does more than write the day's work of his publick Journal' (Mackaness 1953:69). However, John Fryer uses the same distinction implicitly to criticize Bligh's command of the *Bounty* launch, deferring pointedly in his own retrospective journal to Bligh's first-hand narrative: 'I must refer the reader to Captain Bligh's narrative as I would only write the truth to the best of my knowledge and the best of my recollection as I had neither ink nor paper – Mr Bligh made all the necessary remarks – I steerd and rowd in the Boat as any other man.' Fryer continues, 'when we came to Timor I asked Captain Bligh for a ruff coppy of the Log for my own satisfaction and he refused to let me have it' (Fryer 1934:63; for Bligh's launch journal, see Bach 1987). Fryer apologized in similar terms for his retrospective account of the events of the mutiny at the *Bounty* court martial by pointing out that 'our attention from that time to our arrival at Timor [was] so much taken up by the attention to our Preservation that it was not possible for us to make any Note or Memorandum at the time, even if I had had the means' (Rutter 1931:76). Metaphors of honest labour and jealous hoarding are deployed subtly to damn Bligh even as he is described going to great lengths to weigh food rations with even-handedness and to take an equal share of all physical burdens in a situation of extreme distress. Account keeping, then, reveals concerns, not just about authority, but about labour and care, and the relationship between self and other. Yet in the end, all the *Bounty*'s accounts had equal weight.

Proper Returns

> Otaheitia independent of its women had many inducements not only for the sailor but the philosopher. He might cultivate his own ground and trust himself and friends for his defence – he might be truly happy in himself and his happiness would be increased by communicating it to others.
>
> – Robert Southey

I have suggested that friendship and its reciprocal entailments – gifting, loyalty – were key values traded on the deck of the *Bounty* on 28 April 1789. I want further to argue here that the ways in which these terms were bandied imply a relationship to the codes and practices of *taio* that both captain and mutineers had developed during their time in Tahiti. Descriptions of friendships and friendship ceremonies become key moments of disputation in the dialogue between Bligh's, Morrison's and the *Pandora* accounts of Tahiti. In reading *taio*, ostensibly with proto-ethnographic detachment, while also representing their authors as embraced in different ways by its bonds, each of these texts simultaneously stakes a claim to best understanding the breakdown in relations between men that occurs on the *Bounty*.

From the moment the anchor drops in Bligh's 1792 account, the concern is with the politics of securing friendship. Bligh comes equipped with what he believes to be an achieved knowledge of the ways in which exchange and friendship are co-implicated in Tahiti, based on his experiences there during Cook's third voyage. He counts on established friendship links, and the particular diplomatic strategies of his mission have been formulated according to local practices of friendship-making as he has come to understand them. On the first day, as we saw in Chapter 1, he searches in vain among his visitors for people 'of much consequence' (Bligh 1979:61). On the second day 'several chiefs' arrive, and ceremony and exchange may begin:

Among these were Otow, the father of Otoo, and Oreepyah, his brother; also another chief of Matavai, called Poeeno: and to these men I made presents. Two messengers likewise arrived from Otoo, to acquaint me of his being on the way to the ship; each of whom brought me, as a present from Otoo, a small pig, and a young plantain-tree, as a token of friendship. The ship was now plentifully supplied with provisions; every person having as much as he could consume. (Bligh 1979:62–3)

Despite the claim to local knowledge – Bligh initiates ceremony and interprets 'tokens' – there is much improvisation as well as recapitulation in what follows. Poeno, as *ari'i* of Matavai, takes Bligh 'to the place where we had fixed our tents in 1777, and desired that I would now appropriate the spot to the same use' (Bligh 1979:63). Two women, who were staining *tapa* cloth (fabric made from the bark of the paper-mulberry tree), offer refreshments, and when Bligh leaves present him with the mat 'which they put on me after the Otaheite fashion'. Meanwhile, Bligh figures himself as auditor of British largesse, receiving unfavourable reports of the cattle left by Cook, but also having 'the satisfaction to see, that the island had received some benefit from our former visits. Two shaddocks were brought to me, a fruit which they had not, till we introduced it. And among the articles which they brought off to the ship, and offered for sale, were capsicoms, pumkins, and two young goats' (Bligh 1979:63, 64). Exchange relations, in other words, are already fully entangled: the Tahitians bring for trade products that the British have previously gifted to them. Webber's portrait of Captain Cook, left with Tu in 1777, is brought on board to be repaired, and the Tahitians explain that 'Toote [Cook] had desired Otoo, whenever any English ship came, to show the picture, and it would be acknowledged as a token of friendship' (Bligh 1979:64). The British gift, like the friendship it continues to betoken, requires maintenance. Bligh's highly controlled narrative at this point performs what it seeks to depict. Each description is effectively entailed, creating an inventory in favour of the British, into which Bligh's subsequent request for breadfruit can be inserted, diplomatically, as a justified claim – a 'proper return' rather than a 'free gift'. As Bligh concedes in retrospect, 'Perhaps so much caution was not necessary, but at all events I wished to reserve to myself the time and manner of communication' (Bligh 1979:67).

Despite his tight grip of translation and interpretation in these passages, Bligh is all at sea when it comes to the specific rituals of Tahitian friendship. He ultimately seems unsure when official friendship with Tu has been secured, describing two ceremonies that vary in format and degree of formality. The first is a fairly straightforward exchange of names, followed instantly by a carefully tallied gift exchange:

[Otoo] came with numerous attendants, and expressed much satisfaction at our meeting. After introducing his wife to me, we joined noses, the customary manner of saluting, and, to perpetuate our friendship, he desired we should exchange names. I was surprized to find, that, instead of Otoo, the name by which he formerly went, he was now called Tinah. The name of Otoo, with the title of *Earee Rahie*, I was informed had devolved to his eldest son, who was yet a minor, as is the custom of the country. The name of Tinah's wife was Iddeah: with her was a woman, dressed with a large quantity of cloth, in the form of a hoop, which was taken off and presented to me, with a large hog, and some bread-fruit. I then took my visitors into the cabin, and after a short time produced my presents in return. The present I made to Tinah (by which name I shall hereafter call him) consisted of hatchets, small adzes, files, gimblets, saws, looking-glasses, red feathers, and two shirts. To Iddeah I gave ear-rings, necklaces, and beads; but she expressed a desire also for iron, and therefore I made the same assortment for her as I had for her husband. Much conversation took place among them on the value of the different articles, and they appeared extremely satisfied; so that they determined to spend the day with me, and requested I would show them all over the ship, and particularly the cabin where I slept. This, though I was not fond of doing, I indulged them in; and the consequence was, as I had apprehended, that they took a fancy to so many things, that they got from me nearly as much more as I had before given them. (Bligh 1979:65)

As I observed in Chapter 2, name exchange involved an implicit destabilization as well as cementing friendship, enshrining various possibilities of misconstrual – of status, or simply of pronunciation. Here at the very point at which he achieves a *taio* relationship with the man whose preeminence he awaited, Bligh is thrown into confusion about where true authority now lies: is it in fact with the 'minor', Tu? According to Tahitian codes of inheritance, 'kin-Titles' – that is, offices associated with the complexly imbricated official religion and politics – passed immediately to the heir at birth. As Douglas Oliver explains, 'thereafter, the child's father continued to perform the secular jobs associated with his released kin-Titles during his heir's minority, but the religious rights and duties associated with those kin-Titles were transferred to the heir' (Oliver 1988:46). Status is at best divided: more confrontingly, the father may be a mere figurehead, with true control in the hands of one conventionally understood to be his dependant. This sense of destabilized authority is, I think, responsible for the other slips of control in this passage: the sense that Tina may now be, not only a mere cipher of power for the true authority, his son, but for a powerful wife 'Itea, who appears to control the reciprocal prestation, and who rejects Bligh's decorative trinkets and requests replicas of her husband's masculine gifts – tools of iron.[5] Finally, Bligh represents himself as swindled by the very system he has attempted so carefully to exploit: forced through the insinuations of hospitality to offer double what he intended.

The published account differs in small but significant ways from Bligh's log. In the log, where the confusion of name exchange follows more closely the pattern I outlined, mispronunciation is the factor producing subtle shifts of identity: 'He taking the Name of Bligh, which he could pronounce no way but Bry, and I that of Tinah.' The 'red feathers' are more specifically described as 'two very fine red Wings of Flamingoes which I had procured at the Cape of Good Hope for the purpose' (Bligh 1937: I, 373). And the manipulation of gifting is more proliferative: 'He was not satisfied here, for after my showing him the ship, he begged of everyone he met with, took some of the Gentlemens handkerchiefs, and asked for Shirts and other Articles' (Bligh 1937: I, 374). The common denominator in the alterations seems to be an attempt to cement Bligh's authority: not to allow him to be mockable as the captain who puts too much anticipatory thought into his exotic gift, is exposed to the 'bad language' (to adopt Dening's term) of

---

[5] Oliver conveys prepositionally a sense of Tahitian female power as predicated on the successful manipulation of power rather than its direct manifestation: 'Since females did not perform religious duties, and seldom if ever any secular administrative ones, the duties associated with their kin-Titles usually passed *through* rather than *to* or *from* them' (Oliver 1988:46).

mispronunciation, and is unable to protect his crew from Tina's importuning.

The second *taio* ceremony described in the 1792 account, which follows the text of the log much more faithfully, involves a more ceremonial gifting, orchestrated by the Tahitians and resulting in the public proclamation of the *taio* bond. Bligh is summonsed to Tina's brother's house:

> At this place I found a great number of people collected, who, on my appearance, immediately made way for me to sit down by Tinah. The croud being ordered to draw back, a piece of cloth, about two yards wide and forty-one yards in length, was spread on the ground; and another piece of cloth was brought by Oreepyah, which he put over my shoulders, and round my waist, in the manner the chiefs are clothed. Two large hogs, weighing each above two hundred pounds, and a quantity of baked bread-fruit and cocoa-nuts, were then laid before me, as a present, and I was desired to walk from one end of the cloth spread on the ground to the other, in the course of which, Tyo and Ehoah were repeated with loud acclamations. (Bligh 1979:69; compare Bligh 1937: I, 376)

Although once again there is a sense that Bligh is playing to a script he doesn't fully understand, there is much relative comfort in this encounter. The main actors are all men. Bligh finds himself costumed as an *ari'i*. The word *taio* and its synonym, *hoa*, are actually enunciated to describe the ceremony, and greeted with acclaim. However, once again his description is haunted by the notion of proper return:

> This ceremony being ended, Tinah desired I would send the things on board, which completely loaded the boat; we, therefore, waited till she came back, and then I took them on board with me; for I knew they expected some return. – The present which I made on this occasion, was equal to any that I had made before; but I discovered that Tinah was not the sole proprietor of what he had given to me, for the present I gave was divided among those who, I guessed, had contributed to support his dignity; among whom were Moannah, Poeenah, and Oreepyah; Tinah, however, kept the greatest part of what I had given, and every one seemed satisfied with the proportion he allotted them. (Bligh 1979:69–70)

Again, exchange threatens to proliferate in ways that transform Bligh's insider knowledge to paranoia. Tina's ostensible status and largesse may be fragmented, and with that his authority. And this in turn offers an unstable reflection for Bligh's sense of command at the very moment he has been declared Tina's *taio* – effectively, just as he has become Tina. In terminology that exactly replicates that of his log (Bligh 1937: I, 376), and thus, we can be certain, predates the mutiny and its retrospective insights, Bligh falls back on a notion of just measure: all are satisfied with their allotment. The insistence on proper reciprocation according to 'allotted' proportion that emerges from his local knowledge of Tahitian friendship practices has particular resonances for the rupture that ensues on the deck of the *Bounty*.

The name exchange between Tina and Bligh sets up a reflection between captaincy and chieftainship. The logbook includes reflections on the precariousness of Tina's authority that are expunged from the 1792 account, presumably because of their implications for Bligh's ability both to establish and mirror true authority. For instance, in the period intervening between the ceremonies cementing his friendship with Tina ('Otoo'), he writes in the log, 'what I have seen proves evidently what was generally thought of Otoo, (except by Captn. Cook in particular,) and that he is a Man only nominally possessed of power, or otherwise he has not abilities to govern, which may be the Case, as the Cheifs revile him upon all occasions. He has nevertheless consequence' (Bligh 1937: I, 375). Bligh indicates his awareness that the apparent interchangeability of terms such as 'consequence' and 'power' can become a false equation in practice. Although the reference to Cook serves to justify the choice of Tina as his *taio*, perhaps equally, he and Cook, identical in their endorsement of Tina, represent two faces of captaincy – false status and true authority; consequence and power.

That Bligh should judge and forge relationships of power effectively is integral to negotiating for the breadfruit plants that are the *Bounty*'s main object. In the 1792 account he is eager to represent his prior knowledge of the Tahitian friendship–exchange nexus as the key to his diplomatic handling of his mission. However, once again this manifests as a control of accounts, one whose tendency towards paranoia even he is prepared to acknowledge: 'I had given directions to every one on board not to make known to the islanders the purpose of our coming, lest it might enhance the value of the bread-fruit plants, or occasion other difficulties. Perhaps so much caution was not necessary, but at all events I wished to reserve to myself the time and manner of communication' (Bligh 1979:67). Bligh's full directions are worth comparing with Cook's 'Rules', quoted at the beginning of Chapter 2, for the way in which they bring a new level of explicit calculation to bear on familiar injunctions to cultivate friendship and trade equably:

Rules to be observed by every Person on Board, or belonging to the 'Bounty', for the better establishing a Trade for Supplies or Provisions and good Intercourse with the Natives of the South Sea, wherever the Ship may be at.

1st. At the Society, or Friendly Islands, no person whatever is to intimate that Captain Cook was killed by Indians; or that he is dead.

2d. No person is ever to speak, or give the least hint, that we have come on purpose to get the bread-fruit plant, until I have made my plan known to the chiefs.

3d. Every person is to study to gain the good will and esteem of the natives; to treat them with all kindness; and not to take from them by violent means, any thing they may have stolen; and no one is ever to fire, but in defence of his life.

4th. Evry person employed on service is to take care that no arms, or implements of any kind under their charge, are stolen; the value of such thing, being lost shall be charged against their wages.

5th. No man is to embezzle, or offer to sale, directly, or indirectly, any part of the King's stores, of what nature soever.

6th. A proper person or persons will be appointed to regulate trade, and barter with the natives; and no officer or seaman, or other person belonging to the ship, is to trade for any kind of provisions, or curiosities; but if such officer or seaman wishes to purchase any particular thing, he is to apply to the provider to do it for him. By this means a regular market will be carried on, and all disputes, which otherwise may happen with the natives, will be avoided. All boats are to have everything handed out of them at sun-set.

Given under my hand, on board the 'Bounty', Otaheite, 25th Oct. 1788.

Wm. BLIGH (Rutter 1931:8–9)

Bligh refuses to admit Cook's death either explicitly, or implicitly – echoing the text of Cook's '*RULES to be observe'd by every person in or belonging to His Majestys Bark the Endevour*'. At the same time, his reordered priorities and subtle revisions cast himself as Cook's inheritor, declaring an alternative version of authority that itself testifies to the lessons of Cook's death, particularly in the attempt not only to control the terms of trade, but to anticipate and pre-empt eruptions of violence.

Eventually the perfect moment arrives for Bligh to put in his claim. Tina recounts the sorry history of Cook's gifts of cattle and sheep, most of which were appropriated or destroyed by the people of Eimeo (Moorea) after they defeated Tina's party in battle. Although Bligh is aware that Tina's pleasure in witnessing his concern 'for the destruction of so many useful animals' (Bligh 1979:72) arises primarily from the hope he will revenge the attack, Bligh proceeds as though use and exchange were the only principles in operation, insistently refiguring the destroyed animals as an unrecompensed debt:

I replied, that, on account of their good-will, and from a desire to serve him and his country, King George had sent out those valuable presents to him; 'and will not you, Tinah, send something to King George in return?' – 'Yes,' he said, 'I will send him anything I have;' and then began to enumerate the different articles in his power, among which he mentioned the bread-fruit. This was the exact point to which I wished to bring the conversation; and, seizing an opportunity, which had every appearance of being undesigned and accidental, I told him the bread-fruit-trees were what King George would like; upon which he promised me a great many should be put on board, and seemed much delighted to find it so easily in his power to send any thing that would be well received by King George. (Bligh 1979:73)

The reiteration of the term 'power' and its interplay with questions of value here recalls Bligh's logbook allusions to the distinction between power and consequence. What is of consequence to Bligh is easily within Tina's power. While Bligh, through his insistence on his own capacity to manipulate the conversation, asserts that it is his own party's agenda that is being served in this interaction, his apparent success in appearing 'undesigned' may once again have its reflection in Tina's *seeming* 'much delighted'. Breadfruit cuttings are surely in this scenario Tahiti's 'trinkets': *ari'i* and captain may both be working independently here to achieve an atypically cost-free exchange.[6]

It is the role of such hidden agendas that Morrison latches onto in his alternative account of Tahitian encounter and its ethics of friendship. Morrison renders Bligh's version of cross-cultural friendship dubious both morally and ethnographically, and indeed sets up a critical relationship between these two terms. Well before his initial *taio* ceremony with Tina is mentioned in the 1792 account, Bligh makes casual reference to the fact that 'an intimacy between the natives, and our people, was already so general, that there was scarce a man in the ship who had not his *tyo* or friend' (Bligh 1979:67). A contrast between this relatively uncomplicated intimacy and the hedgings and status anxieties of Bligh's friendship negotiations informs both accounts. However, this is not played out as a simple distinction between formal and informal, cultural and natural friendship, but rather as a differently nuanced sense of how an understanding of Tahitian bond-friendship works in practice.

While the *Bounty* is at Matavai Bay collecting breadfruit, the contest over friendship plays itself out in relation to the ever-vexed question of provision. Morrison reports,

The Market for Hogs beginning now to slacken Mr. Bligh seized on all that came to the ship big & small Dead or alive, taking them as his property, and serving them as the ship's allowance at one pound pr. Man pr. Day. He also seized on those belonging to the Master, & killd them for the ships use, tho He had more then 40 of different sizes on board of his own, and there was then plenty to be purchaced: nor was the price much risen from the first, and when the Master spoke to him, telling him the Hogs were his property, he told him that 'He Mr. Bligh would convince him that evry thing was *his*, as soon as it was on board, and that He would take nine tenths of any mans property and let him see who dared say any thing to the contrary', those of the seamen were seized without ceremony, and it became a favour for a man to get a Pound extra of His own hog.

---

[6] The idea that breadfruit cost Pacific islanders nothing in labour was of course a European myth that failed to reflect certain realities of climate and cultivation. For a detailed analysis of this representation, see V. Smith 2006.

The Natives observing that the Hogs were seized as soon as they Came on board, and not knowing but they would be seized from them, as well as the People, became very shy of bringing a hog in sight of Lieut. Bligh either on board or on shore, and watchd all opportunitys when he was on shore to bring provisions to their friends but as Mr. Bligh observed this, and saw that His diligence was like to be evaded, he ordered a Book to be kept in the Binnacle wherein the Mate of the Watch was to insert the Number of Hogs or Pigs with the Weight of each that came into the Ship to remedy this, the Natives took another Method which was Cutting the Pigs up, and wraping them in leaves and covering the Meat with Bread fruit in the Baskets, and sometimes with peeld Cocoa Nuts, by which means, as the Bread was never seized, they were a Match for all his industry; and he never suspected their artifice. By this means provisions were still plenty. (Morrison 1935:29)

The description of Bligh seizing everything as his own contrasts with Bligh's own depiction of Tina's gifts to him as clearly comprised of multiple contributions. Bligh's concern with asserting status and authority here outweighs his sense for the networked aspects of Tahitian friendship. In Morrison's narrative, the struggle between Bligh and the crew members' *taio*s to determine the relationship between gift-giving and friendship plays out as a contest between text and praxis. The Tahitians 'became ... shy' of bringing hogs to the ship – the term shy reflecting the particular co-implication of affect and trade in these fraught relations. They nonetheless seek to continue their established practice of 'bring[ing] provisions to their friends', an attempt which Bligh thwarts by imposing his book of accounts. The Tahitians retaliate by passing off meat as breadfruit, a strategy that has implications for both Bligh's ethnography and his mission. The captain who took such pains to infiltrate his breadfruit interest into Tahitian systems of exchange is oblivious to the ways in which low-status friendships piggyback off his carefully forged alliance, and Tahitian exchange items incorporate false measure. As he gradually fills the ship with breadfruit plants and cramps physical conditions for his crew members, they are shown gaining sustenance at his expense through the bonds they forge on the beach. Friendship is already showing a capacity to interfere with 'an expedition, that there was every reason to hope, would have been completed in the most fortunate manner'.

One of the ways in which the crew is alive to aspects of friendship that Bligh neglects is in its alertness and physical responsiveness to sexual subtexts. As Greg Dening notes, the crew's *taio*s were typically male relations of the women with whom they cohabited (Dening 1992:191). The slippage between sexual and amicable relations is immediately apparent in Morrison's pointed description of the crew's 'easy' friendships:

evry officer and man in the ship were provided with new friends tho none understood the language, yet we found it very easy to Converse by signs at which these people are adepts, and some of the Weomen who came on board became very Intiligent in a short time and soon brought their quondum husbands into a method of discourse by which evry thing was transacted ... (Morrison 1935:30–1)

Here once again Morrison makes the reader aware of a language of signs and physical signals that escapes the logics of diplomacy or accountancy. Instead he is alive precisely to local intelligence – in its associations both of intellect and espionage. Bligh's sexual abstinence in Tahiti leaves him deaf to yet another series of networks and exchange relations bound up within Tahitian friendship: one whose power relations are, once again, negotiated relationally. Women appear to be both instigators and objects of exchange, but this is not the primary question: Morrison's own euphemistically ambiguous language is encompassed by his broader acknowledgement of a language of signs in which the adept and 'Intiligent' communicate outside the constraints of explicit language. The meat is smuggled in under the breadfruit.

I want to distinguish the kind of knowing I am identifying here from the knowingness I have resisted throughout this book: one that might code *all* friendship as sexualized. Morrison's reading of sexual subtexts here is precisely and demonstratively contextual; part of his claim to be a better reader of the Tahitian scene than Bligh. The discussion of *taio* ceremonies is a case in point. In Chapter 2 I quoted Morrison's description of these male nuptials, which he describes as identical in structure to the marriage rituals of virgin spouses. I suggested that *taio* might be seen to represent for Morrison and other Europeans the sanctioned face of relations between men whose unacceptable reflection was the more frankly gender-troubling institution of the *mahu*. Lee Wallace has elegantly argued that Bligh's discussion of the *mahu*, one of the most forthright of European accounts of the institution, contrasts in its directness and indelicacy with what she refers to as 'the excited yet decorous representations of heterosexual contact' in the Pacific contact archive (Wallace 2003:15). Wallace, it might be said, is also making an argument for two types of knowing here. When Bligh 'examines [the *mahu*'s] privacies', measuring the size and texture of his testicles, Wallace suggests that he 'gains an almost shocking intimacy with this transgressive body', and his 'salty reportage reveals a fascination with this possibility at least as strong as his avowed disgust' (Wallace 2003:14). Morrison, who, as I noted earlier, casts his eyes away from the *mahu*, his text consolidating, by its refusal to report, his 'avowed disgust', would in Wallace's terms demonstrate a refusal to be seen to 'know' the *mahu*. I think, rather, that the differences in the two accounts of the *mahu* directly parallel those in Bligh's and Morrison's depictions of the *taio* ceremony. For all the saltiness of his description, Bligh is weighing and measuring a body that is known and distantiated through a mode of scientific investigation. Far from 'prefiguring his own later and continually problematic imbrication in the disciplining of masculine pleasures' (Wallace 2003:14), Bligh's investigation consolidates his distance from the practices he describes. His hand on the *mahu*'s testicles is a testimony to the absence of desire. Morrison's knowledge of the marriage of male friends, on the other hand, implicates him as participant-observer. We know he has sealed such friendship bonds. Exposing his local knowledge exposes him to a reader's knowingness. Like Banks in mourner's garb, he risks being smutted.

George Hamilton, in his account of *taio*, tries to imitate a Banksian blend of scientific and salacious interest, knowledge and knowingness. As surgeon of the *Pandora*, he represents the man of science on a voyage whose otherwise blinkered singleness of purpose led to the loss of opportunities to map new islands and rescue survivors from La Pérouse's ill-fated expedition.[7] He thus structurally occupies the Banks role, which he embraces with gusto: playing participant-observer with particular relish when the topic is local sexual practices, but equally fleshing out Captain Edwards's rebarbatively sparse narrative with descriptions of local agriculture and terrain, to the point where bodies and islands seem fully conflated in his prose: 'we examined Ulitea and Otahah' [Raiatea and Taha'a] (E. Edwards and Hamilton 1915:122). Where Edwards's report makes no mention of *taio*, Hamilton gives a full account of the bond, and the difference between the two *Pandora* texts becomes articulated via this topic as one between a refusal to see and a seeing too much. As I noted in Chapter 2, Hamilton's version of *taio* circles around familiar questions of calculation: are gifts of friendship generous beyond European standards or strategically entailed? Are women objects of exchange or pleasure-seekers exploiting a system of alienable relations? Hamilton's whole account, in its peculiar mixture of revelation and obfuscation, demonstrates nothing more eloquently than the limits of a certain mode of knowingness for understanding intimacy. When he describes the *heiva*:

---

[7] Basil Thompson writes in his introduction to Captain Edwards's bare and factual account of the *Pandora*'s mission to round up the mutineers that 'with a different commander, the voyage would have been one of the most important in the history of South Seas discovery' (E. Edwards and Hamilton 1915:4).

After half an hour's hard exercise, the dear creatures had remüé themselves into a perfect fureur, and the piece concluded by the ladies exposing that which is better felt than seen; and, in that state of nature, walked from the bottom of the theatre to the top where we were sitting on the grass, till they approached just by us, and then we complimented them in bowing, with all the honours of war (E. Edwards and Hamilton 1915:108)

it becomes impossible to distinguish degrees of agency and performativity, public event and private fantasy. The welter of innuendo, peppered with French, the language of sexual knowledge in Tahiti since Bougainville's crew emblazoned their own public sexual performances, signals a kind of connoisseurship that leaves the reader spectacularly uninformed. Friendship, like everything else in Tahiti, is here a cipher for sex. Discussion of purported local practices produces the figure of the consummately knowing observer/interpreter, whose knowledge remains trapped in circles of self-reference.

Alliance

> He says it will show all his enemies that we are good Friends.
> – William Bligh

When Hamilton briefly abandons innuendo to try to describe the more specific valences of Tahitian friendship, female sexuality drops out of his account, and he writes of masculine alliance, co-identity and violence:

The force of friendship amongst these good creatures will be more fully understood from the following circumstance: Churchhill [sic], the principal ringleader of the mutineers, on his landing, became the Tyo, or friend, of a great chief in the upper districts. Some time after the chief happening to die without issue, his title and estate, agreeable to their law from Tyoship, devolved on Churchhill, who having some dispute with one Thomson of the Bounty, was shot by him. The natives immediately rose, and revenged the death of Churchhill their chief, by killing Thomson, whose skull was afterwards shown to us, which bore evident marks of fracture. (E. Edwards and Hamilton 1915:110)

All accounts of the mutineers' sojourn in Tahiti take this as a seminal friendship anecdote: as a way of explaining the unique 'force' and 'circumstance' of the *taio* bond. Even Edwards's restricted report allows itself a brief moment of pseudo-ethnographic speculation when he recounts that 'Churchill, Master at Arms, had been murdered by Matthew Thompson, and that Matthew Thompson was killed by the natives and offered as a sacrifice on their altars for the murder of Churchill, whom they had made a chief' (E. Edwards and Hamilton 1915:30). For Edwards such extreme retributive loyalty must be ascribed to a generalized notion of religious sacrifice. Bligh on the other hand, as self-appointed expert on Tahitian friendship, refuses to sanctify the deaths by reference to cultural practice. In his *Providence* journal he instead restores the double murder to the framework of British justice, which they are seen to have evaded and yet somehow fulfilled: 'thus these two Villains affected their own destruction, and avoided the punishment that awaited them' (Oliver 1988:125).[8]

Morrison traces the relationship between the falling out of the European friends and their Tahitian *taio* loyalties. Thompson and Churchill had moved to the district of Taiarapu with Brown, a beachcomber the mutineers found living at Matavai on their return to Tahiti. As Morrison narrates, 'Soon after their Arrival at Tyarrabboo they had a quarrel (which we were sensible Brown Had fomented) and parted. Thompson making friends with Teetorea the Chief of Towtirra & uncle to Vayheeadooa, and Churchill went to Vyeowtea to a house prepared for him, Brown going to live with Matte who was then at Towtirra' (Morrison 1935:93). Much of Morrison's account of the breakup of the friendship mixes a kind of petty playground politics – best friends split by third parties, jealousy of new intimacies – with a violent revenge logic reminiscent of pre-political *xenia*. However, two aspects of Morrison's reporting of the deaths stand out, both of which are specific to the European encounter with the particularities of the *taio* bond. Morrison rehearses the question of whether property or sentiment lies at the heart of such friendships:

We knew not what to think of this business as we were inclined to think that Thompsons death was more on account of His having the property of both, then for Killing Churchill, but the Natives insisted that it was for killing him who they Acknowleg'd to be a Chief in consequence of His Friendship with the late Vayheeadooa whose Name he also bore. (Morrison 1935:94)

If he seems here to endorse scepticism about Tahitian friendship claims, a more complex commentary on the entailments of name exchange resonates in Morrison's remark that 'Thompson growing Jealous of Churchill threatened to Shoot him if any difference or distinction was made between them' (Morrison 1935:93). While both have befriended powerful *ari'i* at Taiarapu, when Vehiatua, Churchill's *taio*, dies, Churchill's status as embodiment of Vehiatua's identity becomes manifest. This is the moment at which exogenous ties triumph over endogenous similarities. Stranger loyalty takes over from the friendship of fellow

---

[8] In the first version of his journal, Bligh describes Churchill and Thompson as 'unfortunate Wretches', but the words are altered in his amended journal, presumably corrected upon his return to England, with hindsight as to the outcome of the mutineers' trial.

countrymen, fellow crew members, fellow mutineers. 'Difference or distinction was made between' Thompson and Churchill, on no basis of race or class, but according to local ties of friendship.

Greg Dening is a subtle commentator on the way *taio* worked to ramify relations for the returned mutineers in Tahiti. He suggests that within broader Tahitian society, it was 'their relationship to the highly ranked Tahitians that kept at bay much ordinary envy and anger at their presence' (Dening 1992:217). I have in turn tried to suggest that 'ordinary envy and anger' between the mutineers themselves was subject to extraordinary pressures when it encountered the varying rewards offered by the *taio* bond. The kinds of intense loyalty and violent breach that erupted as consequences of these new relationships were in some ways the flip side of mutiny. Where the mutiny called on the politics of allegiance, *taio* manifested a politics of alliance. The two terms are, as the *Oxford English Dictionary* notes, sometimes confounded, but where allegiance declares a relationship of hierarchy, alliance is forged from a relationship of affinity. The former is a relationship between subjects and objects: 'the relation or duties of a liege-man to his liege-lord; the tie or obligation of a subject to his sovereign, or government'; 'the recognition of the claims which anything has to our respect and duty' (*OED*). The latter is a relationship between fellow subjects. Its terms – kinship, consanguinity, friendship – stress the equality of its parties: 'union through marriage or common parentage, relationship, kinship, consanguinity'; 'combination for a common object'; 'community or relationship in nature or qualities; affinity; inclusion in the same class'; 'people united by kinship or friendship; kindred, friends, allies' (*OED*). If the mutiny required the crew members of the *Bounty* to declare their allegiance, for or against government as represented by Bligh's command, *taio* allowed them to formalize an affinity across cultural boundaries that in turn liberated them from the hierarchies of their home culture. It gave explicit recognition to a principle of co-identity inherent in the notion of alliance. But it did so, not by weighing or comparing affinities, but rather by risking and instantiating a bond.

Unsurprisingly, it was this aspect of *taio*, rather than its carefully mastered logic of reciprocity, that seemed to confound Bligh. Upon his return to Tahiti in the *Providence* in 1792, he misread alliance as allegiance, interrogating his former *taio*s as to their links with the mutineers and modifying his subsequent relations with them accordingly. Bligh detected 'a natural degree of affection in Tynah & his Father that gave me much pleasure' (Oliver 1988:74). However Tina's capacity to ally himself with the mutineers was a source of suspicion:

I asked him how he came to be so friendly to Christian, for that proved to me he was not sincere in what he said. He replied – 'I really thought you was living and gone to England untill Christian came back the second time. I was then from home, but all my Friends, as soon as they heard from the Men who came on Shore, on their questioning them, that you was lost, from that time we did not profess any friendship to him, and Christian knew it so well that he only remained a few hours, and went away in such a hurry, that he left a second Anchor behind him . . .' Thus he freed himself from any suspicion on my side, & with his usual good nature and cheerfulness regained my esteem & regard. (Oliver 1988:75)

Once again Bligh is torn between a confidence that he can read the 'natural' signs of genuine sentiment in his old friend, and fear that he is being manipulated by the friendship claim. The dilemma is both immediately practical, and exemplary of the philosophical conundrums we have encountered in Scottish Enlightenment philosophy. For David Hume, the suspicion engendered by the potential gap between professed and genuine sentiment could ultimately only be reconciled by a knowledge of character. In his *Enquiry Concerning the Principles of Morals* (1751), Hume cites two varieties of scepticism, one general:

That all *benevolence* is mere hypocrisy, friendship a cheat, public spirit a farce, fidelity a snare to procure trust and confidence; and that, while all of us, at bottom, pursue only our private interest, we wear these fair disguises, in order to put others off their guard, and expose them the more to our wiles and machinations,

and the other philosophical:

That, whatever affection one may feel, or imagine he feels for others, no passion is, or can be disinterested; that the most generous friendship, however sincere, is a modification of self-love; and that, even unknown to ourselves, we seek only our own gratification, while we appear the most deeply engaged in schemes for the liberty and happiness of mankind. (Hume 2006:90)

Hume's subsequent refutation of both these principles is primarily *ad hominem*. He responds in the first instance: 'What heart one must be possessed of who professes such principles, and who feels no internal sentiment that belies so pernicious a theory, it is easy to imagine.' And in the second, he shows that practice contradicts theory by holding up lived examples against stated principles:

Whoever concludes from the seeming tendency of this opinion, that those, who make profession of it, cannot possibly feel the true sentiments of benevolence, or have any regard for genuine virtue, will often find himself, in practice, very much mistaken. Probity and honour were no strangers to EPICURUS and his sect. ATTICUS and HORACE seem to have enjoyed from nature, and cultivated by reflection, as generous and friendly dispositions as any disciple of the austerer schools. And among the modern, HOBBES and LOCKE, who maintained the selfish system of morals, lived irreproachable lives; though the former lay not under any restraint of religion, which might supply the defects of his philosophy. (Hume 2006:91)

Hume, then, posits a distinction between principle and practice against a thesis that equally distinguishes between public statement and private sentiment. But the confidence he achieves is in turn precarious. It implies a social and philosophical world in which people act very differently from how they profess.

The kind of knowledge adduced here, however, is precisely of a type precluded by the terms of contact. Although Bligh was able to reference the question of whether Tina was genuinely professing friendship or manipulatively courting the dominant visitor against the experience both of previous voyagers and his own previous voyages, these are ultimately transitory rather than embedded encounters. Tina's explanation is not a strong one: surviving mutineers testified that Christian planned his immediate departure from Tahiti prior to dropping off those who chose to remain there; a number of Tahitian *taio*s and women were on the *Bounty* with Christian when it departed Tahiti again, some of whom had already accompanied him to Tubuai, and none of whom appear to have renounced his friendship once they became apprised of his treatment of Bligh. Moreover, Tina was not present when Christian reappeared, and his explanation is devolved in the 'some of my best friends tell me' anecdotal mode. Bligh's eagerness to believe in Tina's fidelity and to confirm the natural sentiment he reads upon his features, is as integral to the exoneration of his own command of the *Bounty* mission as it is to proving Christian's guilt: it shows that Bligh read friendship correctly on his first voyage. Indeed, his renewed affection for Tina here, on whom he reflected more unflatteringly, as we saw earlier, in his *Bounty* log, has a quality of absolution.

The politics of alliance are still strongly at work behind *taio*, however, and Tina does appear to have a hidden agenda. Immediately after asserting his renewed esteem and regard, Bligh writes, 'Pooeno & the Matavai People seem to be objects of great dislike to Tynah and his Father, they requested I would undertake the War with them to destroy those people' (Oliver 1988:75). Poeno, it may be recalled, was Bligh's second *Bounty* chiefly *taio*: his and Tina's wives rivalled each other in their displays of grief after the *Bounty* was threatened by a storm in Matavai Bay (see Chapter 4). There is, then, a symmetry between Bligh's desire for reassurance that Tina turned against Christian, with whom both he and Bligh had formerly friendly relations, and Tina's desire that Bligh take up arms against his former friend Poeno. Bligh manages to explain to Tina that 'it would interfere with the busyness

I was sent on' to turn against Poeno (Oliver 1988:75), an explanation that presumably would not have sufficed to justify any continued support of Christian by Tina. It is Bligh who has forged non-exclusive bonds in Tahiti, played off *ari'i* against one another and divided his alliance. He refuses to identify with his *taio* Tina in the way that Churchill became identified with Vehiatua: to take on his friend's cause.[9] While his journal does not explicitly register any sense of personal conflict over this issue of loyalty, Bligh's subsequent comments on an ensuing gift exchange with Tina suggest that the strict traditional codes of friendship-making have becoming diluted. 'There was very little of the ancient Custom of the Otaheitean; all that was laid aside,' he writes; 'I believe no European in future will ever know what their ancient Customs of receiving Strangers were' (Oliver 1988:75). Bligh also displaces any sense of infidelity back onto Tina, questioning his acquisition of a secondary wife, the younger sister of his wife 'Itia, and in fact the widow of the same Vehiatua whose bond with Churchill proved so definitively binding (Oliver 1988:78). The acquisition of such secondary wives was common practice among the *ari'i*, but is more fundamentally shocking to the English, in their own cultural terms, than breaches of friendship.[10] If Tina's affections can be so fundamentally realigned, the question of his loyalty to Bligh must perhaps after all remain open.

Seeming Friendly

> What reason had you to imagine that John Millward was friendly to you at the time he was placed Centinel over you?
> – He appeared to me to be very uneasy in Mind.
> — Deposition of John Fryer, *Bounty* court martial

Back in England, at the trial of the mutineers, which took place between 12 and 19 September 1792, questions of loyalty and motivation were also being played out. Ten mutineers of the fourteen apprehended by the crew of the *Pandora* made it back to England for trial (four perished when the *Pandora* was wrecked). These were Peter Heywood, midshipman; Joseph Coleman, armourer; James Morrison, boatswain's mate;

---

[9] Bligh does take some degree of issue with Poeno prior to Tina's arrival (Oliver 1988:64–5); however, it is not predicated on identification with Tina. Poeno also had more than one *Bounty* friendship – he became James Morrison's *taio* when the mutineers returned to Tahiti.

[10] George Tobin also comments on Tina's infidelity in his journal – perhaps partly from identification with 'Itia, who was his *taio* – observing 'Poor 'Itia seemed neglected for those charms still in bloom of her younger sister and was seldom allowed to share her lord's bed' (Tobin 2007:79).

Charles Norman, carpenter's mate; Thomas McIntosh, carpenter's crew; and the seamen Thomas Ellison, Thomas Burkitt, John Millward, William Muspratt and Michael Byrn. Coleman, Norman, McIntosh and Byrn were acquitted; Heywood and Morrison were pardoned; and Muspratt was subsequently acquitted on a technicality. The trial, I want to argue, once again pitted account keeping against local knowledge, and attempted to distinguish between cultural fluency and degeneracy. As each accused defended himself, he was above all putting into practice lessons he had learned in Tahiti: how can one distinguish, in the absence of possibilities of direct verbal communication, from expression, tone or the manipulation of objects, whether intentions are friendly? How is goodwill performed?

Primarily, it was inaction that had to be defended. The accused adopted a variety of postures to explain what they claimed was not active malice but fundamental passivity. Morrison, Millward and Burkett argued that their willingness to take weapons into their hands was motivated by an agreement with the Master, Fryer, sealed by whispered words and handshakes, to try to retake the ship. Norman, Coleman and McIntosh, already exonerated by Bligh, and Byrn, the semi-blind fiddler, pleaded a different passivity: forced to remain on board because of their varied skills as carpenters, armourer, and musician, they registered their resistance with cries and tears. Heywood and Ellison, from different ends of the class spectrum, pleaded the innocence of extreme youth: both were seventeen years old at the time of the trial. They claimed in retrospect to have suffered a trauma: they were the, again passive, victims of temporary confusion. The failure of any real assumption of agency leaves both witnesses and defendants grasping at the slippery signs of friendly intention. Fryer claims that he made a signal to John Millward, the Gunner, 'who I thought seemed friendly', and that he had gauged this friendly feeling from the fact that 'He appeared to me to be very uneasy in Mind' (Rutter 1931:74, 79). Morrison was perceived to be an ally when 'his appearance gave me reasons to speak to him to be on his Guard; he appeared to be friendly' (Rutter 1931:81). The accused grasp at every manifestation of both goodwill and confusion, adducing equally their bustle to provision the launch and their willingness to stay behind, their emotion and lack of emotion, as evidence of this elusive friendliness.

Tears, tokens of sensibility that, as we saw in Chapter 4, were taken as indices of genuine Tahitian feeling by Bligh during the *Bounty* voyage, are here significantly evidential. John Fryer testifies: 'Thomas McIntosh, Carpenter's Mate, another of the Prisoners, and Charles Norman, another of the Prisoners, were leaning over the rail apparently to me to be crying – Michael Byrn, another of the Prisoners, in one of the Boats crying' (Rutter 1931:77). Not all such tears are equal, however. When interrogated as to his interpretation of the men's crying, William Cole the Boatswain makes a distinction:

> You have said that you did not see any of the Prisoners shew marks of disapprobation of what was going on – What was the Cause of Coleman, Norman, and Michael Byrn's crying as you have represented them to be? – They wanted to come away; as to Byrn I do not know why he was crying. I suppose for no other reason he was blind he could not see, to my knowledge. (Rutter 1931:87)

Peter Heywood, Thomas Ellison and Thomas Burkett all testify that the officers Hayward and Hallet, who both subsequently spoke particularly vindictively against the mutineers (Hayward had also accompanied Edwards on the *Pandora* voyage and had notably displayed no sympathy towards his former shipmates), shed their own significant tears when told by Christian they could not remain on the *Bounty*:

> I was influenced in my Conduct by the Example of my Messmates, Mr. Hallet and Mr. Hayward, the former of whom was very much agitated and the latter, tho' he had been many years at Sea, yet, when Christian ordered him into the Boat he was evidently alarmed at the perilous situation, and so much overcome by the harsh Command, that he actually shed tears . . .
>
> When the two later Gentlemen Rec'd the order they weep't Bitterly and Mr. Hayward begged to know what he had done to be sent out of The Ship . . .
>
> Mr. Hallett said (with tears in his Eyes), 'I hope you will not insist upon it, Mr. Christian.' (Rutter 1931:139, 176, 187)

Yet if tears in these cases betray ignobility and not merely sentiment, their absence remains more crucially damning. Peter Heywood must account for his dry eyes as an alternative manifestation of agitation. He claims an excess of feeling has stymied its display: 'The Spectacle was as sudden to my Eyes as it was unknown to my Heart – and both were Convulsed at the Scene'; 'It is not in my power to describe my feelings upon seeing the Captain as I did' (Rutter 1931:138). Heywood seems here to draw on Adam Smith's model of 'silent and majestic sorrow', but the 'convulsed' eye that does not weep had proved unconvincing to Bligh, as we saw earlier, when he encountered the mourning Tahitian mother. Like that mother, Heywood has been accused of not merely failing to weep, but laughing (Rutter 1931:143). In his defence, he in turn calls on the spectacle of his own mournful mother: 'My Parents (but I have only one left, a solitary and Mournful Mother who is at home weeping and trembling for the Event of this day)', and indeed a chorus of female relatives whose tears stand in for his own: 'the consolation or settled misery of a dear Mother and two Sisters who mingle their tears

together and are all but frantic for my situation – pause for your Verdict!'
(Rutter 1931:147, 148). If this constitutes an attempt to recast his
apparent lack of emotion, in Adam Smith's terms, as appropriate masculine restraint, Heywood also continues to perform his youth and
innocence here: he appears at the court martial primarily as the boy –
the son and brother – rather than the man.[11]

The trial returns repeatedly to the ambiguous expressions of Heywood
and Morrison during the mutiny. Hayward is asked how he distinguishes
between the motives of Morrison and McIntosh, who both gave practical
assistance to the mutineers, and responds, 'The Difference was in the
Countenances of the People, tho' Opinion may be ill-grounded; the
Countenance of the one was rejoiced and the other depressed.' However,
he suspects Heywood of being on the side of the mutineers, although
when asked, 'Did you observe any Marks of Joy or Sorrow on his
Countenance or Behaviour?' he replies, 'Sorrow', an inconsistency
picked up by the court (Rutter 1931:121). As Greg Dening has shown,
the trial of the mutineers was theatre. The repeated references to 'marks'
of emotion recalls the eighteenth-century acting theory that I discussed
in Chapter 4, and indeed the crew members' defences divide along the
lines of such theory. McIntosh, Norman, Coleman and Byrn assert
the identity of their expression with their feeling of sorrow ('the
Sorrow I expressed at being detained was real and unfeigned' (Rutter
1931:161)), while Heywood and Morrison question the legibility of
emotion in the play of facial feature. Accused of laughter by Hallet,
Heywood asks whether he could 'have been able to particularise the
Muscles of a man's Countenance even at a considerable distance from
him' (Rutter 1931:143). If the testimony of his fellow officers is legitimate, then the connection between face and feeling must be false,
Heywood implies, since 'I am sure, if the Countenance is at all an Index
to the Heart, mine must have betrayed the sorrow and distress he has so
accurately described' (Rutter 1931:146). Morrison's defence goes further. In responding to the accusation, 'My *Countenance* has also been
compared with another employ'd on the *same* business', he asserts, 'This
Honorable Court knows that *all* Men do not bear misfortunes with the
same fortitude or equanimity of Mind, and that the face is *too often* a bad
index to the Heart.' Indeed, his very ability to mask his feelings is
represented as part of his collected endeavour to turn the mutiny
around: 'If there were *No sorrow* mark'd in my Countenance, it was to

[11] John Barrow dwells, in his defence, on the relationship of Peter Heywood with his
mother and sisters, and reproduces some of their correspondence (Barrow
1989:202–218).

deceive those whose *Act* I abhorred, that I might be at liberty to *seize* the *first* Opportunity that *might* appear favourable, to the retaking of the Ship' (Rutter 1931:166). In Diderot's terms, Morrison's capacity for detachment is consummate acting.

Writing as well as performance plays an important role in the trial. The two mutineers whose faces have proven hardest to read, Heywood and Morrison, have a distinct authorial advantage. Both have managed to retain journals. Heywood's has assisted Captain Edwards 'to form my Letter to the Admiralty'; Edwards testifies 'he gave me some Account; I had recourse to his Journals, and he was ready to Answer any Questions that I asked him' (Rutter 1931:156). Morrison wrote up his journal in 1792, first as he awaited trial and then as he recuperated after receiving the king's pardon (Maude 1968:2; Dening 1992:74). Greg Dening has argued that his account was itself instrumental in the outcome of Morrison's trial: that the existence of a manuscript was public knowledge, and that his supporters bargained for pardon on the assurance that it would remain unpublished (Dening 1992:41). (If this was indeed the case, it is perhaps unsurprising that, when he repeated his breadfruit voyage, Bligh was so fearful and punishing of Godolphin's and other alternative journals.) Heywood and Morrison also presented the most literary of the mutineers' defences. Heywood's statement is read by an attorney: he continues to shield himself behind protectors, and paint himself as the sentimental innocent. Morrison's defence is closer to legalistic detective work: he carefully builds his case. Other mutineers are also redeemed or condemned by writing. Muspratt employs a skilful legal counsel to conduct his case, who eventually enables him to evade his sentence on a technicality. Thomas Ellison, who was hanged, is the real boy victim of the court martial: the youngest crew member, he is, whatever his degree of involvement, most poignantly innocent of the literacy that exonerates other mutineers. At the trial he speaks of the debts his illiteracy incurred: 'Capt. Bligh took great pains with me and spoke too [*sic*] Mr. Samule, his Clark, to teach me Writing and Arithmetick and I believe Would have taught me further had not this happend. I must have been very Ingreatfull if I had in any respect assisted in this Unhappy Affair' (Rutter 1931:177–8).

Bligh, not present to hear the words of the accused or their written testimonies, called the mutineers to mind by their 'marks'. At Coupang, after his arduous open boat voyage, he drew up a list, 'made out from the recollection of the persons with me, who were best acquainted with their private marks' (Bligh 1794:277), which included the following portraits of those who stood trial:

Peter Heywood, midshipman, aged seventeen years, five feet seven inches high, fair complexion, light brown hair, well proportioned; very much tattooed; and on the right leg is tattooed the three legs of Man, as it is upon that coin. At this time he has not done growing; and speaks with the Manx, or Isle of Man, accent ...

James Morrison, boatswain's mate, aged twenty-eight years, five feet eight inches high, sallow complexion, long black hair, slender made; has lost the use of the upper joint of the forefinger of the right hand; tattooed with a star under his left breast, and a garter round his left leg, with the motto of 'Honi soit qui mal y pense'; and has been wounded in one of his arms with a musket-ball ...

John Millward, seaman, aged twenty-two years, five feet five inches high, brown complexion, dark hair, strong made; very much tattooed in different parts of the body, and under the pit of the stomach, with a *taoomy* of Otaheite ...

Thomas Burkett, seaman, aged twenty-six years, five feet nine inches high, fair complexion, very much pitted with the small-pox, brown hair, slender made, and very much tattooed ...

William Muspratt, seaman, aged thirty years, five feet six inches high, dark complexion, brown hair, slender made, a very strong black beard, with scars under his chin; is tattooed in several places of his body ...

Thomas Ellison, seaman, aged seventeen years, five feet three inches high, fair complexion, dark hair, strong made; had got his name tattooed on his right arm and dated 25th October 1788 ...

William Byrne [i.e. Michael Byrn], seaman, aged twenty-eight years, five feet six inches high, fair complexion, short fair hair, slender made; is almost blind and has the mark of an issue on the back of his neck; plays the violin.

Joseph Coleman, armourer, aged forty years, five feet six inches high, fair complexion, grey hair, strong made; a heart tattooed on one of his arms.

Charles Norman, carpenter's mate, aged 26 years, five feet nine inches high, fair complexion, light brown hair, slender made, is pitted with the small-pox, and has a remarkable motion with his head and eyes.

Thomas M'Intosh, carpenter's crew, aged twenty-eight years, five feet six inches high, fair complexion, light brown hair, slender made; is pitted with the small-pox and is tattooed.

The four last are deserving of mercy, being detained against their inclinations.
(Bligh 1794:275–7)

The ways in which the mutineers are recorded as marked begin with age and rank, height and complexion, and end with the legacies of disease and deformity, but the most distinguishing markings are those of the tattoos almost all have adopted. There seems to be a correspondence, in Bligh's list, between tattooing and guilt, so that the four 'deserving of mercy' are either untattooed or have minor or unnoticed markings. Heywood's heavy tattooing, on the other hand, comes as a surprise to those who have read his protestations of youth and innocence. Indeed his most memorable marking, the symbol of the 'Isle of Man', seems to encapsulate the ambiguous status between boy and manhood that he manipulates in his defence: although 'not done growing' he has tasted an 'isle of manhood' in Tahiti, but the 'Isle of Man' is also his family seat, referencing the birthright that will eventually be significant to his pardon. Thomas Ellison, on the other hand, has identified himself fully with the new island, inscribing the date of his arrival in Tahiti under his name upon his right arm, while Millward, like Fletcher Christian, has adopted a full Tahitian tattoo, rather than a composite of British and local cultural symbols.

Without wishing to labour a notion of culture 'inscribed on the body', there are ways in which the mutineers can be seen to have adopted a writing and a language that communicate across the codes of ship's law. At a crucial moment during the mutiny, Christian is reported to have attempted to silence Bligh by addressing him in Tahitian. The semi-literate Thomas Ellison is well equipped to translate Christian's words to the court: 'Captn. Bligh Wanted to talk with him, I believe. I heard Mr. Christain [sic] say two or three times "Mammoo, sir," which the meaning of the word is, "Sillance, sir"' (Rutter 1931:175).[12] This address to the captain forms part of Ellison's portrait of a deranged Christian: 'he looked like a Madman, is [sic] long hair was luse, is shirt Collair open'. But even as he appears simply to have forgotten distinctions of rank, Christian asserts that the crew has become bound by a new cultural language. It includes a variety of practices from which Bligh kept himself exempt: tattooing, sexual exchange; as well as others in which he saw himself as expert: vocabulary, gift-giving, making significant friends. For all his careful diplomacy, Bligh appears excluded from this achieved fluency.

Towtow

> He who justly proves himself a friend is man enough nor is he wanting to society. A single friendship may acquit him.
>
> – Shaftesbury

Although he was adopted as a Romantic figure, Christian was, according to Bligh's description, a bowlegged man, 'tattooed on his backside', with whom one might be quite literally reluctant to shake hands: 'He is subject to violent perspirations, and particularly his hands, so that he soils anything he handles' (Bligh 1794:275). If this makes him a distasteful associate and indeed contributes to the picture of his descent into madness in British terms, his willing nativization opens him to a different level of cross-cultural friendship from Bligh's. Despite all the careful parsing of motive, the weighing of allegiance and the rereading of gesture

---

[12] Burkett has Christian addressing the term, less respectfully, to Hayward (Rutter 1931:185).

that takes place at the court martial, James Morrison's equally evidential text makes a simple claim: that Christian understood friendship better than Bligh; that he was a better friend. When the mutineers arrived back at Tahiti to stock themselves with animals and foodstuffs and women for the fortified community they planned to construct at Tubuai, Christian told their Tahitian friends that the ship's crew had met with Captain Cook, that Cook had settled a country called 'Wytootacke' (Aitutake, in what would become known as the Cook Islands), and that Christian and his party were obtaining supplies to join him there. Morrison recounts:

> We remained here till the 16th during which time we were plentifully supplyd with evry necessary by the Natives our old friends nor do I think they would have thought any worse of us had they known the truth of the Story or been any way shy of supplying us as Mr. Christian was beloved by the whole of them but on the Contrary none liked Mr. Bligh tho they flatterd him for His Riches, which is the Case among polishd Nations those in power being always Courted. (Morrison 1935:52)

Christian, Morrison claims, was 'beloved'. He made friendships that testified to genuine sentiment, and transcended the politics of diplomacy. In both Tahitian and European terms, Christian's friendships purportedly prompt an uncalculated giving, far removed from that displayed by and towards Bligh.

The romance and inconclusiveness of his story have made Christian in particular, of all the *Bounty*'s cast, a figure of ongoing speculation. In briefly turning to some of the things known and written about his time on Pitcairn, I simply want to conclude this chapter as I began it, by scrutinizing a claim about friendship. If, as Bligh asserted, the mutiny could be attributed to the 'friendly and endearing behaviour' of Tahitians, and if, as Morrison professed, Christian held the affectionate support of Tahitians not through any principle of abstract justice but through the force of feeling he inspired, 'beloved by the whole of them', then how did this story of cross-cultural friendship play out on Pitcairn Island?

As Alan Frost has shown, accounts of the mutiny offer an inconsistent composite portrait of Christian: 'We learn that Christian was "always cheerful", and that he was "always sullen and morose"; that he was a person who indulged his sexuality liberally, and that he was the very reverse of a sensual man; that he cared about the welfare of his party, and that he treated them capriciously and brutally' (Frost 1994:227). Affectively and interpersonally, Christian appears equally as bad and good friend. Frost is particularly interested in the ways in which Christian's story was taken up by the Wordsworth/Coleridge/Southey Romantic circle (he was also famously and more immediately the subject of

Byron's 'The Island'). Romanticism, however, is quintessentially a literature of narcissism rather than friendship: the image of Christian favoured by Byron, 'Stern, aloof a little from the rest' (Canto IV, 85), is tempered, in the testimonies of his British supporters, by a sentimental tribute to his capacities for inspiring male friendship. Edward Christian's defence of his brother figures him making repeated attempts to do alone what the sympathetic feeling he inspires in the crew instead requires him to do communally: to abandon Bligh. Christian is said to have been, alternatively, carefully planning to slip away from the ship on a raft of spars in the hope of making his way back to Tonga, or contemplating suicide (he is described in two sources wearing a deep sea lead 'concealed in his breast' prior to the mutiny as 'another resource'): either way, he is reported to have told Norman that the mutiny 'never would have happened if I could have left the ship alone' (Barney 1794:252). When the experiment of settlement on Tubuai fails, Christian is again represented as asking to see out his fate alone: '*I desire no one to stay with me*', only once again to find himself joined by a faithful company who declare, '*We shall never leave you, Mr. Christian, go where you will*' (Barney 1794:260). Edward Christian collects 'word for word, some of the unpremeditated expressions used by the gentlemen and people of the *Bounty* in speaking of this unfortunate mutineer', which include fervent testimonies to his capacity to inspire friendship: '*every officer and seaman on board the ship would have gone through fire and water to have served him*'; '*He . . . was dear to all who ever knew him*'; '*beloved by all*' (Barney 1794:262–3).

In literary terms then, Christian may be seen to straddle the types of the sentimental man of feeling and the solitary Romantic hero. He is a sensitive individual in a harsh man's world. Edward Christian depicts his brother as emotionally overwrought in the immediate lead-up to the mutiny: 'tears were running fast from his eyes in big drops'. Yet such tears are irregular and provoked, testimony to the extent of his abuse by Bligh: 'This was the only time he ever was seen in tears on board the ship, and one of the seamen, being asked if he ever observed Christian in tears before, answered, "No, he was no milk-sop"' (Barney 1794:250–1). It is important, however, to note the extent to which his depiction, both as feeling and as manly, is equally reliant on what is understood to be a Tahitian frame of reference. Thus, Edward's defence of Christian as a man who inspired strong male feeling is addressed to popular depictions of his brother as highly sexually, or in turn emotionally, engaged by the women, or a woman, of Tahiti. Edward avers that 'the officers who were with Christian upon the same duty declare that he never had a female favourite at Otaheite, nor any attachment or particular connection among the women. It is true that some had what they called *their girls*, or women with whom they constantly lived all the time they were upon the island, but this was not the case with Christian' (Barney 1794:262). This is pseudo-ethnography in the Hamilton mode, conveniently uniting stereotypes of native female and unruly sailor libido. But multiple sources also cite *taio* bonds as evidence of the kinds of loyalty that Christian inspired.

This is interesting in a number of ways. First, *taio* complicates the adoption of a too straightforward binary opposition between homo-social or homosexual shipboard ties and island female connection in any retrospective assessment of the mutiny (Hough 1973; Wallace 2003:51). *Taio* as we have seen, primarily from Morrison, involves a kind of marriage with, usually, another male, which is understood to formalize a significant friendship bond entailing an exchange of identities. A compelling world of male union, then, called the *Bounty* crew on shore as well as at sea. Secondly, it involves a covert amalgamation of European and Tahitian notions of friendship. Thus when Morrison claims that 'we were plenti-fully supplyd with evry Necessary by the Natives our old friends nor do I think they would have thought any worse of us had they known the truth of the Story or been any way shy of supplying us as Mr. Christian was beloved by the whole of them', he moves seamlessly between an under-standing of the exchange relationship reified by established friendship in Tahiti and a familiar European notion of friendship as liberating forms of trust that exceed legalistic constraints. In order to exonerate Christian from the ignominy of the mutiny, Morrison frees *taio* from both its typically disreputable association with calculation in European accounts and its much attested particularity. Calculation is reserved to describe the local relationship with Bligh, who has in turn been too careful to flatter appropriate powerful figures in bestowing his friendship. Christian on the other hand, it is claimed, inspired a level of goodwill that exceeds the conventions of *taio*. Tahitians would have continued to supply Christian because he was 'beloved by *the whole* of them' (my emphasis), not just a particular friend: because he stimulated a force of feeling that overrode the politics of exchange.

Finally, the complex referencing of *taio* bonds supports my argument that local knowledge, and in particular *taio* as an instantiation of local knowledge, is one of the most significant ways in which the justice of the mutiny is contested. Edward Christian enshrines a moment of this contest in his defence, when he reports:

Captain Bligh sometimes entertained the chiefs of the island, and before all the company used to abuse Christian for some pretended fault or other ... There is no country in the world where the notions of aristocracy and family pride are carried higher than at Otaheite, and it is a remarkable circumstance that the chiefs are naturally distinguished by taller persons, and more open and intelligent countenances, than the people of inferior condition. Hence these are the principle qualities by which the natives estimate the gentility of strangers, and Christian was so great a favourite with them that according to the words of one person, 'they adored the very ground he trod upon'. He was *tyo*, or friend, to a chief of the first rank in the island, whose name, according to the custom of the country, he took in exchange for his own, and in whose property he participated. The chief dined one day with Captain Bligh and was told by him that his *tyo* Christian was only his *towtow*, or servant. The chief upbraided Christian with this, who was much mortified at being thus degraded in the opinion of his friend, and endeavoured to recommend himself again to the chief by assuring him that he, Captain Bligh, and all the officers were *towtows* of the King of Bretane. (Barney 1794:257)

We see Bligh here using his knowledge of Tahitian vocabulary to mark a distinction – possibly even make a pun – between friendship and servitude, from which Christian is in turn forced to exert his own translation skills to redeem himself. Encounter is depicted as its own complex performance space, in which local knowledge is required in order to manifest signs of power. Like Morrison, who claimed that Tahitian *ari'i* flattered Bligh 'for His Riches, which is the Case among polished Nations those in power being always Courted', Edward Christian makes an argument about cultural consensus. However, he sees a natural aristocracy as uniting Christian with the Tahitian noble savage: Tahitian affirmation becomes a validation of Christian's qualities as a gentleman and as a friend.

Yet if his supporters set up *taio* as a key term in Christian's defence, they also establish a basis for condemning the community he established on Pitcairn Island as a failure of principles of friendship. Because on Pitcairn the mutineers' Polynesian *taio*s are definitively recast as *towtow*s. After leaving Tubuai and returning sixteen mutineers to Matavai Bay, Christian and the eight mutineers who cast their lot with him cut the *Bounty*'s cable and departed on the night of 22 September 1789. The Tahitian woman Teehuteatuaonoa, known as 'Jenny', was one of nineteen women, a female child and six men: three from Tahiti, two from Tubuai and one from Raiatea, who were abducted on the ship. (Of the other women, Teehuteatuaonoa reports, one in desperation leapt off the ship and swam back to shore, while six 'who were rather ancient' (Teehuteatuaonoa 1829:590) were dropped off at Moorea.) Teehuteatuaonoa lived on Pitcairn for thirty years before seeking a passage back to Tahiti, subsequently giving two accounts of the Pitcairn community that are unique in enabling some individuation of these 'wives' and *taio*s (Teehuteatuaonoa 1819 and 1829). One of the two Tubuaian men she identifies was Taroamiva, the younger brother of the chief from whom Christian had purchased the land for his proposed Tubuaian settlement, who had left his island believing his existence there to be endangered by his friendship with Christian (Morrison 1935:63–4; Maude 1968:17). The Raiatean was a high-ranking man named Tararo. Teehuteatuaonoa also names Oopee and Teimua among the Tahitian *taio*s taken to Pitcairn. Her own status was a relatively ambiguous one: of all the women who went to Pitcairn she alone remained childless, and Greg Dening describes her as *taio* rather than wife of the mutineer Alexander Smith (later John Adams), 'claimed by him and initialed with a tattoo under her left arm, "AS/1789" ' (Dening 1992:321).

The abduction of *taio*s was only the first stage in a process by which Polynesian friends were degraded to servants, and indeed slaves. None of the Polynesians was given any land on Pitcairn. Teehuteatuaonoa passes over the significance of such a division of resources, reporting with a biblical simplicity, 'They shortly after divided the ground, and allotted to each his proportion' (Teehuteatuaonoa 1829:591); however, this is clearly the moment at which *taio*s, friends bound in a commitment to sharing resources as though they shared identities, were refigured as serfs, labouring without land or property of their own. There were, by Greg Dening's calculation, 'Nine portions, nine mutineers; there was no land for the "blacks" (as they called the natives). Neither the six men from Tubuai, Tahiti and Raiatea nor the twelve women and infant girl from Tahiti were allocated land' (Dening 1992:316). The women in fact become part of the allotment: one each taken as wives by the mutineers, and the remaining three shared between the Polynesian men. I have elsewhere traced in detail the shifts by which, accompanying this division of property, brown-skinned Polynesians were refigured as 'blacks' and noble savage intimates as natural slaves (V. Smith 2003:130–2). The rebellions and reprisals that eventually led to the murders of five of the mutineers and all of the Tubuaian and Society Island men on Pitcairn were all attributable to this material reconfiguration.

If the history of the mutiny has been figured as a cyclical story of the debasement of power, friendship – Bligh's excuse and Edward Christian's defence – has been left out of the picture. But tracing the fluctuating understanding of cross-cultural friendship through the mutiny's archive adds significantly to our understanding of this history. It also maps a wider shift in relations between Europeans and Oceanians as the eighteenth century drew to a close, and visits of exploration were replaced by the tentative early settlement of beachcombers, of whom the *Bounty* mutineers were among the first, and then missionaries and traders. As relationships became more enduringly linked for Europeans to land and property, the exchanges of *taio* became more fraught. Co-identity in cross-cultural friendship was not coterminous with the fashioning of self that seemed to be rendered possible in these later translocations. Possibly this is another factor responsible for the linguistic obsolescence of the term *taio* in the nineteenth century. Rhetorically, the decline of *taio* registered in the early stirrings of what was to become a full-blown literary nostalgia for the immediacy of the first South Seas encounter. When Bligh returned to Tahiti in the *Providence* to complete his breadfruit voyage, he noted, as I mentioned earlier, the decline of traditional practice, that accompanied the creolization of increased contact: 'it is rather a difficulty to get them to speak their own language without mixing a jargon of English, and they are so generally altered, that I believe no European in future will ever know what their ancient Customs of receiving Strangers were' (Oliver 1988:75). Bligh's nostalgia here for the uncompromised Tahitian culture he claims to have observed on earlier visits is clearly tinctured by his own sense of the intervening history of the mutiny. The mutineers had left, with their mixed race progeny, a bastardized Tahitian language and culture, not merely structurally but ethically debased: 'Our Friends here have benefited very little from the intercourse they have had with Europeans since I left them. Our Countrymen must have taken great pains to have taught them such vile & blackguard expressions as are in the Mouth of every Tahitian' (Oliver 1988:62). Yet it was not just criminal contact that had been detrimental: Vancouver's Admiralty-backed exploration voyage had equally participated, in the interim between Bligh's two breadfruit voyages, in changing codes of contact: 'When the Matilda Captain Weatherhead passed Matavai, some of the Natives swam off to him with Notes that some of the Discovery's People had given them to recommend them as Tyo's, these Notes were dated the 12th January 1792, which I suspect was the time they Sailed' (Oliver 1988:61–2). The conversion of *taio* from form of practice to form letter, from exchange to account keeping, is registered even by the punctilious Bligh with regret.

7 'Prizeable companions'

> Those who want friends to open themselves unto, are cannibals of their own hearts.
>
> – Bacon

Edward Robarts deserted the whaler *New Euphrates* at Vaitahu Bay, Tahuata in the Southern Marquesas in December 1798. He claimed that he jumped ship to escape the consequences of a planned mutiny.[1] His flight was facilitated by a Hawaiian, Tama,[2] then resident on the island, and by the chief of Vaitahu, Tainai, who directed him towards Hapatoni, another bay where he would be safe from the captain of the ship. Robarts spent his early months on Tahuata forging friendships that allowed him to acquire the language and explore the island. But between sociable encounters he was left alone, which, he admitted in his journal, 'gives me an oppertunity of peeping and prying about me' (Dening 1974:56). In January and then again in late February 1799, he offered his assistance to the crew of the whaler *London*, which anchored at Tahuata to make repairs. When the ship departed in March, Robarts was displeased to find that 'a stout boy, a native of france, had hid himself among the natives'. Robarts comments of this fellow beach-comber, whose name was Jean Cabri,[3] and whom he would re-encounter later during his stay in the Marquesas, that 'He proved to be a very bad person not worth notice. He departed to live on the other side the Isle. I would not suffer him to be in the same house with me' (Dening 1974:68).

---

[1] The story of his escape is reconstructed by Greg Dening (2004:284), who edited Robarts's journal. It should be noted at the outset that this is not a diary in the strict sense: it was a retrospective account of his time in the Marquesas, 1798–1806, begun in 1810–11 in Calcutta and completed between 1819 and 1824 (Dening 1974:16).

[2] The name 'Tama' was, as Crook explains, an island version of 'Sam'. Crook gives his Hawaiian name as 'Owheve'. Owheve had been renamed Sam in Boston, from where he was returning in the *Alexander* when he was importuned to remain at Tahuata by the local Marquesans (Crook 2007:109).

[3] He was also known as Joseph Kabris.

Immediately after these remarks, Robarts recounts the following story:

Being now a second time left alone I imploy my time by degrees to learn the language among my friends ... One day in the abscence of the family I took a walk to look about me. I observd an old house uninhabited. Out of curiosity I peepd in and espyd a large chest. This enduced me to go into the house. I opend the chest, it not being fast. Here I found some medicinces [sic], a bible and some other good books, an old pair of black breeches, a Keg which once had been full of nails, with several letters written in a Journal. They was numberd. On peruseing them I found they had been wrote by a person of the name Crook, one of the Missionaries that was sent out the first time the Mission Ship *Duff* ... came to the south seas. This discovery gave me a great deal of uneasiness. I could not tell what to think. By the date of some of his papers he had been abscent about eight months. At times I was verry unhappy. Sometimes I thought he had died; other times I thought he had been murdered, as I found several things among the natives I supposed to have been part of the contents of the chest. Oft would I weep in some secret place. How much did I regreet the loss of the company of this good young man. At least his writings was pious [and] gave me to think he would have been a very prizeable companion in my situation. However I found a very good companion in Mr Crooks bible and the other good books I found in his chest. (Dening 1974:68–9)

The house he enters initially strikes Robarts as old and uninhabited. But within it he finds signs of habitation that are at once familiar and alien: a series of cultural objects that he is uniquely placed to read and interpret. Yet he is unclear whether he is trespasser or guest. Like Goldilocks, he seems to fluctuate between intrusion and entitlement, between a sense that he invades a pristine shrine, and a notion that he is the belated but rightful inhabitant of this house full of objects that find their appropriate use and purpose with his arrival. Where the encounter with the French boy Cabri produced feelings of alienation, registered as a visceral inclination to exclude him from his own domestic space, the encounter with Mr. Crook's possessions promotes an instantaneous and regretful identification. Robarts would 'not suffer [Cabri] to be in the same house with [him]', but having refused the offer of friendship with one fellow European, finds an absent, mourned compatriot within a domicile where he is in turn an intruder. Cabri may offer a more immediate reflection to Robarts the fellow beachcomber, but it is an image that is rejected in favour of the idealized missionary. Crook's possessions reinstate a distinction between the purportedly civilized and the savage that Robarts had hitherto negotiated by assimilation. He prizes Crook's distinction, and no longer wishes to be 'hid away' like Cabri among the natives: to pass as a local.

Robarts's peeping and prying, initially turned outwards, towards the new (Marquesan) culture, finds itself travelling home to focus on the traces of a lost version of domesticity. And with his intrusion among these out-of-place things comes a sense of shame, for the distance he has travelled from the kinds of unbending, unassimilable value represented by the pious young man. The passage registers a series of shifts, between alienation and recognition, intimacy and repudiation, the *unheimlich* and *heimweh*. And within these contradictory experiences of affinity and loss, there are claims for authentic emotion: the mention of tears shed in private, the sentimental signifiers of heartfelt grief. The loss that Robarts mourns in Crook is both the loss of a potential friend and of a potential self: and the two losses are intimately connected. The ambiguous phrasing, 'he would have been a very prizeable companion in my situation' expresses simultaneously the desire *for* a companion and the desire to *be* that ideal figure, and thus to be better equipped to cope with the vicissitudes of his 'situation'.

Robarts's evaluation of Crook as 'prizeable companion', which comprises a claim that he knows how properly to value the missionary, is metonymized in his subsequent relationship to Crook's possessions. Robarts's picture of the departed missionary becomes more detailed with each new object he finds: Crook's identity is linked in an immediate and affective way with the signs of civil and domestic culture. The abandoned house provokes a general melancholy ('I was verry unhappy'), betokening inevitably, through its array of foresaken commodities, an absent British subject, whom Robarts both mourns ('How much did I regreet the loss of the company of this good young man') and seeks to replace. He does this by befriending a range of texts deserted by the previous occupant. They include 'Mr Crooks bible and the other good books I found in his chest', but also 'several letters written in a Journal'. In reading these different texts Robarts accesses his imagined friend in two ways: both by 'peeping and prying' at his intimate thoughts and by occupying the space that Crook has vacated as reader. Just as Robarts has begun to find intimacy in a new spoken tongue, literacy is idealized as a form of fraternity.

The feeling of simultaneous recognition and loss that encompasses Robarts among Crook's possessions produces an attendant alienation from the local community on Tahuata. His sense of the uncanny, registered within the empty house, infects the broader island setting so that where he had once felt at home, he now becomes unsettled. A scene of reified domesticity, which initially seemed to position him as culturally equipped inhabitant, ramifies into sites of conscious concealment and potential misappropriation. He 'supposd' that he finds items from the house distributed among the natives. He must now find another 'secret place' in which to weep. The potential eruption of savage violence and the unspoken threat of cannibalism implicit in the complete disappearance of the 'good young man', of whom books, breeches and medicines are the only physical trace, destabilizes Robarts's sense of both the sanctity of this domestic shrine and the benignity of the society in which he has made his alternative home.[4] 'My friends', 'the family' become simply 'the natives': potential murderers. The empty house reminds him of a lost community from which he has become alienated, and simultaneously alienates him from the community within which he has placed himself, where he has been welcomed, introduced, exchanged names and taught the language. The estrangement Robarts suffers after encountering Crook's belongings, is in contrast to his depiction of an idealized Marquesan model of friendship and domestic hospitality in his journal. The first significant relationships that Robarts forges in Tahuata are with the ruling chief of Vaitahu, Tainai, and the chief of Hapatoni, Tehauitafettere. He describes an overwhelming and competitive hospitality that is extended to him in these communities, in terms with which we are by now familiar:

The inhabitants all seemd to try to outdo each other in Kindness to me ... their numbers so pressing round me made their company a burden, every one asking a number of questions. I could only answer with a smile or a nod. At times I was obliged to secret myself till they was gone, which sometimes would be sun sett. I would then return to the house. My friend and his consort very kindly receives me – more like a parent, a brother or some near Kinsman than an entire stranger, and that [from] an uncivilized race of people quite different from enlightened nations! These poor benighted people shews that hospitality not to be meet with among a number of people who call themselves christians. I speak as I have found, and deem it the duty of everyone to greatfully acknowledge the worth of the friendly hut that screens him from want and misery; for this ceartenly was my situation, a stranger in a strange country, among a race of people I could not converse with. (Dening 1974:55)

Robarts's fluctuating sense of his position as both stranger and friend, and as friend by virtue of being stranger, manifests as a need for privacy in the midst of overwhelming welcome. For hospitality in this Oceanic community is, once again, perceived as both consummate and implicitly excessive, its enthusiasm competitive as well as thoughtful ('outdo each other in Kindness'). Robarts's apostrophizing of the 'friendly hut that screens him' manifests this ambivalence, its walls acting as a screen

---

[4] Both Calder 1996 and Wallace 2005 have focused on the relationship between domesticity and alienation in the writings of early missionary settlers in the Marquesas.

between him and want, in the double sense of destitution but also clamorous importuning.

Just prior to this equivocal eulogy Robarts has highlighted an issue of Marquesan etiquette that we can now register as trope rather than simple reportage. Describing his arrival at Hapatoni beach, he writes:

The other natives comes to pay their respects. They are remarkable fond of strangers, several came around me to feel whether I was flesh and bone as they was . . .
I must here beg leave of my fair reader to permit me to relate such matters of fact as are within bounds. My friend took me by the hand and led me to the side of his consort who was sitting on a fine matt. I was a little surpriz'd at this part of the cerimony when he told me I must sleep on the same matt with her. I must confess the ladys artillery was powerfull enough for any man to surrender, but I could not accept of this unrivaled peice of friendship. I ashurd him by sighns that I was perfectly satisfied of his sincear friendship towards me and begd leave to retire at a becomeing distance from his consort, which was granted. I told him it was against the laws of my country to sleep with other mens wives. (Dening 1974:53)

The situation recalls the 'serious inauguration' described by George Hamilton (Chapter 2) when he was required to sleep with the wife of the 'king' of Moorea. Robarts's comments on Marquesan generosity echo Hamilton's eulogy to Tahitian *taio*s: 'the extent of the word friend, by them, is only bounded by the universe' (Hamilton 1793:38–40). Yet once again in Robarts's case we find issues of difference played out through the disposition of domestic space. Robarts argues to be allowed to keep a 'becomeing distance' between himself and the chief's consort, with the chief's 'unrivaled peice of friendship' figured as an assault by phallic women. While he claims to have successfully evaded the 'powerful' artillery of the consort, he eventually also complies with a compromised version of local 'ceremony' by sleeping with a relative of his friend. The anecdote might be read as the Marquesan chief's extended attempt to ascertain his degree of susceptibility: 'whether I was flesh and bone as they was'.

It is against this model of sociality: the open house, the importunate crowd, unfamiliarity registered as over-familiarity, that we can best read the sense of nostalgia that confronts Robarts when he crosses Crook's threshold. Wishfully, Robarts deems his anecdote 'within bounds', but it is a story of breached boundaries. Oceanian generosity is exemplary but also, to Robarts's mind, excessive. The pressures of hospitality dissolve what in his home society are regarded as the appropriate boundaries between men; boundaries manifest in notions of inviolable property, including conjugal property, and in domestic reclusion. The swapping of names has effected a dissolution of the nominal distinction between self and other which sets in play a potentially endless series of exchanges: of goods, of services, of bodies. Although Robarts represents the woman as the object of circulation here, it is more likely that he himself is the sexual object. Marquesan women were able to take as many as fifteen *pekio* or secondary husbands according to polyandrous custom, a fact of which Robarts was aware, writing later in his account, 'In this liberty these people differ from any other class of people that I ever met with. One man may have several women, but for one woman to have several men I think is a pill hard to digest' (Dening 1974:270). The appeal of Crook, the lost friend, constitutes, in this context, the respite of containment; both the sexual containment signalled by his piety, and the containment of things, shored up and hidden away in the large chest, within the house walls. Yet in the very process of recovering the sense of fellow feeling that Crook's abandoned house enables, Robarts has had to invade and intrude. He takes possession of Crook's belongings, and in doing so demonstrates, not just his occupancy of the space Crook left behind, but his assimilation into a society that does not respect the inalienability of things. Even as he identifies with the lost missionary and grows suddenly fearful of savage violence and thievery, it is nonetheless he who breaks open Crook's chest and steals his possessions.

The imagined friendship of Robarts and Crook recapitulates and refigures many of the concerns of this book. It casts its reflection on the cross-cultural friendships that each man succeeded or failed in forging. It reclaims a desire for particular rather than general friendship, pits links of birthplace against cross-cultural allegiance and trades racial hierarchies against those of class. Like the great model friendships of Gaius Laelius and Scipio Africanus, or of Michel de Montaigne and Etienne de la Boetie, Robarts and Crook's lost friendship is reified in mourning ('Sometimes I thought he had died; . . . Oft would I weep in some secret place. How much did I regreet the loss of the company of this good young man'). It invokes and troubles the Ciceronian tradition of friendship as mirror image, and introduces a further Christian philosophical tension between friendship and broader charity. It is both an extreme form of stranger friendship and a plea for cultural familiarity. The brief anecdote within which the friendship is imagined expresses a yearning for affinity, figured as natural, a type of homecoming, through the forgetting of other boundaries, discursive and social, which would have rendered this, in fact unlikely, pair at best equivocal friends. In this final chapter I will pursue some of these resonances in a broader context of early Oceanic missionary encounter. I turn to the period of early settlement, in which Europeans saw themselves as entering and changing, rather than simply visiting and observing, island communities. My focus here shifts from Tahiti to the Marquesas, figured by the end of the eighteenth century as an outpost of genuine savagery in an increasingly known Pacific. Codes and practices of friendship, or their purported absence, emerge as significant factors in this representation. A contest of ascendancy was at this juncture played out between the two main categories of first settlers in Oceania, the beachcombers and missionaries, which was partly dependent upon assertions of cultural expertise. A proto-ethnographic cultural intimacy constituted a formal and lasting expression of superior personal intimacy. Therefore, this chapter attends to the subtle connections between claims for intimate and ethnographic knowledge: for what, together, constitute *insider* knowledge. Finally, it seeks to test as well as affirm those principles of encounter that I have traced throughout this book. It registers the feelings that animate Robarts's response to the loss of Crook, the imagined friend: the binding forces of familiarity and shame that could instantly nullify those very risks and rewards of cross-cultural friendship that I have sought, nonetheless, to represent.

A Powerful Example

Of a commended stranger, only the good report is told by others. Only the good and new is heard by us. He stands to us for humanity. He is what we wish. Having imagined and invested him, we ask how we should stand related in conversation and action with such a man and are uneasy with fear.

– Emerson

The missed encounter of Robarts and Crook, which gives pause to Robarts's vigorous narrative, is also mourned by the missionary, though not by name. Robarts barely makes an appearance in William Pascoe Crook's *Account of the Marquesas Islands*, and when he does the reference makes apparent the unlikelihood of their actual friendship:

Early in December, arrived the Butterworth, then commanded by Lawrence Frazier, & the New Euphrates, Henery Glasspoole, both which vessels had been engaged in the South Wale Fishery; & having met at the Gallipagoes, had kept Company from thence. Having received great damage from a violent Gale on the coast of Colefornia, they remained three weeks at Resolution Bay to make needful repairs. Temoteitei [Timauteitei], the youngest son of Pahouhonu [Pahauhonu], being on board the Butterworth at the time of the Ship's departure, was detained, a boy being wanted on board. On the other hand, the Cook of the Euphrates, named James Roberts, deserted, & was secreted by the Natives at Ennapoo [Anapoo]. His conduct, however, was soon found to be so different from that of Mr. Crook, that he became contemptible to the Islanders; who took from him any thing he procured, as they frequently serve the Women of the poorer sort. (Crook 2007: 116–17)

Once again, the picture of the other is derived from hearsay: Crook has of course left Tahuata when Robarts deserts. News of the latter's arrival must have travelled by word of mouth, couched in the kinds of complimentary reflection that would flatter the hearer, possibly via Timauteitei, one of two Marquesans who travelled back to England with Crook. As we shall see, Crook was not able to offer an effective alternative to Robarts's example of European identity: his inclusion of this report in his account projects his own failure back onto Robarts. Placed beside Robarts's sentimental conjuring of their impossible friendship, Crook's comments here register as a rebuff. Where Robarts pays homage to the traces of Crook, Crook fails to record his name correctly. He pulls local knowledge to castrate Robarts, suggesting that his gifts in Tahuata did not receive 'proper returns', so that contrary to Robarts's account of himself, he figures as poor woman rather than great man.

Crook arrived at Vaitahu Bay on 5 June 1797 in the *Duff*, as part of the first London Missionary Society evangelical voyage to the Pacific. He was twenty-two years old, originally from Dartmouth in Devonshire, and had been a manservant. After his conversion and acceptance as a missionary (initially disputed because of his youth), he had trained briefly as a tin worker.[5] The *Duff* had landed groups of nineteen and ten missionaries, respectively, at Tahiti and Tonga, leaving two missionaries bound for the Marquesas: Crook and a more senior convert, recently ordained, named John Harris. But once the ship reached Tahuata, Harris found those same issues that had discombobulated Robarts – shared blankets, chests of possessions and infringed boundaries – to be thoroughly alienating. Having made their intentions known to Tainai and obtained his support, the pair went on shore with the captain to see what level of hospitality and support they might expect. When the captain later sought 'to know their sentiments of this place, and whether they were still in the same mind to settle' (J. Wilson 1799:132), he found the two differently disposed. Crook had read friendly intentions everywhere and optimistically multiplied the signs of hospitality:

Mr. Crook observed, that he was encouraged by the reception they had met with; thought the chief had behaved exceedingly well, and approved of the house assigned them, the place, and the people; and concluded by saying, that though there was not the same plenty as at other islands, he had no objections

---

[5] This was in accordance with the London Missionary Society priority of sending 'godly mechanics' into the mission field. Among the missionaries of the *Duff*, wrote Wilson, 'we were desirous to obtain some possessed of literary attainments, but especially to procure adepts in such useful arts and occupations as would make us most acceptable to the heathen in that state of inferior civilization to which they were advanced' (J. Wilson 1799:4; see also V. Smith 1998:58; Gunson 1978:32–42; Davies 1961:xxx).

to stay ... However, appearances gave him reason to think that they had their plentiful seasons here as well as at other islands... (J. Wilson 1799:132–3; compare ms journal: Crook [1799]).

Harris, on the other hand, 'delivered his sentiments with hesitation, as if fear had taken possession of his mind: his opinions were quite contrary to Crook's; he disapproved of every thing, and judged the scene before him a solemn one; and, in short, seemed entirely to have lost his firmness and ardour' (J. Wilson 1799:133). While Crook began sleeping on shore the next day, Harris procrastinated for a week before landing with his possessions. When he eventually came ashore, the pair were invited to go with Tainai on an excursion to another valley; Harris chose to remain at Vaitahu Bay, and as Wilson's *Missionary Voyage* relates:

The chief ... desirous of obliging him, not considering any favour too great, left him his wife, to be treated as if she were his own, till the chief came back again. Mr Harris told him that he did not want the woman; however, she looked up to him as her husband, and finding herself treated with total neglect, became doubtful of his sex; and acquainted some of the other females with her suspicion, who accordingly came in the night, when he slept, and satisfied themselves concerning that point, but not in such a peaceable way but that they awoke him. (J. Wilson 1799:141–2)

Everyone seems at this point dissatisfied with Harris's masculinity: Wilson's reference to his failure of 'firmness and ardour' similarly equates a resistance to embracing hospitality with impotence. Disconcerted by the women's investigations, Harris rushed to the shore with his belongings, and 'spent an uncomfortable night sitting upon his chest'. Crook tells the story somewhat differently in his account, omitting any reference to the incident with Tainai's consort, and claiming instead that 'A Crowd of the Natives, gathering round Mr Harris in the night, frightened him away; & broke open & plundered his Chest' (Crook 2007:104), seeking much the prized red feathers that Harris had earlier revealed. Whether Harris's desertion is accounted for purely as a matter of material property or more complexly as an issue of conjugal property, the picture remains of a man traumatized by the relationship he encountered between friendship-formation and exchange.

Belatedly Crook seems to have felt that Harris was right. On 22 May 1798 he was picked up in Vaitahu Bay by Captain Edmund Fanning of the sealing ship the *Betsy*, in a state of distress. As Fanning later reported the encounter,

At 3 P.M. on the lighting up of a rain squall, a small canoe, in which only two persons were to be seen, was observed hastening towards the ship ... As [it] came along side, we were greatly astonished to hear one of the persons exclaim in our mother tongue, 'Sir, I am an Englishman, and now call upon, as I have come to you, to preserve my life.' Words cannot express my surprise at this moment, on hearing so unexpected a claim. The stranger was instantly assisted in getting up the gangway, and no sooner had attained the deck, than observing, 'I am a missionary,' he sank into a seat provided for him on the quarter-deck, and bowed his head for a few minutes. (Fanning 1970:130)

Fanning describes Crook's appearance in nativized mode:

Mr. Crook was at this time dressed in the native garb of the island, having only the maro on (a piece of cloth manufactured by the natives, which wound around the middle of the body ...); the remaining portion of his person, from being continually exposed to the sun, had become tanned nearly as brown as the chiefs themselves were; and this mode of dress he had been under the necessity of submitting to for months past. (Fanning 1970:133)

But if he appears to Fanning first as an islander and then a degenerate beachcomber, Crook's adaptation to local costume had nonetheless been shaped by peculiarly dogmatic reservations. In Tahuata he had in fact 'adopted a dress similar to that of the native Women; as being more decent than that of the Men & more convenient than his own Clothes' (Crook 2007:120). What Fanning terms a necessary submission to local practice was rather an intriguing marriage of convenience with conviction. Crook's appearance on Fanning's deck, emaciated and in drag, comes close to that of one of the 'poorer' women he claimed that Robarts personated in the Marquesas.

Fanning dropped Crook at the Northern island of Nukuhiva, from where he would, after a further nine months in the Marquesas, be taken back to London by the *Butterworth*, companion vessel to the whaling ship the *New Euphrates* from which Robarts had deserted a month earlier at Tahuata. In a letter to the London Missionary Society that Crook penned on board the *Betsy*, he regretted the presumption that had left him in a foreign place without a friend from home. When the *Duff* had left him at Tahuata, he had acknowledged 'that his happiness would have been greatly increased had his devoted situation been with a friendly and agreeable assistant, whose conversation and sympathy might have comforted him in times of trouble' (J. Wilson 1799:142), figuring the blessings of friendship as personal rather than integral to his mission. But his letter from the *Betsy* recognized the instrumentality of company to the very self-constitution of the missionary. He wrote, 'Some perhaps the greatest part of you were of the opinion that the best method of success were to settle in a body ... but some respectable members of your body thought one or two left on an Island might be more eligible I was of the later opinion and finding a door I entered and

came hither. [I have since] altered my views.'[6] He had come to realize
that without a friend from home: a fellow actor, an interlocutor, versed
in the same language, he lacked the evangelist's capacity to set what he
later called a 'powerful example' to the people among whom he resided.
Robarts might have been that friend, just as Crook might have been the
friend who redeemed Robarts for a British audience. They might have
legitimated one another. As Alex Calder puts it, Crook longed 'to
reconstitute his identity in the confirming look of someone who knows
how to read him rightly' (Calder 1996:145). He also needed to be read
in a more immediate sense. He required a partner in order to demonstrate the technology of writing, in support of his claim to represent not
just spiritual but cultural advancement (V. Smith 1998:1–5). Robarts,
Crook's reader, arrives too late, to read his messages alone and in
private, not as performance but as billet-doux. His fetishization of
Crook's Bible as substitute companion, however, might have been
instantly comprehensible in local terms. Crook reports that:

Finding Mr. Crook frequently retiring, & occupied with the perusal of his bible,
the Natives imagined that he grieved for his separation from all his friends; & that
his book was some kind of Memorial of his former connections which excited his
sympathetic Affections. A crowd of them, chiefly women, had collected near his
house, the day after the Ship had sailed; & Teinae being asked by him what
was their intention, answered that doubtless it was to lament with him for his
separation from his kindred & friends. (Crook 2007:105)

What Calder calls Crook's 'flustered letter' from the *Betsy* also contained a loaded confession: 'I desire to blush and be confounded before
the Lord for ever temptation has been of such strange sort that I am
perswaded it would be the greatest presumption in any one knowing
them to encounter.' It is an admission beguiling to interpretation, that
has evoked compelling readings, both from Calder himself, who sees
Crook's confusion as a desire 'to be confounded by the proper symbolic
system' (Calder 1996:145), and from Greg Dening, who suggests that
Crook felt the hubris of the European who is offered a kind of worship
(Dening 2004:277–9) – a temptation whose fatal attraction was proven
by his almost namesake Cook. Both Calder and Dening propose that
Crook desires a reminder of the familiar to place his experience of the

---

[6] Crook 1798; published in Peacocke 1995:162–3 and Crook 2007:165–6. There was
some division among the directors of the missionary society as to how missionaries
might best make an impact on Oceanians. Dr Thomas Haweis had argued for the
settlement of all missionaries sent out in the *Duff* in a consolidated group in Tahiti,
while Samuel Greatheed advocated their spreading out among the islands (Houghton
1990:105).

As I have already remarkd, these people are remarkable fond of strangers. Particularly a white man was a great novelty among them ... My haveing made a tollerable progress in learning the language, [I] could converse fluently ... I past some time at this place in a state of flying happiness as I was always on the move, not stopping long in a place; for the more I traveld among these people, the more I dived into their manners and customs. [For] by confineing myself to one place and one family I could not be acquainted with their general temper and dispositions. (Dening 1974:86)

Again the complete, indeed visceral, reconciliation of sentiment and calculation is notable here. Friendship is prefigured as bridge in Robarts's reference to 'manners and customs', that staple of the travel account that he hoped would be his passport back to society. It is of course possible to read his eschewal of particular friendship in favour of a mode of intimacy that allows him to generalize character as a refusal of individual connection in favour of proto-anthropological typification. However, this would be to ignore the less reflexive, more explicitly affective or embodied aspects of his prose – his 'state of flying happiness'; his 'dive' into custom. Moreover, it would discount his awareness of his own value as 'novelty': as object of reciprocal interest to his hosts.

Crook, unlike Robarts, had difficulty making friends in the Marquesas. Also unlike Robarts, his first friendships on Tahuata were his most awkward. It was only by the time he reached Nukuhiva that he appears to have understood the way in which Marquesan friendship worked, and how integral the practice of name exchange was to being fed and housed and protected. At Nukuhiva he was thus finally to forge a relatively sustaining bond friendship with the chief Kiatonui, whereas at Tahuata he was unable to capitalize on his bond with Tainai even for basic sustenance. In journal entries written before the *Duff* sailed, he termed Tainai and his other hosts at Tahuata 'our Friends', and described himself, as Robarts was to, as so crowded by enthusiastic locals that he 'despaired of having a moment alone' (Crook 1797: 11 June). But in his retrospective account he reassesses this friendship as calculated: 'Teinae evidently piqued himself upon the residence of an European under his charge, & would not, on any account, have been deprived of so flattering a distinction at that time' (Crook 2007:105). Indeed, his account is one long narrative of disillusionment, proto-ethnographically articulated. Before the *Duff* departs he expresses the hope 'that they had their plentiful seasons as well as at the other islands' (J. Wilson 1799:133), that 'the People appear kind, friendly, and teachable but very childish' and that 'They have no human sacrifices' (Crook 1797: Remarks, 15 June). Having found himself instead so hungry and unprovided for that he had to swim out to sea towing a line to catch fish, having made neither friend nor convert, and having been exposed to an unrepentant and performative cannibalism, he constructs a retrospective account that crystallizes his sense of disappointed hospitality and retracted friendship into cultural fact. He writes at length of a failure of human relations on every level: marital, familial and intimate:

The Nature of their Marriages, & the ways of living of the different Sexes, precludes in general, the exercise of Conjugal Affections; instances of which are rare in the extreme, partialities toward one man, or one Woman, being chiefly discovered by jealousy. It is natural to suppose that Paternal Affection, likewise, cannot be very strong. Fathers often treat their nominal Children very harshly, yet they seem to place a pride in having a numerous family; and Children are, not uncommonly, much fondled. As they grow up, little care however is taken, even as to their necessary sustenance. The Children are early inured to the most barbarous spectacles; & amuse themselves by playing with the mangled limbs, & private parts, of naked bleeding corpses. Among the men & women, there are persons who discover much more benevolence of disposition than others do; but real disinterested friendship, or even genuine compassion, is almost utterly unknown.

They have the custom, which seems to be universal in the Pacific Ocean, of exchanging names with others, by way of forming friendships, but those have not the same force or durability, which is said to characterize the Tiyos of Otahite. The names thus assumed are called by them e noa tatappa [*inoa tatapa*]. They likewise assume the name of any person whom they have killed, whether males or females. (Crook 2007:86)

We might contrast this enumeration of modes of failed intimacy with Robarts's sense, on departing Tahuata, of having been reared by his friends. Crook is clearly identified with the child whose fondling does not intimate real sustenance, while his elevation of the Tahitian *taio* bond over its Marquesan equivalents is full of regret for the destination he passed up when he chose to stay in the Marquesas alone. And we might compare this formulation of ethnography from narcissistic injury with Cook's misnaming of the Friendly Islands, or his misunderstanding of Australian aboriginal indifference to Europeans as indifference to their land, or with Crook's own extrapolation from his personal experience of two Marquesan islands, 'The history of Nuguheva is, happily, much less portentous than that of Tahouatta' (Crook 2007:136). The progressive European record of Oceanic places and cultures is, as I noted in the Introduction, a map of achieved, failed or false intimacy.

The local practice of name exchange emerges as a key factor for thinking about why the missionary failed at friendship in the Marquesas where the beachcomber succeeded. Alfred Gell has observed that, if name exchange was common practice in Tahiti and the Society Islands, 'Marquesans developed this transactional mode to an extraordinary degree.' He notes that exchanging names was 'normal practice for those who wished to maintain social relationships outside their own community'; specialist craftsmen, for example, 'needed a complete network of name-exchangees, whose identity (i.e. kinship affiliations, wife, children, possessions etc) they assumed for the duration of their visit', a practice they reciprocated when visited by their fellow craftsmen. As Gell elaborates, 'name-exchange annulled differences': it disseminated identity. He concludes that 'in practice, identity was extraordinarily labile; a man with an extended network of name-exchange partners was, in effect, a multiple person' (Gell, 175, 176). The beachcomber was categorically comfortable with labile identity: it had in most cases been his condition for crossing the beach. He was open to multiple conversions. The evangelical missionary, on the other hand, sought to convert. His religion's version of name exchange was christening: the one-way gift of a new name as symbol of initiation. He was invested in a spiritually reconstituted, singular and inviolable self, and his mission was not to trade identities strategically, but to subordinate local practices to his own. In Crook's case, this manifested as a dogged literalism; a refusal to insinuate.

Crook, bearing an invisible gift – the Word – whose worth was both absolute and utterly provisional, and espousing a theology that equated showing friendship with exemplary disinterestedness, exchanged tentatively. Ideologically committed to an ideal of cultural transformation rather than cultural exchange, he was left isolated, out of circulation: lacking a companion with whom he could perform an example; lacking a reader to make sense of him; missing the friend he never knew. But having come to the Marquesas alone and on a mission, Crook could only understand friend to mean convert. Robarts is not the only potential friend to whom his account is blind. Tama, the Hawaiian who later helped Robarts to jump ship, asked Crook to teach him to read and write:

Some pains were taken with him, but his attention could not be fixed, & in a few days he left off learning. He acted, however, in a friendly manner to Mr. Crook; whom the Natives begun to treat with comparative contempt, saying he could do nothing but pore over his book; while Tama could throw a Stone, or a Spear, farther than any of them. This change inclined Mr. Crook to remove his residence to Anateiteina [Hanatetena], & he slept one night in the house where Duteitei [Tutete] was lodged, proposing to accompany him. Tama discovered much concern upon the account, & followed Mr. Crook to the house, with tears in his eyes, saying, 'You go way Anateiteina, me go too, me no tay here; you tay, me tay.' Tama then returned to Teinae, & talked very sharply with him on his neglect of Mr. Crook, who finally resolved upon remaining at Witahhu [Vaitahu]. (Crook 2007:110)

It is subsequently acknowledged that 'from Tama's Example, Mr. Crook derived considerable advantage, as to his mode of sustenance; which he found might have been more comfortable, if he had previously been better acquainted with the manners of the Natives' (Crook 2007:111). However, Tama also set himself up as an alternative preacher, telling 'the Natives that the English had no Gods; for he had been in their country (meaning America), & never saw any; but that at Whihe [Hawaii], his Country, they had Gods, about whom he conversed' (Crook 2007:111), and thus ultimately forfeited friendship with Crook. There is a pattern of exchange here, but only one gift of value in Crook's eyes; there are tears and wounded feelings, but only one mode of genuine friendship.

In Nukuhiva Crook was able to profit retrospectively from Tama's instruction. He made a proper friendship bond with Kiatonui, sacralized in what he refers to as 'a tedious Ceremony', exchanging names with Kiatonui's grandson Pakauoteii, 'by which name Mr Crook was always called at Nuguheva; & as the Chief himself bore the same name, it elevated him to equal Rank with either of them' (Crook 2007:139). More importantly, he came to understand the kinds of entitlement that such friendship conferred:

> he found the knowledge he had already acquired, of the language & manners of the Islanders, incomparably more useful than any articles of property would have been. Had he possessed them here, they would, indeed, probably, been of some disadvantage; as he might then, as before have been unable to attain any thing, but by exchanging them. Whatever he now asked for he had given to him; & he found his Situation so much preferable, with respect to the abundance of provision, & the conduct of the Natives, that he determined upon remaining at this Spot. (Crook 2007:139)

Crook learnt how to ask in local terms. Bereft of possessions, he no longer clung, with the anxiety of so many European visitors in Oceania, to a sense of the exploitable value of things from home. He developed a willingness to be implicated as recipient and not merely donor of culture and hospitality. But the missionary trained to believe that those without his God are benighted still found it difficult to acknowledge the 'friendly hut' and the 'Bridge that conveys me safe over'. The closest he came to friendship on Nukuhiva was with a man who approximated to a convert. Granted land by virtue of his bond with Kiatonui, he was instructed in the selection and cultivation of the site by 'Hee-hue [Hiihui], a thoughtful & friendly man, ... [who] was fond of conversing with Mr. Crook, and frequently called upon him' (Crook 2007:141). Unable to reciprocate this generosity and pleasure in his friend's company, Crook co-opted the relationship to his own sense of mission: 'Mr. Crook availed himself of opportunities to converse with Heehue on subjects of religion; both with the view of instructing his friendly assistant, and of qualifying himself to address the Natives publicly' (Crook 2007:142). If Crook recognized Hiihui as more intimate than his bond-friend and provider Kiatonui, this was not because he demonstrated the much sought-after virtue of non-calculated affection, but because he was prepared to receive instruction. His own expressed interest slips easily from the particular friend Hiihui to an imagined public in terms of which Hiihui could only ever figure in anticipation as metonym and in retrospect as inadequate substitute. When Crook departed he left behind this friend, 'who was desirous to have accompanied Mr. Crook to England' (Crook 2007:150): we learn that he was between forty and fifty, and considered too old to be taken aboard by the captain of the *New Euphrates*. Assuring the reader that he paid his dues: 'Heehue, whose Services Mr. Crook had recompensed with an adze, and other articles that were not disposed of in barter' (Crook 2007:151), Crook returns to a notion of friendship as service and account keeping that confirms even as it seeks to compensate his abandonment of his friend.

In February and March of 1825 Crook revisited the Marquesas from Tahiti, where he had been a pastor for nine years, in order to establish a cohort of Tahitian teachers in the islands. He published a report on his visit to Tahuata in the *Transactions of the Missionary Society* for 1826. His initial response to the Marquesans was alienated, indeed traumatized. Coming into Vaitahu Bay the party found itself surrounded by islanders swimming out from shore and he confesses, 'I felt alarmed at the moment, and wished to turn back, fearing we should be swamped, or perhaps ill-treated' (Crook 1826:230). His description initially gives no hint of his former connection with Tahuata, reinforcing a sense of his complete dissociation from his previous 'acquaintance' with the local community: 'the native men, with their disfigured faces, and savage antic manners, make a very unpleasant impression upon the mind at first, but after a little acquaintance, they appear more gentle' (Crook 1826:231). Five days later the current chief of Hema, Toteitei – Tainai's heir – 'recognized me as his *cousin*. He and his people were highly interested while we were discoursing concerning events which happened during the time of my former residence here' (Crook 1826:232). The Marquesans acknowledged both a formal bond relationship and the mutual history that entails. Their interest in pursuing shared memories in turn engaged some level of affective response in Crook: 'I find myself quite at home with him and his people, and they regard me as one of themselves' (Crook 1826:232). Yet ultimately he resisted the embrace of this recognition. Having established some of the Tahitian teachers (whom he refers to collectively as 'the Natives' (Crook 1826:229)) at Tahuata, he took the opportunity to return immediately to Tahiti in a passing ship, claiming that 'my long absence from home began to lie heavy on my mind, and I expected, if I did not return by the present opportunity, to be detained two or more months from my large and beloved family, the numerous members of the church, and the many souls committed to my charge' (Crook 1826:237). Church and family members are indistinguishable in Crook's prose. The feeling of being 'at home' for the missionary ultimately has charge only where he finds himself settled in a body of those whose origins and values make him 'one of themselves'.

Adam von Krusenstern, whose Russian expedition visited Nukuhiva in 1804, and who encountered Robarts and Cabri, wrote of the relative merits of Robarts and Crook as powerful examples:

> I have no doubt that he [Robarts] would effect more good than the missionary Crook, who remained for some time upon this island, was able to perform; for the latter had no other idea than that of converting the Nukahiwers to Christianity, without recollecting that it was first necessary to make them men: for this purpose Robarts appears to me more proper, as well on account of the example he afforded, and of his activity, as the esteem which they universally bore him, than either Crook or any other missionary whatever. (Krusenstern 1968:175)

Robarts was, in Crook's terms, alone – especially after Krusenstern's consort vessel the *Neva* accidentally kidnapped his fellow European Cabri and took him back to Europe via Kamchatka.[9] His exemplarity lay in his capacity to forge exogenous rather than endogenous ties: in his marriage and his broader friendships, the wide esteem in which he was held. To set a powerful example also, it seems, required a gift for friendship.

Disinterest

> Our religion takes no notice of it.
>
> – Jeremy Taylor

The missionary enterprise of which Crook found himself a disaggregated representative was predicated on a claim to disinterested friendship: to uncalculated and selfless concern for heathen souls. In dedicating the *Missionary Voyage* to George III, the Directors of the London Missionary

---

9 Although Cabri was clearly foe rather than friend to Robarts, Krusenstern felt that their national enmity should have been overridden by racial sympathy, writing, 'Here, too, the innate hatred between the French and English appeared ... As they had been placed by fate among a people, whom they themselves represented as false, cruel, and faithless; by friendship and harmony alone could they avail themselves of their superior knowledge to hold all the inhabitants at defiance; while, on the contrary, in the manner they were now living, they could only expect from day to day to fall a sacrifice to each other's hatred' (Krusenstern 1968:111–12).

Society distinguished their own interest in imparting the Gospel from the 'peculiarly' calculated concerns of science and commerce:

Your MAJESTY's subjects felt themselves peculiarly interested, whether their views lead them to consider these discoveries as tending to enlarge the bounds of science, or as opening a field of commercial speculation. A nobler object, Sire, has engaged the attention of the Missionary Society, who, believing CHRISTIANITY to be the greatest blessing ever imparted to mankind, desired to communicate that inestimable gift, with all its happy effects, to these unenlightened regions. (J. Wilson 1799: front matter)

Missionary enterprise is figured here as gift rather than gain. It is disinterested in the primary sense: unbiased by personal interest, free from self-seeking (*OED*). In the Instructions to Captain Wilson, the Directors call the Gospel 'a blessing beyond the power of calculation to estimate' (J. Wilson 1799:xcii–xciii). Yet missionaries such as Crook appear, in their relationships with islanders such as Hiihui, to be disinterested in the looser sense: lacking in interest or concern. Their generalized friendship registers as disengaged, without pulse. This sense of disengagement is, paradoxically, inseparable from the way in which gifting figured in the missionary enterprise. The roles of prestation and reception were perceived as inherently culturally divided: the heathen was always the recipient, the missionary always donor. Exchange became invisible or disavowed, and this accounts for the curious ingratitude that registers in so many missionary accounts. Coupled to this sense of unidirectional donation was a refusal to countenance the possibility of cross-cultural friendship. When the Directors commended the missionaries to Captain Wilson's care, they asked him to remember that 'Having forsaken their friends and their country for the love of Christ, and with the desire of spreading the honours of his name among the heathen, they will seek in your kind attention an equivalent for the endearing connexions they have relinquished' and urged him to act, Christ-like, as 'the universal friend, in whose bosom they will deposit their diversified cares' (J. Wilson 1799:xc). Friendship is one of the sacrifices that missionaries are seen to make when they leave their homeland on an endeavour that anticipates no foreign friend.

Debate about the role and value of friendship has a deep tradition within Christian theology. Christian thinkers parsed the mode of relationship that I have termed disinterested, negotiating between singular friendships and a more communal *caritas*, and between friendship to men and to God. Secular relationships tended to be regarded as poor shadows of an idealized friendship with God, and were represented either as a worldly distraction from the distribution of non-individuated Christian love, or as fellowship, capable of figuring forth a more transcendent mode of relation. St Augustine wrestles with both these conceptions in his *Confessions*, in describing a 'very dear friend' of his youth. As Kuisma Korhonen has pointed out, Augustine's evocation of his friendship draws on expressions and quotations from Cicero, challenging Cicero's *amicitia* with Christian *caritas* (Korhonen 2006:251). Like the classical authors on friendship, Augustine focuses on the qualities of likeness and proximity that drew the pair together: 'We were both the same age, both together in the heyday of youth, and both absorbed in the same interests. We had grown up together as boys, gone to school together, and played together ... There was a sweetness in our friendship, mellowed by the interests we shared.' Yet Christianity must negotiate an insistent third term in the friendship calculation. Friendship is no longer the simple union of one like-minded and stationed individual with another, but the union of these two through God and the Holy Spirit: 'Yet ours was not the friendship which should be between true friends, either when we were boys or at this later time. For though they cling together, no friends are true friends unless you, my God, bind them fast to one another through that love which is sown in our hearts by the Holy Ghost' (Augustine 1961:75). Augustine here figures friendship without God as a kind of co-dependency. When his friend becomes ill and is baptized, the terms of friendship are altered. Augustine teases him about the baptism, but 'He looked at me in horror as though I were an enemy, and in a strange, new-found attitude of self-reliance he warned me that if I wished to be his friend, I must never speak to him like that again' (Augustine 1961:76). A relationship with God replaces the co-dependent 'clinging' of secular friendship with a novel sense of and fear for the self.

Once the individual has undergone conversion, his secular friend becomes potential 'enemy'. But Christian theology further destabilizes the friend/foe distinction by refiguring the enemy as friend. St Thomas Aquinas teases out this problem in his *Summa Theologiae* (34, Questions 23 and 25, 'On the nature and objects of charity'). Aquinas acknowledged that it is natural to love friends and hate enemies, and that 'it seems as perverse to love one's enemies, as it would be to hate one's friends' (Aquinas 1975:105). However, he cites the Gospel injunction to '*Love your enemies* and, in the same breath, *Do good to those that hate you*' in support of the argument that felt and not merely formalized friendship be shown to one's enemies: 'The outward marks and demonstrations of charity flow from the love within us and are proportioned to it. Now the commandment absolutely insists that we have this interior love for our enemies in general' (Aquinas 1975:105). If it is hard to muster this feeling spontaneously ('it is only with a friend that a friend is friendly'), this is once again achieved *through* God. God represents the perfect friend, for the sake of whose virtue we extend friendship to those God loves, including our enemies: 'In a friendship of true worth we love principally a man of virtue, though out of regard for him we love all who belong to him, even if they are not virtuous' (Aquinas 1975:7, 9). In such formulations, however, relationship to God appears to follow the pattern of (Aristotelian) friendship, even as it sets the mould for Christian friendship.

Aquinas raises the question of the relationship between ethics and feeling that lies dormant in classical formulations of friendship. Where Aristotle and Cicero suppose a seamless relationship between the perception of virtue and friendly sentiment, Aquinas's acknowledgement of the circularity of friendship lodges it primarily in feeling. And with this recognition he is prepared, at least briefly, to disequilibriate the ledger of classical thinking on friendship,[10] objecting that:

Love can be unequal in two ways: first on the part of the good we wish our friend. In this respect we love all men equally out of charity: because we wish them all one same generic good, namely everlasting happiness. Secondly love is said to be greater through its action being more intense: and in this way we ought not to love all equally.

Or we may reply that we have unequal love for certain persons in two ways: first, through our loving some and not loving others. As regards beneficence we are bound to observe this inequality, because we cannot do good to all: but as regards benevolence, love ought not to be thus unequal. (Aquinas 1975:8–9)

In Aquinas's terms, the effort of the Christian lies in rebalancing the equation of friendship in a new way: by offering more (necessarily) to those who deserve less. This is achieved by making God the mediating term in all friendship. Friendship for the Christian must always be primarily for the sake of the relationship to God, and the relationship with God must subordinate all friendship. Yet in the process of reaching this conclusion, Aquinas acknowledges an impulse of immediate fellow feeling that exists outside of the logic of Christian friendship, and against which Christian friendship is depicted as counterintuitive, 'perverse'.

Religious thinkers of the seventeenth century followed Aquinas in seeking to counter the classical model of idealized friendship with a Christian version of broader charity. The most influential early modern tract on the subject was Jeremy Taylor's *Discourse of the Nature, Offices and Measures of Friendship, with Rules of Conducting it* (1657), addressed to the

---

[10] Daniel Schwartz claims that Aquinas's notion of friendship 'is more flexible and more able to accommodate disagreement and lack of mutual knowledge than that promoted by Aristotle' (Schwartz 2007:viii).

poet Katharine Philips. Issues of interestedness permeate this text. Taylor opens with the question of the right of 'interested persons' to offer advice on given topics, as a means of complimenting his interlocutor, a woman he acknowledges to be 'eminent in friendships'. Taylor suggests that:

> Wherever the interest is secular or vicious, there the bias is not on the side of truth or reason, because these are seldom served by profit and low regards. But to consult with a friend in the matters of friendship, is like consulting with a spiritual person in religion; they who understand the secrets of religion, or the interior beauties of friendship, are the fittest to give answers in all inquiries concerning the respective subjects; because reason and experience are on the side of interest; and that which in friendship is most pleasing and most useful, is also most reasonable and most true; and a friend's fairest interest is in the best measure of the conducting friendships. (Taylor 1662:9)

Friendship is like religion for Taylor in two important respects. First, it absolves 'interest' from the taint of calculation. And secondly, by doing so, it legitimates closed conversation – a conversation between initiates (the kind of conversation regretted by Crook).

But Taylor goes on to declare another kind of disinterest: the disinterest of New Testament Christianity in the very concept of friendship as it has previously been understood. 'The word "friendship,"' he writes, 'in the sense we commonly mean by it, is not so much as named in the New Testament; and our religion takes no notice of it.' This contradiction of humanist expectation requires some elaboration, and Taylor continues:

> There is mention of 'friendship with the world', and it is said to be 'enmity with God'; but the word is no where else named, or to any other purpose in all the New Testament. It speaks of friends often; but by friends are meant our acquaintance, or our kindred, the relatives of our family, or our fortune, or our sect; something of society, or something of kindness, there is in it; a tenderness of appellation and civility, a relation made by gifts, or by duty, by services and subjection; and I think I have reason to be confident, that the word 'friend' (speaking of human intercourse) is no otherways used in the Gospels or Epistles, or Acts of the Apostles: and the reason of it is, the word friend is of a large signification; and means all relations and societies, and whatsoever is not enemy. (Taylor 1662:10–11)

The problem posed by friendship for New Testament theology seems here to be primarily linguistic. The term is too comprehensive: synonymous with almost any type of relationship, all-encompassing, and yet ultimately best defined negatively. But Taylor anticipates that Philips is concerned to inquire into that model of friendship adumbrated by the classical philosophers: one understood to be superlative and exemplary. This type of exceptional friendship, he explains, 'Christianity hath new christened' as charity.

other Oceanic, makes clear that both are the products of ethical systems: of laws negotiating with historical change. But it also indicates why Christian missionaries and Oceanians, the former seeking to disseminate disinterested charity towards a group of potential converts, the latter seeking a particularized bond that had from earliest contact been suspected of self-interest, fail to record successful cross-cultural friendships.

Friendly Footing

> There is no love, no friendship, without the intercourse of conversation.
>
> – Jeremy Taylor

Taylor translates superlative friendships – those comprising 'the greatest love, and the greatest usefulness, and the most open communication, and the noblest sufferings, and the most exemplar faithfulness, and the severest truth, and the heartiest counsel, and the greatest union of minds', into charity, 'new christen[ing]' friendship, but in the process converting it to a different concept, one which Shaftesbury finds to be self-serving. The task of translation was central to the work of missionaries, a fundamental step towards conveying their message. But since missionaries were relative latecomers to Oceania, language acquisition was already an inherently compromised process. As Crook's ship the *Duff* voyaged from England to Tahiti in 1796, the men and women on board made efforts to master 'a manuscript vocabulary of the Otaheitean language' which the captain, James Wilson, explained, had been 'providentially ... preserved' during the fraught journey of the *Bounty* mutineers to England on the *Pandora* (J. Wilson 1799:13–14). The vocabulary, along with James Morrison's 'Account of the Island of Tahiti and the Customs of the Islanders' had been given to London Missionary Society Director Samuel Greatheed by Peter Heywood. As I noted in the previous chapter, the documents may have been instrumental in securing the King's Pardon for these two men accused of mutiny. They also played a role in determining the choice of Tahiti as the site of the first London Missionary Society enterprise. In the 'Instructions to Captain Wilson', the Directors highlighted the pivotal importance of these texts to the mission: 'We recommend to your attentive perusal the papers which have been committed to you ... To this subject belongs the consideration of the safety of our women, probability of introducing our improvements, supply of provisions, the products of the island in sugar, cotton, sandal-wood, &c' (J. Wilson 1799:xcvii). The reprobate documents have become converted to potential instruments of paternalism and commerce. Morrison's account, as we have already seen, was in turn informed by layered relationships and incremental conversations with Tahitian *taio*s.

A quarter of a century earlier the Spanish friars Jerónimo Clota and Narciso González, in attempting to establish a mission at Tautira between November 1774 and November 1775, had employed the translation skills of a marine Máximo Rodríguez, though the friars were antipathetic to Rodríguez spiritually and socially. Rodríguez had travelled on the Spanish expedition to Easter Island in 1770 (Gonzalez 1908), where, Oliver Berghof speculates, he may have picked up rudimentary Polynesian dialect, and had been a crew member on the first voyage of the *Aguila* to Tahiti in 1772 under Domingo Boenechea. However, it was from two Oceanic travellers, Pautu and Tetuanui, who went to Lima on the *Aguila* and spent two years as the guest of the Peruvian viceroy, that he eventually 'learned enough Tahitian to allow him to converse freely and compile a short dictionary' (Berghof 2004:70). Again, conversations in the context of bonded relationships became translated into texts exchanged between collaborators whose ethics and lifestyles were antagonistic. In editing the combined texts of the Spanish mission, Glanville Corney emphasized the superiority of Rodríguez's over the missionary accounts. He recognized the opportunities for intercultural observation opened up by both the author's humble status and capacities for friendship: 'the *padres*' diary throw[s] little ... light' on the character and politics of Tahitian chiefs with whom 'one gains a closer acquaintance ... from the Narrative of the Interpreter-marine, Máximo Rodríguez, who lived on terms of intimate good-fellowship with them both, and wrote his notes day by day with the simplicity and artlessness natural to a youth of his humble birth and position, and without thought of their being ever committed to print' (Corney 1913–18: II, xxxvi). Friendship is offered as hermeneutic key: to enable the reader to gain 'closer acquaintance', the narrator must necessarily be endowed with a gift for intimacy. Similarly, we have seen that affinities are the weave as well as the concern of Robarts's writing.

It is worth taking a brief detour into Rodríguez's account, because it represents a situation in which sacred and secular ambition became explicitly intertwined. Where Robarts and Crook form a hypothetical counterpoint through the friendship that one imagined and the other failed to envisage, Rodríguez lived with the missionaries in an endorsed but unharmonious alliance: as he wrote, 'From what I can see we are in continual conflict among ourselves' (Corney 1913–18: III, 95). Rodríguez is very explicit about the fact that 'there is no bond' between marines and padres, but rather a revolving theatre of discontent: 'since each one considers himself alone, so that when some are quarelling the others are mere lookers on' (Corney 1913–18: III, 105). The lack of consensus produces a dysfunctional monstrosity: 'the one saying it ought to be done a certain way, and the other not so: from which it appears that we are all heads, and that we cannot get along for lack of feet' (Corney 1913–18: III, 99). Rodríguez's facility with language means that, like Tupaia among the Maori, he is understood to be a prestigious member of his group. This in turn enables him to make highly strategic friendship bonds. He is selected by Tu as *taio*: 'Otù showed such a friendly attachment towards me that in a little while he adopted me as his brother, and as a son to his own parents and other kinspeople; and he exchanged his name for mine, an act which, among these folk, is the bond of highest favour' (Corney 1913–18: III, 6). Moreover he comprehends the full implications of this role – both affective and authoritative. When he is invited to participate in a mourning ceremony for an adopted relative, he is given 'to understand that I must share in their sorrow because I was related to the deceased *arii*, inasmuch as he was related to all the Chiefs' (Corney 1913–18: III, 31). And when some canoeists 'began to be afraid lest the *arii* Otù should take them to task for bringing me; . . . I told them not to worry about that, because I was the *arii*'s brother' (Corney 1913–18: III, 37).

Just as Krusenstern's comments indicated that Robarts made the more effective cultural and indeed religious ambassador to the Marquesans because of his capacity to generate esteem, so David Samwell, in his journal of Cook's third voyage, reported of the Spanish mission to Tahiti:

> [They] left three Spaniards behind them on the Island to examine it & cultivate the good will & Friendship of the Natives; one of them was a common Person whom the Indians called Marteemoo, he was very much liked by them & had during his abode here rendered himself by far the most noted of any of the Spaniards, the other was a priest, whose Function they made known to us by imitating him in a ludicrous Manner in [saying] Grace before meat & counting his Beads & perfor[ming] other Ceremonies of the Romish Church; the thir[d] was a Servant who attended upon them. (Cook 1967: 1054; compare Corney 1913–18: III, xvii)[11]

Like Robarts, 'Marteemoo' (that is, the 'maritimo' Rodríguez) succeeds where missionaries fail, in cultivating friendship. He is emphatically well liked. Moreover, he seems, also like Robarts, to have offered a more effective example of Christian values. Again, this exemplarity emerges within his account through competing versions of disinterest and

---

[11] In perhaps unconscious tribute to the effectiveness of Rodríguez's example, Samwell's first statement here echoes the terms of his own Admiralty's instructions for Cook's voyages: 'You are to endeavour by all proper means to cultivate a friendship with the Natives.'

self-interest. Rodríguez describes a 'wrangle' (Corney 1913–18: III, 162) that took place between the padres and Vehiatua, the ari'i in whose territory they resided, when Vehiatua failed to compensate Narcisco after he 'succoured him in his illness'. When Rodríguez in turn cured a relative of Vehiatua, he preached a very different example:

> Vehiatua sent for me to make me a present on behalf of his sick relative, for he was now better; but I would not accept anything, and made them understand that it was our duty to assist the sick, from lowest to highest. And when I told them that our Sovereign also did it, and gave alms to such as had no means of getting attended to in their homes, for whom he maintained hospitals, they were lost in wonder. (Corney 1913–18: III, 163)

Rodríguez preaches a secular charity, strategically aligning himself with sovereign rather than church in requiring no compensation for his gift. Like so many other Europeans in Oceania, he has previously had to learn that refusal of gifts does not 'meet the sentiments' of Oceanic friendship. When he earlier attempted to repudiate the status of chief offered because of his name exchange with Tu, he caused offence: 'On my disclaiming the title of arii, and declaring myself merely a friend of them all, they took it amiss' (Corney 1913–18: III, 52). By aligning himself here however with the king of Spain, Rodríguez redefines non-reciprocation as a sign of largesse.

While this is clearly in part canny political manoeuvre, Rodríguez is also fashioning his own model of friendly relations: not a lukewarm charity disguising self-interest, but a disinterest that proceeds from affective engagement, and that can advertise the exemplary generosity of his sovereign through astute negotiation with local friendship values. His friendliness is part of a broader interest in the place in which he finds himself. It is ethnographic. As Samwell recorded,

> Marteemo made the Tour of the Island & lived upon a very friendly footing with the Natives, conforming himself to their customs & manners & indulging himself with those pleasures which the Island afforded, more particularly among the Girls, which last Circumstance was so agreeable to the Genius of these People that they looked upon him on this account to be the best Fellow among his Countrymen, who preserved a haughty Distance in their Behaviour to the Indians. (Cook 1967: 1054)

Although it is tempting here simply to focus on the confounding of ethnographic with sexual experience familiar from the example of Banks, the order of Samwell's construction is significant. Living on 'a very friendly footing' leads to a desire, not to convert the Tahitians, but to conform to *their* 'customs & manners'. This in turn allows for indulgence in pleasure. In Aristotelian terms, lesser forms of friendship (the personal benefits of use and pleasure) flow from an entry into a relationship perceived as based on likeness. Friendliness promotes feelings of interest and results in cultural understanding. However, when Rodríguez returns from his tour of the island, having visited all its districts, forged friendships and observed customs, he notes, 'I presently arrived home and found nothing noteworthy, except the *Padres'* lack of interest in my journey' (Corney 1913–18: III, 175). His extended circuit of the island encounters an affective short-circuit: where he had found engagement and hospitality outside, on returning to the mission enclosure he is met with unfriendliness and lack of interest. In Rodríguez's account, the padres' disengagement with the outside world is conflated, not with sexual abstinence, but with lack of Christian charity and of friendly feeling.

The equation, both by Rodríguez himself and by Samwell, of a capacity for friendship with a capacity for ethnographic observation, anticipates something of Malinowski's model of participant observation, as outlined in the preface to *Argonauts of the Western Pacific*. The subsequent publication of Malinowski's *Diary in the Strict Sense of the Term* (posthumously, in 1967), which exposed the simmering negative affect and libidinized engagement of the participant-observer with his subjects, has obscured the degree of friendly feeling that Malinowski incorporates into his modelling of an anthropological scientific methodology: seeming instead to expose a Janus-faced enterprise in which a false friendliness disguises familiar spectres of racism and sexual appetite. But Malinowski advocates a methodology fundamentally based in a tentative, partially repudiated feeling of friendship. His prefatory remarks to *Argonauts of the Western Pacific*, confessions rendered 'scientific' through the application of an apparently oxymoronic 'methodological candour', reprise the shifts of emotion experienced by Robarts as he first encountered signs of a more 'natural companion' in Crook's abandoned house, and then returned to his involved life with the Marquesans of Tahuata:

For the native is not the natural companion for a white man, and after you have been working with him for several hours, seeing how he does his gardens; or letting him tell you items of folk-lore, or discussing his customs, you will naturally hanker after the company of your own kind. But if you are alone in a village beyond reach of this, you go for a solitary walk for an hour or so, return again and then quite naturally seek out the natives' society, this time as a relief from loneliness, just as you would any other companionship. And by means of this natural intercourse, you learn to know him, and you become familiar with his customs and beliefs far better than when he is a paid, and often bored, informant. (Malinowski 1961:7)

'Natural intercourse' is firmly distinguished here from contracted information. Such terms of course recall the numerous disavowals of exchange within cross-cultural friendship that we have looked at throughout this book. Indeed, what we see modelled here is not simply new science but conventional friendship. As he becomes more established among the Trobriand Islanders of Omarakana, Malinowski experiences an increasingly engaged interest in their lives:

I began to take part, in a way, in the village life, to look forward to the important or festive events, to take personal interest in the gossip and the developments of the small village occurrences; to wake up every morning to a day, presenting itself to me more or less as it does to the native ... Quarrels, jokes, family scenes, events usually trivial, sometimes dramatic but always significant, formed the atmosphere of my daily life, as well as of theirs. It must be remembered that as the natives saw me constantly every day, they ceased to be interested or alarmed, or made self-conscious by my presence ... Also, over and over again, I committed breaches of etiquette, which the natives, familiar enough with me, were not slow in pointing out. I had to learn how to behave, and to a certain extent, I acquired the feeling for native good and bad manners. With this, and with the capacity of enjoying their company and sharing some of their games and amusements, I began to feel that I was indeed in touch with the natives, and this is certainly the preliminary condition of being able to carry on successful field work. (Malinowski 1961:7–8)

Malinowski admits to personal interest. He figures himself as a gossip, as inept. And he says he enjoys the islanders' company and recreations. These elements, typically understood to be antipathetic to scientific analysis, become the basis of his methodology. Like Robarts, it is 'in a state of flying happiness' that he 'dive[s] into their manners and customs'. Affective engagement is crucial to observation from within. The fact that this domestic picture also incorporates imagery of the hunt: 'the Ethnographer has not only to spread his nets in the right place, and wait for what will fall into them. He must be an active huntsman, and drive his quarry into them and follow it up to its most inaccessible lairs' (Malinowski 1961:7), should not obscure the significance of Malinowski's friendly methodology – and not least because the hunt is his metaphor, while friendship is his practice. The textual/subtextual relationship here is precisely *not* friendship/racist denigration, but rather new science trying to authorize itself, once again, through a complex mixture of friendship and its disavowal.

In attending to the friendly contexts of Oceanic encounters, this book has attempted to interrogate the reflexive assumption that contact can only become legible when we assume that professions of friendship disguise their opposite, that friendship is always calculating on other goals. I have analysed something of the long western philosophical tradition in which such suspicion of friendship is embedded. I have shown that Oceanic cultures also framed and articulated discourses of friendship, and that the conjunction of these with European values through rough and ready acts of friendship-formation on the beach begged questions of those values. I have attempted to articulate the kinds of European double-think about friendship that were exposed by these encounters, without obscuring the affective register of European investment in friendship. In suggesting, in these final chapters, that better friends made better cultural observers, I hope to move the notion of cultural observation away from the panoptic and towards the reciprocal, the dialectical and the partial. To see it a little less like either science or sentiment, and more perhaps like *taio* might have been: a model created between cultures.

Crook brought back from his nineteen months in the Marquesas the outlines of a Marquesan vocabulary. It was, his recent editors suggest, an inherently problematic document, for the following reasons:

It is most difficult to determine the quality of Crook's comprehension of his informants in the Marquesas, those who furnished him with his base vocabulary and grammar ... It often appears that Crook misunderstood a good deal of what was being explained to him. For example, *pohoa* has to be the 'scent of a meal, cooking aromas', not Crook's 'baking fish to preserve it'. It seems that Crook often interpreted situational, non-objective concepts in a rather free fashion ... Many of Crook's definitions may be regarded as misunderstandings or outright mistakes. (Crook, Greatheed and Tima'u Te'ite'i 1998:xliii)

The editors focus on Crook's inability to understand vocabulary contextually – as aroma, not recipe: as something registered situationally. Fortunately, when ultimately assembling his *Essay Toward a Dictionary and Grammar of the Lesser-Australian Language, according to the Dialect used at the Marquesas,* Crook had the assistance of two collaborators: the erudite Samuel Greatheed and, most importantly, a fellow-traveller, Timauteitei, one of two Marquesans who had accompanied him to England on the *Butterworth*. As his recent editors observe, the contribution of Timauteitei, not only to the dictionary but to interpreting the ethnological data that informed Crook's account, cannot be underestimated. If this relationship was, in the end, the closest Marquesan friendship Crook forged (the evidence is simply of collaboration), it also allowed him most closely to approach ethnographic understanding.

Robarts, despite his nostalgic friendly feeling for the missionary Crook, pauses during an account of Marquesan warfare to reflect,

The polished part of the world have some thousands of teachers, but these have none. Or, at least, those that did come did not stop long. I do not wish to dip my pen among thorn, or pretend to explain the reason any further then [that], I suppose, of course, [in] the few months that Mr Crook was among them (as, by his own writings, he could not get hold of the language), his situation became irksome, haveing no one to converse with. (Dening 1974:78)

Robarts makes an equation between friendly relations and the ability both to transmit and receive cultural knowledge, that shows Crook to disadvantage. Though Crook wrote to the Directors of the Missionary Society from the *Betsy* that he was well embarked on his Marquesan vocabulary, his intimate journals, left behind at Tahuata and coded in a form of language that only he and Robarts shared, exposed his incapacity for communication. He may have been gathering words, but they had not formed sentences. His word lists did not become conversations. He wrote, but could not speak. In imagining what this might be like – 'supposing' a situation so different from his own quick initiation through friendship bonds into linguistic exchange – Robarts begins to grasp what troubled him on entering Crook's abandoned home: the inhospitality of the familiar; the chill at the heart of recognition. In Robarts's simplistic, and yet perhaps ultimately valid perception, Crook became sick of his own company. He taught nothing because he went home. And he went home because he made no friends.

Bibliography

[A. B. C. Esq.] (1773) *An Epistle from Mr. Banks, voyager, monster-hunter, and amoroso, to Oberea, Queen of Otaheite. Transfused by A. B. C. Esq. Second Professor of the Otaheite, and every other unknown Tongue. Enriched with the finest Passages of the Queen's Letter to Mr. Banks*, 2nd edn, London: John Swan and Thomas Axtell

Adams, Henry (1976) *Tahiti: Memoirs of Arii Taimai e Marama of Eimeo, Teriirere of Tooarai, Terrinui of Tahiti, Tauraatua i Amo*, ed. Robert E. Spiller, New York: Scholars' Facsimiles and Reprints (Paris, 1901)

Adams, Rebecca G., and Graham Allan (1998) *Placing Friendship in Context*, Cambridge: Cambridge University Press

Agamben, Giorgio (2004) 'Friendship', *Contretemps*, 5, December, 2–7

Agnew, Vanessa (2008) *Enlightenment Orpheus: The Power of Music in Other Worlds*, Oxford: Oxford University Press

Alexander, Michael (1977) *Omai: 'Noble Savage'*, London: Collins and Harvill

[Anon] (1778) *New Discoveries concerning the World and its Inhabitants, in two parts*, London: J. Johnson

(1790) *The History of Prince Lee Boo, a Native of the Pelew Islands. Brought to England by Captn Wilson. A New Edition*, London: E. Newbery

(1810) *The Interesting and Affecting History of Prince Lee Boo*, London: H. Bryer

(1820) *The History of Prince Lee Boo, to which is added, The Life of Paul Cuffee, a man of colour, also, some account of John Sackhouse, the Esquimaux*, Dublin: C. Crookes; Miami, FL: Mnemosyne, 1969

(1829) *The Story of Aleck, or Pitcairn's Island, being a true account of a very singular and interesting colony*, Amherst, MA: J. S. & C. Adams

(1841) *'Prince Lee Boo', Chambers's Miscellany of Useful and Entertaining Tracts*, Edinburgh: William and Robert Chambers

(1849) *Friday Christian; or the First-Born on Pitcairn's Island, by a poor 'member of Christ'*, New York: D. Appleton and Co

Aquinas, St Thomas (1975) *Summa Theologiae, vol. 34, Charity (2a2ae. 23–33)*, ed. R.J. Batten, London: Blackfriars and Eyre and Spottiswoode

Aristotle (1998) *Nicomachean Ethics*, trans. D.P. Chase, London: J. M. Dent, Toronto: Dover, 1911

Ashton, Thomas (1959) *Economic Fluctuations in England, 1700–1800*, London: Oxford University Press

Augustine (1961) *Confessions*, Harmondsworth: Penguin

Bach, John (ed.) (1987) *The Bligh Notebook: 'Rough Account – Lieutenant Wm Bligh's voyage in the* Bounty*'s Launch from the ship to Tofua & from thence to Timor' 28 April to 14 June 1789. With a draft list of the BOUNTY mutineers*, Sydney: Allen & Unwin

Banks, Joseph (1962) *The Endeavour Journal of Joseph Banks 1768–1771*, ed. J.C. Beaglehole, 2 vols., Sydney: Public Library of New South Wales/Angus & Robertson

Barish, Jonas (1981) *The Antitheatrical Prejudice*, Los Angeles: University of California Press

Barker-Benfield, G.J. (1996) *The Culture of Sensibility: Sex and Society in Eighteenth-Century Britain*, Chicago: University of Chicago Press

Barney, Stephen (1794) *Appendix Containing A full account of the real Causes and Circumstances of that unhappy Transaction, the most material of which have hitherto been withheld from the Public*, London: J. Deighton, in William Bligh and Others, *A Book of the 'Bounty'*, London: J. M. Dent and Sons, 1938, 246–66

Barrow, Sir John (1989) *The Eventful History of the Mutiny and Piratical Seizure of H.M.S* Bounty*: its cause and consequences*, London: John Murray (1831)

Barrows, Susan (1981) *Distorting Mirrors: Visions of the Crowd in Late Nineteenth-Century France*, New Haven, CT: Yale University Press

Bataille, Georges (1997) *The Bataille Reader*, ed. Fred Botting and Scott Wilson, Oxford and London: Blackwell

Beechey, F.W. (1831) *Narrative of a Voyage to the Pacific and Beering's Strait, to co-operate with the Polar Expeditions: performed in His Majesty's ship* Blossom, vol. I, London: Henry Colburn and Richard Bentley

Beer, Gillian (1996) *Open Fields: Science in Cultural Encounter*, Oxford: Oxford University Press

Bell, Sandra, and Simon Coleman (eds.) (1999) *The Anthropology of Friendship*, Oxford: Berg

Benedict, Barbara M. (2001) *Curiosity: A Cultural History of Early Modern Inquiry*, Chicago: University of Chicago Press

Benjamin, Walter (1983) *Charles Baudelaire: A Lyric Poet in the Era of High Capitalism*, trans. H. Zohn, London: Verso

Berghof, Oliver (2004) 'Tahiti 1767–1777: the view from the shore', in Byron R. Wells and Philip Stewart (eds.), *Interpreting Colonialism*, Oxford: Voltaire Foundation

Berlant, Lauren (ed.) (1998) 'Intimacy: a special issue', *Critical Inquiry*, 24:2, Winter

Bewell, Alan (1996) ' "On the Banks of the South Sea": botany and sexual controversy in the late eighteenth century', in Miller and Reill (1996), 173–93

Bhabha, Homi (1994) *The Location of Culture*, London: Routledge

Blanchot, Maurice (1997) *Friendship*, trans. Elizabeth Rottenberg, Stanford, CA: Stanford University Press (1971)

Bligh, William (1794) *An Answer to certain Assertions contained in the Appendix to a Pamphlet entitled Minutes of the Proceedings on the Court Martial held at Portsmouth, 12 August 1792, on Ten Persons charged with Mutiny on Board*

(1969) *The Journals of Captain James Cook on his Voyages of Discovery, vol. II, The Voyage of the* Resolution *and* Adventure *1772–1775*, ed. J.C. Beaglehole, extra series no. 35, Cambridge: Hakluyt Society

Cooper, John M. (1977) 'Aristotle on the Forms of Friendship', *Review of Metaphysics* 30:4, 619–48

Corney, Bolton Glanville (ed. and trans.) (1913–18) *The Quest and Occupation of Tahiti by Emissaries of Spain during the years 1772–1776*, 3 vols., London: Hakluyt

Crain, Caleb (2001) *American Sympathy: Men, Friendship, and Literature in the New Nation*, New Haven, CT: Yale University Press

Crook, William Pascoe (1797) *Journal*, 12 April to 15 June 1797, dealing with experiences at Tongatabu and voyage on the *Duff* to Christina, MS A1963, Mitchell Library Sydney

 (1798) *Letter to Directors of the Missionary Society*, 23 May. Photocopy. Sydney, Mitchell Library, State Library of NSW

 (1826) 'Mr. Crook's Late Voyage to the Marquesas', *Transactions of the Missionary Society*, October, South Seas, 225–38

 (2007) *An Account of the Marquesas Islands 1797–1799*, forewords by Greg Dening, Hervé-Marie Le Cleac'h, Douglas Peacocke and Robert Koenig, Tahiti: Haere Po

Crook, William Pascoe, Samuel Greatheed and Tima'u Te'ite'i (1998) *An Essay Toward a Dictionary and Grammar of the Lesser-Australian Language, according to the Dialect used at the Marquesas* (1799), ed. H.G.A. Hughes and S.R. Fischer, Auckland: Institute of Polynesian Languages and Literatures

Dapp, Kathryn Gilbert (1939) George Keate, Esq., Eighteenth Century English Gentleman (Ph.D. thesis, University of Pennsylvania)

Darby, Madge (1965) *Who Caused the Mutiny on the Bounty?*, Sydney: Angus and Robertson

Davies, John (1961) *The History of the Tahitian Mission 1799–1830*, ed. C.W. Newbury, Cambridge: Hakluyt

Daws, Gavan (1968a) 'Kealakekua Bay Revisited: a note on the death of Captain Cook', *Journal of Pacific History*, 3, 21–3

 (1968b) *Shoal of Time: A History of the Hawaiian Islands*, Honolulu: University of Hawaii Press

Delano, Amasa (1817) *A Narrative of Voyages and Travels in the Northern and Southern Hemispheres: comprising three voyages round the world; together with a voyage of survey and discovery, in the Pacific and Oriental islands*, Boston, MA: E. G. House; facs. edn, Upper Saddle River NJ: Gregg Press, 1970

Dening, Greg (1974) (ed.) *The Marquesan Journal of Edward Robarts*, Canberra: Australian National University Press

 (1980) *Islands and Beaches: Discourse on a Silent Land, Marquesas 1774–1880*, Honolulu: University of Hawaii Press

 (1992) *Mr Bligh's Bad Language: Passion, Power and Theatre on the* Bounty, Cambridge: Cambridge University Press

 (1996) *Performances*, Chicago: University of Chicago Press

 (1998) 'Writing, Rewriting the Beach: an essay', *Rethinking History*, 2:2, 143–72

(2001) 'Ó Mai! This is Mai: a masque of a sort', in [NLA] (2001), 51–6

(2004) *Beach Crossings: Voyagings across Time, Cultures, and Self*, Philadelphia: University of Pennsylvania

Derrida, Jacques (1994) *Given Time: I. Counterfeit Money*, trans. Peggy Kamuf, Chicago: University of Chicago Press (1991)

(1997) *Politics of Friendship*, trans. George Collins, London: Verso

(2000) *Of Hospitality: Anne Dufourmantelle Invites Jacques Derrida to Respond*, trans. Rachel Bowlby, Stanford, CA: Stanford University Press

(2001) *The Work of Mourning*, ed. Pascale-Anne Brault and Michael Naas, Chicago: University of Chicago Press

Dettelbach, Michael (1996) ' "A Kind of Linnaean Being": Forster and eighteenth-century natural history', in J. Forster (1996), lv–lxxiv

Diderot, Denis (1957) *The Paradox of Acting*, trans. Walter Herries Pollock, New York: Hill and Wang (1830)

(1993) 'Supplement to Bougainville's Voyage', in *This is not a Story and other Stories*, trans. P.N. Furbank, Oxford: Oxford University Press

Du Rietz, Rolf (1962) 'Three Letters from James Burney to Sir Joseph Banks. A Contribution to the History of William Bligh's "A Voyage to the South Sea" ', *Ethnos* 27, 115–25

(*c.* 1981) *Fresh Light on John Fryer of the 'Bounty'*, Uppsala: Dahlia Books

Dunmore, John (ed.) (2002) *The Pacific Journal of Louis Antoine de Bougainville 1767–1768*, London: Hakluyt Society

Dunphy, Jocelyn (1982) 'Insurrection and Repression: Bligh's 1790 narrative of the mutiny on board *H. M. Ship* Bounty', in Frances Barker et al. (eds.), *1789: Reading Writing Revolution: Proceedings of the Essex Conference on the Sociology of Literature, July 1981*, Colchester: University of Essex

Durkheim, Emile (2001) *The Elementary Forms of Religious Life*, trans. C. Cosman, Oxford: Oxford University Press (1912)

Edmond, Rod (1997) *Representing the South Pacific: Colonial Discourse from Cook to Gauguin*, Cambridge: Cambridge University Press

Edmond, Rod, and Vanessa Smith (eds.) (2003) *Islands in History and Representation*, London: Routledge

Edwards, Edward, and George Hamilton (1915) *Voyage of H.M.S.* Pandora, *despatched to arrest the mutineers of the* Bounty *in the south seas, 1790–91: being the narratives of Captain Edward Edwards, R.N. the commander and George Hamilton, the surgeon*, ed. Basil Thomson, London: Francis Edwards

Edwards, Philip (1994) *The Story of the Voyage: Sea-Narratives in Eighteenth-Century England*, Cambridge: Cambridge University Press

Eger, Elizabeth (2009) 'Paper Trails and Eloquent Objects: bluestocking friendship and material culture', *Parergon* 62:2, 109–38

Ellingson, Ter (2001) *The Myth of the Noble Savage*, Berkeley and Los Angeles: University of California Press

Elliot, John, and Richard Pickersgill (1984) *Captain Cook's Second Voyage: The Journals of Lieutenants Elliott and Pickersgill*, ed. Christine Holmes, London: Caliban

Ellis, Markman (1996) *The Politics of Sensibility: Race, Gender and Commerce in the Sentimental Novel*, Cambridge: Cambridge University Press

Ellis, William (1783) *An authentic narrative of a voyage performed by Captain Cook and Captain Clerke, in His Majesty's ships* Resolution *and* Discovery *during the years 1776, 1777, 1778, 1779 and 1780: in search of a North-West passage between the continents of Asia and America: including a faithful account of all their discoveries, and the unfortunate death of Captain Cook,* London: G. Robinson, J. Sewell and J. Debrett

Ellis, William (1967) *Polynesian Researches, during a residence of nearly six years in the South Sea islands,* 2 vols., London: Dawsons of Pall Mall (1829)

Ellison, Julie (1999) *Cato's Tears and the Making of Anglo-American Emotion,* Chicago: University of Chicago Press

Elsner, John and Roger Cardinal (eds.) (1994) *The Cultures of Collecting,* London: Reaktion

Engels, Friedrich (1952) *The Condition of the Working Class in England in 1844,* trans. F.K. Wischnewetzky, London: Allen & Unwin (1845)

Fanning, Edmund (1970) *Voyages to the South Seas, Indian and Pacific Oceans, China Sea, North-West Coast, Feejee Islands, South Shetlands, &c,* Upper Saddle River, NJ: Gregg Press

Favazza, Armando R. (1996) *Bodies under Siege: Self-Mutilation and Body Modification in Culture and Psychiatry,* 2nd edn, Baltimore, MD, and London: Johns Hopkins University Press

Ferdon, Edwin N. (1981) *Early Tahiti as the Explorers Saw It,* Tucson: University of Arizona Press

Ferguson, Adam (1999) *An Essay on the History of Civil Society,* Cambridge: Cambridge University Press

Ferguson, Frances (1988) 'Malthus, Godwin, Wordsworth, and the Spirit of Solitude', in *Literature and the Body: Essays on Populations and Persons,* ed. E. Scarry, Baltimore, MD: Johns Hopkins University Press, 106–24

Finney, Ben (1964) 'Notes on Bond-Friendship in Tahiti', *Journal of the Polynesian Society* 73:4, 431–5

Fitzgerald, John T. (1997) *Graeco-Roman Perspectives on Friendship,* Atlanta, GA: Scholar's Press

Folger, M. (1813) Letter from M. Folger to the Lords of the Admiralty, Mar 1, giving an account of a visit to Pitcairn Island, Discovery of Pitcairn Islanders, Public Records Office Letters, 1813–14

Forster, E.M. (1951) *Two Cheers for Democracy,* London: Edward Arnold

Forster, George (2000) *A Voyage Round the World,* ed. Nicholas Tomas and Oliver Berghof, 2 vols., Honolulu: University of Hawaii Press

Forster, Johann Reinhold (1982) *The* Resolution *Journal of Johann Reinhold Forster, 1772–1775,* ed. M. Hoare, 4 vols., London: Hakluyt Society

(1996) *Observations Made during a Voyage round the World,* ed. Nicholas Thomas, Harriet Guest, Michael Dettelbach, Honolulu: University of Hawaii Press

Fraisse, Jean-Claude (1974) *Philia: la notion d'amitié dans la philosophie antique: essai sur un problème perdu et retrouvé,* Paris: J. Vrin

Freud, Sigmund (1984) *On Metapsychology: The Theory of Psychoanalysis,* trans. James Strachey, The Pelican Freud Library, vol. 11, London: Penguin

Frost, Alan (1994) 'Tahiti, the *Bounty* Mutiny, and the English Romantic Poets', in *Dangerous Liaisons: Essays in Honour of Greg Dening*, ed. Donna Merwick, Melbourne: University of Melbourne

Frow, John (1997) *Time and Commodity Culture: Essays in Cultural Theory and Postmodernity*, Oxford: Clarendon Press

Fryer, John (1934) *The voyage of the* Bounty*'s launch as related in William Bligh's despatch to the Admiralty and the journal of John Fryer*, ed. Owen Rutter, London: Golden Cockerel Press

Fullerton, W. Y. (n.d.) *The Romance of Pitcairn Island*, London: Carey Press

Gallagher, Catherine (1986) 'The Body versus the Social Body in the Works of Thomas Malthus and Henry Mayhew', *Representations*, 14, 83–106

Gandhi, Leela (2006) *Affective Communities: Anticolonial Thought, Fin-de-siècle Radicalism, and the Politics of Friendship*, Durham, NC: Duke University Press

Gascoigne, John (1994) *Joseph Banks and the English Enlightenment: Useful Knowledge and Polite Culture*, Cambridge: Cambridge University Press

(2007) *Captain Cook: Voyager between Worlds*, London: Continuum

Gell, Alfred (1993) *Wrapping in Images: Tattooing in Polynesia*, Oxford: Clarendon

Ginnekin, Jaap van (1992) *Crowds, Psychology and Politics 1871–1899*, Cambridge: Cambridge University Press

Goldie, Matthew Boyd (2009) *The Idea of the Antipodes: Place, People and Voices*, London: Routledge

Gonzalez, Captain Don Felipe (1908) *The Voyage of Captain Don Felipe Gonzalez in the Ship of the Line* San Lorenzo, *with the Frigate* Santa Rosalia *in company, to Easter Island in 1770 1: preceded by an Extract from Mynheer Jacob Roggeveen's Official Log of his Discovery and Visit to Easter Island in 1722*, ed. and trans. Bolton Glanville Corney, Cambridge: Hakluyt

Goring, Paul (2005) *The Rhetoric of Sensibility in Eighteenth-Century Culture*, Cambridge, Cambridge University Press

Gregory, Chris (1982) *Gifts and Commodities*, London: Academic Press

Guest, Harriet (1992) 'Curiously Marked: tattooing, masculinity, and nationality in eighteenth-century British perceptions of the South Pacific', in *Painting and the Politics of Culture: New Essays on British Art 1700–1850*, ed. John Barrell, Oxford: Oxford University Press

(1996) 'Looking at Women: Forster's observations in the South Pacific', in J. Forster (1996), xli–liv

(2007) *Empire, Barbarism, and Civilization: Captain Cook, William Hodges, and the Return to the Pacific*, Cambridge: Cambridge University Press

Gunson, Niel (1964) 'Great Women and Friendship Contract Rites in Pre-Christian Tahiti', *Journal of the Polynesian Society*, 73:1, March, 53–69

(1978) *Messengers of Grace: Evangelical Missionaries in the South Seas, 1797–1860*, Melbourne: Oxford University Press

Gutiérrez, Ramón A. (2001) 'What's Love Got to Do with It?', *Journal of American History*, 88:3, December, 866–9

Hackforth-Jones, Jocelyn, with David Bindman, Romita Ray and Stephanie Pratt (2007) *Between Worlds: Voyagers to Britain 1700–1850*, London: National Portrait Gallery

Hall, Catherine (ed.) (2000) *Cultures of Empire, A Reader: Colonizers in Britain and the Empire in the Nineteenth and Twentieth Centuries*, New York: Routledge

Hamilton, George (1793) *A Voyage Round the World in His Majesty's Frigate Pandora. Performed under the Direction of Captain Edwards in the Years 1790, 1791, and 1792*, Berwick: W. Phorson, B. Law and son

Harrison, Mark (1988) *Crowds and History: Mass Phenomena in English Towns, 1790–1835*, Cambridge: Cambridge University Press

Haseldine, Julian (ed.) (1999) *Friendship in Medieval Europe*, Stroud: Sutton

Hau'ofa, Epeli (1993) 'Our Sea of Islands', in *A New Oceania: Rediscovering our Sea of Islands*, ed. Eric Waddell, Vijay Naidu and Epeli Hau'ofa, Suva: University of the South Pacific

    (1995) 'Pasts to Remember', Oceania Lecture, University of the South Pacific, Fiji

    (1998) 'The Ocean in Us', *Contemporary Pacific*, Fall

Hauser-Schäublin, Brigitta (1998) 'Exchanged Value: the winding paths of the objects', in *James Cook: Gifts and Treasures from the South Seas: The Cook/ Forster Collection, Göttingen*, ed. Brigitta Hauser-Schäublin, Gundolf Krüger and Christian F. Feest, Munich and New York: Prestel

Hawkesworth, John (1773) *An Account of the Voyages Undertaken by the Order of His Present Majesty for Making Discoveries in the Southern Hemisphere, and successively performed by Commodore Byron, Captain Carteret, Captain Wallis, and Captain Cook, In the* Dolphin, *the* Swallow, *and the* Endeavour: *Drawn up from the Journals which were kept by the several Commanders, And from the Papers of Joseph Banks, Esq.*, 3 vols., 2nd edn, London: W. Strahan, T. Cadell

Henry, Teuira (1928) *Ancient Tahiti*, Honolulu: Bernice P. Bishop Museum

Herman, Gabriel (1987) *Ritualised Friendship and the Greek City*, Cambridge: Cambridge University Press

Hewes, Gordon (1974) 'Gesture Language in Culture Contact', *Sign Language Studies*, 4, 1–34

Hill, Aaron (1754a) 'The Art of Acting', in *The works of the late Aaron Hill, Esq; in four volumes. Consisting of letters on various subjects, and of original poems, moral and facetious. With an essay on the art of acting*, vol. 3, London

    (1754b) 'An Essay on the Art of Acting', in *The works of the late Aaron Hill, Esq; in four volumes. Consisting of letters on various subjects, and of original poems, moral and facetious. With an essay on the art of acting*, vol. 4, London

Hill, John (1750) *The Actor: A Treatise on the Art of Playing. Interspersed with Theatrical Anecdotes, Critical Remarks on Plays, and Occasional Observations on Audiences*, London: R. Griffiths

Home, Henry, Lord Kames (1972) *Elements of Criticism*, 6th edn, 2 vols., New York: Garland (1885)

Hough, Richard (1973) *Captain Bligh and Mister Christian*, New York: Dutton

    (1979) *The Murder of Captain James Cook*, London: Macmillan

Houghton, Greg (1990) 'The Voice of One Crying in the Wilderness', in Cathcart et al. (1990), 101–30

Howard, June (1999) 'What is Sentimentality?', *American Literary History*, 11:1, Spring, 63–81

Howe, K. R. (1984) *Where the Waves Fall: A New South Sea Islands History from First Settlement to Colonial Rule*, Honolulu: University of Hawaii

Hulme, Peter (1986) *Colonial Encounters: Europe and the Native Caribbean, 1492–1797*, London: Routledge

Hulme, Peter and Ludmilla Jordanova (eds.) (1990) *The Enlightenment and its Shadows*, London: Routledge

Hume, David (1985) *A Treatise of Human Nature*, London: Penguin
(2006) *An Enquiry Concerning the Principles of Morals: A Critical Edition*, Oxford: Clarendon

Hutcheson, Francis (2004) *An Inquiry into the Original of Our Ideas of Beauty and Virtue*, ed. Wolfgang Liedhold, Indianapolis: Liberty Fund

Hutson, Lorna (1994) *The Usurer's Daughter: Male Friendship and Fictions of Women in Sixteenth-Century England*, London: Routledge

Hutter, Horst (1978) *Politics as Friendship: The Origins of Classical Notions of Politics in the Theory and Practice of Friendship*, Waterloo, Ont.: Wilfred Laurier Press

Hyatte, Reginald (1994) *The Arts of Friendship: The Idealization of Friendship in Medieval and Early Renaissance Literature*, Leiden: Brill

Jameson, Fredric (1981) *The Political Unconscious: Narrative as a Socially Symbolic Act*, Ithaca, NY: Cornell University Press

Jaussen, Mgr. Tepano (1987) *Dictionnaire de la langue tahitienne, 6e edition, revue et augmentée*, Papeete: Société des Etudes Océaniennes

Joppien, Rüdiger (1979) 'Philippe Jacques de Loutherbourg's Pantomime "Omai, or, a Trip round the World" and the Artists of Captain Cook's Voyages', in *The British Museum Yearbook: Captain Cook and the South Pacific*, ed. T.C. Mitchell, vol. 3, London: British Museum Publications

Kamakau, Samuel (1992) *Ka Po'e Kahiko: The People of Old*, trans. Mary Kawena Pukui, ed. Dorothy Barrere, Honolulu: Bishop Museum Press

Kaplan, Steven Laurence (1976) *Bread, Politics and Political Economy in the Reign of Louis XV*, 2 vols., The Hague: Martinus Nijhoff

Keate, George (2002) *An Account of the Pelew Islands*, ed. Karen L. Nero and Nicholas Thomas, London and New York: Leicester University Press

Kendon, Adam (2004) *Gesture: Visible Action as Utterance*, Cambridge: Cambridge University Press

Kenny, Anthony (1992) *Aristotle on the Perfect Life*, Oxford: Clarendon

Kerckhoff, Alan C. (1970) 'A Theory of Hysterical Contagion', in *Human Nature and Collective Behavior: Papers in Honor of Herbert Blumer*, ed. Tamotsu Shibutani, New Brunswick, NJ: Prentice-Hall, 81–93

King, Preston, and Heather Devere (eds.) (2000) *The Challenge to Friendship in Modernity*, London: Frank Cass

Kirkpatrick, John (1983) *The Marquesan Notion of the Person*, Ann Arbor, MI: UMI Research Press

Knellwolf, Christa (2001) 'Comedy in the *OMAI* Pantomime', in [NLA] (2001), 17–22

Konstan, David (1997) *Friendship in the Classical World*, Cambridge: Cambridge University Press

And enriched with Historical and Explanatory Notes, 2nd edn, London: J. Almon

Sedgwick, Eve Kosofsky (1985) *Between Men: English Literature and Male Homosocial Desire*, New York: Columbia University Press

(1990) *Epistemology of the Closet*, Berkeley: University of Califormia Press

Sennett, Richard (1977) *The Fall of Public Man*, New York: Alfred A. Knopf

Shaftesbury, Anthony Ashley Cooper, Third Earl of (1999) *Characteristics of Men, Manners, Opinions, Times*, ed. Lawrence E. Klein, Cambridge: Cambridge University Press

Sheldon, Richard (2004) 'Bread Politics and Political Economy at the Accession of George III', paper delivered at the session *Of Bread and Corn: dialogue sur le blé* at The American Society for Eighteenth-Century Studies 35th Annual Meeting, 24–28 March

Shelton, Walter J. (1973) *English Hunger and Industrial Disorders: A Study of Social Conflict during the First Decade of George III's Reign*, London: Macmillan

Shillibeer, John (1817) *A Narrative of the Briton's Voyage to Pitcairn's Island*, Taunton: printed for the author

Silver, Allan (1989) 'Friendship and Trust as Moral Ideals: an historical approach', *European Journal of Sociology*, 30, 274–97

(1990) 'Friendship in Commercial Society: eighteenth-century social theory and modern sociology', *American Journal of Sociology*, 95, 1474–504

(1997) ' "Two Different Sorts of Commerce", or, Friendship and Strangership in Civil Society', in *Public and Private in Thought and Practice: Perspectives on a Grand Dichotomy*, ed. Jeff Weintraub and Kishan Kumar, Chicago: University of Chicago Press, 43–74

SLNSW MITCHELL MSS (1786) Series 23.01 Anonymous letter received by Joseph Banks, 13 December 1786, Women – Tahiti

Smith, Adam (2002) *The Theory of Moral Sentiments*, ed. Knud Haakonssen Cambridge: Cambridge University Press

Smith, Bernard (1985) *European Vision and the South Pacific*, 2nd edn, New Haven, CT, and London: Yale University Press

Smith, Howard M. (1975) 'The Introduction of Venereal Disease into Tahiti: a re-examination', *Journal of Pacific History*, 10, 38–45

Smith, Vanessa (1998) *Literary Culture and the Pacific: Nineteenth-Century Textual Encounters*, Cambridge: Cambridge University Press

(2003) 'Pitcairn's Guilty Stock: the island as breeding ground', in Edmond and Smith (2003), 116–32

(2004) 'Costume Changes: passing at sea and on the beach', in *Sea Changes: Historicizing the Ocean*, ed. Bernhard Klein and Gesa Mackenthun, New York: Routledge, 37–53

(2005) 'Crossing the Beach at Taipivai: the psychogeography of islands and beaches', *ESQ: A Journal of the American Renaissance*, 51:1–2, 104–13

(2006) 'Give Us Our Daily Breadfruit: bread substitution in the Pacific in the eighteenth century', *Studies in Eighteenth-Century Culture*, 35, 53–75

Smyth, Arthur Bowes (1979) *The Journal of Arthur Bowes Smyth: Surgeon, Lady Penrhyn 1787–1789*, Sydney: Australian Documents Library

Sparrman, A. (1953) *A Voyage Round the World With Captain James Cook in H.M.S. 'Resolution'*, trans. H. Beamish and A. Mackenzie-Grieve, London: Robert Hale

Stallybrass, Peter, and Allon White (1986) *The Politics and Poetics of Transgression*, London: Methuen

Stanhope, Philip Dormer (1998) *Lord Chesterfield's Letters*, Oxford: Oxford University Press

Stannard, David E. (1989) *Before the Horror: The Population of Hawai'i on the Eve of Western Contact*, Honolulu: University of Hawaii Press

Stern, William Louis (1993) 'The Uses of Botany, with Special Reference to the 18th Century', *Taxon*, 42:4, 773–9

Stern-Gillet, Suzanne (1995) *Aristotle's Philosophy of Friendship*, New York: State University of New York Press

Stoler, Anne Laura (2001a) 'Tense and Tender Ties: the politics of comparison in North American history and (post) colonial studies', *Journal of American History*, 88:3, December, 829–65

    (2001b) 'Matters of Intimacy as Matters of State: a response', *Journal of American History*, 88:3, December, 893–7

Strathern, Marilyn (1988) *The Gender of the Gift: Problems with Women and Problems with Society in Melanesia*, Berkeley: University of California Press

Tadmor, Naomi (2001) *Family and Friends in Eighteenth-Century England: Household, Kinship, and Patronage*, Cambridge: Cambridge University Press

Taillemite, Étienne (ed.) (1977) *Bougainville et ses compagnons autour de monde 1766–1769*, 2 vols., Paris: Imprimerie Nationale

Tambiah, Stanley J. (1996) *Leveling Crowds: Ethnonationalist Conflicts and Collective Violence in South Asia*, Berkeley: University of California Press

Taylor, Jeremy (1662) *A Discourse of the Nature, Offices and Measures of Friendship with Rules of Conducting it, in a letter to the most ingenious and excellent Mrs. Katharine Phillps*; reprint London: Chapman and Hall, 1920

Tcherkézoff, Serge (2004) *Tahiti 1768. Jeunes filles en pleurs: la face cachée des premiers contacts et la naissance du mythe occidental (1595–1928)*, Tahiti: Au Vent des Iles

Teehuteatuaonoa (Jenny) (1819) [Narrative I], *Sydney Gazette*, 17 July
    (1829) [Narrative II], *United Service Journal*, 589–93

Terrell, Jennifer (1982) 'Joseph Kabris and his Notes on the Marquesas', *Journal of Pacific History*, 17:2 101–12

Thomas, Nicholas (1991) *Entangled Objects: Exchange, Material Culture and Colonialism in the Pacific*, Cambridge, MA: Harvard University Press

    (1994a) *Colonialism's Culture: Anthropology, Travel and Government*, Cambridge: Polity

    (1994b) 'Licensed Curiosity: Cook's Pacific voyages', in Elsner and Cardinal (1994), 116–36

    (1996) '"On the Varieties of the Human Species": Forster's comparative ethnology', in J. Forster (1996), xv–xl

    (1997) *In Oceania: Visions, Artifacts, Histories*, Durham, NC: Duke University Press

(2002) ' "The Pelew Islands" in British Culture', in Keate (2002), 27–40

(2003) *Cook: The Extraordinary Voyages of James Cook*, New York: Walker

Thompson, E. P. (1971) 'The Moral Economy of the English Crowd in the Eighteenth Century', *Past and Present*, 50, 76–136

Tilly, Charles (2003) *The Politics of Collective Violence*, Cambridge: Cambridge University Press

Tobin, George (2007) *Captain Bligh's Second Chance: An Eyewitness Account of his Return to the South Seas*, ed. Roy Schreiber, Sydney: UNSW Press

Todd, Janet (1980) *Women's Friendship in Literature*, New York: Columbia University Press

Tomkins, Silvan (1963) *Affect, Imagery, Consciousness, Volume II: The Negative Affects*, New York: Springer

Turnbull, David (1998) 'Cook and Tupaia, a Tale of Cartographic *Méconnaissance*?', in Lincoln (1998), 117–32

Vancouver, George (1984) *A Voyage of Discovery to the North Pacific Ocean and Round the World 1791–1795*, ed. W. Kaye Lamb, 4 vols., London: Hakluyt Society (1798)

Velásquez, Eduardo A. (ed.) (2003) *Love and Friendship: Rethinking Politics and Affection in Modern Times*, Lanham, MD: Lexington Books

Vernier, Charles (1948) 'Les Variations du vocabulaire tahitien avant et après les contacts européens', *Journal de la Société des Océanistes*, 3:3, December, 57–85

Vernon, Mark (2005) *The Philosophy of Friendship*, Basingstoke: Palgrave Macmillan

Vincent-Buffault, Anne (1991) *The History of Tears: Sensibility and Sentimentality in France*, trans. Teresa Bridgeman, New York: St Martin's Press

Wallace, Lee (2003) *Sexual Encounters: Pacific Texts, Modern Sexualities*, Ithaca, NY, and London: Cornell

(2005) 'A House is not a Home: Marquesan encounter, gender and everyday life, 1833–4', *Journal of Pacific History*, 40:3, 265–88

Wallis, Samuel (1766–8) 'Log of Captain Samuel Wallis on the *Dolphin* during his voyage round the world 1766 to 1768', Sydney: Mitchell Library, State Library of NSW, MSS CY Safe 1/98; microfilms FM4/1355

Weiner, Annette B. (1992) *Inalienable Possessions: The Paradox of Keeping-While-Giving*, Berkeley: University of California Press

White, Carolinne (1992) *Christian Friendship in the Fourth Century*, Cambridge: Cambridge University Press

Williams, Glyndwr (2003) 'Tupaia: Polynesian Warrior, Navigator, High Priest – and Artist', in *The Global Eighteenth Century*, ed. Felicity Nussbaum, Baltimore, MD, and London: Johns Hopkins University Press

Williams, Glyndwr (ed.) (2004) *Captain Cook: Explorations and Reassessments*, London: Boydell

Williams, Glyn [Glyndwr] (2008) *The Death of Captain Cook: A Hero Made and Unmade*, Cambridge, MA: Harvard University Press

Williams, Raymond (1984) *Keywords*, Oxford: Oxford University Press

Williamson, Robert R. (1939) *Essays in Polynesian Ethnology*, ed. Ralph Piddington, Cambridge: Cambridge University Press

Wilson, Elizabeth (2004) *Psychosomatic: Feminism and the Neurological Body*, Durham, NC, and London: Duke University Press

Wilson, James (1799) *A Missionary Voyage to the Southern Pacific Ocean, performed in the years 1796, 1797, 1798, in the Ship* Duff, *commanded by Captain James Wilson*, London: published for the benefit of the society, printed by S. Gosnell for T. Chapman; reprinted, introduction by Irmgard Moschner, New York: Frederick A. Praeger, n.d. [1979?]

Wilson, Kathleen (2003) *The Island Race: Englishness, Empire and Gender in the Eighteenth Century*, London and New York: Routledge

Wilson, Kathleen (ed.) (2004) *A New Imperial History: Culture, Identity, and Modernity in Britain and the Empire, 1660–1840*, Cambridge: Cambridge University Press

[Wolcot, John] (1789) *Sir Joseph Banks and the Emperor of Morocco. By Peter Pindar*, Dublin: P. Byrne

Wolf, Eric R., (1966) 'Kinship, Friendship, and Patron–Client Relations in Complex Societies', in *The Social Anthropology of Complex Societies*, ed. Michael Banton, London: Tavistock, 1–22

Worthen, William B. (1984) *The Idea of the Actor: Drama and the Ethics of Performance*, Princeton, NJ: Princeton University Press

Young Robert (1995) *Colonial Desire: Hybridity in Theory, Culture and Race*, London and New York: Routledge

Index